Network Access, Regulation and Antitrust

T0298449

The rapid growth of network industries has generated much comment amongst academics and policymakers. This timely volume takes an inter-disciplinary, case-study based, approach to examining a wide range of network issues and experiences in order to develop recommendations that are useful in informing antitrust, regulatory, and legislative policy. Legal, economic, political, and institutional aspects of network access problems are identified.

Part I focuses on five key topics that are fundamental to reasoned analysis of the access problem in antitrust enforcement actions or regulatory policy: natural monopoly and network externalities, tipping, essential facilities, access pricing and access remedies. Part II presents ten case studies of network access: freight railroads, electricity transmission, natural gas pipelines, local telecommunications, long distance telecommunications, broadband, automated teller machines, internet browsers, internet-based airline and travel services, and online music. Part III draws out relevant comparisons and contrasts from the key topics and case studies to develop a number of policy recommendations.

Network Access, Regulation and Antitrust will prove invaluable to students of business, economics, law and economics, and industrial economics. This book will also be of interest to policymakers and academics working in this field.

Diana L. Moss is Vice President and Senior Research Fellow at the American Antitrust Institute.

The Economics of Legal Relationships
Edited by Nicholas Mercuro and Michael D. Kaplowitz
Michigan State University

*Volumes 1, 2 and 3 are published by and available from Elsevier.

The Economics of Legal Relationships

Sponsored by the Michigan State University College of Law

STATEMENT OF SCOPE

The Economics of Legal Relationships is a book series dedicated to publishing original scholarly contributions that systematically analyze legal-economic issues. Each book can take a variety of forms:

- It may be comprised of a collection of original articles devoted to a single theme, edited by a guest volume editor.
- It may be a collection of refereed articles derived from the Series Editors' "call for papers" on a particular legal-economic topic.
- An individual may wish to (co)author an entire volume.

Each book in the series is published in hardback, approximately 250–300 pages in length and is dedicated to:

- Formulate and/or critique alternative theories of law and economics — including — the new law and economics, the economics of property rights, institutionalist and neoinstitutionalist law and economics, public choice theory, or social norms in law and economics.
- Analyze a variety of public policy issues related to the interface between judicial decisions and/or statutory law and the economy.
- Explore the economic impact of political and legal changes brought on by new technologies and/or environmental and natural resource concerns.
- Examine the broad array of legal/economic issues surrounding the deregulation-reregulation phenomena.
- Analyze the systematic effects of legal change on incentives and economic performance.

CALL FOR AUTHORS/VOLUME EDITORS/TOPICS

An individual who is interested in either authoring an entire volume, or editing a future volume, of *The Economics of Legal Relationships* should submit a 3–5 page prospectus to one of the series editors. Each prospectus must include: (1) the prospective title of the volume; (2) a brief description of the organizing theme of the volume, whether single authored or edited; (3) an identification of the line of literature from which the proposed topic emanates; and (4) either a table of contents or, if edited, a list of potential contributors along with tentative titles of their contributions. Send prospectus to either series editor. Please note that the series editors only accept individual manuscripts for publication consideration in response to a specific "Call for Papers."

Send prospectus directly to either series editor:

Professor Nicholas Mercuro
Michigan State University
College of Law
East Lansing, MI 48824
phone: (517) 432-6897
e-mail mercuro@msu.edu

Professor Michael D. Kaplowitz
Michigan State University
Department of Community Agriculture, Recreation, and Resource Studies
East Lansing, MI 48824
phone: (517) 355-0101
e-mail kaplowit@msu.edu

Network Access, Regulation and Antitrust

Edited by Diana L. Moss

American Antitrust Institute

Routledge
Taylor & Francis Group

LONDON AND NEW YORK

First published 2005
by Routledge
2 Park Square, Milton Park, Abingdon, Oxon OX14 4RN

Simultaneously published in the USA and Canada
by Routledge
711 Third Ave, New York, NY 10017

First issued in paperback 2012

Routledge is an imprint of the Taylor & Francis Group

Typeset in Baskerville by Wearset Ltd, Boldon, Tyne and Wear

British Library Cataloguing in Publication Data
A catalogue record for this book is available from the British Library

Library of Congress Cataloging in Publication Data
A catalog record for this book has been requested

ISBN 978 0 4156 5039 7

Contents

Figures

Tables

Contributors

Donald I. Baker is Senior Partner with Baker & Miller, an independent practice with a focus on antitrust and competition policy issues. Mr. Baker is a former Assistant Attorney General in charge of the Antitrust Division, U.S. Department of Justice, Professor of Law at Cornell Law School, and partner of two major Washington, D.C. law firms.

Richard M. Brunell is Visiting Professor at Roger Williams School of Law and Adjunct Professor at Boston College Law School. Mr. Brunell is formerly counsel at Foley Hoag LLP, an attorney in the Antitrust Division of the Justice Department, and an Assistant Attorney General in the Massachusetts Attorney General's Office.

D. Adam Candeub is Assistant Professor of Law at Michigan State University College of Law. Previously, Professor Candeub was an attorney-advisor for the Federal Communications Commission in the Media Bureau and Competitive Pricing Division of the Common Carrier Bureau, and a litigation associate for the Washington, D.C. firm of Jones, Day, Reavis & Pogue.

Harry First is Charles L. Denison Professor of Law and Director of the Trade Regulation Program at New York University School of Law. Professor First also served as Chief of the Antitrust Bureau in the Office of the New York State Attorney General, and was twice a Fulbright Research Fellow.

Albert A. Foer is the President of the American Antitrust Institute. Previously, he practiced law at Hogan & Hartson and Jackson & Campbell, held the position of Assistant Director and Acting Deputy Director of the Federal Trade Commission's Bureau of Competition, and was the Chief Executive Officer of a mid-sized chain of retail jewelry stores for 12 years.

Peter Fox-Penner is Principal and Chairman of the Board of the Brattle Group. Previously, Dr. Fox-Penner was Principal Deputy Assistant Secretary for Energy Efficiency and Renewable Energy in the U.S.

Department of Energy, Senior Advisor in the White House Office of Technology and Science Policy, Vice President at Charles River Associates, and served in the Illinois Governor's Office of Consumer Services.

Norman Hawker is Associate Professor in the Haworth College of Business at Western Michigan University. Formerly, Professor Hawker was of counsel at Farhat Tyler & Associates, P.C. and Assistant Attorney General for the State of Michigan Department of Attorney General. Mr. Hawker has also served as Research Fellow for the American Antitrust Institute, and as a visitor on the University of Toledo College of Law and University of Michigan Business School faculties.

John E. Kwoka is the Neal F. Finnegan Distinguished Professor of Economics at Northeastern University. Formerly, Professor Kwoka was the Columbian Professor of Economics and Co-Director of the Research Program in Industry Economics and Policy at George Washington University, has served on the faculties at University of North Carolina at Chapel Hill, Northwestern University, Harvard University, the Brookings Institution, and at Harvard University's Kennedy School of Government, and has held various positions at the Federal Trade Commission, the Antitrust Division of the Department of Justice, and the Federal Communications Commission.

Diana L. Moss is Vice President and Senior Research Fellow of the American Antitrust Institute. Formerly, Dr. Moss was Senior Economist and coordinator for competition analysis in the Office of Markets, Tariffs and Rates at the Federal Energy Regulatory Commission, and a consulting economist at the National Economic Research Associates and Putnam Hayes and Bartlett. Dr. Moss is Adjunct Professor of Public Policy at the Georgetown University Graduate Public Policy Institute.

Richard P. O'Neill is the Chief Economic Advisor of the Office of Markets, Tariffs and Rates at the Federal Energy Regulatory Commission (FERC). Previously, Dr. O'Neill served as Chief Economist and Director of the Office of Economic Policy and Director of the Commission's Office of Pipeline and Producer Regulation at FERC, directed oil and gas analysis at the Energy Information Administration, and served on the computer science and business faculty at Louisiana State University and on the business school faculty at the University of Maryland.

Michael D. Pelcovits is a Principal with Microeconomic Consulting and Research Associates, Inc. (MiCRA). Formerly, Dr. Pelcovits was Vice President and Chief Economist for MCI Communications Corporation and WorldCom, a founding principal of the consulting firm of Cornel, Pelcovits and Brenner, Senior Staff Economist at the Federal Communications Commission, and served at Civil Aeronautics Board, Bureau of International Aviation.

Rudolph J. R. Peritz is Professor of Law at New York Law School. He has visited at the University of Essex, U.K., the PALLAS Program in European Business Law, Netherlands, and Libera Universita Internazionale degli Studi Sociali (LUISS), Rome, Italy. Professor Peritz has also been a Langdell Fellow at Harvard Law School, Senior Research Fellow at the American Antitrust Institute, and Director, Computer-Assisted Enforcement Program, Antitrust Division, Attorney General of Texas.

Jonathan L. Rubin is a Research Fellow at the American Antitrust Institute. Formerly, Dr. Rubin was an Assistant Professor of Economics at KVL University in Copenhagen. Previously, Dr. Rubin was in private practice as a trial lawyer in Florida. He also practiced law in Washington, D.C., specializing in antitrust law and economics. Dr. Rubin is Adjunct Professor of Law at the George Washington University Law School.

Lawrence J. White is the Arthur E. Imperatore Professor of Economics at New York University's Stern School of Business. Professor White has previously served as Board Member, Federal Home Loan Bank Board, Director of the Economic Policy Office, Antitrust Division, U.S. Department of Justice, and on the Senior Staff of the President's Council of Economic Advisers.

Acknowledgments

The editor and publishers wish to thank *Ohio Northern University Law Review* for granting permission to reproduce:

"Open Windows: The Essential Facilities Doctrine and Microsoft," by Norman Hawker, 25 Ohio N.UL. Rev. 115, 1999.

Introduction

Diana L. Moss and Peter Fox-Penner[1]

In the New Economy, as in the Old, many important industries are characterized by their reliance on networks. Some observers espouse the view that networks are generally efficiency-enhancing because of the unique economies they enjoy and, therefore, intervention in situations where access to a network has (or is likely to) become a competitive problem is unwarranted. Others in this camp argue that certain network industries should be allowed to function, unfettered, as monopolies because they constantly face the threat of wholesale replacement from newer, more technologically advanced networks.[2] This group faces off against those arguing that networks raise the specter of market failure and can give rise to competitive problems that will ultimately harm consumers, thus warranting pre-emptive policy intervention. Some critics have even argued that these industries are so different from non-networked industries that U.S. antitrust laws are not equipped to deal with the competitive problems they can create. Other voices in the network access debate argue that the antitrust laws are suitably flexible, but great care clearly is needed when analyzing network industries to ensure that their differences from traditional industries are sufficiently taken into account. Yet others have argued that regulation, not antitrust, is the best arena in which to deal with cases of problematic network access.

Adding to the complexity, the network access problem is appearing in distinctly non-traditional and more interesting forms, such as virtual networks. Thus, access issues relating to physical networks such as railroads, electricity transmission, gas pipelines, telecommunications, and airlines—Old Economy industries—are increasingly complemented by those cropping up in internet browsers, software applications, and internet-based distribution of products and services.[3] In virtual networks, the linkages between "nodes" on the network are not physical, as in the case of railroad tracks or telephone wires, but *invisible*. Shapiro and Varian note that these linkages, however, are "no less critical for market dynamics and competitive strategy."[4] This distinction reminds policymakers that, while real and virtual networks have significant differences, they are viewing variations of essentially the same problem.

Thus, each turn in the evolution of markets that rely on a network or networks generates challenging new legal and economic issues for policy-makers and industry participants. Networks are the subject of a burgeoning political economy literature.[5] Access problems are part of antitrust enforcement and regulatory actions in the U.S. and in other jurisdictions, including South America, Japan, and Europe. In the U.S. and elsewhere, public influence over the vital sectors of the economy that display network properties remains strong, so there is a compelling reason to resolve the tensions in today's public policy governing network industries.[6]

What does this all mean for how antitrust and regulation handle network access problems? There is now a good deal of practical experience in dealing with network access problems through some combination of legislation, regulation, or antitrust. But these experiences tend to be very different—regulation is pre-emptive while antitrust is reactive. Legislation is often resorted to when all else fails. The administrative costs and burdens of implementing access initiatives and remedies affect how courts address access issues relative to regulators. Regulators often promote related policy agendas in the process of addressing access problems, such as jump-starting or fostering the development of markets—as in electricity and telecommunications. Increasingly, antitrust "monitoring" of access issues is playing a larger role in shaping outcomes in formative or dynamic industries such as internet-based products and services. Most recently, and as discussed in detail in Part II, a key U.S. Supreme Court decision seemingly diminished the role of antitrust enforcement in refusals to deal cases involving network access in local telecommunications, raising questions about the role of antitrust in other network industries where regulation has been a key driver of access policy.

Models of network access

Many of the foregoing issues are better understood with the added context of how network industries are organized and how the role of integration into complementary markets affects a network owner's incentives. Network industries are organized in a number of different ways, each of which poses different questions, challenges, and implications for network access policy. One model is a vertically-integrated industry with a central bottleneck (sometimes an essential facility) and competitive complementary markets upstream and/or downstream from the network. These networks almost always involve the potential for significant consumer harm if the access problem is left unremedied. Rivals in complementary markets must gain access to the bottleneck to remain viable and so it is typically regulated to provide equal access to all competitors on reasonable terms. The switched telephone network follows this model, with the local exchange generally viewed as the bottleneck and the long distance portion as competitive. In this model, regulation and antitrust both have important roles but face challenges.

A second model is one of multiple competing end-to-end networks, such as ATM networks, internet-based airline and travel products and services, and online music.[7] Rivalry between competing networks can encourage technological innovation but strong network effects in these industries may also provide many opportunities for strategic behavior.[8] Usually, industries that fit the second model are not subject to profit, price and entry regulation. Instead, socially desirable outcomes, including maximum consumer welfare, are ensured through enforcement of competition laws.

A third organizational model is a more realistic representation of many complex networks today. Most of these networks have certain elements that are costly to bypass and for which there are limited alternatives. Portions of the network may remain fully regulated, other portions are regulated using less direct methods such as licenses or self-regulation, and still others are left to competition and its enforcers. Gas pipelines, for example, fit into this category. This model thus updates the traditional "binary" view of network access markets, recognizing that it is increasingly hard to find network models that reside at the ends of the spectrum. Rather than finding a monopolized network or, conversely, a competing end-to-end network, we find that most modern network markets have a mixture of attributes such as physical and virtual network components and competitive and non-competitive characteristics. In this "mixed model," antitrust and regulation are also not mutually exclusive alternatives—they must co-exist in order to accomplish the objectives of network access policy. Alfred Kahn alluded to this concept over 30 years ago:

> The decision to regulate never represents a clean break with competition. No regulatory statute to the author's knowledge completely abandons reliance on competition as one guarantor of good performance. The determination of the proper mixture of competitive rivalry and government orders in the formula for social control is or ought to be the central, continuing responsibility of legislatures and regulatory commissions.[9]

"Mixed model" network industries have often been the subject of deregulation, whereby price regulation in complementary products markets is lifted or softened and/or regulation of the network moves from cost-based to performance-based. But many experiments with deregulation have stumbled, so it is "regulatory reform" or "restructuring" that characterizes ongoing efforts to transition these industries to the point where the network market and/or complementary markets are more competitive. Thus, the question is how to approach reform in many traditional network industries such as electricity transmission and telecommunications.[10]

Regulation must be agile enough to adapt to the changing needs of complementary markets above and below the bottleneck. Many argue that efforts to reform current regulatory regimes in these industries are hampered because policymakers will not yield sufficient ground to "let the market work." Proponents of this view allege that the first model is used too often, or that regulation of the bottleneck is too heavy-handed or ineffective in either the first or third models. Many of the case studies in Part II will address these issues.

The extent to which all segments of the production chain are controlled by a single, vertically-integrated firm in the first and third models has significant implications for competitive outcomes in network industries. Is access less of a problem when the network owner is not vertically integrated into complementary markets? To be sure, an unintegrated network can raise competitive issues if the network owner chooses not to treat all comers equally. Such discrimination can result in "bargaining" for access to the network or in favoritism on the part of the network owner. But there are fewer examples of competitive harm involving unintegrated—as opposed to integrated—networks.

With vertical integration, the network owner's possession of "incentive and ability" to lessen competition are requisite conditions for concern. Harm to competition can be accomplished through sabotage, refusals to deal, or conduct designed to foreclose rivals from—or raise their costs of access to—network facilities or services.[11] The extent of vertical integration determines the complexity in establishing interoperability between links in the production chain *and* between competing chains.[12] Indeed, decisions to integrate (or not) can be driven by the freedom to choose common or different interoperability standards, the degree of which is a function of complex strategic and technological determinants.[13] Interoperability issues can be the primary source of competitive harm, as in the case of the Microsoft operating system and competing applications software and AT&T's standardization of telephone technology. Thus, the form of network industry organization and the degree of vertical integration are critical factors in assessing the extent and severity of the access problem. Integration and interoperability between links in the production chain are key analytical features of many case studies in Part II.

Study contributors

The Network Access Project (NAP) was launched in late 2001 with a preliminary list of possible case studies and key topics. Contributors from academia, government, and industry offered a wide and valuable range of experience and expertise in network access in industries where network access has been a central policy issue. In early 2002, contributors and other participants met at Northeastern University to discuss their preliminary findings. A year later, at a second NAP workshop at Northeastern, contributors and other participants met to discuss the common themes across cases and to formulate policy recommendations. These findings were presented and critiqued in the summer of 2003 at the annual American Antitrust Institute (AAI) conference. In early 2004, a third and final workshop was held at Northeastern to share updates to various cases, discuss new developments, and to finalize policy recommendations.

Without the generous support of John Kwoka at Northeastern University and various chapter contributors (listed in the following section), this study would not have been possible. We also owe many thanks to individuals that participated in workshops; provided comments on interim findings at AAI's 2003 annual conference, research support, and administrative support; and served as advisors and reviewers. These include: Joseph Brodley (Boston University), Stacey Dogan (Northeastern University Law School), Glenn Kaplan (Massachusetts Office of the Attorney General), Michael Dworkin (Vermont Board of Public Utilities), Simon Wilke (University of California—Berkeley), Suzanne Robblee (Northeastern University), Cheryl Fonville (Northeastern University), Zhongmin Wang (Monash University), Amery Pore (University of Colorado), Janie Chermak (University of New Mexico), Steven Morrison (Northeastern University), David Gabel (Queens College—SUNY), Robert Loube (Rhoads & Sinon, LLC), Robert Lande (University of Baltimore), and George Hay (Cornell University).[14]

Organization of the book

To say something about the roles of antitrust and regulation in network access, we need to understand the network access problem well enough to fashion credible and useful policy recommendations. A logical first inquiry might therefore be: What is an appropriate approach to take in studying the network access experience and fashioning recommendations that would guide future policy making? The proliferation and complexity of networks warrant an approach that examines the economic, legal, political, and institutional aspects of the network access problem across a wide range of experience.[15] This study thus takes a multidisciplinary, case-study approach to analyzing the access problem. The goal is to identify common themes, along with prominent contrasts across these experiences to produce better-informed policy recommendations that will be useful for guiding antitrust, regulatory, and legislative policy. The study aims to answer a number of key questions about the access problem and its possible solutions:

- Under what circumstances is network access a competitive problem, particularly in the context of different models of network organization?

- When is a "wait and see" approach better than more immediate intervention, particularly in the face of rapid technological change that may both create and destroy market power?
- In what situations should antitrust be used to address competitive problems in networks, as opposed to regulation—particularly in "mixed" cases where parts of the production chain are competitive while the network remains a bottleneck?
- When should vertical separation of the network owner's complementary market interests be used to remedy network access problems, versus implementing a system of compulsory access?
- What, if any, should be the rules for facilitating access to a privately-owned or controlled network under a compulsory access regime?

In attempting to answer these questions, the book proceeds as follows. Part I discusses the foundations for network access analysis (including the basics of network architecture). This section focuses on several key topics in network access that are fundamentally important to the access debate and policy development and provide the underpinnings of reasoned analysis in antitrust enforcement actions or regulatory policy. These include:

- Natural monopoly and network externalities—John Kwoka, Northeastern University
- Tipping—Rudolph Peritz, New York Law School
- Essential facilities—Norman Hawker, University of Western Michigan
- Access pricing (efficient component pricing rule)—Lawrence White, New York University
- Access remedies after *Trinko*—Jonathan Rubin, American Antitrust Institute, Norman Hawker, University of Western Michigan, and Adam Candeub, Michigan State University.

Part II presents ten case studies of network access. The cases display a range of characteristics that are relevant for a comprehensive assessment of access policy and that have been addressed in very different ways by antitrust and regulation. Several of the case studies are classic network examples involving railroads, electricity, gas transportation, and telecommunications. These industries have long been recognized as natural monopolies. There are also several case studies of access issues resolved in the formative stages of the industry; dynamic access problems; and those raising competitive concerns that could have, but never materialized. These include automated teller machines (ATMs), broadband, internet browsers, online music, and internet-based airline reservations. In total, the case studies include:

- Freight railroads—John Kwoka, Northeastern University and Lawrence White, New York University

- Electricity transmission—Diana Moss, American Antitrust Institute
- Natural gas pipelines—Richard O'Neill, Federal Energy Regulatory Commission
- Local telecommunications—Jonathan Rubin, American Antitrust Institute
- Long distance telecommunications—Michael Pelcovits, MiCRA Inc.
- Broadband—Richard Brunell, Roger Williams Law School
- Automated teller machines—Donald Baker, Baker and Miller
- Internet browsers—Norman Hawker, University of Western Michigan
- Internet-based airline and travel services—Albert Foer, American Antitrust Institute
- Online music—Harry First, New York University.

Part III pulls together the key topics and case studies by drawing relevant comparisons and contrasts across the case studies. These are then used to fashion a number of policy recommendations to answer the questions posed at the outset of this introduction. Space limitations precluded the inclusion of several additional cases and key topics involving network access. They will likely be the subject of subsequent work. In that respect, as well as for their own use, the chapters in this volume represent an excellent foundation for the analysis of access issues in network industries.

Notes

1 Vice-president and Senior Research Fellow, American Antitrust Institute and Chairman, the Brattle Group. Many thanks to Albert Foer and John Kwoka for helpful review and comments.
2 See generally, R. B. McKenzie, *Trust on Trial*, Cambridge, Massachusetts: Perseus Publishing, 2001.
3 See generally, M. Mueller, "On the frontier of deregulation: New Zealand telecommunications and the problem of interconnecting competing networks," in *Opening Networks to Competition: The Regulation and Pricing of Access*, D. Gabel and D. Weiman (eds), Boston: Kluwer, 1998. W. B. Tye and C. Lapuerta, "The economies of pricing network interconnection: theory and application to the market for telecommunications in New Zealand," *Yale Journal on Regulation* 13, 1996, pp. 419–500; and J. Farrell and P. J. Weiser, "Modularity, vertical integration, and open access policies: towards a convergence of antitrust and regulation in the internet age," Institute for Business and Economic Research Working paper No. E02–325, Berkeley, California: University of California, Berkeley, 2002.
4 C. Shapiro, C. and H. R. Varian, *Information Rules: a Strategic Guide to the Network Economy*, Cambridge, Massachusetts: Harvard Business School Press, 1999, p. 174.
5 See generally, J. J. Laffont, P. Rey, and J. Tirole, "Network competition: II. price discrimination," *Rand Journal of Economics* 29, 1998b, pp. 38–56; N. Economides and L. J. White, "One-way network, two-way networks, compatibility, and public policy," in *Opening Networks to Competition: The Regulation and*

Pricing of Access, D. Gabel and D. F. Weiman (eds), Boston: Kluwer, 1998; N. Economides, "The economics of networks," *International Journal of Industrial Organization* 14, 1996, pp. 673–99; L. J. White, *U.S. Public Policy Toward Network Industries*, Washington: AEI-Brookings Joint Center for Regulatory Studies, 1999; and J. Rifkin, *The Age of Access*, New York: Tarcher/Putman, 2000.

6 Network access issues have arisen in antitrust enforcement and restructuring initiatives in the European Union, South America, and New Zealand.

7 Government policy has sometimes encouraged (e.g., ATMs and credit card companies) the existence of multiple end-to-end networks, even when a single network might be more efficient.

8 M. L. Katz and C. Shapiro, "R&D rivalry with licensing or imitation," *American Economic Review* 77, 1987, pp. 402–20 and M. H. Riordan, "Regulation and pre-emptive technology adoption," *Rand Journal of Economics* 23, 1992, p. 334.

9 A. E. Kahn, *The Economics of Regulation: Principles and Institution—Volume 11*, Cambridge, Massachusetts: MIT Press, 1971, pp. 113–14.

10 For early discussion on regulatory reform and network industries see S. Breyer, *Regulation and Its Reform*, Cambridge, Massachusetts: Harvard University Press, 1982.

11 See generally, D. L. Rubinfeld and H. J. Singer, "Vertical foreclosure in broad-band access," *Journal of Industrial Economics* 49, 2001, pp. 299–318; W. G. Shep-herd, "Problems in creating effective competition," in *Opening Networks to Competition: The Regulation and Pricing of Access*, D. Gabel and D. F. Weiman (eds), Boston: Kluwer, 1998; D. L. Weisman, "The incentive to discriminate by a vertically-integrated regulated firm: a reply," *Journal of Regulatory Economics* 14, 1998, pp. 87–91; D. L. Weisman, "Access pricing and exclusionary behavior," *Economics Letters* 72, 2001; and G. A. Woroch, F. R. Warren-Boulton, and K. C. Baseman, "Exclusionary behavior in the market for operating system software: the case of Microsoft," in *Opening Networks to Competition: The Regulation and Pricing of Access*, D. Gabel and D. F. Weiman (eds), Boston: Kluwer, 1999.

12 The most widely accepted theory of vertical integration, attributable to Williamson (see O. E. Williamson, *Markets and Hierarchies—Analysis and Antitrust Implications: A Study in the Economics of Internal Organization*, New York: The Free Press, 1985), is that vertical integration occurs precisely because it is physically and technologically inefficient to try to standardize or coordinate successive stages of production.

13 Compatibility encompasses relationships with other producers in vertical chains and with consumers using the technology. In network industries, firms make ongoing decisions about merger, divestiture, or retooling to become part of a different compatible chain, to fend off challenges from new technolo-gies, or to respond to pricing or marketing by rivals. In partially deregulated utility industries, where a substantial portion of the industry remains under direct or indirect regulatory control, regulators tend to have more say about standards and compatibility and antitrust enforcement deals with competitive abuses stemming from market power.

14 Thanks also to: Rick Warren-Boulton (MiCRA, Inc.), Robert Reynolds (Brattle Group), Gary Taylor (Brattle Group), Atreya Chakraborty (Brattle Group), Phillip Weiser (University of Colorado), Michael Salinger (Boston University), Amil Petrin (University of Chicago), Mary Freely (Massachusetts Office of the

Attorney General), Michael Pollitt (Cambridge University), Jeff Ballou (Northeastern University), and Tran Nam Son (Office of the Government, Vietnam).

15 Studies of network access typically focus on particular aspects of the problem. See generally, A. D. Melamed, "Network industries and antitrust," *Harvard Journal of Law & Public Policy* 23, 1999, pp. 147–57. The "case-study" approach to networks is a well-used and valuable form of analysis. Peltzman and Winston look at four cases involving the deregulation of network industries (see S. Peltzman and C. Winston, eds, *Deregulation of Network Industries: What's Next?* Washington, D.C.: AEI-Brookings Joint Center for Regulatory Studies, 2000). Kwoka and White (2003) include a number of cases that analyze network access from an antitrust policy perspective (see J. E. Kwoka, Jr. and L. J. White, eds, *The Antitrust Revolution: Economics, Competition, and Policy,* 4th edn, New York: Oxford University Press, 2003). Gabel and Weiman (1998) collect nine studies that focus on the regulation and pricing of access in both the U.S. and abroad (see D. Gabel, and D. F. Weiman, eds, *Opening Networks to Competition: The Regulation and Pricing of Access,* Boston: Kluwer, 1998). The American Economic Association's Papers and Proceedings (2001) contain a number of case studies on network access (see *American Economic Association Papers and Proceedings* 91, 2001).

Part I

Key topics

Preface to part I

A number of key issues are central to an analysis of network access. Part I presents essays on five of the more important issues: natural monopoly, tipping, essential facilities, access pricing, and remedies for the access problem. A good starting point for the discussion to follow is a brief overview of network architecture. How networks are configured often sets the stage for the types and magnitude of issues that are likely to be encountered in evaluating and remedying an access problem.

Networks are made up of links that connect nodes. There are a number of possible configurations. One is a "star" network with a central hub, as shown in Figure I.1. This configuration could represent an airline with the central node as the hub and outer nodes as smaller airports. Another possibility is a local electricity distribution system where the central node is a generator; the outer nodes are consumers, and the links are distribution lines. Another possible network configuration involves two "stars" connected through a trunk line, as shown in Figure I.2. This configuration implies that transactions flow *between* two distribution systems. Each star,

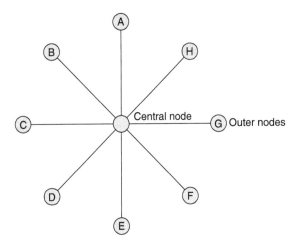

Figure I.1 A star network.

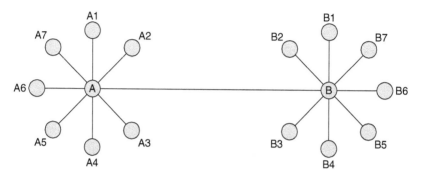

Figure I.2 Two star networks connected by a trunk line.

for example, could represent a local telephone system connected with a long-distance line or more complex network systems, e.g., personal computers and applications software.

The networks in Figures I.1 and I.2 can have a number of important characteristics. For instance, networks can display supply-side economies. For instance, if there is sufficient capacity at the central node, adding nodes to the network reduces average costs through economies of scale, thus lowering prices to all customers. However, since there are a limited number of possible routes through the network, short-run capacity constraints can create congestion, manifested in interruptions or delays in service. All transactions are routed through the central node in "star" networks. In electricity and similar examples, traffic flows only from the central node (which initiates a transaction) to an outer node that receives the transaction, thus making it a one-way network. One-way networks can display particularly strong economies of scale. In airline and similar examples, the outer nodes can receive *and* initiate transactions so that transactions can flow back and forth between any two outer nodes via the central node. Thus, it is a two-way network.

The nature of the central node can also be an important feature of network architecture. The central node must be sized appropriately to accommodate demand in the market. Moreover, compatibility between nodes and among links is essential for the network to operate.[1] The central node can be a bottleneck or, in more extreme cases, an essential facility. In the latter case, access is necessary for suppliers and consumers to operate in the market. Here, we make the traditional distinction between "essential facility" and "bottleneck." If a facility is "essential," it is the one and only facility to which firms in complementary markets must gain access to ultimately reach consumers. A bottleneck, on the other hand, implies that the access problem is only one of degree, i.e., that there are substitutes, although they may not be sufficient to ensure workable competition.

Finally, some networks display demand-side economies or "network effects." Network effects result when the network is configured such that when an additional user joins the network, other users benefit. Thus, the value consumers derive from consuming a product complementary to the network increases as the number of users on the network increases. Because two-way networks allow users to "interact" by initiating and receiving transactions, network effects can be particularly strong.[2] There are numerous examples of network effects. The more customers a bank has on its ATM network, the more machines it will install and the more consumers will value ATM services. The same is true of the telephone system and arguments for the widespread benefits of universal service. Network effects are often critical to the economic survival of the firms comprising the network industry. "Tipping" occurs when subscribership to a particular network technology or product reaches a critical mass so that consumers gravitate toward that technology. Moreover, rival networks may engage in strategic behavior to alter the degree and nature of competition which can promote tipping.[3]

The five essays in Part I address many of the foregoing issues that relate directly to the competitive situations that are influenced by the underlying network architecture. In the opening essay on networks and natural monopoly, John Kwoka explains how differences in demand- and supply-side economies have critical implications for network access. Rudolph Peritz looks more closely into the implications of tipping for access policy in the second key topics essay. In the third essay on essential facilities, Norman Hawker discusses in detail the origins of and legal economics of the essential facility doctrine. Access pricing can be a controversial issue, with much of the debate focusing on the tension between incentives for efficient entry and the perpetuation of monopoly rents for the network owner. Lawrence White presents the elements of this debate in the fourth key topics essay on the efficient component pricing rule. In a final and timely essay, Jonathan Rubin, Norman Hawker, and Adam Candeub assess the relevant history and implications of access remedies after *Trinko*. Antitrust enforcement of network owners' "refusals to deal" with competitors in attempting to gain access to networks has important implications for the essential facilities doctrine. This essay looks carefully at the implications if the U.S. Supreme Court's recent decision in the *Trinko* local telecommunications case, which codified a very limited role for antitrust in cases involving legislated compulsory access implemented by a regulatory agency.

Notes

1 Investments in new network equipment or technology are typically sunk, i.e., they cannot be transferred to another network.
2 Arguably, however, there may be exceptions to the one-way/two-way network

distinction and the presence of network effects. For example, newspaper distribution is a one-way network. However, if readers read articles in one local newspaper and can discuss those same articles with other readers, they thereby encourage new subscribers to join the newspaper's "network." This is a network effect.

3 O. Shy, *The Economics of Network Industries*, Cambridge: Cambridge University Press, 2001, pp. 3–4.

Topic 1

Networks and natural monopoly

John E. Kwoka[1]

A monopoly is said to be "natural" when the most efficient structure of an industry consists of a single seller. This outcome is usually identified with economies of scale, that is, cost advantages of a size so great as to preclude even a second seller. More recently, considerable attention has been paid to a different mechanism whereby a single seller, or only a few sellers, may arise. This mechanism is rooted in what are called demand-side economies of scale or network effects.

This chapter will outline the economics underlying these two sources of natural monopoly and distinguish their various sources. Then it will discuss strategies that can be used to exploit network effects to the detriment of market operation.

Cost-based natural monopoly

The conventional case of a natural monopoly is rooted in economies of scale, or what are now sometimes termed supply-side economies of scale. It is helpful in thinking about this case to envision a single-product firm whose long-run average cost curve declines at least up to the output level given by the intersection of demand and long-run average cost, as shown in Figure I.1.1.[2] As is well understood, equilibrium of the unfettered market in this case consists of a single firm: Any smaller second firm would suffer higher unit cost and be forced to exit the market. Any second firm that sought to achieve the same low cost as the large firm would find the market oversupplied, forcing one of the firms out. In either case only one firm, serving the entire market, would survive.

From the standpoint of cost efficiency, this equilibrium is optimal: In the face of such strong economies of scale, no other organization of the supply sector—that is, no division of output into two or more sources—results in lower total costs of producing market-required output. Indeed, if demand were to grow, that new demand (at least up to some point) should also be served by the natural monopoly producer. Not only are the additional units produced more cheaply by that firm than by any other, but increasing that firm's total output creates a cost externality:

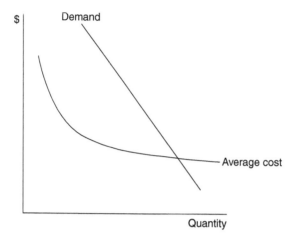

Figure I.1.1 Supply-side economies of scale.

The unit cost of all previous output declines, with potential benefits to consumers.

While strong economies of scale characterize many production processes, it is noteworthy that some apparent natural monopoly markets are served by more than one producer. For example, despite seeming large economies, some rail freight routes are served by two railroads, there are multiple long distance carriers, and a number of cities have two local newspapers. The railroad case illustrates the fact that, in markets of sufficient demand density, all economies may be exhausted, thereby permitting a second cost-competitive producer. A corollary to this proposition is offered by the telecom example: Some apparently natural monopoly markets may transition to non-monopoly status, as demand growth overtakes economies of scale, or as technological change reduces necessary scale. Newspapers illustrate how a second firm may survive in certain markets by offering a differentiated product or service for which consumers are prepared to pay a somewhat higher price. [3]

Cost-based economies and the natural monopolies or oligopolies they imply derive from characteristics of the production process—indivisibilities, geometric properties, massed reserves, and the like. Quite different considerations come into play in the case of network industries.

Networks and natural monopoly

Networks are often discussed as if they were a single phenomenon. In reality there are several different types of supposed networks, distinguished by the origins of their advantage to size (somehow defined). In addition, as we shall see, the different cases raise somewhat different competitive concerns.

The communications paradigm

The classic example of a network is communications, whereby all individuals in the same group are linked so as to be able to engage in two-way communication with each other. This is best illustrated by a local exchange telephone network. In such a network the value to each consumer is a function of the number of others who are simultaneously on the same network, since that group defines the set of persons with whom communication is possible.[4]

Consumers in the group may be linked in various ways, two of which are illustrated in Figure I.1.2. Panel A describes a network of bilateral linkages between nodes, representing consumers, at A, B, C, D, and E. As the number of consumers increases, this network architecture consisting of all possible bilateral linkages is not likely to be cost efficient. Instead, the network may employ a star architecture, as shown in Panel B. Now Points A through E are linked through a switch at the common point S, which routes calls between all possible pairs of consumers using fewer and shorter links.[5]

There are three important features of such networks, regardless of the architecture. First, if there are multiple networks serving the same consumers, any individual consumer will value a larger network more than a smaller network. This follows immediately from the assumption that the value of a network to any consumer is a function of the number of people who are already (or prospectively) members of that network.[6] Hence, consumers will rationally choose the larger network, which is therefore likely to become ever larger. Second, the act of joining any network confers an external benefit on existing members, since they now have an additional

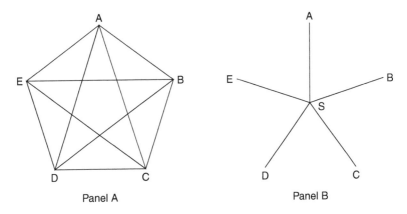

Figure I.1.2 A communications network.

person with whom they can communicate. This phenomenon is a demand-side economy of scale (sometimes called a consumption external-ity), a benefit of scale that derives from demand aggregation. Note that even if unit production costs were constant—that is, if there were no cost economies whatsoever—demand-side economies could nonetheless result in industry concentration. Third, the total value to a community of users of a single large network is greater than with multiple smaller networks. To see this, recall the assumption that the value to each member of the network is proportional to the total number of others in the network. Letting that total number be n, the total value to all users is related to $n \cdot (n-1) = n^2 - n$. This expression is maximized when all n takes on its largest possible value, that is, when all users are aggregated into a single network. Put differently, any division of these same n people among two or more networks results in diminished total value.[7] Hence, a single network is optimal.

This last proposition makes clear the close relationship between the condition for a cost-based natural monopoly and a demand-side natural monopoly. In the former case any division of total output between two or more producers results in higher total cost, while in the latter any division of consumers between two or more networks reduces the total value of networking.

As noted, this paradigm applies directly to local telephone service, but it also captures the network properties of other communications activities, such as faxing, emailing, instant messaging, and file transfer. In each case consumers value network membership because it is the network, defined by a platform or protocol, that allows them to reach others. This demand-side economy represents the defining characteristic of a network effect and a network industry.

The transport paradigm

A second case generally described as a network involves transport and dis-tribution industries such as airlines, postal delivery, and electricity distrib-ution. Using the example of airlines, production architecture in this case is illustrated in Figure I.1.3, where points S and T denote hub airports. These are connected by trunks, into and out of which there are collection and feeder lines, or spokes. Such industries resemble the previously dis-cussed communications networks not only in their graphical depiction, but also in some of their economic characteristics. Three deserve mention.

First, consumers seeking transportation from point A to point T gener-ally prefer to remain on the same carrier for both segments, creating what may appear to be a network effect. Second, there are likely to be signific-ant economies of joint production for segments A–S and S–T relative to their production by separate sellers. Finally, these interdependencies on

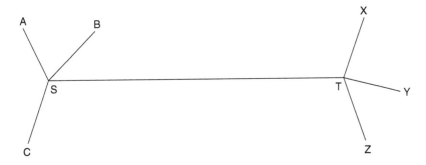

Figure I.1.3 A transport network.

the demand and supply side may lead to concentration throughout a system even when parts of the system would seem to support many providers. This can occur when strong cost economies cause one segment to be served by few or perhaps a single seller, and economies of integration undermine standalone production on other segments.

Despite these seeming similarities, the transport case does not exhibit true demand-side economies. For example, while consumers may wish to remain on the same carrier, this does not imply any added value for being on the same network (carrier) as other consumers—not even the carrier with the most other consumers. The benefit arises whether the through-carrier is large or small. The second and third factors just mentioned are fairly conventional multiproduct economies—an economy of scope in one case, and an economy of vertical integration in the other.[8] Neither constitutes the key ingredient of a network economy—a demand-side externality that causes consumers to concentrate their purchases.

One final phenomenon, however, does raise some possible demand-side economies. In some industries the seller that offers the largest number of product alternatives garners a more-than-proportional share of consumers and sales. In the airline industry, for example, the so-called S-curve shown in Figure I.1.4 describes the larger share of bookings on one carrier from a city as the number of flights offered by that carrier increases. Either of two forces may underlie this phenomenon. First, there may be consumer information and transaction costs which are minimized by more frequently contacting the dominant provider for a range of travel needs. Thus, if one carrier is known to have the most departures to a desired destination, the first telephone call that an airline travel consumer makes is likely to be to that carrier, and unless the quoted fare is unacceptable on its face, the consumer may purchase the ticket without checking with an alternative carrier.

Second, travel agents make a large fraction of reservations (especially for business consumers), and carriers often provide incentives to travel

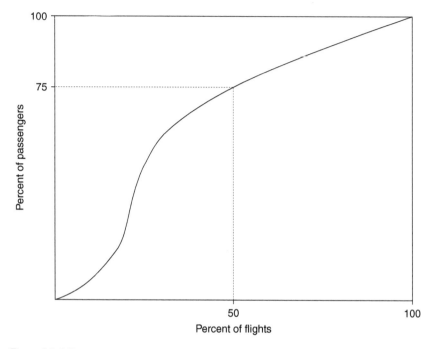

Figure I.1.4 S-curve.

agents in a city to book a disproportionate number of flights on that carrier. These nonlinear commission schedules may distort purchase patterns in favor of a high percentage of passengers on the dominant carrier.[9]

To the extent that it reflects true consumer benefit from choosing the dominant provider, the S-curve would appear to be a network effect. True consumer benefit characterizes those choices made by consumers that minimize their search and transactions costs. Nonlinear travel agent commission schedules do not obviously represent cost savings, much less informed consumer choices, and hence where the S-curve results from such nonlinearities, no such conclusion holds. Indeed, such payment schedules would appear to be a pecuniary transfer or even strategic behavior by the dominant seller, neither of which qualify as true consumer gains.

Thus, while most of the forces that characterize the transport case are familiar economies of scale, scope, and density, consumer search and purchase behavior described by the S-curve may represent a network effect.

The hardware/software paradigm

The final network case involves strongly complementary products, in many cases conditioned by important dynamic considerations. This case is perhaps best described by the example of a personal computer. While a consumer's benefit from a PC is not directly affected by how many others buy the same equipment—there are no true demand-side economies to PCs—the number of other PC purchasers is likely to influence the supply of software written to run on it.[10] Since consumer benefit derives only from hardware-plus-software, a "virtual network" of users with interests in related or complementary goods arises.

Two further assumptions are required to observe network effects. First, there must be significant production economies of scale in the related "software" industry. Absent that condition, there would be no impediments to proliferation of functionally equivalent software written for all platforms, and potential buyers of PCs would no longer need to be concerned about software availability.[11] Something more is required for true network effects.

The second, and crucial, assumption is best explained by extending the example of a PC purchase. Since the PC is durable and there is typically a flow of new software designed for it, today's consumers make decisions based not only on the current availability of complementary software, but also on their *expectations* about future new software. But the supply of the future software in turn depends upon software writers' expectations of the likely future purchase decisions of prospective consumers of PCs. This feedback effect creates important dynamics based on the expectations of PC buyers and of software developers. The resulting equilibrium is more complicated, involving the fulfillment of consumer expectations.[12]

Examples of these hardware/software issues abound. The most important intertemporal effects arise in many common entertainment systems—video games, music formats (cassettes, CDs), and, as a historical example, VCRs (Beta vs. VHS). A different type of intertemporal issue is raised in cases where post-purchase service is important for a good (e.g., cars), and in instances where post-purchase inputs are required (e.g., automotive fuel, ink cartridges for printers). While future expectations clearly affect these durable goods purchase decisions, other hardware/software systems may not involve intertemporal issues quite so powerfully. An example where current availability of the complementary good is crucial is credit card networks. Since the network of merchants accepting a card changes only slowly, current acceptability largely determines consumers' choice of credit card.

In hardware/software markets, the equilibrium may involve only one or a small number of networks, as consumers individually and rationally choose to align themselves with what they anticipate to be—and thereby ensure will be—the dominant platform. But as the economics literature notes (and many businesses have discovered), there may be also be an equilibrium involving no buyers. If a buyer expects few others, there will be little incentive for software writers, and hence buyers' initial expectations are fulfilled.

Despite some special features, the hardware/software case does rest on demand-side economies. Consumers gain added value from adopting the same hardware as most others—not in this case for reasons of communication between hardware devices, but because of the strong complementarities with related goods. This case does therefore represent a network phenomenon.

Networks, competition, and policy

The above discussion has identified three types of possible network effects, defined as those flowing from demand-side economies: (1) consumption externalities, (2) search and purchase economies, and (3) dynamics. In principle, actual network industries can be classified into one of these types. Practice is often more complicated, however, since the relevant distinctions are not always easy to discern and some industries may embody more than one such characteristic.

An important example of overlapping considerations concerns intertemporal effects. Consider the earlier discussion of the communications paradigm, which argued that a new consumer would join the largest network. So long as there are switching costs between networks, the rational consumer will join that network which *will* be the largest in the most relevant time frame, rather than the largest network at the time of purchase. Hence expectations about the evolution of competing networks may influence current consumer choice even in the classical case of network communications.[13]

Here we offer some observations about the competitive implications of networks, highlighting matters of potential concern. First, in the classical case of communications and in most other networks, as noted previously, there are forces propelling the market to an equilibrium consisting of a single provider. By itself this is not objectionable, since it may well be in consumers' own interests to become members of the dominant network. That said, it is well understood in the economics literature that the dominant network may not in fact be socially optimal, since aggregation advantages may cause consumers to make choices that result in persistent dominance by an inferior technology.

Second, an important force resisting the emergence of a single provider is product differentiation. Much as with traditional economies of scale, consumers' preference for variety may sustain two or more providers of (e.g.) telecommunications services in some form of competition. Unit costs may be above the social minimum as a result, but to the extent that this outcome reflects consumers' willingness to pay for alternative differentiated service, this is unobjectionable. Indeed, the resulting competition may result in net benefits in terms of cost efficiency and innovation.

Third, product differentiation offers some opportunity for new entry into the market, although de novo entry into network industries is quite difficult. Most networks involve high sunk costs, multiple related products, and switching costs to consumers. Overcoming these barriers requires that the entrant's product offer a significant improvement over the incumbent system. That can be and has been done: CDs supplanted record albums and cassettes, and DVDs represent the next technology in this progression.

The discussion thus far has presumed there is a "natural" incompatibility between competing networks, effectively requiring consumers to choose between alternatives. In other cases rivals may engage in strategic behavior to alter the degree and nature of competition. The following examples illustrate a range of such behavior. First, one company may simply exclude its rivals from a crucial aspect of the service, thereby degrading its rivals' quality or cost position, or in the limit, its ability to offer a competitive service at all. This strategy raises issues of bottleneck services and essential facilities, concepts dating back to the controversy and court case involving Terminal Railroad of St. Louis.[14]

Another possibility is that a company may deliberately create and enforce technological incompatibility between systems or among components of a system, thereby undermining a rival's ability to enter selectively. Such has been the allegations involving AOL's Instant Messaging, as well as Microsoft's behavior with respect to independent applications software.[15] Finally, a company may engage in "expectations management," so that customers are induced to wait for the offering of that company in the belief that in so doing they are choosing the dominant system. IBM was frequently accused of pre-announcing products in efforts to limit customer switching to rival products.

Since each of these strategies is designed to constrain a rival firm's operation, it is the dominant firm that is most likely to adopt them. A smaller firm, by contrast, generally wishes for a system that allows entry, access to necessary inputs, and access to consumers. In some cases compatibility may nonetheless emerge: Rivals may come to an agreement about standards and protocols when they value the resulting product variety more than incompatibility.[16] Or, third parties may develop adapters and converters that render components compatible.[17]

In other cases, however, public policy intervention may be required in order to foster competition on behalf of consumers. This policy can take several forms representing varying degrees of intervention: (1) policy can simply require firms to guarantee compatibility between rival systems, without specifying the mechanism; (2) somewhat more aggressively, policy can establish common protocols and standards that ensure that products can interact; and (3) a yet more aggressive policy would mandate access to a rival's crucial input, as with colocation requirements in telecom.

The choice among these policies will depend upon the nature of the product or service, the number and capabilities of rivals, and the degree of transparency of the dominant firm's behavior. Whether any policy is necessary at all further depends upon the nature of the underlying network effects as well as any market adjustments and responses to those forces. In any case, whether due to endogenous forces or policy, network industries are generally found to have multiple providers, strongly suggesting the social benefits of such competition as may be viable in network industries.

Notes

1 Neal F. Finnegan Professor of Economics, Northeastern University.
2 This is helpful but incomplete, since most interesting real-world firms produce multiple products and the stated condition based on average cost cannot be generalized to the multiproduct case. Equally importantly, this is not a definition of natural monopoly since a single firm may be the most efficient organization of production for market sizes at least slightly greater than that where the firm's average cost curve reaches its minimum. Technically, natural monopoly is given by subadditivity of the cost function. For the single product case, a declining LRAC is a sufficient (but not a necessary) condition. See, for example, J. Tirole, *The Theory of Industrial Organization*, Cambridge, Massachusetts: MIT Press, 1988.
3 Note that both firms face higher unit costs as a result of fragmented production, resulting in higher equilibrium prices.
4 This formulation of a communications network was originally due to J. Rohlfs, "A theory of interdependent demand for a communications service," *Bell Journal of Economics* 5, 1975, pp. 16–37. We postpone discussion of interconnection between networks.
5 The advantage of the star architecture, of course, is dependent on the relative costs of the switch vs. bilateral linkages.
6 The value to one person of joining a network with no others on it is zero. AT&T's efforts to introduce PicturePhone failed due to its inability to create a network of users. The role of prospective membership and expectations will be discussed more fully below.
7 This result has been labeled Metcalfe's Law, after Bob Metcalfe, inventor of Ethernet.
8 For a discussion of this perspective, see N. Economides and L. White, "Networks and compatibility: implications for antitrust," *European Economic Review* 38, 1994, pp. 651–62.
9 For further discussion, see S. Borenstein, "The evolution of U.S. airline competition," *Journal of Economic Perspectives* 6, 1992, pp. 45–73.
10 Here we assume incompatibility among systems, an assumption to be examined below.
11 Alternatively, there might be vertical integration between PC and software manufacturers, but with a proliferation of alternatives the outcome would still approach competitive equilibrium.
12 For this reason, the common use of the term "systems" for this case does not

fully capture the relevant issue, namely, the dynamics of demand. For extensive discussion of this case, see M. Katz and C. Shapiro, "Systems competition and network effects," *Journal of Economic Perspectives* 8, 1994, pp. 93–115.

13 Clearly, the consumer might also postpone the purchase decision altogether, in order to ensure selection of the dominant network.

14 *U.S. v. Terminal Railroad Association of St. Louis,* 224 U.S. 383 (1912).

15 See G. Faulhaber, "Access and network effects in the new economy," pp. 453–75 and D. Rubinfeld, "Maintenance of monopoly: Microsoft," pp. 476–501 in *The Antitrust Revolution,* J. Kwoka and L. White (eds), 4th edn, New York: Oxford University Press, 2004.

16 For discussion of these issues, see C. Matutes and P. Regibeau, "Mix and match: product compatibility without network externalities," *Rand Journal of Economics* 19, 1988, pp. 221–34.

17 See J. Farrell and G. Saloner, "Converters, compatibility, and the control of interfaces," *Journal of Industrial Economics* 40, 1992, pp. 9–35.

Topic 2
Tipping

Rudolph J. R. Peritz[1]

Introduction

For lawyers, tipping can have a wide range of meanings—from liability for insider trading to the constitutionality of regulating exotic dancers (posted sign: "Keep 10 foot distance from patrons and no tipping!"). A recent Westlaw search brought back 5028 case opinions with references to tipping of one sort or another. Physical and social scientists have studied precipitous change—whether Stephen J. Gould's punctuated equilibrium theory of natural selection or sociologists' investigations of white flight from cities to suburbs. In the 1970s, French mathematician René Thom developed a topology of discontinuous change whose English translation is Catastrophe Theory. It could just as well have been called tipping theory. About ten years later, a group of off-center academics, among them economists Kenneth Arrow and Brian Arthur, began to publish papers and proceedings of the Santa Fe Institute. They wanted to develop a mathematical language to describe the discontinuities of precipitous transitions among chaos, complexity and stability.

More broadly, images of tipping have been commonplace. There is the barking dog whose behavior suddenly turns to fight or flight. Or the multiple personality disorders whose victims snap into and out of different persona. Perhaps the best known image is the straw that broke the camel's back. The image of the barking dog portrays an abrupt change of state without any build-up to the turn.[2] The trope of the last straw depicts the final step in a gradual process that nonetheless culminates in an abrupt change in the camel's back.

In market economics, there have been several notions of tipping, where tipping is taken to mean a predisposition toward winner-takes-most outcomes. Recent examples include the triumphs of digital disc technologies over analogue tapes, VHS over Beta in the videotape wars, and, of course, Microsoft over rivals in PC operating systems, web browsers, word processing software, and, perhaps, media players. Over 100 years ago, economist Henry Carter Adams wrote about industries whose high start-up costs and low operating costs naturally led to monopoly, whether single firms or cartels. Similar arguments of ruinous competition to justify a cartel were heard in *Trans Missouri Railroad Association*, the first antitrust case decided on the merits by the Supreme Court.

Another economic conception of tippy markets has been around for many years but has influenced antitrust policy only since the mid-1980s. That is Joseph Schumpeter's "perennial gales of creative destruction"—his metaphor for the emergence and triumph of "the new" and for the overthrow of current monopolies and incumbent technologies. In recent years, "the new" has been associated with innovation and, thus, with competition on the merits. But those associations have long had their critics. In the 1930s, economist Edward Chamberlin's influential work raised distinctions between innovation and product differentiation, between substantial improvement and mere surface changes. In the 1980s, economists Ordover & Willig wrote of predatory innovation.

In the mid-1980s, a newer economic notion of tipping was developed in articles by Arthur, Farrell, Katz, Saloner, Shapiro, and others. This newer economics shifted focus from supply side to demand side economies of scale. The fundamental insight was that tipping was more likely to occur in industries organized into networks because network membership tended to become more valuable as network size increased. The increasing value to both current and prospective members is called network effects or positive returns to demand. Its graphical representation is the S-shaped adoption curve or "logistic" pattern of growth.

But here, too, limits have been recognized. On the demand side, some current patrons might enjoy diminishing network effects fairly quickly. Moreover, supply side economies of scale remain important, as do pricing strategies. Finally, network size and network saturation can produce increasing transaction costs that result in negative returns to demand.

Network effects have provided the rationale for concerns expressed in numerous workshops, hearings, white papers, public statements, and in matters pursued by the FTC and the Antitrust Division in the 1990s: From requiring ATM network access or software porting to resolving the FTC's two *Intel* matters—one involving access to interface information and the other assuring the continued viability of DEC's Alpha chip technology after their merger. In Europe, the Commission stopped Microsoft from gaining joint control, at least directly, of a U.K. cable network on the rationale that the increased likelihood of the network's adopting Microsoft's operating system for TV set-top boxes would give Microsoft a head start and, thus, raise the threat of tipping the entire European O.S. market for TV set-top boxes toward a Microsoft monopoly.[3] More recently, the Commission issued findings followed by a decree requiring Microsoft to unbundle its Media Player from Windows and to make confidential information about Windows available to competitors in the market for low-end network server operating systems in order to allow servers running non-Windows operating systems to interoperate smoothly with PCs running Windows.

Tipping is not limited to network industries, whether largely physical networks such as pipelines or largely virtual networks such as the Microsoft Windows customer base. Indeed, one of the most familiar stories of tipping is the VHS–Beta rivalry in the VCR market, which is not strictly a network industry but a systems market of bundled products. We will turn to the VCR story shortly. For now, it is useful to review the basic positive feedback scenario of network effects and the associated tendency toward tipping in the systems context: increasing sales of VHS format machines and, thus, increasing requests for pre-recorded VHS tapes prompted video rental shops to increase VHS inventories, which then provoked increasing sales of VHS machines, and back around in what has been called a "virtuous circle": More of each VHS system component kept making the other more valuable to current and future VHS patrons. Hence, future customers were more and more likely to choose VHS, especially if Beta systems lagged behind in the production of virtuous circles. Eventually, potential patrons did not even consider Beta systems a viable alternative, regardless of price and quality.

Potential customers had to choose one or the other format because VHS and Beta systems were incompatible. The costs of switching between them produced an either/or choice that hardened the VHS equilibrium. In short, having made the VHS choice, customers were locked in to the VHS standard . . . until a substitute would emerge to offer value sufficiently higher than the perceived costs of switching to that substitute (or replacing the old technology at the end of its useful life despite an inventory of non-staple complements). This, of course, is the unfolding DVD story.

What more can be said about lock-in and its relationship to tipping? First, despite the VCR story, lock-in and tipping seem to be relatively independent phenomena. Neither one requires the other. The marketing strategy literature is replete with examples of successful strategies to segment markets and lock-in customers, with no mention of tipping. And tipping does not require lock-in, at least not always. Perhaps the best example of that proposition is the browser market dominance of Internet Explorer. Internet Explorer and Netscape Navigator are not incompatible from the browser user's perspective. (Their differences can raise compatibility issues for website developers and other applications programmers.) And what of WORD and WordPerfect? For file sharing purposes, they are (imperfectly) compatible. But WORD nonetheless dominates the market. Why the dominance of IE and WORD? The complete answer is complex, but part of the answer seems to be some low level of switching costs that is still high enough to tip the IE and WORD customer bases toward weaker equilibria of lock-in. Indeed, the strategic marketing literature does counsel that even low switching costs can effectively lock in customers. The recent struggle in the FCC over cell phone number portability is evidence of the importance of even small switching costs. When, if ever, should strategies to trigger tipping or to provoke lock-in raise antitrust concerns? Restated, what should antitrust make of a non-dominant firm's primary purpose to raise rivals' costs rather than to improve a product?

The cost structures of network and systems markets raise further antitrust questions about strategic conduct, particularly pricing strategies intended to induce tipping. First, given the exceedingly low marginal costs associated with network industries and information goods industries generally, how should antitrust policy treat penetration pricing? What of predatory pricing doctrine, whether the current standard of pricing below some measure of cost or recent arguments for closer scrutiny of some above-cost pricing strategies? Does condoning penetration pricing tilt the playing field to favor financially powerful firms and exert pressure to transform, for example, software development, into a needlessly concentrated industry? Second, should a distinction be made between physical and virtual networks because physical networks such as railroads and pipelines typically entail much higher sunk costs than software development usually does? In consequence, should market concentration in software development be looked at more closely than concentration in railroads, despite seemingly similar cost structures? Should courts in software cases consider more seriously remedies that create competitive structures than they do in railroad or pipeline or telecommunications industries?

As we know, not all systems are cut from the same mold. Scholars have posed useful definitions and distinctions in the conceptual terminology of systems: For example, systems versus networks, communications systems versus hardware/software systems, actual versus virtual versus physical systems, unidirectional versus multidirectional networks, network effects versus network externalities, and meritorious versus accidental outcomes. We have addressed a few of these distinctions. There is not enough time to discuss them all but their significance will emerge in comparative readings of the case studies in this collection. It is useful to conclude with perhaps the most controversial distinction—merit versus chance.

Brian Arthur, in his path-breaking article entitled "Competing technologies, increasing returns, and lock-in by historical events," used as an example the competition between VHS and Beta formats for video recording and playback. Like the barking dog, the market for VCRs was destined to tip one way or the other. Traditional market economists attributed the VHS result to merit. The better technology won. Schumpeterian competition carried the day. That the VHS format won so convincingly was seen as the result of network effects and, perhaps, a greater agility in developing economies of scale in production and distribution. But Arthur told a different story, a story of chance rather than one of merit.[4]

Brian Arthur's story is intriguing for the very reason it remains controversial. He called into question the causative agency of merit. It was entirely possible, he claimed, for the better technology to lose. It was possible because the phenomenon of positive returns could develop from *random* clusters of market events, generating ever larger and more power-ful spirals of positive feedback entirely out of proportion to the size of the inciting events. Random clusters of VHS machine purchases could co-occur, purely by accident, to prompt increases in pre-recorded VHS tape inventories, and vice versa. Positive feedback loops would begin to take shape. If those random loops emerged earlier or grew faster than random Beta system loops, then the winner would have been VHS . . . based not on merit but on chance or historical accident.

In his article, Arthur cited studies claiming that Beta systems produced superior audio and video quality. The controversy over Arthur's work involves both his theory and his evidence. His theory emerges out of a sto-chastic or probabilistic methodology that is very different from the statics and comparative statics of the dominant market economics. Perhaps this methodological difference explains why Arthur's claims about probabili-ties are sometimes misunderstood as assertions about necessary outcomes. Other times, his theory is rejected on its own terms as an unconvincing view of markets reflecting positive returns, his critics taking issue with his evidence (like the VCR story), claiming that in every instance he cites, the better technology did in fact win.

What is at stake in this debate is the causative relationship between innovation and market success. To put it in the older language of econo-mist Edward Chamberlin, when is product change improvement and when is it only differentiation? How that question should be resolved pre-sents difficult issues of political economy and conjures images of industrial planning. Certainly the Patent Office resolves such questions every day. But the debate has centered on the federal courts' recent treatment of antitrust issues surrounding licensing, bundling and product integration, which raise questions of merit even more broadly—not only innovation versus mere differentiation but also a third category of predatory or anti-competitive product change. This third category, at least, invokes a tradi-tional antitrust doctrine that calls for the very judgments that we are uncomfortable making. Is the right approach to be found in the D.C. Circuit's tying doctrine and its deference to technological change—whether the greater deference granted in the three-judge panel's treat-ment of the 1995 Microsoft consent decree or the lesser deference given in the circuit's en banc opinion in the more recent Microsoft monopoliza-tion case? Or should the answer to the question of competition on the merits turn on the slippery notions of *mens rea* or primary purpose? What of attempted monopolization cases? And merger or joint venture cases? Should there be a preliminary market power screen in rule of reason cases—a particularly difficult question in the context of dynamic markets? These few questions, and others, should provoke useful discussion.

Notes

1 Professor of Law, New York Law School.
2 Some observers claim that "ears back" means flight and "ears up" means fight.
3 M. Monti, "Competition and information technologies," speech for Kangaroo Group's *Barriers in Cyberspace* conference, September 18, 2000. Online. Available HTTP: <http://europa.eu.int/rapid/pressReleasesAction.do?reference=SPEECH/00/315/0/RAPID&format=HTML&aged=&language=EN&guiLanguage=en> (accessed November 4, 2004).
4 There is also a third story—one of strategic marketing.

References

Adams, H. C., *The Relationship of the State to Industrial Action*, in 1 Publication of the American Economic Association 471, 1887.

Arrow, K. J., "Economic welfare and the allocation of resources for invention," in *The Rate and Direction of Inventive Activity: Economic and Social Factors*, Princeton, N.J.: Princeton University Press, 1962, pp. 609–25.

Arthur, W. B., "Competing technologies, increasing returns, and lock-in by historical events," *Journal of Economics* 116, 1989, pp. 116–31.

Arthur, W. B., *Increasing Returns and Path Dependence in the Economy*, Ann Arbor, Michigan: University of Michigan, 1994.

Chamberlin, E., *The Theory of Monopolistic Competition*, Cambridge, Massachusetts: Harvard University Press, 1933.

Farrell, J. and Katz, M. L., "The effects of antitrust and intellectual property law on compatibility and innovation," *Antitrust Bulletin* 43, 1998, pp. 609–50.

Farrell, J. and Saloner, G., "Standardization, compatibility, and innovation," *Rand Journal of Economics* 16, 1985, pp. 70–83.

In re Intel Corp., 1999 F.T.C. LEXIS 145 (August 3, 1999) (complaint, Docket No. 9288); FTC Decision and Order. Online. Available HTTP: <http://www.ftc.gov/os/1999/08/intel.do.htm> (accessed June 14, 2004).

Katz, M. L. and Shapiro, C., "Network externalities, competition, and compatibility," *American Economic Review* 75, 1985, pp. 424–40.

Katz, M. L. and Shapiro, C., "Systems competition and network effects," *Journal of Economic Perspectives* 93, 1994, pp. 93–115.

Liebowitz, S. J. and Margolis, S. E., "Network externality: an uncommon tragedy," *Journal of Economic Perspectives* 8, 1994, pp. 133–50.

"Microsoft in Telwest retreat," Online. Available HTTP: <http://news.bbc.co.uk/1/hi/business/820933.stm> (accessed June 14, 2004).

Ordover, J. A. and Willig, R. D., "An economic definition of predation: pricing and product innovation," *Yale Law Journal* 91, 1981, pp. 8–53.

Peritz, R. J. R., *Competition Policy in America: History, Rhetoric, Law*, revised edn, New York: Oxford University Press, 2001.

Peritz, R. J. R., "Antitrust policy and aggressive business strategy: a historical perspective on understanding commercial purposes and effects," *Journal of Public Policy and Marketing* 21, 2002, pp. 237–42.

Schumpeter, J. A., *Capitalism, Socialism and Democracy*, New York: Harper and Row, 1950.

Shapiro, C. and Varian, H. R., *Information Rules: A Strategic Guide to the Network Economy*, Cambridge, Massachusetts: Harvard Business School Press, 1999.

Thom, R., *Stabilité Structurelle et Morphogenèse*, Paris: Intereditions, 1972.

United States v. Microsoft, 84 F.Supp.2d 9 (D.D.C. 1999) (Findings of Fact), 87 F.Supp.2d 30 (D.D.C. 2000) (Conclusions of Law), judgment aff'd in part & rev'd in part, 253 F.3d 34 (D.C. Cir. 2001) (en banc).

United States v. Microsoft, 147 F.3d 935 (D.C. Cir 1998), reversing 980 F. Supp. 537 (1998).

United States v. Trans-Missouri Freight Ass'n, 166 U.S. 290 (1897).

Topic 3

The essential facility doctrine
A brief overview

Norman Hawker[1]

"The report of my death was an exaggeration."[2]

Introduction

Despite the misgivings of some commentators, the essential facilities doctrine is not dead. The doctrine consists of four elements: (1) control of the essential facility by a monopolist; (2) a competitor's inability to duplicate the essential facility; (3) the denial of the use of the facility to a competitor; and (4) the feasibility of providing the facility. In the wake of *Verizon Communications Inc. v. Law Office of Curtis V. Trinko, LLP*,[3] successful application of this doctrine may depend not only on what the plaintiff alleges as the essential facility, but also the absence of a non-judicially mandated means of access. Nonetheless, the Supreme Court did not overrule essential facilities doctrine, and lower courts continue to apply the doctrine.[4]

Development of the doctrine

Contrary to some assertions,[5] the essential facility doctrine is not a recent development in antitrust. The doctrine dates back to the 1912 decision in *United States v. Terminal R.R. Ass'n of St. Louis*.[6] A group of railroads, through their ownership of the Terminal Association, controlled all the available terminals for railway traffic to enter or pass through St. Louis.[7] Competing railroads could not afford to build their own facilities,[8] especially given St. Louis's peculiar "geographical and topographical" conditions.[9] This gave the owners of the Terminal Association the power "to impede free competition from outside companies."[10] As a prophylactic measure, the Court required the Terminal Association to provide access to its facilities by non-owner railroads "upon such just and reasonable terms and regulations as will ... place every [railroad] upon as nearly an equal plane as may be."[11] Although the issue had been framed in terms of a restraint of trade,[12] the Court went out its way to state that the conduct would also constitute an attempt to monopolize in violation of section 2 of the Sherman Act.[13]

For the next half century, cases that could be characterized as group boycotts dominated the development of the essential facilities doctrine.[14] The Court in *United States v. Griffith*[15] reaffirmed, at least in *dicta,* that a single firm monopolist must share essential facilities with competitors in other markets to prevent "the use of monopoly power, however lawfully acquired, to foreclose competition, to gain a competitive advantage, or to destroy a competitor."[16]

In 1973, the Supreme Court resolved doubts about the applicability of the essential facilities doctrine to unilateral refusals to deal by holding that a single firm monopolist must deal with its competitors in *Otter Tail Power Co. v. United States.*[17] Otter Tail sold electricity in the retail and wholesale markets of the upper Midwest.[18] For many of the towns, Otter Tail owned the only transmission lines connected to wholesale electric power sources.[19] When several towns voted to replace Otter Tail with their own municipal systems in the retail market,[20] i.e., they decided to compete with Otter Tail at the retail level, Otter Tail "refused to sell the new systems energy at wholesale and refused to agree to wheel power from other suppliers of wholesale energy."[21] Without access to wholesale electricity from Otter Tail or through its transmission lines, the new municipal systems could not obtain electricity to sell to their retail customers.[22] Although the Court did not specifically use the phrase "essential facility," it did find that Otter Tail had violated section 2 and required Otter Tail to deal with the municipal systems.[23]

The essential facilities doctrine crystallized in *MCI Communications Corp. v. AT&T.*[24] Summarizing nearly three-quarters of a century of case law, the Seventh Circuit formulated the doctrine's four basic elements: (1) control of the essential facility by a monopolist; (2) a competitor's inability practically or reasonably to duplicate the essential facility; (3) the denial of the use of the facility to a competitor; and (4) the feasibility of providing the facility.[25]

Although the doctrine remains controversial, and different courts have applied these factors in different ways, virtually every court that has considered the essential facility doctrine over the past eighteen years has relied on the *MCI* formulation.[26] At issue in *MCI* was the extent to which AT&T had to open up its local telephone exchange to its competitors in the long distance telephone market.[27] MCI had built a long distance telecommunications network, but MCI needed to connect its network to local telephone facilities in each of the cities that was served by AT&T.[28]

The Seventh Circuit found all of the elements of the essential facility doctrine present. First, AT&T had a monopoly over the local telephone facilities, and MCI could not provide to certain long distance services without access to local telephone facilities.[29] Second, MCI could not duplicate the local telephone facilities, both because it "would not be economically feasible" to do so and because MCI could not obtain regulatory authorization "for such an uneconomical duplication."[30] Third,

AT&T conceded that it had denied MCI access to the local telephone facilities.[31] Fourth, it was "technically and economically feasible for AT&T to provide the interconnections."[32] AT&T, moreover, did not have any legitimate business or technical reasons for denying MCI access to the local exchanges.[33]

The Supreme Court has never formally adopted the essentially facilities doctrine, and in *Trinko,* where the doctrine had been successfully used in the court below,[34] the Court declined the opportunity to "recognize it or repudiate it."[35] *Trinko* concerned the refusal of Verizon to provide interconnection with competing telephone companies in violation of the Telecommunications Act of 1996. The Court stated that the doctrine should not apply because the 1996 Act contained its own "extensive provision for access."[36] While this statement calls the holding of *Otter Tail* into question,[37] to date the lower courts have not read *Trinko* as a repudiation of the essential facilities doctrine as outlined in *MCI.*[38]

Rational for the doctrine

The essential facilities doctrine appears to be a special application of the leveraging doctrine.[39] Consequently, to prevent a monopolist from extending "monopoly power from one stage of production to another, and from one market to another,"[40] the essential facilities doctrine creates an exception to the general rule that even a monopolist has discretion as to the customers with whom he will deal.[41] The essential facilities doctrine differs from leveraging in that it requires proof that a competitor needs access to compete and the business justifications defense appears to be more limited.[42]

Sullivan and Grimes have identified some important criticisms of the essential facilities doctrine. They point out that it "collides" with several concepts:

> [1] not even a monopolist need give positive assistance to competitors; [2] innovation should be encouraged and rewarded; and [3] the law should not turn against those that competition has encouraged merely because they have thoroughly prevailed.[43]

Sullivan and Grimes also fear that as formulated, the doctrine could apply to any essential facility and would limit the doctrine to cases where "the market power attained is attributable in significant part to sources other than the skill, initiative and innovation of the owner."[44] On the other hand, a monopolist's denial of access to its competitors also bears the characteristics of monopoly leverage identified by Sullivan: it is exploitive, it is restrictive, and it ultimately obscures the source of the monopolist's power.[45]

Elaboration for the doctrine's elements

With nearly a century of experience with this doctrine, the reasonably mature jurisprudence has developed for each of the four elements.

Control of the essential facility by a monopolist

This element raises three issues: (1) whether the defendant is a monopolist, (2) whether the defendant controls a facility, and (3) whether the facility is essential. As to the issue of a facility, at least one commentator has suggested that only physical structures may constitute facilities.[46] In *Bellsouth Advertising & Publishing Corp. v. Donnelley Information Publishing, Inc.*,[47] however, one of the few cases to directly address this issue, the plaintiff and defendant competed in the telephone directory market. When the plaintiff sued for copyright and trademark infringement, the defendant responded by alleging that the plaintiff's refusal to provide the defendant with updated listings violated the essential facilities doctrine. The court held that the doctrine applied to both tangible and intangible property since the "effect in both situations is the same: a party is prevented from sharing in something essential to compete."[48]

Subsequent cases have also refused to limit the definition of facilities to physical structures. In *Advanced Health Care Services, Inc. v. Radford Community Hosp.*,[49] for example, the Fourth Circuit held that access to hospital patients could constitute a facility.[50] Similarly, the district court in *American Health Sys. v. Visiting Nurse Ass'n*[51] applied the essential facilities doctrine to hospital referrals.[52] Another district court indicated that services could constitute a facility in *Sunshine Cellular v. Vanguard Cellular Systems, Inc.*[53]

Exactly what makes a facility essential has stirred a great deal of debate. If the word "essential" is to have any many meaning, then competitors must suffer "more than inconvenience or even some economic loss" from the denial of access,[54] but courts have differed in just how much more important access must be.

To the extent that it has addressed the issue, the Supreme Court has suggested a relatively easy standard. In *Associated Press v. United States*,[55] for example, the government challenged the Associated Press' prohibition on the distribution of stories to competitors of its member newspapers. Although non-members could turn to alternative news services[56] and "some competing papers have gotten along without AP news,"[57] the Court upheld the grant of summary judgment for the government on grounds that access to the stories collected and distributed by the defendant "gives many newspapers a competitive advantage over their rivals."[58] Ultimately, however, the Associated Press' control over the stories represented collective action by its members. The Court relied on the competitive advantage test in *Otter Tail*,[59] an unambiguous case of single firm monopoly. But one could argue this was mere dicta given the fact that it would have been all but impossible for Otter Tail's competitors to sell electricity without access to the utility's transmission lines.

Nonetheless, most courts that have addressed the issue since MCI have used much tougher standards than "competitive advantage" to determine whether the facility is essential. The Ninth Circuit Court of Appeals, for example, has stated that a facility "will be considered 'essential' only if control of the facility carries with it the power to eliminate competition" in other markets.[60] Requiring proof that it is literally impossible to compete without access to the facility seems a bit extreme,[61] but the district court in *Paladin Associates, Inc. v. Montana Power Co.*,[62] recently followed this rule in granting summary judgment against a natural gas marketer who was denied access to Montana Power's pipeline system.[63] Some courts have required that an essential facility be "not merely helpful but vital to [a firm's] competitive viability,"[64] while other courts have required that denial of access "inflicts severe handicap on potential market entrants."[65] Perhaps the most lenient formulation in use simply asks whether "competitors need access if they are to compete effectively."[66]

It is not altogether clear that the choice of standard makes a difference in practice. For example, in *Florida Mun. Power Agency v. Florida Power & Light Co.*,[67] the district court began its analysis by quoting the Ninth Circuit test, then stated the plaintiff must "at a minimum" prove the "severe handicap" test, and ultimately ruled against the plaintiff's motion for summary judgment because it did not show that "an alternative to facility was not feasible."[68]

Without any discussion of the standard, *CTC Communications Corp. v. Bell Atlantic Corp.*,[69] the district court refused to grant summary judgment on a claim that access to the defendant's voice mail services constituted an essential facility for the plaintiff, a reseller of local telephone services. Instead, the court simply found sufficient evidence of the number of business users who would not switch to a reseller such as the plaintiff without access to the defendant's voice mail services.[70]

A competitor's inability practically or reasonably to duplicate the essential facility

The second element of the essential facilities, which requires an inability of competitors to duplicate the essential facility, overlaps with the first factor.[71] After all, if duplication were practical or reasonable, then duplication would be an alternative to use of the monopolist's facility and one could not consider the facility essential.[72] This does not mean that a competitor must find it literally impossible to duplicate the facility, rather the test is whether it is economically and practically feasible for a competitor to duplicate the facility.[73]

The denial of the use of the facility to a competitor

Even as it declined to recognize or reject the essential facility doctrine, the Court in *Trinko* elevated the importance of the third element, stating that "the indispensable requirement for invoking the doctrine is the unavailability of access to the 'essential facilities'; where access exists, the doctrine serves no purpose."[74] The doctrine's third element consists of three basic components. First, the doctrine only applies when the person denied access to the facility competes with the monopolist.[75] In *America Online, Inc. v. GreatDeals.Net,*[76] where an advertiser sought access to AOL's subscribers, the court dismissed the essential facilities claim because the AOL did not compete with the advertiser, nor did AOL have any financial stake in an advertiser.[77]

Similarly, the Federal Circuit reversed the district court and held that Intel could deny Intergraph, a computer workstation manufacturer, access to critical information because the two did not compete.[78] Intergraph held the patents to the Clipper microprocessor, but the court held that this could not establish a competitive relationship because "Intergraph had abandoned the production of Clipper microprocessors . . ., and states no intention to return to it."[79] Even had the court accepted a competitive relationship in the microprocessor market, Intergraph would almost certainly have failed to establish an essential facilities claim because it needed the information from Intel to compete with other workstation manufacturers, not to compete with Intel in the microprocessor market.[80]

Second, at least in private litigation, the plaintiff must show that the defendant actually denied the plaintiff access to the essential facility.[81] The doctrine does not require an unequivocal refusal to deal under any terms,[82] but rather a refusal to provide access on reasonable, nondiscriminatory terms.[83] In *Zschaler v. Claneil Enterprises, Inc.,*[84] for example, the plaintiff competed with defendants in offering lodgings in a ski resort area. The defendants also owned the reservation system used by the vast majority of consumers.[85] Although the reservation system listed the plaintiff's lodgings, the court found that the defendants had "effectively denied" the plaintiffs access to this essential facility because the reservation system diverted consumers to the defendant's lodgings.[86] Although absolute equality of access is not required,[87] provision of access on a nondiscriminatory basis lies at the very heart of the doctrine.[88]

In contrast to private plaintiffs,[89] the government may seek prophylactic relief. In *Terminal R.R. Ass'n*, the Association had not in fact denied any competitor equal access to its terminal facilities,[90] but yet the government still won an injunction to prevent the Association from denying access to competing railroads.[91]

Finally, *Trinko* appears to have established a third component, the absence of an alternative legal mechanism for compelling access. The Court in *Trinko* ruled that the essential facility doctrine did not apply to

Verizon's refusal to provide interconnections for competing telephone companies because the Telecommunications Act of 1996's "extensive provision for access makes it unnecessary to impose a judicial doctrine of forced access."[92]

Lower courts have already begun to incorporate and apply this third component. In *Nobody In Particular Presents, Inc. v. Clear Channel Communications, Inc.*,[93] the plaintiff, a Denver area concert promoter, alleged that the defendant, who promoted concerts and owned four of Denver's six radio stations, had denied the plaintiff access to "rock radio advertising and promotional support" that was essential for concert promotion. The defendant argued that *Trinko* required dismissal of the plaintiff's claim. The court, however, found that *Trinko* actually supported the plaintiff's claim because there was "no government agency... compelling [the defendant] to allow access to its airwaves."[94] Consequently, antitrust law "is the only mechanism by which [the defendant's] behavior may be policed,"[95] and, therefore, the defendant's behavior "does fall into the limited category of cases where refusal to deal implicates the Sherman Act."[96]

The feasibility of providing the facility

Courts generally treat the question of feasibility as having two components. First, it must be technologically and practically feasible for the monopolist to give its rivals access to the facility.[97] Second, even if the capability to share the facility exists, a monopolist may still raise a business justification for refusing to deal with competitors.[98]

Technical feasibility

The test for technical feasibility is a practical one.[99] For example, the facility consists of a limited resource, the monopolist is not required to stop its use of the facility to make the resource available for competitors.[100]

Business justification defense

Although technically an affirmative defense,[101] courts often deal with business justifications under the rubric of the essential facilities doctrine's fourth element.[102] In *City of Anaheim v. So. Calif. Edison Co.*,[103] for example, the Ninth Circuit held that a utility did not have to provide competitors with access to a particular inexpensive source of electricity if doing so would impair the utility's ability to access the same source for the utility's own retail customers.[104]

Morris Communications Corp. v. PGA Tour, Inc.,[105] presents a more recent application of the business justification defense that attempts to incorporate the *Trinko* decision. The defendant refused to grant access to its media center, which included its relay system for real-time scores at PGA golf tournaments, unless the plaintiff agreed to restrictions on the redistribution of the scores. The court found that the defendant had valid business justification because granting access would have given the plaintiff a free ride on the defendant's proprietary system.[106] The plaintiff argued that proffered free rider defense was a pretext and the defendant's real motivation was "economic."[107] The court distinguished between granting access to a distribution channel controlled by the defendant and access to a product created by the defendant, and the court believed that *Trinko* fell into the latter category.[108] Since access to the media center would only allow the plaintiff to resell a product created entirely by the defendant's efforts, the court felt that the free rider problem was not pretextual and noted that the prevention of free riding "is an inherently economic motivation."[109]

What makes *Morris Communications* so troubling is that the essential facility does not create a free rider problem. The doctrine only requires non-discriminatory, not free, access to the facility.

Anticompetitive intent and effects

MCI distinguished the doctrine from other section 2 cases involving refusals to deal that "focus on the intent and competitive effect of the refusal to deal; not on whether the facility itself is 'essential.'"[110] Thus, the doctrine establishes a quasi-per se monopolization offense insofar as a successful claim does not require additional proof of anticompetitive intent or effect.[111]

The presumption of anticompetitive effect and intent is consistent with the need for antitrust laws to protect the "competitive process, and their application does not depend in each particular case upon the ultimate demonstrable consumer effect."[112] When a firm cuts off its rival's access to an essential facility, then the firm will monopolize the market, not by virtue of "superior skill, foresight and industry,"[113] but by making it impossible for its rivals to engage in the competitive process.

This is not to say that the essential facilities doctrine abandons traditional section 2 concepts altogether. For example, one cannot tell whether the defendant who owns the facility is a monopolist or whether competitors have access to alternatives without defining the relevant markets.[114] Thus, in an unpublished opinion, the Ninth Circuit upheld the grant of summary judgment against the plaintiff in *Reiser v. Microsoft Corp.*,[115] when the plaintiff failed to show the existence of a downstream market where he would compete with Microsoft.[116]

Conclusion

The essential facility doctrine seems to have weathered the *Trinko* decision in relatively fine shape. Contrary to the fears that *Trinko* may have placed the doctrine "on a respirator,"[117] it appears that *Trinko* merely limited application of the doctrine to cases where there is no other legal means of compelling access.

The reaction to *Trinko*, however, begs a fundamental question about the essential facility doctrine, i.e., why do the lower courts continue to embrace this doctrine in the face of continuing skepticism from the Supreme Court and unrelenting hostility from commentators? After all, as one of the few favorable commentaries on the doctrine pointed out, if "U.S. scholarship were the last word on the subject, one would be led to conclude that the essential facilities doctrine should be described narrowly or fully abandoned."[118] While a full exploration of the issue is not possible here, a few tentative ideas are in order. First, unlike traditional rule of reason analysis under section 2, the essential facility doctrine provides a clear and easy test for courts to administer. Second, the doctrine has an intuitive appeal. This is not a throw back to populism,[119] but a recognition that the purpose of antitrust law is to preserve and promote competition.[120] A court does not require extended economic analysis to see that denying a rival firm access to an essential facility necessarily reduces competition in the market that the rival sought to enter. Compelling access to the essential facility ensures that market forces, not the discretion of the monopolist who controls the essential facility, will determine the success or failure of the rival's product. Finally, the essential facility doctrine does provide a way of addressing monopolistic harms that are not easily addressed by economic models based on price theory.[121] For example, "pure" exclusionary harms may not lead to "deadweight" consumer welfare losses,[122] but they could result in a reduction of consumer choice.[123]

Notes

1 Associate Professor of Strategy, Law and Ethics, Haworth College of Business, Western Michigan University, and American Antitrust Institute Research Fellow.

2 M. Twain, untitled handwritten note, May 1897. Online. Available HTTP: <http://www.twainquotes.com/Death.html> (accessed May 1, 2004). See also B. Mikkelson, *And Never the Twain Shall Tweet*, Urban Legends Reference Pages, 2002. Online. Available HTTP: <http://www.snopes.com/quotes/twain.htm> (accessed May 1, 2004).

3 124 S. Ct. 872 (2004).

4 See, for example, *Nobody In Particular Presents, Inc. v. Clear Channel Communications, Inc.*, U.S. Dist. LEXIS 5665 (D. Colo. 2004).

5 See, for example, *Flip Side Prod., Inc. v. Jam Prod., Inc.*, 843 F.2d 1024, 1032 (7th Cir. 1988); *TCA Bldg. Co. v. Northwestern Resources Co.*, 873 F. Supp. 39 (S.D. Tex. 1995); S. D. Makar, "The essential facility doctrine and the health care industry," *Fla. St. U. L. Rev.* 21, 1994, pp. 913–43.

6 *United States v. Terminal R.R. Ass'n of St. Louis*, 224 U.S. 383 (1912). See M. L.

Azcuenga, "Essential facilities and regulation: court or agency jurisdiction," *Antitrust Law Journal* 58, 1990, p. 883 (referring to *United States v. Terminal R.R. Ass'n of St. Louis* as "the granddaddy of all essential facilities cases").

7 Ibid., 397.

8 Ibid., 395.

9 Ibid., 397, 404, 405, and 398.

10 Ibid., 401.

11 Ibid., 411.

12 Ibid., 394.

13 Ibid.

14 See, for example, *Associated Press v. United States*, 326 U.S. 1 (1945); *Silver v. New York Stock Exch.*, 373 U.S. 341 (1963).

15 334 U.S. 100 (1948).

16 Ibid., 107.

17 *Otter Tail Power Co. v. United States*, 410 U.S. 366 (1973).

18 Ibid., 368.

19 Ibid., 370.

20 Ibid., 371.

21 Ibid.

22 Ibid., 378.

23 It has been suggested that *Trinko* "overturns *Otter Tail*," "Impact of Trinko case is focus of seminar in ABA spring meeting," *Antitrust & Trade Reg. Rep. (BNA)* 86, 2004, p. 350 (remarks of E. Fox), but the Court in *Trinko* evidently did not see it that way, since the Court pointed to *Otter Tail* as a good case for compelling access because, unlike the defendant in *Trinko*, the defendant in *Otter Tail* "was already in the business of providing a service to certain customers... and refused to provide the same service to certain other customers." *Verizon Communications Inc. v. Law Office of Curtis V. Trinko, LLP*, 124 S. Ct. 872, 880 (2004).

24 *MCI Communications Corp. v. AT&T*, 708 F.2d 1081 (7th Cir. 1983).

25 Ibid., 1132–33.

26 See, for example, *Caribbean Broad. Sys. v. Cable & Wireless PLC*, 148 F.3d 1080, 1088 (D.C. Cir. 1998); *Delaware & Hudson Ry. Co.v Consolidated Rail Corp.*, 902 F.2d 174, 179 (2d Cir. 1990); *Ideal Dairy Farms, Inc.v. John Labatt, Ltd.*, 90 F.3d 737, 748 (3d Cir. 1993); *Advanced Health Care Services, Inc. v. Radford Community Hosp.*, 910 F.2d 139. 150 (4th Cir. 1990); *City of Anaheim v. So. Calif. Edison Co.*, 955 F.2d 1373 (9th Cir. 1992); *Aspen Highlands Skiing Corp. v. Aspen Skiing Co.*, 738 F.2d 1509, 1520 (10th Cir. 1984), *aff'd on other grounds*, 472 U.S. 585 (1985); *Metronet Services Corp. v. Qwest Corp.*, 2001 U.S. Dist. LEXIS 7436 at pp. 7–8 (W.D. Wash., April 16, 2001); *Morris Communications Corp. v. PGA Tour, Inc.*, 117 F. Supp. 2d 1322, 1327 (M.D. Fla. 2000); *Florida Mun. Power Agency v. Florida Power & Light Co.*, 81 F. Supp. 2d 1313, 1330 (M.D. Fla. 1999); *America Online, Inc. v. GreatDeals.Net*, 49 F. Supp. 2d 851, 862 (E.D. Va. 1999). The Eighth Circuit reworked the formulation by combing the third and fourth elements. See *City of Malden v. Union Elec. Co.*, 887 F.2d 157, 160 (8th Cir. 1989) ("The doctrine requires (1) control of an essential facility by a monopolist; (2) the inability to practically or economically duplicate the facility; and (3) the unreasonable denial of the use of the facility to a competitor when such use is economically and technically feasible"); *Willman v. Heartland Hosp. East*, 34 F.3d 605, 613 (8th Cir. 1994).

27 MCI also sought access to AT&T's long distance network for the cities not reached by MCI's long distance network in *MCI Communications Corp. v. AT&T*, op. cit., 1147. Not surprisingly, however, the Seventh Circuit rejected this claim. First, denial of access to this network had not "inflicted a severe handicap on [long distance] market entrants" (*MCI Communications Corp. v. AT&T*, op. cit., 1148). Second, MCI could not credibly claim that it could not practically or reasonably duplicate the facility since MCI's primary business was to duplicate AT&T's long distance network. Ibid.

28 Ibid., 1131.

29 Ibid., 1133.

30 Ibid.

31 Ibid.

32 Ibid.

33 Ibid.

34 *Law Offices of Curtis V. Trinko v. Bell Atlantic Corp.*, 305 F.3d 89 (2d Cir. 2002).

35 *Verizon Communications Inc. v. Law Office of Curtis V. Trinko*, op. cit., 881.

36 Ibid.

37 Remarks of E. Fox, op. cit., p. 350.

38 See, for example, *Nobody In Particular Presents, Inc. v. Clear Channel Communications, Inc.*, op. cit.

39 But see S. F. Ross, *Principles of Antitrust Law*, Westbury, New York: Foundation Press, 1993, p. 97 (denial of access to an essential facility "is generic predation"); Criticism of leveraging generally extends to the essential facilities doctrine because "the rationale of the essential facility doctrine is exactly the same as that of the leveraging cases." G. J. Werden, "The law and economics of the essential facility doctrine," *St. Louis U. L. J.* 32, 1987, p. 460; D. Reiffen and A. N. Kleit, "Terminal Railroad revisited: foreclosure of an essential facility or simple horizontal monopoly?" *Journal of Law and Economics* 33, 1990, pp. 420–1; D. J. Gerber, "Rethinking the monopolist's duty to deal: a legal and economic critique of the doctrine of 'essential facilities,'" *Va. L. Rev* 74, 1988, p. 1083; cf. IIIA P. E. Areeda and H. Hovenkamp, *Antitrust Law: An Analysis of Antitrust Principles and Their Application*, New York: Aspen Law and Business, 1996, p. 174; *Blue Cross & Blue Shield United of Wisconsin v. Marshfield Clinic*, 65 F.3d 1406, 1413 (7th Cir. 1995) ("Similarly, if the practice of medicine in some sparsely populated county of north central Wisconsin is a natural monopoly, consumers will not be helped by our forcing the handful of physicians there to affiliate with multiple HMOs. Those physicians will still charge fees reflecting their monopoly") (Posner, J.). Judge Posner's criticism of the essential facilities doctrine in Marshfield Clinic is especially surprising because he had wholeheartedly endorsed the doctrine (although not its application) in *Olympia Equip. Leasing Co. v. Western Union Tel. Co.*, 797 F.2d 370, 376 (7th Cir. 1986) ("Some cases hold . . . that a firm which controls a facility essential to its competitors may be guilty if it refuses to allow them access to the facility. We accept the authority of these cases absolutely") (Posner, J.).

40 *MCI Communications Corp. v. AT&T*, op. cit., p. 1132; accord *Advanced Health Care Services, Inc. v. Radford Community Hosp.*, op. cit., 139; *Twin Lab., Inc. v. Weider Health & Fitness*, 900 F.2d 566 (2d Cir. 1990); *Florida Mun. Power Agency v. Florida Power & Light Co.*, op. cit., 1330.

41 *United States v. Colgate & Co.*, 250 U.S. 300, 307 (1919).

42 S. B. Opi, "The application of the essential facilities doctrine to intellectual property licensing in the European Union and the United States: are intellectual property rights still sacrosanct?" *Fordham Intell. Prop. Media & Ent. L. J.* 11, 2001, pp. 421–2.

43 L. A. Sullivan and W. S. Grimes, *The Law of Antitrust: An Integrated Handbook*, St. Paul, Minnesota: West Group Publishing, 2000, p. 112.

44 Ibid., p. 114. Note that in the government's litigation to date, the courts have assumed that Microsoft acquired its OS monopoly.

45 "The term leverage generally refers to a tactic by which a firm with power in one market exploits that power in another. The term also refers to leveraging power from one product to another, as in the tying cases. . . . Leverage tactics have three characteristics in common: first, all are efforts to maximize monopoly returns (they are 'exploitive'); second, all impede the competitive process in ways that straightforward monopoly pricing does not (they are 'restrictive'); third, the restrictive impact of the conduct is felt at a point removed from the source of power. Leverage cases have another quality in common. They are a favorite target of Chicago School theorists who regard them as perverse." L. A. Sullivan and A. I. Jones, "Monopoly conduct, especially leveraging power from one product or market to another," in *Antitrust, Innovation, and Competitiveness*, T. M. Jorde and D. J. Teece (eds), New York: Oxford University Press, 1992, pp. 171–2.

46 G. J. Werden, op. cit., pp. 452–3; see also *North American Soccer League v. National Football League*, 465 F. Supp. 665, 676 n.20 (S.D.N.Y. 1979), *rev'd on other grounds*, 670 F.2d 1249 (2d Cir.), *cert. denied*, 459 U.S. 1074 (1982) (suggesting that the essential facilities doctrine may be limited to "tangible physical objects").

47 *Bellsouth Advertising & Publishing Corp. v. Donnelley Information Publishing, Inc.*, 719 F. Supp. 1551, (S.D. Fla. 1988), *rev'd on other grounds*, 999 F.2d 1436 (11th Cir. 1993).

48 Ibid., 1566. The court in Bellsouth relied on dicta in two other district court decisions to the effect that services as well as physical structures could constitute facilities. *Driscoll v. City of New York*, 650 F. Supp. 1522, 1529 (S.D.N.Y. 1986); *Mid-South Grizzlies v. National Football League*, 550 F. Supp. 558, 571 n.32 (E.D. Pa. 1982), *aff'd*, 720 F.2d 772 (3d Cir. 1983), *cert. denied*, 467 U.S. 1215 (1984). *Mid-South's* dicta is somewhat ambiguous on the definition of a facility. Although the *Mid-South* found no difficulty treating both "physical structures or discreet [sic] services" as facilities, the court expressed skepticism that membership in the National Football League would constitute a facility. *Id.*

49 *Advanced Health Care Services, Inc. v. Radford Community Hosp.*, op. cit.

50 Ibid., 150–1.

51 *American Health Sys. v. Visiting Nurse Ass'n*, 1994–1 Trade Cas. (CCH) ¶70,633 (E.D. Pa. 1994).

52 Ibid., 72,440.

53 *Sunshine Cellular v. Vanguard Cellular Systems, Inc.*, 810 F. Supp. 486, 497 (S.D.N.Y. 1992).

54 *Twin Lab., Inc. v. Weider Health & Fitness*, op. cit., 570. Similarly, a court cannot treat a facility as essential when competitors have access to reasonable

alternatives. *Id.* ("a plaintiff must show . . . that an alternative to the facility is not feasible").

55 *Associated Press v. United States*, op. cit.

56 Ibid., 17.

57 *Associated Press v. United States*, op. cit., 18.

58 Ibid. (emphasis added).

59 *Otter Tail Power Co. v. United States*, op. cit., 377 ("Otter Tail used its monopoly power [to] gain competitive advantage . . . in violation of the antitrust laws"); *accord United States v. Griffith*, 334 U.S. 100, 107 (1948) ("the use of monopoly power . . . to gain a competitive advantage . . . is unlawful").

60 *Alaska Airlines, Inc. v. United Airlines, Inc.*, 948 F.2d 536, 544 (9th Cir. 1991) (emphasis in the original). One problem with the way the Ninth Circuit applied the test was it seemed to allow the defendants "to weaken competition by slow erosion" because there had been no "immediate exclusion." Sullivan and Grimes, op. cit., p. 130.

61 But see Opi, op. cit., pp. 321–2; see also, *Advanced Health-Care Services, Inc. v. Giles Memorial Hosp.*, op. cit., 498.

62 *Paladin Associates, Inc. v. Montana Power Co.*, 97 F. Supp. 2d 1013, (D. Mon. 2000).

63 *Paladin Associates, Inc. v. Montana Power Co.*, op. cit., 1038. The court also relied on evidence that (1) Montana Power did not have control over all of the relevant pipelines, (2) the plaintiff and Montana Power did not compete in some of the secondary markets, and (3) the plaintiff had been granted access to Montana Power's pipeline for at least one of the secondary markets. *Id.*

64 *Monarch Entertainment Bureau, Inc. v. New Jersey Highway Auth.*, 715 F. Supp. 1290, 1300 (D.N.J.), aff'd, 893 F.2d 1331 (3d Cir. 1989)

65 *Hecht v. Pro-Football, Inc.*, 570 F.2d 982, 993 (D.C. Cir. 1977); *see also* Twin Lab., Inc. v. Weider Health & Fitness, op. cit., 568 (emphasizing that the denial must inflict a "*severe handicap*" on market entrants); *Directory Sales Management Corp. v. Ohio Bell Telephone Co.*, 833 F.2d 606, 612 (6th Cir. 1987) (quoting *Hecht* with apparent approval); *Fishman v. Estate of Wirtz*, 807 F.2d 520, 539 (7th Cir. 1986); *TCA Bldg. Co. v. Northwestern Resources Co.*, op. cit., 39; *Florida Fuels, Inc. v. Belcher Oil Co.*, 717 F. Supp. 1528, 1533 (S.D. Fla. 1989).

66 *Monarch Entertainment Bureau, Inc. v. New Jersey Highway Auth.*, op. cit.; *Delaware Health Care, Inc. v. MCD Holding Co.*, 893 F. Supp. 1279, 1287 (D. Del. 1995).

67 *Florida Mun. Power Agency v. Florida Power & Light Co.*, op. cit.

68 Ibid., 1330–32. Although the plaintiff lost its motion for summary judgment, it survived the defendant's cross motion. So this case should be considered a victory for the plaintiff.

69 *CTC Communications Corp. v. Bell Atlantic Corp*, 77 F. Supp. 2d 124, (D. Me. 1999).

70 Ibid., 147–48.

71 *City of Anaheim v. So. Calif. Edison Co.*, op. cit., 1380; Ross, op. cit., p. 96, n.38.

72 See *Twin Lab., Inc. v. Weider Health & Fitness*, op. cit., 570; *Kramer v. Pollock-Krasner Found.*, 890 F. Supp. 250, 257 (S.D.N.Y. 1995). In *McKenzie v. Mercy Hosp. of Independence, Kansas*, 854 F.2d 365, 370–71 (10th Cir. 1988), for example, the court found that the plaintiff's ability to render obstetrical and emergency medical services from his office defeated the plaintiff's claim that the

essential facilities doctrine applied to the defendants refusal to give the plaintiff access to the defendant's emergency room and obstetrical care facilities.

73 See *Delaware & Hudson Ry. Co. v Consolidated Rail Corp.*, op. cit., 179 (suggesting that physical duplication is not required when it "would be an impractical and unreasonable project to undertake"); *Directory Sales Management Corp. v. Ohio Bell Telephone Co.*, op. cit., 612; *Sunshine Cellular v. Vanguard Cellular Systems, Inc.*, op. cit., 498–99; *Florida Fuels, Inc. v. Belcher Oil Co.*, op. cit., 1532.

74 *Verizon Communications Inc. v. Law Office of Curtis V. Trinko*, op. cit., 881.

75 *Caribbean Broad. Sys. v. Cable & Wireless PLC*, op. cit., 1088–89; *Interface Group v. Mass. Port Auth.*, 816 F.2d 9, 12 (1st Cir. 1987) ("it is difficult to see how denying a facility to one who . . . is not an actual or potential competitor could enhance or reinforce the monopolist's market power") (Breyer, J.); *Ferguson v. Greater Pocatello Chamber of Commerce, Inc.*, 848 F.2d 976, 983 (9th Cir. 1988) (because "the Fergusons are not in competition with ISU . . ., ISU has not refused to deal with a competitor"); *Kramer v. Pollock-Krasner Found.*, op. cit., 257; D. J. Gerber, op. cit., p. 1076.

76 *America Online, Inc. v. GreatDeals.Net*, op. cit.

77 Ibid., 862–3.

78 *Intergraph Corp. v. Intel Corp.*, 195 F.3d 1346, 1356–58 (Fed. Cir. 1999).

79 Ibid., 1355.

80 Ibid., 1357.

81 *MCI Communications Corp. v. AT&T*, op. cit., 1132.

82 *Metronet Services Corp. v. Qwest Corp.*, op. cit., *11; G. J. Werden, op. cit., p. 456.

83 See *City of Vernon v. So. Calif. Edison Co.*, 955 F.2d 1361, 1367 (9th Cir. 1992) (defendant's insistence on a provision giving it the right to refuse access "until it felt like it" constituted a refusal to deal); *Delaware & Hudson Ry. Co.v. Consolidated Rail Corp.*, op. cit., 179–80 (indicating that a price increase of 800 percent could constitute a refusal to deal under the essential facilities doctrine); *City of College Station, Tex. v. City of Bryan, Tex.*, 932 F. Supp. 877, 888 (S.D. Tex. 1996); *Sunshine Cellular v. Vanguard Cellular Systems, Inc.*, op. cit., 498.

84 *Zschaler v. Claneil Enterprises, Inc.*, 958 F. Supp. 929 (D. Vt. 1997).

85 The court said that "over 800 percent" of the area's lodging reservations were made through the defendants' "Central Reservation" system. *Zschaler v. Claneil Enterprises, Inc.*, op. cit., 944. Since the largest possible market share is 100 percent, this must be a typographical error by the court. Presumably, the court meant 80 percent.

86 *Zschaler v. Claneil Enterprises, Inc.*, op. cit., 945.

87 See *Southern Pac. Communications Co. v. AT&T*, 740 F.2d 980, 1009 (D.C. Cir. 1984) ("Absolute equality of access . . . is not mandated by the antitrust laws).

88 See *Illinois Bell Telephone Co. v. Haines and Co., Inc.*, 905 F.2d 1081, 1087 (7th Cir. 1990) (the doctrine imposes an "obligation to make the facility available to competitors on nondiscriminatory terms"); *Ferguson v. Greater Pocatello Chamber of Commerce, Inc.*, 848 F.2d 976, 983 (9th Cir. 1988) (the doctrine imposes "a duty to make that facility available . . . on a nondiscriminatory basis").

89 *Contra Intergraph Corp. v. Intel Corp.*, op. cit., 1346. The court denied Intergraph's request for a preliminary injunction not because Intel had yet to deny

access, but because Intel did not compete with Intergraph. *Accord, Paladin Associates, Inc. v. Montana Power Co.*, op. cit.

90 *United States v. Terminal R. R. Ass'n of St. Louis*, op. cit., 400.

91 Ibid., 411.

92 *Verizon Communications Inc. v. Law Office of Curtis V. Trinko*, op. cit., 881.

93 *Nobody in Particular Presents, Inc. v. Clear Channel Communications, Inc.*, op. cit.

94 Ibid., *188.

95 Ibid.

96 Ibid., *189.

97 See *Hecht v. Pro-Football, Inc.*, op. cit., 992–93; *Southern Pac. Communications Co. v. AT&T*, op. cit. (quoting, *Hecht*).

98 *City of Anaheim v. So. Calif. Edison Co.*, op. cit., 1380.

99 See *Hecht v. Pro-Football, Inc.*, op. cit., 992–93; *Southern Pac. Communications Co. v. AT&T*, op. cit. (quoting, *Hecht*).

100 See *City of Vernon v. So. Calif. Edison Co.*, op. cit.; G. J. Werden, op. cit., p. 457.

101 *Florida Fuels, Inc. v. Belcher Oil Co.*, op. cit., 1535; *cf., City of Vernon v. So. Calif. Edison Co.*, op. cit., 1367.

102 See, for example, *City of Anaheim v. So. Calif. Edison Co.*, op. cit., 1380; *State of Illinois, ex rel. Burris v. Panhandle Eastern Pipe Line Co.*, op. cit., 1483; *cf.* G. J. Werden, op. cit., p. 457.

103 *City of Anaheim v. So. Calif. Edison Co.*, op. cit., 1380.

104 Ibid., 1381; *cf., Hecht v. Pro-Football, Inc.*, op. cit., 992–93; *Southern Pac. Communications Co. v. AT&T*, op. cit. (quoting, *Hecht*).

105 *Morris Communications Corp. v. PGA Tour, Inc.*, 2004 U.S. App. LEXIS 5915 (11th Cir. 2004).

106 Ibid., see also C. M. Seelen, "Comment: the essential facilities doctrine: what does it mean to be essential?" *Marq. L. Rev.* 80, 1997, p. 1124.

107 Ibid., *23. Although the court did not elaborate, the plaintiff probably meant that the defendant could have no other motivation for denying access than to hold on to the economic rents generated by the absence of competition in the market for the sale of real time scores.

108 Ibid., *22–24.

109 Ibid., *24–26.

110 *MCI Communications Corp. v. AT&T*, op. cit., 1148.

111 *Cf.* Opi, op. cit., p. 422; A. Kezsbom and A. V. Goldman, "No shortcut to antitrust analysis: the twisted journey of the 'essential facilities' doctrine," *Colum. Bus. L. Rev.* 1996, p. 1. Although they criticize the essential facilities doctrine as having "little independent, substantive content" (ibid., p. 34), these commentators concede that when the doctrine "functions as a res ipsa loquitur-type signal" such that "the court may infer the existence of a defendant's 'willful acquisition or maintenance of monopoly power' (monopolization) or 'intent' to monopolize (attempted monopolization)" (ibid., p. 35). But see Sullivan and Grimes, op. cit., pp. 251–2. Sullivan and Grimes argue that at least in the context of an essential facility controlled by more than one, but less than all competitors, "a plaintiff must prove harm to competition in a defined market" (ibid., p. 251).

112 *Fishman v. Estate of Wirtz*, op. cit., 536.

113 *United States v. Aluminum Co. of Am.*, 148 F.2d 416, 430 (2d Cir. 1945); *see also United States v. Grinnell Corp.*, 384 U.S. 563, 570–71 (1966) (the acquisition of

monopoly power "as a consequence of superior product, business acumen, or historic accident" does not violate section 2 of the Sherman Act).

114 *Paladin Associates, Inc. v. Montana Power Co.*, op. cit., 1037; *Flip Side Prod., Inc. v. Jam Prod., Inc.*, op. cit., 1033; *cf.* W. Blumenthal, "Three vexing issues under the essential facilities doctrine: ATM networks as illustration," *Antitrust Law Journal* 58, 1990, pp. 858–60 (market definition is required to determine the existence of the first and second elements of the doctrine); see also *Nobody In Particular Presents, Inc. v. Clear Channel Communications, Inc.*, op. cit., *176–81.

115 *Reiser v. Microsoft Corp.*, 2000 U.S. App. LEXIS 5901 (9th Cir. 2000).

116 Ibid., *3

117 "Impact of Trinko cases is focus of seminar in ABA spring meeting," remarks of Janet L. McDavid, *Antitrust & Trade Reg. Rep.* (BNA) 86, pp. 350, 2004.

118 R. Pitofsky, *et al.*, "The essential facilities doctrine under U.S. antitrust law," *Antitrust L.J.* 70, 2002, p. 443.

119 See Ross, op. cit., p. 97.

120 *Cf. Mid-South Grizzlies v. National Football League*, op. cit., 787. See also R. Pitofsky, op. cit., p. 443.

121 See J. R. Ratner, "Should there be an essential facility doctrine?" *U. C. Davis L. Rev.* 21, 1988, pp. 327–82.

122 See E. M. Fox, "What is harm to competition? Exclusionary practices, and anticompetitive effect," *Antitrust Law Journal* 70, 2002, pp. 371–411.

123 See R. H. Lande, "Consumer choice as the ultimate goal of antitrust law," *U. Pitt. L. Rev.* 62, 2001, pp. 503–35.

Topic 4

Access pricing and the "efficient component pricing rule"

Lawrence J. White[1]

Introduction

The pricing of access to bottleneck facilities by potential (or actual) providers of complementary components continues to be a serious and bedeviling policy problem for network industries, such as rail, telephone, and electricity. Most economic analyses of this problem have concluded that marginal-cost-based prices are the correct solution, with additional complications that may be necessary to deal with the special problems of economies of scale of the bottleneck facility. An alternative "solution" offered to this problem has been the "efficient component pricing rule" (ECPR).[2] It is a specific regulatory prescription for the pricing of access.

This chapter will argue that, though there are some circumstances where the ECPR yields efficient outcomes, it generally will *not* yield glob-ally efficient outcomes.[3] Accordingly, the ECPR is not a generally sensible policy prescription. The remainder of this chapter will expand on these themes.

A description of the ECPR

The ECPR is best illustrated through a stylized diagrammatic example and some simple arithmetic. In Figure I.4.1, an incumbent owns a bottleneck facility, represented by line segment AB. This segment could represent a monopoly rail route or marshalling yard; a local telephone exchange switch or local wire lines; or a local electricity distribution system. The incumbent also owns a complementary facility represented by line segment BC. This segment could be a connecting rail line; local or long distance telephone wire lines; or electrical generating facilities. Thus the incumbent can provide the integrated product or service ABC, which could be (if we continue with our examples) an integrated (or through) rail service from A to C (via B); completed local or long distance tele-phone calls; or electricity service to users.

A second firm ("the entrant") wishes to supply the complementary service BC, but needs to purchase the complementary bottleneck service AB in order to satisfy customer demands for the integrated ABC service.

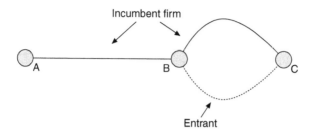

Figure I.4.1 The bottleneck incumbent and the entrant.

What price should the bottleneck incumbent be permitted to charge the entrant for providing access?

The ECPR states that the incumbent should be permitted to charge a price that is equal to the incumbent's opportunity costs of providing access, *including any lost net revenues that the incumbent experiences as a consequence of the entrant's gaining sales at the expense of the incumbent.* The goal of the ECPR is to ensure that the entrant gains sales at the expense of the incumbent only when the entrant is more efficient (has lower costs) than the incumbent in the production of the complementary component.

The logic of the ECPR can be illustrated with the following numerical example, based on Figure I.4.1. Suppose that the marginal cost of providing access service from the bottleneck facility itself (AB) is $5 per unit, that the incumbent has marginal costs of $2 per unit in supplying the complementary component BC, and that the monopolist sells the integrated service ABC for $10 per unit.[4] Then the ECPR would allow the monopolist to charge the entrant a price of $8 per unit for access: $5 for the marginal costs of the access itself plus $3 for the forgone net revenues (profit) that the incumbent loses for every unit of ABC that the entrant sells. Quick arithmetic calculations will show that the entrant will find entry worthwhile only if its unit costs of providing service BC are at or below $2—i.e., only if the entrant's unit costs are at or below the incumbent's marginal costs for BC.

The logic of the ECPR is seductive. It prevents the entry of inefficient firms. Who could oppose that? And, indeed, there is one limited circumstance under which the ECPR prescription does yield an efficient outcome: where the price of the integrated (ABC) service is itself regulated and the complementary components (BC) produced by the entrant and the incumbent are perfect substitutes, so that the *only* relevant consideration is the minimization of the cost of producing the complementary component. It is worth noting, however, that even in this case the ECPR involves a "tax" paid by the entrant to the incumbent.[5] To the extent that this tax reduces the profitability of the entrant, which thereby inhibits its ability to invest in its productive activities (because of likely difficulties in raising external capital that an entrant may well face, due to asymmetric-information-based problems), and the entrant's technology involves cumulative-volume-based learning-by-doing, then even in this case of a regulated price the ECPR may discourage the entry of a more efficient competitor for the complementary component BC.

More generally, when the price of ABC is not regulated, then under the simple terms just described the ECPR is insensitive to the market power that has generated the mark-up (of $3) that the incumbent is earning by selling ABC at a price of $10 per unit *and the consequent allocative efficiency* imposed on consumers of ABC. The ECPR guarantees that this $3 mark-up, and its associated allocative inefficiency will persist, *even if the entrant is more efficient than the incumbent*. Further, in the presence of market power by the incumbent there are quite general circumstances under which the entry (or threat of entry) by *even an inefficient entrant* could improve global efficiency. In addition, application of the ECPR yields inefficiencies when the complementary components (BC) produced by the entrant and the incumbent are imperfect substitutes; when economies of scale are present in the entrant's production of the complementary component or in the incumbent's production of the bottleneck service; or when the incumbent's costs of production are observed imperfectly. Thus, in many (arguably, most or even nearly all) realistic real-world circumstances the ECPR prescription fails a global efficiency test. The remainder of this essay will demonstrate briefly the problems that arise with the ECPR when any of the circumstances described above are present.

The general problems of the ECPR

The incumbent's price represents the exercise of market power

Suppose, as in the numerical example above, that the incumbent's $10 price for the service ABC includes a monopoly margin of $3. Then, as explained above, even if the entrant is more efficient than the incumbent and does succeed in gaining access and providing the integrated ABC service, the going-forward price will continue to include that $3 monopoly margin, with the consequent allocative inefficiency.

Further, even if the entrant were less efficient than the incumbent, entry could still be socially beneficial if the improved allocational efficiency that would follow from the lower post-entry price exceeded lost efficiency on the production that is displaced from the incumbent to the entrant. This outcome is most clearly seen in the limiting case where the *threat* of entry causes the incumbent to lower its price to a level just below what the entrant could sustain. Thus, continuing with the numerical example, even if the entrant has unit costs for segment BC of, say, $3 but could purchase access to segment AB solely at its marginal cost of $5, the threat of its entry would cause the incumbent to lower its price to just below $8. A clear improvement in allocative efficiency occurs.[6]

More generally, as Economides and White observe, "An 'entry tax' that required entrants to reimburse incumbents for their forgone revenues would quickly be seen as a protective and anticompetitive device and would likely receive little support from policy-oriented economists, despite any claims that the tax would preclude inefficient production. The ECPR is just this type of entry tax."[7]

The incumbent's and entrant's complementary components are imperfect substitutes

In most circumstances the entrant's provision of the complementary component BC will be perceived as differentiated from the incumbent's provision of component BC, because of differences in service quality (e.g., speed, reliability, frequency, company reputation, etc.) and will be branded as a way of encouraging that differentiation. In these circumstances, even the productive efficiency argument in support of the ECPR loses its force. Where two products are differentiated, comparisons of efficiency that are based solely on unit costs make little economic sense; a comparison of the unit costs of producing apples with the unit costs of producing oranges rarely yields useful insights.

Of course, the ECPR could still be applied.[8] But now the relevant criterion would not be how the entrant's unit costs compare with the incumbent's unit costs (since this comparison has little meaning); instead, entry would be determined by whether there are customers for the entrant's component who are willing to pay a price that is sufficiently above the entrant's unit costs (including the marginal costs of segment AB) so as to cover the incumbent's mark-up (the $3 in the numerical example). Regardless of whether there are or aren't such customers, however, the ECPR would again ensure allocative inefficiency by shutting out any potential customers of the entrant who would be willing to pay a price that is between the entrant's relevant marginal costs and the mark-up inclusive price.

Non-constant returns to scale

The relevant concern here is the presence of economies of scale in production. We will address economies of scale in both the production of the complementary component and the production of the bottleneck service itself.

Economies of scale in the production of the complementary component

If the entrant's technology involves economies of scale, then the artificial mark-up or margin that is inherent in the ECPR will inhibit the entrant's scale of production and thus will inhibit even relatively efficient entrants.

Economies of scale in the production of the bottleneck service

If the bottleneck service is produced under conditions of economies of scale, then marginal cost pricing of the bottleneck service itself will not fully cover the costs (including capital costs) of the facility. The globally efficient price or prices that will cover all costs will involve some margin above marginal cost[9] and, if demanders can be segmented, some form of price discrimination. One version of this price discrimination would involve up-front access fees (scaled so as not to discourage light users) plus marginal prices that are equal to marginal costs; another version would involve Ramsey prices that are inversely proportional to individual demanders' price elasticities.[10]

Under either version, global efficiency does call for the entrant to pay a price for access that is in excess of the direct marginal costs of the bottleneck facility. *But only by chance would these higher efficiency-based mark-ups over marginal costs be identical to the ECPR mark-up.* Generally, if the incumbent has been unconstrained in its pricing of the integrated service, the ECPR charge will be *greater* than a Ramsey-related price (since the incumbent would be maximizing profits, while the Ramsey price would just try to cover the bottleneck costs, including capital costs).[11]

The incumbent's costs cannot be observed accurately

Even if the entrant has lower costs than the incumbent for the production of component BC, the incumbent may nevertheless wish to exclude it from providing the BC service. This could arise if the incumbent perceives the entrant to be a potential challenger to the incumbent's activities in other markets—perhaps in the AB bottleneck market itself, or in connected CD, CE, CF markets (not shown in Figure I.4.1)—*and* the potency of the entrant's threat in these other markets is related (because of economies of scale or scope) to its viability in the BC segment.[12] In this event, the incumbent would want to *understate* its true marginal costs of producing segment BC, so as to increase its apparent mark-up on the BC component and thus increase the ECPR charge.

As a second possibility, suppose that the incumbent is constrained by rate regulation to earn zero excess profits in the bottleneck market. In that case, the incumbent would like to use "creative accounting" to transfer some of its true costs of producing the complementary component to the bottleneck service, thereby understating the former costs and similarly overstating the latter costs, so as to justify larger revenues (and higher implicit profits) for the bottleneck service.[13] The lower apparent costs for producing the complementary component will also mean a higher ECPR charge and thus a distortion of productive and allocative efficiency.

Conclusion

Despite its seductive logic, the ECPR has an extremely limited applicability as an efficient method for determining the charge that an entrant, who wants to produce and sell a complementary component, should pay to an integrated incumbent for access to the incumbent's bottleneck facility. Though "opportunity cost" usually has the ring of efficiency, the operative concept should be *social* opportunity cost, not private opportunity cost. Unfortunately, the ECPR embodies the latter, not the former. Instead of the ECPR, regulated rates for access should embody marginal cost concepts, with the inclusion of Ramsey (or similar) pricing concepts when appropriate.

Notes

1 Arthur E. Imperatore Professor of Economics, New York University Stern School of Business.
2 See W. J. Baumol, "Some subtle issues in railroad regulation," *International Journal of Transportation Economics* 10, August 1983, pp. 341–55; W. J. Baumol and J. G. Sidak, "The pricing of inputs sold to competitors," *Yale Journal of Regulation* 11, 1994, pp. 171–202; W. J. Baumol and J. G. Sidak, *Toward Competition in Local Telephony*, Cambridge, Massachusetts: MIT Press, 1994; and R. D. Willig, "The theory of network access pricing," in *Issues in Public Utility Regulation*, H. M. Trebing (ed.), Proceedings of the Institute of Public Utilities Tenth Annual Conference, East Lansing: Division of Research, Graduate School of Business Administration, Michigan State University, 1979, pp. 109–52.
3 See N. Economides, "The tragic inefficiency of the M-ECPR," Working Paper No. 98–01, Department of Economics, Stern School of Business, New York University, December 1997. Economides shows that the "M-ECPR," a modest modification of the ECPR that has been advocated by Sidak and Spulber (1996), has the same flaws (see J. G. Sidak and D. F. Spulber, "The tragedy of the telecommons: government pricing of unbundled network elements under the Telecommunications Act of 1996," *Columbia Law Review* 97, 1996, pp. 1081–161).
4 We assume here a fixed proportions model where one unit of bottleneck service (AB) plus one unit of the complementary component (BC) is necessary to produce the integrated service ABC.
5 See F. Ramsey, "A contribution to the theory of taxation," *Economic Journal* 37, 1927, pp. 47–61. The justification for a Ramsey oriented "tax" will be discussed below.
6 The outcome is cloudier if the inefficient entrant actually does enter, since then the improved allocative efficiency is offset to a greater or lesser extent by the decreased productive efficiency of the entrant. Economides and White (N. Economides and L. J. White, op. cit., pp. 557–79 and N. Economides and L. J. White, "The inefficiency of the ECPR yet again: a reply to Larson," *Antitrust Bulletin* 43, 1998, pp. 429–42) show the conditions, using a standard set of oligopoly models, under which global efficiency improves subsequent to the entry of an inefficient entrant.

7 N. Economides and L. J. White, "Access and interconnection pricing: how efficient is the 'efficient component pricing rule'?" *Antitrust Bulletin* 40, 1995, pp. 569–70.
8 Under some circumstances, a one-for-one substitution of the entrant's component (BC) for the incumbent's component might still apply; but more generally, an elasticity of substitution between them would have to be determined.
9 Unless a subsidy is provided from public funds.
10 Ramsey, op. cit.
11 Note also that the Ramsey-type pricing and its associated mark-up should be directly linked to the charge for the use of the bottleneck facility, rather than determined (as is true of the ECPR) from the mark-up on the integrated service ABC.
12 J. A. Ordover and R. D. Willig, "Access and bundling in high-tech markets," in *Competition, Innovation and the Microsoft Monopoly: Antitrust in the Digital Marketplace*, J. A. Eisenach and T. M. Lenard (eds) Boston: Kluwer, 1999, pp. 103–28; L. J. White, "Microsoft and browsers: are the antitrust problems really new?" in ibid., pp. 129–54; and L. J. White, "A $10 billion solution to the microsoft problem," *UWLA Law Review* 32, Symposium 2001, pp. 69–80.
13 This was one of the arguments underlying the antitrust suit against AT&T that resulted in the 1982 agreement to divest the bottleneck local service from the complementary equipment and long distance parts of the company. See R. G. Noll and B. M. Owen, "The anticompetitive uses of regulation: *United States v. AT&T* (1982)," in *The Antitrust Revolution: The Role of Economics*, J. E. Kwoka, Jr., and L. J. White (eds), 2nd edn, New York: HarperCollins, 1994, pp. 328–75; T. J. Brennan, "Why regulated firms should be kept out of unregulated markets: understanding the divestiture in *United States v. AT&T*," *Antitrust Bulletin* 32, 1987, pp. 741–93; T. J. Brennan, "Cross-subsidization and cost misallocation by regulated monopolists," *Journal of Regulatory Economics* 2, 1990, pp. 37–51; and T. J. Brennan, "Is the theory behind *U.S. v AT&T* Applicable Today?" *Antitrust Bulletin* 40, 1995, pp. 455–82.

References

Armstrong, M. and Vickers, J., "The access pricing problem with deregulation," *Journal of Industrial Economics* 46, 1998, pp. 115–21.

Armstrong, M., Chris, D., and Vickers, J., "The access pricing problem: a synthesis," *Journal of Industrial Economics* 44, 1996, pp. 131–50.

Laffont, J. J. and Tirole, J., "Access pricing and competition," *European Economic Review* 38, 1994, pp. 1673–710.

Laffont, J. J., Rey, P., and Tirole, J., "Network competition: i. overview and nondiscriminatory pricing," *Rand Journal of Economics* 29, 1998a, pp. 1–37.

Laffont, J. J., Rey, P., and Tirole, J., "Network competition: ii. price discrimination," *Rand Journal of Economics* 29, 1998b, pp. 38–56.

Topic 5

Access remedies after *Trinko*

Jonathan L. Rubin, Norman Hawker, and
D. Adam Candeub[1]

Introduction and background

One of the principal purposes of the Telecommunications Act of 1996[2] (the "1996 Act," or simply, the "Act") is to require incumbent local telephone monopolists (incumbent local exchange carriers, or "ILECs") to open their markets to entry by competitive carriers.[3] As of this writing, competitive local exchange carriers ("CLECs") provide nearly 15 percent of the U.S.'s approximately 185 million switched telephone lines.[4] Whether, after eight years since passage into law, this competitive market share evinces the "success" of the 1996 Act is difficult to judge, but at least part of the reason that the CLECs' share is not higher is due to the apparently widespread reluctance of the ILECs to provide access to their networks in a manner consistent with the requirements of the law.[5]

The 1996 Act puts an end to antitrust supervision of the telecommunications industry by the district court for the District of Columbia and places jurisdiction of the markets once dominated by the AT&T Bell System under the Federal Communications Commission ("FCC"). But the Act contains an antitrust-specific savings clause that provides, "nothing in this Act shall be construed to modify, impair, or supersede the applicability of any of the antitrust laws."[6] The savings clause would seem to ensure the availability of antitrust remedies for parties injured in case an incumbent monopolist decides to frustrate competition. However, the recent Supreme Court decision in *Verizon Communications Inc. v. Trinko*[7] holds otherwise. After *Trinko*, the remedy for denial of access in local telephone markets may be in the exclusive province of the 1996 Act and its implementing regulations.

This chapter evaluates *Trinko* in the context of the telecommunications industries, and also examines its broader implications for claims based on denial of access under Section 2 of the Sherman Act. In particular, we look at the implications on the law applicable to the refusal of a monopolist to grant existing or potential competitors access to its property or some element of its "infrastructure."

Cases-in-controversy, including Supreme Court cases, deliver legal rules limited by their nature to their own particular facts and circumstances. Some "play" in the assessment of the significance of the legal rules announced in any particular case is to be expected. Because *Trinko* raises more questions than it answers, however, conclusions from *Trinko* must be carefully qualified. Some of the Court's reasoning supports a narrow view that *Trinko* is a decision confined to regulated telecommunications carriers engaged in trading unbundled network elements. But the opinion can also be read as a watershed event in the history of Section 2 jurisprudence. The Court's short but wide-ranging opinion could support either polar caricature of interpretation. The significance of the opinion could be profound, but it could just as easily be reined-in.

The rest of this chapter proceeds as follows. In the next section we set the background by describing the dispute in *Trinko*. The following section analyzes the rationales given by the Majority and the Concurring Opinions for dismissal. It sets forth the analysis of the Majority's first rationale, the peculiar circumstances in the telecommunications industry. This section also provides an analysis of the broader antitrust argument, including the Court's journey to the "outer boundaries of Section 2." Although these boundaries are not well-demarcated, the Court found them clear enough relative to Verizon's conduct to conclude that the conduct was not anticompetitive. This has implications for the essential facilities and monopoly leveraging doctrines, which the Court professed to have left undisturbed. The third section examines the standing issues found in the Concurring opinion. Finally, the fourth section sets forth some brief conclusions in an attempt to assess the fallout of *Trinko* for Section 2 jurisprudence in other industries.

The dispute in *Trinko*

The *Trinko* case pitted a local incumbent monopolist telephone company, Bell Atlantic (an original "Bell operating company" now owned by Verizon), against the local customers of a CLEC (AT&T). The plaintiff-consumers alleged an antitrust injury—the failure to obtain the benefits of competitive local telephone service—which, they claimed, was the result of slow order-filling and other non-price conduct by Bell Atlantic that amounted to "denying" AT&T access to its local network and which the plaintiffs characterized as "exclusionary."

The 1996 Act opens local telecommunications markets to competition by, *inter alia*, requiring ILECs to lease parts of their local networks (called "unbundled network elements") to "requesting carriers" (primarily CLECs) at below-retail rates. Another provision of the law permits ILECs, previously barred from offering long distance services, to enter the long distance market upon a sufficient showing of competition in their local service areas. To further competition, the Act imposes on ILECs various duties to share their local network at government-supervised rates, in fulfillment of which Bell Atlantic entered into interconnection agreements with AT&T and other CLECs. Bell Atlantic's record of service under these agreements, however, was so poor that the CLECs filed complaints with the FCC and the New York Public Service Commission ("PSC"). Bell Atlantic entered into a consent decree with the FCC requiring a "voluntary contribution" to the U.S. Treasury of $3 million, and the New York PSC entered orders finding Bell Atlantic liable to the CLECs for $10 million in compensation.

The *Trinko* antitrust case was filed one day after the entry of the consent decree with the FCC. The plaintiff, on behalf of a class of similarly-situated New York CLEC customers, sued Bell Atlantic for anti-competitive conduct cognizable under Section 2. Relying on *Goldwasser v. Ameritech Corp.*,[8] in which the Seventh Circuit found that allegations involving similar claims against an ILEC failed to state a Section 2 cause of action, the U.S. District Court of the Southern District of New York dismissed the case for failure to state a legal claim.[9] The United States Court of Appeals for the Second Circuit reversed and reinstated the antitrust claim, suggesting that, depending on the proof, the facts alleged in the amended complaint could support Section 2 liability under either an essential facilities theory or under a theory of monopoly leveraging.[10] The Supreme Court granted *certiorari* to decide the sole question of whether the Second Circuit erred in reinstating the antitrust claim.

The rationale in the main opinion and the concurrence

In reversing the Second Circuit's reinstatement of the antitrust claim, Justice Scalia, speaking for six members of the Court,[11] relied on two principal lines of argument. First, if two conflicting federal statutes pertain to the same subject matter, one of statute must yield to the other.

For its second rationale the Majority found that under existing antitrust principles the amended complaint did not state a Section 2 claim. No antitrust action for Verizon's wrongful conduct was available, as the district court had ruled. Three Justices joined a concurring that expressed a third rationale supporting dismissal,[12] that the consumers who brought the claim in *Trinko* lacked standing to sue under the antitrust laws. With three competing rationales all supporting dismissal, it is easy to see how *Trinko* can be all things to all people, either a results-driven decision intended to prohibit the use of the antitrust laws to enforce specific unbundling provisions of the 1996 Act, or profoundly important for the future direction of monopolization law.

The first rationale: statutory conflicts, legal and practical

At a minimum, *Trinko* is a results-driven case, narrowly applicable to transactions involving unbundled network elements, trade in which was created by and is supervised under the 1996 Act. This minimalist view attributes the *Trinko* decision to policy or prudential grounds based on the impracti-calities of enforcing two conflicting sets of federal statutes. The Court first set out to "determine what effect (if any) the 1996 Act has upon the appli-cation of traditional antitrust principles."[13] The Court saw both legal and practical conflicts between the two laws.

The legal conflict: implied immunity

The legal conflict involves the issue of implied antitrust immunity, which was repudiated by the savings clause. Implied immunity bars antitrust claims where there is "a convincing showing of clear repugnancy between the antitrust laws and the regulatory system."[14] The Court quickly decided that it could not interpret that the intent of Congress was to grant antitrust immunity to the firms regulated under the 1996 Act. While the majority's recognition of the legal effect of the savings clause was imme-diate their disappointment at not being able to legally immunize monopo-lies regulated under the 1996 Act was not well disguised. The Court found the 1996 Act to be a "detailed regulatory scheme" which was a "good can-didate" for the implication of antitrust immunity.[15] Thus it appears that a majority of the Supreme Court believes that the 1996 Act and the antitrust laws are clearly repugnant.

But the legal doctrine of implied immunity is simply an attempt to apply an inferred legislative intent, and Congress clearly did not intend the 1996 Act to preempt the antitrust laws. Although the 1996 Act replaced the judicial oversight created by the consent decree in the Department of Justice's antitrust case AT&T, that case had focused on competition in the long distance market and the goals of that case were largely accomplished by 1996. Consequently, the 1996 Act's transfer of jurisdiction to the FCC could not support a finding that Congress intended to bar antitrust intervention in the still monopolistic local exchange market. More importantly, the savings clause undoubtedly indic-ates that Congress did *not* mean to imply that firms subject to the 1996 Act should be immune from the antitrust laws, so it follows that the drafters of the Act did not view the two statutes as presenting conflicting legal regimes. The notion of co-existence between the antitrust laws and the regulation in the 1996 Act, therefore, cannot be ruled out by the language of the savings clause. Thus, the Majority correctly found that Congress had "precluded" an interpretation of the 1996 Act as an effort by the legis-lature to immunize the telecommunications industry from liability under the antitrust laws.[16]

The practical conflict: judicial economy

Although Majority could not apply the doctrine of implied immunity as a matter of Congressional intent, there remained a prudential doctrine that depended on judicial economy, an important antecedent of which is found in Judge (now Justice) Breyer's opinion in *Town of Concord, Ma. v. Boston Edison Co.*[17] In *Town of Concord*, the First Circuit had to decide whether "price squeeze" conduct violated antitrust law "when it takes place in a fully regulated industry."[18] The First Circuit held that the price squeeze did not violate the antitrust laws, because "regulation [made the] critical difference in terms of antitrust harms, benefits, and administrative considerations."[19] In other words, antitrust intervention could not as a practical matter improve the situation given the regulatory oversight provided by the administrative agency.

The *Trinko* Court in a similar fashion considered the "economic and legal setting" to avoid application of antitrust laws even without implied immunity. Not only is the regulatory goal of 1996 Act "more ambitious" in eliminating existing monopolies than the traditional antitrust goal of preventing new monopolies by means of anti-competitive conduct, but the Court seems to find that the two statutes work at cross-purposes. The 1996 Act was designed to eliminate lawful monopolies, while the antitrust laws merely seek to prevent unlawful monopolization. "It would be a serious mistake," Justice Scalia warns, "to conflate the two goals." Principles of antitrust illegality must yield to the more detailed and comprehensive approach of the 1996 Act.

Three principal factors appeared to motivate the majority's application of the *Town of Concord* rule in *Trinko*. First, because the 1996 Act fulfills an antitrust function, the probability of an antitrust violation is low in the markets governed by the Act. Consequently, there is little risk of harm from a "false negative" under antitrust law. Second, the required antitrust remedies are burdensome, perhaps, suggests the Court, to the point of irremediability. Finally, and in light of the first two factors, antitrust litigation is not cost effective, since it would yield only a small marginal benefit at the cost of burdensome remedies.

THE ANTITRUST FUNCTION

The Majority concluded that the 1996 Act created a regime with a "structure designed to deter and remedy anticompetitive harm,"[20] and that this structure had succeeded in serving as "an effective steward of the antitrust function"[21] that "'significantly diminishe[d] the likelihood of major antitrust harm.'"[22] The Majority pointed to the Act's detailed implementing regulations, the FCC's complex pricing formula, and the elaborate procedures to make agreements and settle disputes, and observed that Congress' legislative and regulatory approach to the market for local exchange services in the 1996 Act was obviously designed to yield competitive benefits. Such benefits were not necessarily promoted by the antitrust laws. More importantly, the Majority found that administrative remedies had worked.

Unfortunately, the majority's vaunted opinion of the efficacy of the antitrust function of the 1996 Act has not been borne out in practice. The FCC itself has disparaged the administrative remedies as insufficient to deter anticompetitive conduct, and the ILECs may have treated this level of fines as an acceptable a cost of doing business. The number of complaints brought before antitrust courts also suggests that the 1996 Act had not successfully fulfilled its antitrust function.

ADMINISTRABILITY AND IRREMEDIABILITY

The perceived difficulty in administering forced-access remedies also led the *Trinko* Court to apply the *Town of Concord* analysis. Forced sharing places on antitrust courts the difficult burden of the "central planning" required to decide price, quantity, and the other terms of dealing. Such remedies require the "continuing supervision of a highly detailed decree."[23] Section 2 litigation can be "difficult."[24] The cases will be "technical" and "extremely numerous."[25] The Court suggests that when compulsory access requires the court to assume day-to-day control characteristic of a regulatory agency, antitrust courts should deem the problem before them "irremediable."[26]

In other words, courts cannot create workable interconnection regimes, and, therefore, this job should be left to regulators. This concern has a remarkable and unacknowledged history harkening back to the last time there was vibrant competition in local telephony in the United States, after the expiration of the principal Bell patents in 1893–94 and before the Mann-Elkins Act of 1910 and the Kingsbury Agreement of 1916, which ultimately established the Bell System as a regulated monopoly. During this competitive period, large local exchange carriers were under no legal duty to interconnect. Competitors argued that as common carriers, the Bell companies had an obligation to provide service to all comers, including competitors charging the same regulated rate, but the courts refused to judicially mandate interconnection. The courts agreed with the common carrier principle to the extent that anyone had a right to receive retail service. Thus, the Bell companies had to transmit messages to competitors that purchased telephone service from a Bell company, provided competitors sought network access in the same manner as a member of the public. Otherwise, one telephone company had a duty to call the central office of another telephone company to tell them to inform its subscriber of the call.[27]

In a controversy reminiscent of the current voice-over-internet-protocol ("VoIP") debate, telephone companies in that period refused to permit telegraph companies to subscribe to their networks despite their duties as common carriers. The price of a long distance phone call was so high that telegraphy offered a competitive alternative. When consumers called their local telegraph offices to recite their long distance telegraph messages, the phone company lost business. Courts ruled that as common carriers phone companies could not refuse interconnection to these competitors, consistent with Supreme Court precedent that telegraph companies were required to receive messages from all.[28]

While courts can order that a regulated, established rate be charged to everyone including competitors, courts have difficulty setting rates for interconnection between competitors. The problem faced in the early common carriage cases and in *Trinko* is identical; a competitor cannot economically interconnect through retail access. But the history of telecommunications deregulation suggests that courts can effectively mandate interconnection. Competitive long distance markets were established through just such a judicial decree, although the price paid for interconnection initially involved substantial judicial wrangling.

As with the antitrust function in the 1996 Act, the *Trinko* Court appears to have an exaggerated opinion of the ability of the regulatory regime to do the job. The FCC has so far drafted three sets of unbundling rules, only to have each of them vacated in substantial measure by the federal courts. Among the difficulties faced by the FCC is the need to tailor rules to each local market on an individual basis. Courts are better suited to evaluate such case-by-case requirements, so the majority's rejection of antitrust litigation on the grounds of irremediability may have elevated form over substance.

ANTITRUST (IN-)EFFICIENCY

The third important element of the doctrine in *Town of Concord* is the manner in which regulation "dramatically alters the calculus of antitrust harms and benefits."[29] Having established the competitive benefits of the de-monopolization scheme in the 1996 Act, the *Trinko* majority balanced the benefits of antitrust against a "realistic assessment of its costs." Here, the judicial burden, awkwardness, and inconsistent goals of antitrust minimized any marginal contribution of antitrust litigation. In light of the comprehensiveness and competitive safeguards in the 1996 Act, the Court concluded that the "additional benefit to competition provided by antitrust enforcement will tend to be small." That is, antitrust law in local exchange markets governed by the Act would be inefficient. The majority concludes that, on balance, the antitrust laws have nothing or little to add to the rules and relief already provided for by the 1996 Act.

The majority found that the costs of antitrust include the risk of "false positives" in antitrust fact-finding, the prospect of which "chills" pro-competitive conduct, and the potential for deleterious effects on the incentives of firms to invest in infrastructure in order to engage in facilities-based competition. While it is indisputable that vigorous lawful competitive activity in some circumstances can be indistinguishable from unlawful monopolization, the risk of false positives in the context of

Trinko seems small. The conduct at issue was specifically repudiated in the 1996 Act, which condemns an ILEC's refusal-to-deal in unbundled network elements as anticompetitive, so such violations are easy to identify.

The other perceived cost, that forced sharing "may lessen the incentive for the monopolist, the rival, or both to invest in those economically beneficial facilities," is also difficult to justify. The duties of the ILECs to interconnect may lessen the short term incentives for CLECs to duplicate ILEC network elements, but these duties reflect a judgment already extant in the 1996 Act.[30] Moreover, interconnection may promote the incentives for CLECs to offer other new and improved services not available from the ILECs by opening markets for discounted service, internet service providers (ISPs), providers of VoIP, security services, and other providers for whom it would be prohibitively expensive or uneconomical to build local loop facilities. Punishing the failure of the ILECs to interconnect with antitrust liability is unlikely to affect this balance of incentives.

Finally, what may be most perplexing about the invocation of *Town of Concord* in the context of the *Trinko* case is the fundamentally opposite situation faced in each of the cases. While the essential rationale in the former case was based on the presence of a regulatory scheme designed to lessen or ameliorate the risks of antitrust-type violations, the *Trinko* case involved a transition *away* from regulation toward competitive markets. Withholding antitrust scrutiny may make sense where regulations specifically exist for the purpose of ensuring that anticompetitive conduct is discouraged, but the same cannot be said where regulations are being abandoned in favor of a competitive marketplace. The Majority seems to want to have its cake and eat it too: withholding antitrust liability where a protective regulatory scheme is in place (*Town of Concord*) and also withholding antitrust liability where such regulations are being abandoned to effectuate a transition to competition (*Trinko*). The reasoning in *Town of Concord* cuts in favor of applying the antitrust laws to a telecommunications industry subject to the 1996 Act, not, as the Majority does, in favor of abandoning the protections that antitrust can afford.

The second rationale: the non-cognizability of the antitrust claim

Because the implied immunity doctrine was unavailing, the Majority felt compelled to proceed to the merits of Verizon's alleged violation of Section 2. After separately analyzing this antitrust claim, the Court essentially concluded that Verizon had not engaged in predatory conduct cognizable under Section 2.

Strictly speaking, the Court did not have to engage in a substantive discussion of monopolization law. It could have nullified the antitrust laws on the grounds of its non-immunity judicial economy argument or, for that matter, on the grounds of lack of standing adopted by the concurrence.

But by characterizing Verizon's conduct as something beyond the traditional boundaries of Section 2, the Court could claim that the savings clause itself precluded the antitrust case.

The significance of the antitrust holding for the savings clause

The Majority's antitrust result feeds back to the savings clause, because it leads to the result that the duty of the ILECs to deal with its rivals does not arise from antitrust principles, so it must arise out of the 1996 Act. If the antitrust claim was available at all, it was only by dint of the de-monopolization program in the 1996 Act. Because entertaining such a "new claim[] that go[es] beyond the existing antitrust standards" would be "equally inconsistent" with a prohibition against anything in the Act that might "'modify, impair, or supersede the applicability' of the antitrust laws," the savings clause prohibited the antitrust claim as surely as it prohibited implied immunity. Verizon's conduct may only be judged, condemned, and remedied under the provisions of the Act, and not under the antitrust laws. Thus, the *Goldwasser* rationale carries the day, *sub silentio*. Conduct that was not an antitrust violation before the Act does not become, by operation of law, an antitrust violation after the Act.[31]

Counter-intuitively, the savings clause emerges as a *reason* to withhold the application of the antitrust laws. By the same reasoning, two ILECs could fix prices or allocate markets and escape antitrust scrutiny by pointing out that before the Act no such violation could have occurred because the two firms could not have been potential competitors.[32] The clear message sent by Congress through the savings clause was that the 1996 Act would *not* be inconsistent with the antitrust laws. What the Supreme Court heard is that it *must be*.

Because reaching the antitrust analysis and indulging in a substantive discussion of Section 2 was an exercise of the Court's discretion not required on the undeveloped record before it, the Court invites the impression that its opinion represents a significant statement about the direction of Section 2.

The Section 2 analysis

According to the Court's antitrust analysis, Section 2 does not apply under "existing antitrust standards" to the facts plead in the amended complaint, so the claim in *Trinko* would have to be dismissed regardless of the 1996 Act. Several facets of the Court's antitrust analysis have helped to fuel the notion that *Trinko*'s reach might extend beyond the regulated telecommunications market.

The first is the Majority's view of lawful monopoly and infrastructure. From the existence of lawful monopoly, the Court concludes that monopoly-maintaining conduct represents welfare-enhancing profit-seeking of the type the antitrust laws are intended to promote. The second important facet of the Court's Section 2 analysis is its reliance on the "sacrifice test" to detect predatory conduct, which would seem not only to narrow the range of what may constitute predatory—i.e., actionable—conduct, but also to provide an efficiency defense for nearly any refusal-to-deal. Third, the Majority's definition of predatory conduct rekindles an old debate about the importance of proving intent as opposed to demonstrating effects in Section 2 cases. Finally, although they appeared to have been left largely undisturbed, future application of the essential facilities and monopoly leveraging theories may have been undermined.

THE COURT'S VIEW OF LAWFUL MONOPOLY

Under Section 2, a firm shall not monopolize or attempt to monopolize. The statute prohibits unlawful monopoly willfully acquired or maintained. Lawful monopoly, however, due to a "superior product, business acumen, or historic accident" (a distinction drawn in *United States v. Grinnell Corp.*[33]), is beyond the reach of Section 2. The Court seizes on the existence of lawful monopoly and elevates its status to something more than a sub-optimally organized industry in which the dominant firm is *not to be sued* under the antitrust laws.

To the *Trinko* majority, the dream of monopoly is an important incentive, the "opportunity to charge monopoly prices—at least for a short period—is what attracts 'business acumen' in the first place," because "[i]t induces risk taking that produces innovation and economic growth."[34] Lawfully acquired monopoly, therefore, is not merely to be left alone by the antitrust laws but something the antitrust laws should *promote.* The need to "safeguard" this monopolistic motive was one reason, according to the *Trinko* Court, that there is no "judicial doctrine" of forcing legal monopolies to share with their rivals.[35]

This monopoly-centric view of incentives, which confuses monopoly rents with quasi-rents, suggests an indifference to even uncontroversial economic reasoning. Clearly, economic return must be adequate to induce firms to innovate and invest in risky ventures. In conventional economic models the quasi-rent payoffs from winning an innovation gamble are surplus returns that reward innovation. No additional "kicker" of monopoly rents, which are earned by a dominant firm with an anti-competitive hold on a monopolized relevant market, is necessary. The transitory surplus returns from successful innovation are very different from the allocation of consumer surplus which a monopolist may capture. The former is consistent with a dynamically competitive market, the latter is not. Successful innovation is incentive enough, without the prospect of the absence of competition or market determined prices. Nonetheless, in the Majority's view, forcing a monopolist to share elements of a lawfully acquired monopoly would create a disincentive for activity the antitrust laws were intended to promote. Lawful monopolies include, at a minimum, the ILECs, but potentially also *any firm* with a large or efficient enough infrastructure, or control over an essential input, to dominate its market. From this perspective, a firm's large infrastructure or its control of a competitive gateway is a competitive advantage in league with a superior product, business acumen, or historical good fortune, which should not, in the Court's view, be subject to forced sharing under the antitrust laws.

There are some flaws in the Majority's "monopoly incentive" analysis. As already indicated, it is a mistake to enter into antitrust law the notion that innovation and risk-taking require temporary "monopoly rents" as an incentive. But, such reasoning seems particularly out of place where, as in the local exchange markets, the monopolists have acquired their infrastructure by governmental fiat as opposed to any particular conduct that society might want to encourage. No legal incentive can promote such an historical accident.

Equally problematic is the idea that the emoluments of a legal monopoly are sacrosanct because they were legally obtained. The Majority's interpretation of Section 2, that "the possession of monopoly power will not be found unlawful unless it is accompanied by an element of anticompetitive *conduct*,"[36] is uncontroversial. But the Majority severely limited its application in this context by combining it with the requirement that the defendant satisfy the "sacrifice test," i.e., a "willingness to forsake short-term profits to achieve an anticompetitive end."[37] Under the Majority's view of legal monopoly this test could rarely if ever be satisfied by a monopolist's refusal-to-deal because the failure of a monopolist to grant access to lawfully acquired infrastructure is immediately economically self-justified. Thus, rather than constituting anticompetitive conduct necessary to trigger the antitrust laws, Verizon's conduct is seen as an understandable "reluctance to interconnect," rationally motivated by the desire of the firm to deny its rivals access to its competitive advantage, and not involving any short term profit sacrifice. The Majority fails to limit its reasoning to industries under supervisory regulation in any express way, so an unregulated firm with a dominating infrastructure, or the owner of essential intellectual property, may see *Trinko* as a shield against a range of procompetitive remedies wherever competitive injury results from a refusal-to-deal.

THE SACRIFICE TEST

The Court begins its analysis of Verizon's conduct with the "general rule," based on a fragment from *United States v. Colgate & Co.*,[38] that the antitrust laws do not restrict the "long recognized right of [a] trader or manufacturer *** freely to exercise his own independent discretion as to parties with whom he will deal."[39] The *Colgate* decision makes clear that the antitrust laws have nothing to do with political or other personal motivations for business practices. But in this case, the *Trinko* Court twisted the language of *Colgate* out of context[40] in order to frame its inquiry as whether Verizon's alleged anticompetitive conduct qualified as a narrow exception to the generally available freedom to deal.

The Majority then distinguished the situation in *Trinko* from the circumstances in *Aspen Skiing Co. v. Aspen Highlands Skiing Corp.*,[41] which it referred to as the leading case for Section 2 liability based on "refusal to cooperate with a rival." The Court emphasized that the refusal to deal in *Aspen* involved the discontinuance of a "voluntary (*and thus presumably profitable*) course of dealing which suggested a willingness to forsake short-term profits to achieve an anticompetitive end."[42] By contrast, Verizon's alleged wrongdoing resulted from its failure to initiate a compelled (and thus presumably *un*profitable) course of dealing. As a result, the amended complaint could not have alleged the sacrifice of short term profits, and so did not state a Section 2 cause of action.

The Majority then borrowed the notion of short term profit sacrifice from the standard employed to detect predatory pricing in *Brooke Group Ltd. v. Brown & Williamson Tobacco Corp.*[43] For several reasons, however, its application to the type of non-price conduct alleged in *Trinko* is conceptually flawed. In *Brooke Group* the Court faced the difficult problem of differentiating between lawful, pro-competitive price-cutting and unlawful, anti-competitive predatory pricing. The Court, therefore, required a predatory pricing plaintiff to demonstrate that the defendant incurred some measure of short term profit loss in a rational hope (accompanied by a reasonable possibility of success) of earning long term monopoly rents. But, for reasons already given, the risk of a false positive in the *Trinko* context is substantially less.

Despite its role in *Trinko*, the sacrifice test is not likely to become the global standard for anticompetitive conduct. First, anticompetitive conduct does not occur *only* in the presence of such a sacrifice. For example, when regulation or other constraints not related to market influences shape business behavior, there may be other reliable evidence of anticompetitiveness, even in the absence of a sacrifice of short term profits. The *Trinko* case presented just such a context. Also, some activities, such as "dirty tricks," disparaging a competitor, or manipulating a trade or standards body, can inflict substantial competitive harm without involving the loss of short term profits. Other activities, such as promotions or pure research, may involve substantial profit-sacrifice without any anticompetitive effect. Thus, it is neither necessary nor sufficient to detect anticompetitive non-price conduct.

Universal application of such a test would create a serious pleading burden, requiring information usually only available to the defendant. Moreover, it would foreclose antitrust law's ability to incorporate more refined economic understandings of and approaches to anticompetitive conduct that may develop in the future. In addition, not all industries or markets are likely to be amenable to the same standard for anticompetitive conduct. For these reasons, and doubtless others, it is not sensible to merge the sacrifice test applicable to predatory pricing with the standard for judging refusals-to-deal or other non-price predation. Antitrust law should encourage, not stifle, advances in economic analysis.

THE ROLE OF INTENT AND EFFECT

A more limited interpretation is that the Majority invoked the sacrifice test because other evidence of specific anticompetitive intent or motive is often lacking in Section 2 refusal-to-deal cases. This interpretation places the sacrifice test in the service both of preventing false negatives and ensuring the absence of an efficiency justification for the defendant's conduct.

One commentator suggests that *Trinko* may be read as a retreat from the Court's opinion in *Eastman Kodak Co. v. Image Technical Services, Inc.,*[44] a case decided after *Aspen* in which the Court held that a refusal-to-deal with anticompetitive effects is unlawful unless rebutted by a plausible efficiency justification.[45] Justice Scalia issued a sharp dissent in *Kodak* but the case was not cited in the majority's opinion in *Trinko.* By adopting the sacrifice test—or some other indicium of willfulness—as a pleading requirement, the *Trinko* decision may have shifted the burden of going forward with evidence of an efficiency justification from the defendant to the plaintiff, who must now plead the absence of such a justification.

Trinko's discussion of intent may represent an even greater retreat from the decision in *Brooke Group Ltd. v. Brown & Williamson Tobacco Corp.*[46] The plaintiff in *Brooke Group* alleged that the defendant had engaged in predatory pricing in an effort to discipline the plaintiff for introducing low cost, generic cigarettes. Prior to *Brooke Group,* antitrust law had defined predatory pricing largely in terms of the defendant's intent to injure competition.[47] Although the record in *Brooke Group* contained "sufficient evidence from which a reasonable jury could conclude that [the defendant] envisioned or intended this anticompetitive course of events," the Court nonetheless held that the defendant had not engaged in predatory pricing "because no evidence suggests that [the defendant]—whatever its intent...—was likely to obtain the power to raise the prices for generic cigarettes above a competitive level."[48] Predatory intent, even when coupled with below cost pricing, suggested the Court, "is insufficient as a matter of law" to support a finding of anticompetitive conduct.[49] As one commentator suggested, *Brooke Group* "goes very far in the direction of making intent evidence irrelevant."[50]

Trinko, however, seems to resurrect predatory intent as the hallmark of anticompetitive conduct. Had the Majority in *Trinko* replicated the analysis in *Brooke Group,* it would have looked for allegations of objective evidence to support a conclusion that the defendant received or maintained monopoly power (or reasonably could have expected to receive or maintain monopoly power) as a result of its conduct. The defendant's actual motive would have been irrelevant. Not only did the Majority in *Trinko* largely eschew this type of analysis, it relied heavily, if not exclusively, on the issue predatory intent to distinguish *Trinko* from *Aspen*. The *Aspen* defendant's decision to discontinue a course of dealing "revealed a distinctly anticompetitive bent," but the *Trinko* defendant's "reluctance" to initiate a new course of dealing "tells us nothing about dreams of monopoly."[51] At the very least, the Majority's opinion suggests that the presence or absence of subjective predatory intent demarcates the outer boundaries of liability under Section 2 of the Sherman Act.

WITHER THE ESSENTIAL FACILITIES AND MONOPOLY LEVERAGING?

While the Majority's opinion revealed some hostility to the essential facilities doctrine by favorably citing the critical article on the doctrine by Professor Areeda,[52] the Court saw no need to either "recognize or repudiate" it. Although the case gives little or no explicit guidance about the viability of the essential facilities doctrine as the basis of Section 2 claims in the future in rejecting the refusal-to-deal claim, however, the Court also rejected the essential facilities argument.

By considering the refusal of a lawful monopolist to grant access to its infrastructure on a par with other efficiency-generating conduct, the Majority may have raised the bar on essential facilities. Such denials may henceforth be argued to be inherently self-justifying. The one avenue that remains open, the satisfaction of the sacrifice test, is likely to be impossible to establish in most refusal-to-deal cases.

The Court similarly made no express contribution to the monopoly leveraging doctrine, except to reaffirm in a footnote that it should be regarded as a version of attempt to monopolize requiring a dangerous probability of success, as announced in *Spectrum Sports, Inc. v. McQuillan*,[53] and to reject it on the same grounds as the Section 2 claim itself, i.e., the lack of demonstrable anticompetitive conduct.

While the Court cannot be said to have made any express holding with respect to the essential facilities or monopoly leveraging Section 2 theories, the tone of the opinion is decidedly negative. Given the open-ended nature of the main opinion, it creates an opportunity for lower courts to rely on *Trinko* in the future to justify hostility to such theories. This development is counterproductive in an environment in which large, legal monopolies seem to be proliferating, and in which more and creative means of extending market power appear on an almost daily basis. While these theories are by no means dead, they are, in the words of one commentator, on life-support. The *Trinko* opinion seems to have attenuated the oxygen supply ever so slightly, ensuring their slow but eventual expiration.

The concurrence and the issue of standing

Justice Stevens, in a concurring opinion joined by Justices Souter and Thomas, agreed that dismissal was warranted, but because the plaintiff lacked antitrust standing, based on the principles in *Associated General Contractors of Cal., Inc. v. Carpenters,*[54] an opinion authored by Justice Stevens some 20 years earlier. Since the plaintiffs' injury was "purely derivative" of the injury suffered by AT&T the plaintiffs did not satisfy the definition of a "person" entitled to sue for a violation of the antitrust laws in §4 of the Clayton Act.[55]

It is difficult to establish that the claim in *Trinko* was purely derivative of the injury suffered by AT&T, because its customers suffered different or additional damages from those incurred by AT&T itself. The injuries to AT&T from Verizon's refusal to grant access would have been in the nature of lost profits, while the plaintiffs' damages were due to the absence or inadequacy of AT&T's service. The factors that usually defeat antitrust standing, the problems attendant to duplicate recoveries, apportionment of damages, and the remoteness of the injury, are entirely absent in the *Trinko* case. Moreover, the two-pronged relationship of AT&T to Verizon, at once a wholesale customer and a retail competitor, obscures the standing issue.

Ordinarily, the Court would opt to let its decision rest on the grounds of standing. In this case, by standing mute on the issue and reaching the merits, the Majority suggested that customers of firms denied access may indeed sue for antitrust injury.

Conclusion

The indeterminacy in the significance of *Trinko* for judicially mandated network access is not likely to be overcome until the Court decides another case in which a firm's refusal-to-deal or denial of access is claimed to violate Section 2. Until then, its significance is still unclear, particularly for unregulated markets and for "incentive" markets for patents or copyrights.

In telecommunications and other regulated industries, *Trinko* will likely lead to preemption of the antitrust laws based on *Town of Concord.* However, if the applicable regulatory scheme lacks an adequate antitrust function and the plaintiff can demonstrate that the sacrifice test has low power to detect the type of non-price predatory conduct alleged, the preemption may be overcome, particularly where there are substantial pro-competitive benefits from antitrust litigation.

In regulated industries prognostication is particularly difficult. The aspect of the *Trinko* case most likely to have a significant impact on network access issues is the Majority's view of lawful monopoly, which regards large infrastructure as a legitimate competitive advantage. Under this approach, the failure to share infrastructure with a rival is self-justified on efficiency grounds, potentially raising the prospect that a refusal-to-deal can never constitute anticompetitive conduct. This perspective can potentially extend beyond infrastructure to, for example, essential intellectual property. For instance, if a monopolist's blocking patent is similarly regarded as a legitimate competitive advantage, there are few if any circumstances in which the patentee will be required to grant access under antitrust principles. At the very least, the opportunity to employ antitrust law to achieve pro-competitive access to the network or property of a monopolist has become, after *Trinko*, substantially more uncertain.

Notes

1 Research Fellow, American Antitrust Institute, Associate Professor of Strategy, Law and Ethics, Haworth College of Business, Western Michigan University, and AAI Research Fellow, and Assistant Professor, Michigan State University College of Law.

2 Pub. L. 104–104, 110 Stat. 56 (1996), codified at 47 U.S.C. et seq. For further details of the Act's provisions relating to the introduction of competition into the local exchange market, see Jonathan Rubin, pp. 121–41 this volume.

3 The principal ILECs include the former Bell System monopolists, Verizon Communications, Inc., BellSouth Corp., SBC Communications, Inc., and Quest Communications. Inc., and other existing local exchange providers operating prior to passage of the Act.

4 The CLECs include the interexchange (long distance) carriers, AT&T, MCI, and Sprint, and several hundred other new entrants. They are identified in resources available at the FCC and at the website of the dominant CLEC trade association, CompTel/Ascent, at www.comptelascent.org, or the dominant ILEC trade association, United States Telecom Association, at www.usta.org.

5 The antitrust claims filed or pending in the U.S. district courts against the ILECs by CLECs and others are now too numerous to be listed exhaustively. At least one case, *Covad v. BellAtlantic*, 201 F.Supp.2d 123 (D.C.D.C, 2002), now on appeal to the D.C. Circuit Court of Appeals, alleges a "price squeeze," in which a vertically-integrated monopolist lowers its retail prices and/or raises its wholesale prices to eliminate the wholesale–retail spread that permits a competitor to earn a profit. But most complaints over ILEC conduct resemble *Trinko*, in the sense that the complained of conduct is non-price in nature, such as failing to fill orders or impeding CLEC operations. The Eleventh Circuit Court of Appeals recently upheld a price squeeze suit by Covad against Bell South, allowing it to proceed to trial. See *Covad v. Bell South*, No. 01–16064, 2004 WL 1418405 (11th Cir. June 25, 2004).

6 110 Stat. 143, 47 U.S.C. §152, note.

7 540 U.S. 398 (2004) (*"Trinko"*).

8 222 F.3d 390 (7th Cir., 2000) (*"Goldwasser"*).

9 *Law Offices of Curtis V. Trinko, LLP v. Bell Atlantic Corp.*, 123 F. Supp. 2d 738 (S.D.N.Y. 2000).

10 *Law Offices of Curtis V. Trinko v. Bell Atlantic Corp.*, 305 F.3d 89 (2d Cir. 2002).

11 Joining the majority were Chief Justice Rehnquist and Associate Justices O'Connor, Kennedy, Ginsburg, and Breyer.

12 The concurrence was authored by Justice Stevens, joined by Justices Souter and Thomas.

13 *Trinko*, op. cit., 877.

14 *U.S. v. Nat'l Ass'n of Sec. Dealers*, 422 U.S. 694, 719–20 (1975).

15 *Trinko*, op. cit., 878.

16 Ibid., 878.

17 915 F.2d 17 (1st Cir., 1990) (*"Town of Concord"*).

18 *Town of Concord*, op. cit., 18.

19 Ibid., 23.

20 *Trinko*, op. cit., 881.

21 Ibid., 882.

22 *Trinko*, op. cit., 881, quoting *Town of Concord* at 25.

23 *Trinko*, op. cit., 883.

24 Ibid., 882.

25 Ibid.

26 Ibid., 883.

27 *Wisconsin Tel. Co. v. R.R. Comm'n of Wis.*, 156 N.W. 614, 616 (Wis. 1916); see also *Mich. State Tel. Co. v. Mich. R.R. Comm'n.*, 161 N.W. 240, 243 (Mich. 1916); *Pac. Tel. & Tel. Co. v. Anderson*, 196 F. 699, 703 (D.C. Wash. 1912).

28 See *Western Union Telegraph Co. v. Call Publishing Co.*, 181 U.S. 92 (1901); see also *Delaware & A. Tel. & Tel. Co. v. Delaware*, 50 F. 677, 679–80 (3d Cir. 1892); *Postal Cable Tel. Co. v. Cumberland Tel. & Tele. Co.*, 177 F. 726, 727 (C.C. Tenn. 1910); *Missouri el rel. Baltimore & Ohio Tel. Co. v. Bell. Tel. Co.*, 23 F. 539, 540 (C.C.E.D. Mo. 1885).

29 *Town of Concord*, op. cit., 25.

30 The monopolists' incentives are discussed in Section V.B.1., *infra*.

31 *Goldwasser*, op. cit., 400. (The 1996 Act contains duties and obligations of affirmative assistance that "go well beyond anything the antitrust laws would mandate on their own.")

32 Market definition issue: Seems like they are allocating markets now, but one could argue that Verizon wireless competes with SBC land in Kalamazoo.

33 384 U.S. 563, 570–571 (1966).

34 *Trinko*, op. cit., 879.

35 Ibid.

36 Ibid., p. 879 (emphasis in original).

37 Ibid., p. 880. See Section V.B.2., *infra*.

38 250 U.S. 300 (1919) (*"Colgate"*).

39 *Trinko*, op. cit., p. 879, quoting *Colgate*, at 307.

40 The Majority in *Trinko* argued that the *Colgate* doctrine flowed in part from the fear that "compelling negotiations between competitors may facilitate the supreme evil of antitrust: collusion." *Trinko*, op. cit., 879. *Colgate*, however, stated that the "purpose of the Sherman Act is to prohibit monopolies" as well as collusive actives from interfering with "the free exercise of their rights by those engaged, or who wish to engage, in trade or commerce—in a word to preserve the right of freedom to trade" (*Colgate*, op. cit., 307). Furthermore, the Majority only quoted a portion of the doctrine stated in *Colgate*. The complete statement found in *Colgate* holds that the dealer with monopoly power

does not have an unqualified right of refusal under the Sherman Act: "*In the absence of any purpose to create or maintain a monopoly, the act* does not restrict the long recognized right of trader or manufacturer engaged in an entirely private business, freely to exercise his own independent discretion as to parties with whom he will deal" (the portions omitted by the Majority in *Trinko* have been italicized).

41 472 U.S. 585 (1985) ("*Aspen*").
42 *Trinko*, op. cit., p. 880 (emphasis in original).
43 509 U.S. 209 (1993) ("*Brooke Group*").
44 504 U.S. 451 (1992) ("*Kodak*").
45 R. A. Skitol, "Correct answers to large questions about *Verizon v. Trinko*," *The Antitrust Source*, May, 2004. Online. Available HTTP: <http://www.antitrust-source.com> (accessed July 19, 2004).
46 509 U.S. 209 (1993) ("*Brooke Group*").
47 See, *Utah Pie Co. v. Continental Baking Co.*, 386 U.S. 685 (1967).
48 *Brooke Group*, op. cit., 231.
49 *Brooke Group*, op. cit., 243.
50 H. Hovenkamp, *Federal Antitrust Policy: The Law of Competition and Its Practice*, 2nd edn, St. Paul, Minnesota: West Group, p. 355. See also, L. A. Sullivan and W. S. Grimes, *The Law of Antitrust: An Integrated Handbook*, St. Paul, Minnesota: West Group, 2000, p.155 (*"Brooke Group* appears to invite the Court to disregard intent evidence"); K. L. Glazer, "Predatory pricing and beyond: life after Brooke Group," *Antitrust Law Journal* 62, 1994, p. 627 (*Brooke Group* may not have completely rendered intent "a dead letter in antitrust law," but "it is difficult to deny that the case tends to diminish the importance of intent").
51 *Trinko*, op. cit., p. 880.
52 P. Areeda, "Essential facilities: an epithet in need of limiting principles," *Antitrust Law Journal* 58, 1989, p. 841.
53 506 U.S. 447 (1993).
54 459 U.S. 519 (1983).
55 15 U.S.C. §15.

Part II
Case studies

Preface to part II

The cases present a relatively wide cross-section of access issues that appear in network industries. They include classic access examples that pose relatively straightforward competitive problems and the more novel and dynamic examples in which it is less clear whether such problems will develop. The case studies also cover a range of issues associated with the timing of intervention, method of intervention, and types of remedies. Moreover, the several cases involving compulsory access highlight the many decisions that policy makers must grapple with in crafting appropriate, workable, and effective forced access regimes.

John Kwoka and Lawrence White begin in the first case study by examining access issues in freight railroads and proposing various approaches to the ongoing problem of providing non-discriminatory access. In the second case study, Diana Moss examines the long history of "incremental" access policy in electricity transmission, where many second- and third-generation policies are designed to adjust for past failures and ongoing market and technological developments. In the third case study, Richard O'Neill evaluates the access issue in a leading example of an oligopolized network industry—natural gas pipelines. Jonathan Rubin goes on to assess the complexity of the access problem in a fourth case study on local telecommunications, where interconnection and access pricing are key policy components. Michael Pelcovits assesses one of the more unique examples of remedying access problems through vertical separation in the fifth case study on long distance telecommunications.

In some networks, the availability of access alternatives and the pace of technological change have important implications for policy development. In the sixth case study, Richard Brunell writes on broadband, a distinctive example of a "wait and see" regulatory approach to access. Donald Baker goes on to discuss a leading example of relatively early resolution to access issues in the seventh case study, on automated teller machine networks. He notes that access policies led to a high level of access, perhaps at the expense of too little network competition. Norman Hawker looks at a key example of virtual access that raises significant interoperability issues in the eighth case study, on internet browsers.

The final two case studies examine whether online services are dynamic new entrants competing with other forms of distribution, or whether they represent movement to concentrated, vertically-integrated distribution that could potentially foreclose the market to competing distributors. In the ninth case study, Albert Foer looks at access issues in joint venture agreements involving internet-based airline and travel services. Harry First concludes with the tenth case study—an assessment of access issues potentially arising in online music joint ventures.

Case 1

Freight railroads

John E. Kwoka and Lawrence J. White[1]

Introduction

Railroads are among the earliest examples of a network industry in the U.S. economy. From its origin in the mid-1800s, freight rail service[2] has involved the collection of shipments from scattered locations, their aggregation into multi-car trains at centrally located terminals, their dispatch over trunk lines to other terminals, and finally their distribution to final destinations. A stylized picture of a rail transport network is shown in Figure II.1.1. Points A, B, and C represent points of origin, from which shipments are aggregated at a terminal or yard (denoted T_1), then move to a second terminal T_2, from which they are distributed to final destinations X, Y, and Z.

This production process involves two types of physical facilities. "Below the wheel" are the rights of way, trackage, switches, etc.—inputs with high fixed and sunk costs. "Above the wheel" inputs are the locomotives and cars (the "rolling stock"), also characterized by high fixed costs but not generally sunk with respect to a particular route or shipment. Despite these cost considerations, until recently railroads have been characterized by a significant number of carriers and competition. In some places this was due to shipment densities that were sufficiently high to support multiple trunk lines. Elsewhere it was due to aggressive competition for the

Figure II.1.1 A stylized rail network.

business of specific high volume shippers. For much of the 1900s, it was also due to regulatory impediments to the abandonment of unprofitable lines. And throughout, railroads increasingly had to compete with truck and barge transportation for some types of business.

Also common were railroad mergers, which reduced the number of large ("Class I") railroads from 186 in 1920 to 39 by 1980. In the latter year the Staggers Act was passed, substantially deregulating railroads and granting them wide pricing discretion. The Interstate Commerce Commission (ICC) continued to approve mergers, leaving just eleven Class I railroads by 1995, with but four major railroads in the east and three in the west. The service effects of the round of mergers in the mid-1990s—especially the Union Pacific (UP) and the Southern Pacific (SP) merger that was approved in 1996 by the ICC's successor, the Surface Transportation Board (STB)—were so adverse that the STB imposed a moratorium on mergers, issued new guidelines, and promised to scrutinize future consolidations more critically.[3] Observers nonetheless think it inevitable that the two remaining east coast carriers and the two remaining west coast railroads will pair off, creating two coast-to-coast rail freight systems.

The issues

Throughout its history, freight rail service has raised issues of network access and competition. Three of these deserve mention—compatibility, terminals, and interline competition.

Fifty years after the initial development of the U.S. rail system, different track gauges were still employed. The single most common was the English "standard gauge" of 4 feet, 8.5 inches, which was widespread in the North but accounted for only about half of all track in the country. A wider gauge prevailed in the South, while the Mountain states employed a narrower gauge. Shipments into or out of these regions required either offloading and reloading ("break bulk"), use of car hoists that shifted cars onto different gauge carriages, variable tread rail cars, or three-rail lines. Each of these alternatives had disadvantages, and collectively this system fragmented rail transport and protected regional carriers from incursions by rivals.

In the 1880s, under the impetus of westward expansion, the three major Midwestern railroads decided to switch to the standard gauge, followed soon by most of the southern railroads.[4] At that point it was said that standardization had made southern railroads "truly... part of the national network. An immediate dividend [was] increased efficiency [from] more extensive car interchange... among the railroad companies."[5] Apparently, with no dominant railroad, each found private cost savings more advantageous than the strategic benefit of excluding a competitor, though the details of the process by which this agreement was struck remain unclear.

Clearer competitive concerns were raised by various consolidations and inter-corporate agreements at the turn of the century. The most famous of these was the Terminal Railroad Association, which controlled the sole rail bridge across the Mississippi at St. Louis, as well as switching yards on both sides of the river. This was purchased by Jay Gould and owners of fourteen railroads, a group that did not include all railroads transiting St. Louis. To the extent that the latter were granted access to the terminal facilities at all, such access was said to be at discriminatory rates. Given the economic infeasibility of any other river crossing, the Supreme Court held that Terminal Railroad controlled an "essential facility" and required that non-members be given the right to buy an ownership interest or, alternatively, provided with access to the facilities on fair terms.[6]

Foreclosure and related issues have arisen frequently in the context of competition between single-line and interline railroads. This circumstance—depicted in Figure II.1.2—arises when an entire route O–D is served by one railroad (the single line firm), with one portion (O–T) also served by a second carrier. The latter must therefore "interline" at point T, transferring its shipment to the single-line carrier to complete the movement and thereby compete for the O–D business. The single-line carrier can blunt or eliminate competition by denying the O–T rival access or discriminating in the price charged for the T–D movement (a "price squeeze"). These circumstances became more frequent with the proliferation of end-to-end mergers during the 1970s and 1980s—that is, mergers in which one of two railroads serving the O–T segment merged with the sole T–D railroad, creating a single-line O–D carrier that still faced a competitor on the O–T segment.[7]

Casting this as a simple issue of vertical pricing, relying upon the Chicago School proposition that the monopoly firm can extract all profit from the bottleneck T–D segment, and ignoring the protests of shippers, the ICC concluded that such mergers could not cause incremental market distortion. Any distortion was due to the pre-existing T–D monopoly, and since there were generally efficiency benefits from single-line service to shippers, the ICC approved a wave of such mergers. Empirical evidence, however, has established that interline competition does constrain

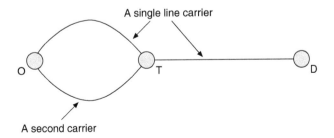

Figure II.1.2 The problem of access.

pricing.[8] Likely reasons include standard pricing practices that do not entail prior full extraction of profit from T–D, greater opportunity for secret contracting in the presence of an interline rival, and the threat of more comprehensive entry. The implication is that discriminatory access or outright foreclosure of the interline competitor in the scenario described in Figure II.1.2 has significant economic consequences.

Access arrangements

There are, in principle and in practice, only a few ways of dealing with access: (1) free market "neglect" (with the hope of entry); (2) regulated rates/tariffs for the sale/purchase of access services; (3) the entrant "rents" the access facilities from the bottleneck carrier; (4) the firms reciprocally cooperate (voluntarily), when each wants/needs access to the other's bottleneck facilities; (5) joint ownership of bottleneck facilities; (6) mandated divestiture of duplicative facilities; and (7) vertical separation. We will address each remedy, in turn.

Free market neglect

One possible response to bottleneck access problems is to neglect or ignore them. This has been the response of the ICC/STB for the past two decades. In some instances this neglect is not serious, because potential entry is a sufficient threat so as to temper the exercise of market power that could otherwise be exercised by the bottleneck carrier. Such tempering occurs when a shipper's location is sufficiently close to another rail carrier's facilities that the threat of building a rail extension to those facilities is a realistic one.[9] In the absence of such realistic threats, however, the neglect of the access problem clearly yields market power for the bottleneck carrier.[10]

Regulated rates for access

This has been the traditional response to bottleneck problems in many network industries, such as rail, telephone, and electricity; such regulation has receded, especially in rail, over the past two decades. The rate regulation, in principle, recognizes the exercise of market power that would otherwise occur and tries to establish rates that would be consistent with a more competitive structure. The actual setting of rates, however, is itself bedeviled with difficult conceptual and factual issues, as well as being subject to political forces.[11] And misguided rate regulation can end up being as distortionary (or more so) as unregulated monopoly bottleneck control over access.

The entrant "rents" access facilities from the bottleneck carrier

In instances when a rail merger has created an access problem—e.g., where two rail carriers merge and some of their shippers previously could ship on either carrier but now would become "captive" to the merged carrier—one regulatory response by the ICC/STB has been to mandate that the merged entity grant "trackage rights" to a third rail carrier to serve those shippers.[12] In essence, the third carrier is permitted access to—permitted to run its trains over—the merged carrier's rail lines in order to serve the otherwise captive shipper. The third carrier (which we will call "the entrant") pays fees to the merged entity for this privilege.[13]

This form of remedy has been popular with the ICC/STB, which has apparently believed that such arrangements provide a completely equivalent substitute for the competition that has been eliminated by the merger. Closer analysis, however, reveals substantial flaws in this type of arrangement.

With trackage rights, the entrant carrier is, in essence, a tenant on the bottleneck carrier's tracks, renting access from the latter. In the absence of any further regulatory intervention, the bottleneck carrier "landlord" holds all of the cards and can structure the price and non-price terms of the arrangement so as to limit the tenant's ability to challenge the market power of the landlord.[14]

With respect to price, the landlord carrier can set fees that are sufficiently high so that the tenant carrier cannot effectively set rates that are below the monopoly level.[15] As for non-price elements, since the landlord carrier controls the dispatching and access to complementary facilities, it can effectively degrade the tenant carrier's service quality sufficiently so as to further mute any competitive threat that might otherwise be forthcoming from the tenant. Further, as trackage rights become more extensive and involve longer hauls by the tenant carrier over the landlord carrier's tracks, the tenant becomes more dependent on the landlord for support facilities (e.g., crew change facilities), making the exercise more costly and less worthwhile for the tenant. Finally, the extensive sharing of information that would be involved in a trackage rights arrangement could well encourage coordinated, noncompetitive behavior.

Reciprocal voluntary access

In many metropolitan areas, where carriers have located marshalling yards that are in close proximity to each other, they have often worked out "reciprocal switching" arrangements with each other. Under these arrangements, though a shipper (or a recipient) may have a direct rail connection to only one carrier's tracks, that carrier permits the switching locomotives of a neighboring carrier to pick up (or deliver) rail cars from that shipper (or to that recipient). These arrangements apply only to trips of short distances within these metropolitan areas. The carriers negotiate these arrangements with the expectation that the balance of traffic (either within that metropolitan area or across all such arrangements) will be roughly even and thus that each carrier will generally benefit from the greater flexibility and access that is thereby gained.[16] Though the ICC/STB has had the power to require reciprocal switching in places where it is not present, the agency has generally not used this power.

Joint ownership

In a few instances (e.g., terminal facilities in St. Louis and Chicago), a number of railroads have jointly owned the facility.[17] For the joint owners, access is no longer a problem.[18] For non-owners, the access problems remain.[19]

Divestiture of duplicative facilities

Sometimes mergers (outside of the railroad industry) threaten to create market power in one or more product and/or geographic markets. A standard antitrust remedy in such instances is to require the merging entity to divest sufficient duplicative facilities in those markets to viable purchasers, so as to reduce market concentration sufficiently to sustain adequate competition.[20] For example, if a merger were proposed between two banks that had extensive branching structures and overlaps in some metropolitan areas that would create high levels of concentration, the requirement of the divestiture of some branches in those areas (sufficient to sustain adequate post-merger competition) is near-automatic.[21]

Divestiture has not been a common remedy for similar merger-created problems in the railroad industry. The merging carriers always argue that the duplicative facilities have important value in reducing congestion or improving the quality of service to shippers, and the ICC/STB has accepted these arguments. Instead, as noted above, the ICC/STB has either ignored the resulting market power or has tried to remedy them with trackage rights arrangements.[22]

Vertical separation

A more radical proposal to resolve these incentive problems involves vertical de-integration of railroads: the creation of one company comprising track and related infrastructure, and a separate *set* of companies that own and operate the rolling stock and do the actual shipping. The operating companies would pay the track company for use of its facilities, but by virtue of a prohibition on its involvement in transport, the track company would have no reason to favor any one purchaser of its services; discriminatory access would cease to be an issue. With appropriate regulation, some economists and policy-makers have argued, the track company can be made to provide cost-based, non-discriminatory service, facilitating the emergence of a viable competitive transport sector.[23]

Until recently there have been no actual examples of this arrangement for rail, but Sweden, Argentina, and the U.K. have now adopted versions of this, and there has been a legislative proposal for U.S. passenger rail service with some similarities.[24] The U.K. unbundled British Rail in 1994, and privatized the various elements in 1997. Railtrack was constituted as the single owner of infrastructure, contractually serving dozens of freight transport companies and two passenger rail companies. It is widely believed that regulation of Railtrack gave it little incentive to maintain track, leading to deterioration of conditions and service (including major accidents), and ultimately to Railtrack's bankruptcy in 2001. Railtrack is now being reconstituted.[25]

In the U.S., dissatisfaction with the performance of rail passenger service has led to a recent proposal that Amtrak be divided into two companies. One would own the infrastructure that Amtrak inherited in the Northeast—the only region where it owns track—while the second would operate passenger train service.[26] At some future date additional franchised passenger service on the same track is foreseen.

Summary

There are potential solutions to the access problem, but none are perfect. In the context of mergers, divestiture of duplicative facilities is the strongest remedy; but it is the remedy that the ICC/STB has generally eschewed. Instead, the agency has generally embraced the creation of trackage rights for a third carrier; but, as we argued above, this is a weak remedy indeed.

Where to go from here

This survey of freight rail makes clear that this industry faces significant issues of providing non-discriminatory access and ensuring bona fide competition. We think at least the following issues could usefully be studied further. One issue is the record of access and prices under trackage rights. There is a record of shipper and competitive carrier complaints, and much economic reason for concern, but systematic evidence on contracts, prices, service, characteristics of haul, etc., is lacking.[27] A second priority is an evaluation of the access experience following the BN–SF and UP–SP mergers of the mid 1990s. Partly this evaluation would relate to the trackage rights research just discussed. But the opponents to these mergers claimed that the trackage rights granted did not fully address many access problems. Finally, experience with vertical separation should be studied. The "clean" break of separation often is muddied by the difficulty of establishing the correct incentives for all parties. The experiences of Argentina, Sweden, and the U.K. bear further examination.

Notes

1 John E. Kwoka is Neal F. Finnegan Professor of Economics, Northeastern University; Lawrence J. White is Arthur E. Imperatore Professor of Economics, New York University Stern School of Business.

2 Passenger rail service in the U.S. is also a network industry, but since Amtrak is presently the sole provider, no competitive access issues arise. Implications of proposed changes in Amtrak's structure are discussed below.

3 See J. E. Kwoka and L. J. White, "Manifest destiny? The Union Pacific and Southern Pacific railroad merger (1996)," in *The Antitrust Revolution: Economics, Competition, and Policy,* J. E. Kwoka, Jr. and L. J. White (eds), 4th edn, New York: Oxford University Press, 2004, pp. 27–51. Many questioned the STB merger guidelines and doubted the determination of the STB to enforce sound antitrust standards. See, for example, J. E. Kwoka and L. J. White, "Letter to Linda J. Morgan, Chair, Surface Transportation Board," November 17, 2000. Online. Available HTTP: <http://www.antitrustinstitute.org/recent/89.cfm (accessed June 15, 2004).

4 One of them—the Illinois Central—deployed 3,000 workers to shift all 550 miles of its line south of Cairo to the narrower gauge between dawn and 3 pm on a single day in July, 1881. Several southern railroads in concert shifted 13,000 miles of track in two days in 1886. See J. F. Stover, *American Railroads,* Chicago: University of Chicago Press, 1961 and C. Shapiro and H. R. Varian, *Information Rules: A Strategic Guide to the Network Economy,* Boston: Harvard Business School Press, 1999.

5 Stover, op cit.

6 See *U.S. v. Terminal Railroad Association of St. Louis,* 224 U.S. 383 (1912).

7 L. J. White, *U.S. Public Policy toward Network Industries,* Washington, D.C.: American Enterprise Institute, 1999.

8 See generally C. Winston, T. M. Corsi, C. M. Grimm, and C. A. Evans, *The Economic Effects of Surface Freight Deregulation.* Washington, D.C.: Brookings, 1990. C. M. Grimm, C. Winston, and C. S. Evans, "Foreclosure of railroad markets: a test of Chicago leverage theory," *Journal of Law & Economics* 35, 1992, pp. 295–310.

9 Such extensions are sometimes described as a "build out" or a "build in," depending on who constructs and owns the extension.

10 Further analysis can be found in W. Tye, "Post-merger denials of competitive access and trackage rights in the rail industry," *Transportation Practitioners' Journal* 53, 1986, pp. 413–27 and H. McFarland, "The economics of vertical restraints and relationships between connecting railroads," *Logistics and Transportation Review* 23, 1987, pp. 207–22. The STB's decision in *Central Power & Light v. Southern Pac. Transp. Co.,* 1 S.T.B. 1059, 1996 and 2 S.T.B. 235 (1997), reflects the agency's general unwillingness to intervene where there are (from shippers' or recipients' perspectives) existing access problems.

11 One such conceptual approach to regulated rates for access, the "efficient component pricing rule" (ECPR), is the subject of Topic 4 in this volume.

12 In the case of the UP/SP merger that the STB approved in 1996, the UP/SP arranged prior to the merger for an extensive trackage rights arrangement with the Burlington Northern Santa Fe (BNSF), which the STB then blessed (but added to) in its approval decision. See Kwoka and White (2004), op. cit.

13 A discussion of trackage rights, as well as other forms of carrier access arrangements, can be found in J. A. Pinkepank, "When (and where and why) railroads share track: a primer on trackage rights, interchange, detouring, joint track, paired track, and car-handling contracts," *Trains,* January 1979, pp. 20–9.

14 The parallels between the problems of trackage rights arrangements in rail and the problems of the leasing of unbundled network elements (UNEs) in telephony are quite close.

15 ICC/STB criteria for pricing trackage rights are set out in *St. Louis Southwestern Ry. Co. Compensation—Trackage Rights* 1 ICC 2nd 776 (1984), et seq. Tenant carriers have long complained that the discretion granted by these rules to the landlord carrier often precludes effective competition.

16 As a theoretical matter, it seems likely, however, that if the structural arrangements were that there was a dominant carrier and one or more smaller carriers, the dominant carrier's incentives would be to avoid reciprocal switching arrangements, in the hopes that this impediment to access would sufficiently weaken the smaller carriers so as to lead to their demise (or to their willingness to merge with the dominant carrier on terms that were favorable to the latter).

17 There is a parallel here with the multi-firm ownership of the Trans Alaska Pipeline (TAP).

18 There is, though, the danger that the joint ownership could become the vehicle for restricted competition among the owners. It could be the means by which extensive information is shared. Or it could levy high marginal fees on the carriers' operations, thereby raising effective prices above competitive prices, and then return the fees in a non-marginal fashion.

19 Indeed, it was the joint ownership of the St. Louis terminal facility that gave rise to the "essential facilities" doctrine in 1912; see *U.S. v. Terminal Railroad Association of St. Louis.*

20 Ensuring that a viable firm purchases the facilities is a crucial and sometimes difficult part of effective antitrust enforcement, since the merging entity would usually prefer that the purchaser quickly disappear from the market. For further discussion, see Federal Trade Commission, "A study of the Commission's divestiture process," Washington, D.C., 1999 and A. Foer, "Toward guidelines for merger remedies," *Case Western Reserve Law Review* 52, 2001, pp. 211–30.

21 Divestiture is far more rare as a remedy in monopolization cases; but it does occur, as in the 1982 AT&T consent decree and in the initial district court decision in *U.S. v. Microsoft.*

22 To illustrate again the competitive problems with trackage rights arrangements, let us continue with the bank-merger-and-branches example. Suppose instead of requiring the divestiture of branches in the problematic metropolitan areas, the Antitrust Division instead simply required that the merging bank provide rental space in those branches to an entrant; few (if any) antitrust analysts would consider that to be an adequate remedy for the market power problems that could arise.

23   In an important sense, vertical separation currently characterizes truck transport: The roads are public facilities (plus a handful of private toll roads), while separate truck companies own and operate their equipment, and all have equal access to the roads. Vertical separation also characterizes the theory behind the divestiture of AT&T in 1982: The bottleneck local operating companies remained regulated and were to be kept separated from the long distance companies, so as to ensure non-discriminatory access by the latter. And the same idea applies to the current ideas in electricity, of separating (regulated) bottleneck local distribution from competitive generation, so as to ensure non-discriminatory access for the latter.

24   *Regulating Privatized Rail Transport*, Policy Research Working Paper No. 2064, Washington, D.C.: World Bank, Economic Development Institute, February 1999.

25   *Accountability of Railtrack*, London: Office of Rail Regulator, May 2001.

26   *Action Plan for the Restructuring and Rationalization of the National Intercity Rail Passenger System*, Report to Congress, Washington, D.C.: Amtrak Reform Council, February 7, 2002.

27   Amtrak's experience in securing passage for its trains might be examined as a benchmark, since the companies from which it contracts for passage are freight railroads that do not compete with Amtrak. This example is muddied, however, by the fact that freight railroads often find that passenger service disrupts their scheduling of freight traffic on the same lines.

Case 2

Electricity transmission

Diana L. Moss[1]

Introduction

Access to electricity transmission networks in the U.S. electricity industry raises traditional and novel economic and legal issues. In the U.S., the system of compulsory access that promotes rival generators' access to the transmission systems of vertically-integrated utilities has proceeded incrementally over the last 30 years. This progress has been powered by a combination of legislative initiatives, regulatory policies, some antitrust enforcement, and remedies for problematic mergers. As will become apparent, reliance on a pervasive regime of compulsory access in electricity—implemented largely by the Federal Energy Regulatory Commission ("FERC" or the "Commission")—has created a difficult tension between regulatory and antitrust enforcement.

As a result of various initiatives, there are now fewer impediments to gaining access to transmission, and wholesale markets are more competitive. But the access problem in electricity is far from resolved. A number of problems pose ongoing and novel challenges to policy makers, which are complicated by restructuring woes. These challenges include balkanization of the state/federal jurisdictional system (particularly in regard to siting and expanding transmission facilities) and a persistent reluctance by Congress and FERC to mandate structural separation of generation and transmission. Market power analysis and enforcement continues to be a key issue. Exclusionary anticompetitive conduct now shares the stage with classical market power (e.g., "strategic" generation withholding). The current threat of vertical reintegration raises novel theories of competitive harm and brings into question the adequacy of competitive analysis performed by the Federal Energy Regulatory Commission. Finally, large scale outage problems have placed reliability at the top of the energy policy agenda and put renewed emphasis on access. The magnitude of these problems may well signal the need for alternative approaches to access in electricity transmission.

The protracted and transitional nature of restructuring efforts thus far makes several basic questions about the success of access in electricity difficult to answer at this time. First, it is not clear to what extent consumers have benefited from transmission access in the form of lower prices and greater choice. An empirical assessment that disaggregates the effects of network access from other parameters underlying broader industry restructuring would be helpful to gauge progress to date. Second, pervasive regulation of transmission, coupled with fundamental changes in electricity markets, have complicated the basic problem that access initiatives were originally designed to cure. For example, there is now a greater diversity in electricity market participants, more intensive use of the transmission grid, and powerful incentives for firms to minimize costs as a result of competition. Thus, vertically-integrated transmission owners are increasingly resistant to expanding their systems for use by rivals or are operating their systems in novel discriminatory ways. As a result, there are a number of regional markets that are transmission-constrained with high concentration of generation ownership. In these areas, the development of competitive markets will continue to be impeded without more aggressive structural reforms that reduce concentration and ease entry barriers.

This chapter provides an assessment of the network access problem in electricity. It begins with a brief history of the electricity industry and moves on to describing key issues in network access, followed by an analysis of the incremental approach to solving the access problem. The chapter concludes with observations on the success of network access and the policy challenges posed by the numerous tensions in the restructuring industry.

Historical perspective

For decades, the electricity industry was characterized by a high degree of vertical integration. Single firms owned all levels of production—generation, high-voltage transmission, and low-voltage local distribution. Regulation of the industry has been motivated by the pervasive view that electric utilities are natural monopolies in their local service areas. Regulation of profits and prices by state and local authorities was therefore instituted in exchange for the utility's exclusive right to serve local markets. This last condition precluded denial or curtailment of service to retail customers, thus creating an "obligation to serve."

Since 1935, U.S. states have had jurisdiction over retail sales of electricity to end-users such as industrial, commercial, and residential customers. Retail sales are typically made at a "bundled" rate.[2] Bundling combines the prices for generation, transmission, distribution, and all other services necessary to deliver the product to the customer. At the retail level, competition between utilities for large industrial loads or other "fringe" customers often resulted in discounting. In places where electricity supply areas intersect or where electricity competes with natural gas in end-use applications (e.g., heating, cooking) or industrial processes, there is also more aggressive pricing.

With the passage of the Federal Power Act (FPA) in 1935, Congress gave the Federal Power Commission in Section 201(b) the authority to regulate the industry beyond the reach of state commissions to "provide effective federal regulation of the expanding business of transmitting and selling electric power in interstate commerce."[3] From 1935 on, the states thus remained the primary regulators of retail electricity markets and the federal government effectively stepped in to regulate the wholesale electricity markets. Before the 1970s, competition in wholesale markets was minimal. The boundaries of wholesale markets were established in accordance with the physical constraints imposed by physical and thermal limits on the high voltage grid and the economics of regional generation cost-differentials and losses associated with transmitting power over long distances.[4]

Two major types of transactions made up the bulk of wholesale trading. "Requirements" sales occurred between transmission-owning utilities and transmission-dependent entities with demand obligations in the utility's "control area." Municipals and cooperatives serving rural and urban areas accounted for the bulk of these entities. Rates for requirement service were, and still are, regulated on a cost-of-service basis. "Coordination" sales, on the other hand, were those made between neighboring utilities and were more loosely regulated given higher levels of competition in regional markets. These transactions allowed utilities to (1) purchase power for less than they could generate themselves, thus lowering costs, and (2) defer expensive capacity additions.

The development of wholesale power markets depends critically on the ability of rival generators to compete with the vertically-integrated transmission owner by gaining access to the high-voltage transmission grid. Vertical integration potentially creates the incentive for the transmission network owner to frustrate rivals' access to the network, since by doing so the firm can drive up electricity prices and collect those higher prices on its own generation sales. Mechanisms for frustrating access take numerous forms and include: (1) curtailing rivals' transmission transactions (on the basis of retail demand priority or reliability), (2) favoring transmission requests from affiliates over non-affiliated generators, (3) understating the amount of transmission capacity available for wholesale transactions, and (4) denying or frustrating interconnection to the grid.

Anticompetitive conduct of the sort described above generally falls under the category of vertical restraints. Such restraints formally include foreclosure, raising rivals' costs, discrimination, and refusals to deal. From an economic perspective, they have much in common in that they involve exclusionary market power, exercised by inflicting injury on rivals and harming competition. But different types of vertical restraints are treated differently under the antitrust laws, which creates some tension between the economic and legal disciplines.

Concern over exclusion formed the basis of the Supreme Court's 1973 decision in *Otter Tail*.[5] In *Otter Tail*, the Justice Department contended that the utility (which sold electricity in Minnesota and the Dakotas) had monopolized the sale of electricity by: (1) refusing to sell wholesale power to towns that sought to displace *Otter Tail* with municipally-owned distribution systems; and (2) declining to wheel (i.e., for a competing seller) power to those towns over its transmission lines.[6] The high court's decision to uphold a lower court's finding of *Otter Tail*'s liability was also the first application of the essential facility doctrine in the electricity industry. The doctrine prevents a monopolist from refusing to allow access to a facility in cases where its availability is critical to the ability of rivals to compete in upstream or downstream markets.[7] In *Otter Tail*, the Supreme Court allowed the federal government to seek antitrust remedies against an electric utility that refused to sell wholesale power to municipalities or to wheel power over its own transmission lines. Thus, the case formally established regulatory and antitrust venues for addressing the transmission access problem.

Key issues in transmission access

The access problem in electricity raises some unique issues not often found in other contexts. For example, access has been plagued by the need to prioritize use of the network. In practice, this translates into which customers and transmission services take precedence over others.[8] The major tension has been in assessing priority for transmission services utilized by wholesale versus retail customers. Federal regulatory initiatives have been challenged by the states for potentially undermining the *quid pro quo* embodied in retail customers' ability to depend (without curtailment) on bundled sales in exchange for a utility's exclusive grant to sell in a franchised service area. As discussed later, FERC's recent proposal to standardize the design of electricity markets goes the farthest of any regulatory initiative in eliminating the "pecking order" associated with transmission priorities—a feature vigorously opposed by the states.

A second unique feature of network access in electricity is the friction between the market-expanding effects of access policies and inadequate transmission investment and congestion. In some cases, constraints produce small markets, dominated by one or more vertically-integrated firms. In more extreme cases, demand within transmission-constrained areas can, at certain times (e.g., periods of high demand), exceed the area's import capacity. At these times, demand can be met only with generation from inside the constrained area and in which generation ownership is highly concentrated. Without intervention, these markets would produce grossly inefficient outcomes.[9] But addressing these issues when the exercise of market power is fleeting and time-variant is difficult. The interdependence between generation and transmission is also an important factor. In some cases, the vertically-integrated firm can strategically operate generation so as to create transmission constraints, a concern that has been alleged in a number of merger cases.

Alleviating transmission constraints in some cases is an almost intractable problem. This is because, among other factors, transmission siting is subject to the vagaries of state regulatory commissions; environmental compliance and other market rules force non-economic operation of certain generators; and governance of reliability organizations is not divorced from the underlying member utilities.[10] Moreover, in the failed 2003 Energy Bill, Congress made clear that transmission siting authority would remain largely in the hands of the states.[11] Subsequent successful bills are unlikely to specify anything different, at least on this issue.

A third difficult issue is the likely mixed effect of access policies on economic efficiency and consumer welfare. Without doubt, access has stimulated the large scale growth of wholesale power markets. In virtually every rulemaking involving transmission network access, FERC cites the expansion of markets and growth in trade, entry of new market participants, and new uses for the transmission system. In crafting standards of conduct that would govern relationships between transmission providers and affiliated generation sellers, FERC specifically noted an increased number of power marketers with market-based rates, an increased market for transmission capacity, a surge of online trading, and significant entry of power marketers and independent generators.[12]

Development of certain types of new products and services has paralleled market expansion and more intense competition. The inevitable price volatility that flows from more freely functioning wholesale markets has given rise to a host of market participants and services related to risk management. It is worthwhile to note, however, that one result of current higher levels of regulatory, financial, and competitive risk has been the exit of many of those firms. But products and services that emerge in response to pressures for firms to manage the risks of competition are fundamentally different than those consumed by the final user. Today, there is not a significantly greater diversity of wholesale (or retail) products than there were several years ago. Moreover, there has not been large scale adoption of retail demand–response products and services such as real-time metering that would better allow consumers to cut consumption in response to periodic high prices.

At the same time, the pressures of more competitive markets have stimulated the development of more efficient generation and transmission technologies.[13] These include smaller, modular generators that can be added to better manage growth in demand and transmission technologies that relieve constraints on the network at lower costs than adding new transmission lines. Thus, cognizable gains in some areas and stasis or even retrenchment in others complicates the metrics of measuring the effectiveness of network access.[14]

Compulsory access in electricity transmission

While the vertical ownership structure of transmission and generation is the source of the network access problem in electricity, its preservation is embodied in the incremental compulsory access policies that have been promulgated over the last 30 years. Absent a more aggressive approach, the tension between the success of compulsory access and competition in wholesale markets will continue.

Legislative and regulatory policy initiatives

As mentioned earlier, numerous initiatives involving transmission access followed the *Otter Tail* decision. Congress's first step was the Public Utility Regulatory Policy Act (PURPA) of 1978. PURPA sought to promote the development of new generators (and reduce consumption of fossil fuels) by giving FERC authority to require utilities to purchase electricity from cogenerators and small power producers at the utility's "avoided cost."[15] PURPA gave rise to a host of regulatory disputes about the calculation of avoided cost and private antitrust suits alleging discrimination against PURPA generators. By the late 1980s, many utilities were locked into PURPA contracts negotiated when natural gas prices were high and paying avoided costs that exceeded their marginal costs of production.[16]

In 1992, Congress took a second step with the passage of the Energy Policy Act (EPAct). The EPAct amended Section 211 of the FPA to give FERC authority to order a transmission-owning utility to provide services to third parties, and amended Section 212 to require wheeling rates that promoted efficient generation and transmission.[17] FERC exercised its new authority only a handful of times, but so cumbersome were the 211 proceedings that the agency ultimately addressed the wholesale wheeling issue through a generic rulemaking. Efficient pricing of transmission service was addressed more specifically by the Commission in its 1994 *Transmission Pricing Policy Statement*.[18] The statement developed the concept of "comparability," later codified in Order No. 888's *pro forma* open access tariff. Comparability meant that a transmission provider was required to charge itself for transmission service on the same or comparable basis that it charged others for the same service. This concept was a central feature of the Commission's 1994 decision in *American Electric Power Service Corporation*, in which it found that an open access tariff that was not "unduly discriminatory or anticompetitive" should be based on the concept of comparability.[19]

Order No. 888 was issued in mid-1996 after a lengthy process involving numerous stakeholders.[20] In the so-called "open access" rule, FERC acknowledged that ongoing discrimination by electric utilities violated Section 205 of the FPA. Order No. 888 thus required utilities to "functionally" unbundle wholesale generation and transmission services. This meant that a public utility had to take transmission service under the same tariff as applied to others; state separate prices for generation, transmission, and ancillary services; and rely on the same electronic information network used by transmission customers when buying or selling power.

Functional unbundling fell short of corporate unbundling (i.e., vertical separation), which would have forced divestiture of generation or transmission. Similar functional unbundling requirements were imposed on unbundled (but not bundled) retail transmission in interstate commerce. Comparability requirements were codified in a generic *pro forma* tariff. Accompanying Order No. 888 was Order No. 889, or the "open access same time information system" (OASIS) and standards of conduct applicable to transmission providers.[21] This system mandated the formation of internet-based sites containing current information on the availability of transmission capacity (including capacity reserved by a vertically integrated utility's generation affiliate) and usage of the transmission system. This effort was designed to improve transparency in the process through which transmission capacity is reserved and to curb potential abuse by vertically-integrated utilities. The accompanying standards of conduct were designed to prevent employees of a public utility from obtaining preferential access to pertinent transmission-related information not available to all customers at the same time.

The initial splash of Order Nos. 888 and 889 was somewhat short-lived. Even as compulsory access was implemented, transmission owners began exploiting loopholes in the rules, thus necessitating ongoing adjudication, revision, and fine-tuning. For example, in *Wisconsin Public Power Inc.*, a municipal utility (WPPI) had difficulty in obtaining access to a key transmission interface jointly owned by Wisconsin Public Service and Wisconsin Power & Light. WPPI alleged that owners of the interface violated the terms of their "open access" transmission tariffs by granting their affiliated generators' requests for access while denying WPPI's requests and failing to disclose information concerning their own use of the transmission interface. FERC granted WPPI's request for relief, requiring WPS and WPL to release transmission capacity improperly reserved for their own use and to recalculate available capacity and make it available on a first come, first serve basis.[22]

Many of the ongoing problems with the access rule provided the stimulus for the next major regulatory initiative—Regional Transmission Organizations (RTOs).[23] Issued in late 1999, Order No. 2000 acknowledged massive restructuring activity, increases in bulk power trade, and more intensive and novel use of the transmission grid. FERC's objective was for all transmission-owning entities, including non-public entities, to place their transmission facilities under the control of RTOs that met certain characteristics in a "timely manner."[24] RTOs allegedly addressed operational and reliability issues in the industry and eliminated residual discrimination in transmission services that could occur when the system is controlled by a vertically integrated utility. Underlying the RTO rule was an implicit assessment that the benefits from relinquishing control of transmission to independent entities outweighed the costs of foregoing head-to-head competition (revealed in transmission price discounting) at the transmission network level. While there are many examples of network competition (even in industries with heavy sunk costs), however, electricity is not one of the stronger ones. But if governance of the RTO was truly divorced from the interests of the underlying member firms, planning for network expansion and congestion management would be independent.[25]

FERC's most recent attempt to address network access was a proposal to create a standard market design (SMD) for electricity markets in the U.S. In a proposed rulemaking issued in mid-2002, the Commission again recognized that vertically integrated transmission owners and operators continued to use their interstate transmission facilities in ways that inhibit competition in both wholesale markets *and* in retail markets where states have implemented retail choice. The premise behind SMD was that standard market rules and inter- and intra-merger practices would eliminate the discrimination that created barriers to new low cost producers. In the SMD proposal, FERC proposed—in an expanded version of Order No. 888's requirements—a nondiscriminatory open access tariff that would encompass a single service applicable to *all* users of the interstate network, including wholesale, unbundled retail, and bundled retail customers. The proposal also made the case for "locational marginal pricing" as an efficient approach to transmission congestion management (coupled with tradable financial rights to manage risk associated with congestion pricing) and proposed market monitoring and mitigation procedures. Finally, in light of the foot-dragging created by the voluntary nature of the Commission's RTO requirements, FERC reiterated its priority for public utility membership in independent transmission organizations.

In the last round of access initiatives, FERC issued in early 2004 two rules that address specific aspects of the problem. The first of these efforts set out standards of conduct designed to prevent the anticompetitive sharing of information between a transmission company and its energy affiliates with business interests in complementary product markets.[26] Such information sharing, if unimpeded, could enable the transmission owner to frustrate rivals' access to the network or to otherwise discriminate in favor of its affiliate. The second initiative was stimulated in large part by complaints that generators had difficulty getting interconnected without requesting delivery, were treated in a discriminatory manner, and experienced interconnection delays because of a lack of binding commitments in *pro forma* tariffs.[27] In the interconnection rule, FERC acknowledged the critical nature of correct incentives underlying interconnection of generators to the grid and set forth standards for interconnection agreements and procedures. Standard interconnection procedures, FERC argued, would encourage investment, ease entry for competitors, ensure efficient generation siting, and limit opportunities for transmission owners to favor affiliated generation.

It is clear from the preceding discussion that access to electricity transmission in the U.S. has been dealt with largely through regulatory policy initiatives. There are few recent significant federal antitrust cases involving network access in electricity. Most of these cases not involving agreements that could lessen competition would be prosecuted under Section 2 of the Sherman Act.[28] One reason for this may be that when conduct-based complaints arise, the antitrust agencies (DOJ, in particular, which would lay claim to most cases) tend to rely on regulatory enforcement by FERC because of the pre-existing access framework and the agency's superior institutional knowledge. This approach has tended to characterize merger review, as discussed in the next section.

Mergers and network access

In the last 15 years, FERC and the antitrust agencies have conditionally approved or challenged a number of mergers under Section 203 of the FPA. A number of features of problematic merger cases are important to note. First, most of the problematic mergers were vertical in nature—they combined either: (1) generation- and transmission-owning utilities (electric–electric mergers), or (2) a generation and transmission-owning utility and a gas pipeline (electric–gas mergers). The first category of mergers generally posed competitive issues relating to electric transmission access while the second category raised issues focused on gas transportation access. Second, at least over the period from the early 1990s to the present, the antitrust agencies only challenged electric–gas mergers while FERC conditionally approved only one gas–electric merger and two electric–electric mergers. Thus, in the context of merger review and enforcement, FERC again took the lead on addressing the transmission access problem.

The first merger case to present significant network access issues was the combination of Ohio Edison and Centerior, two vertically-integrated utilities with adjacent service territories in the Midwest. The effect of the merger was to "internalize" transmission interfaces that interconnected the two utilities, thus removing them from the Commission's open access purview. Opponents alleged this would give the merged company significantly more latitude in discriminating against third party users of its transmission system, since transmission could be made unavailable due to retail load obligations or reliability concerns. The merger also combined two large generation portfolios, significantly increasing concentration in the relevant market. The Commission expressed concern about post-merger access to transmission and anticompetitive planning and operation of the merged system.[29] In addition to accepting the merging parties' commitments regarding access to, availability and pricing of internal transmission capacity, the Commission encouraged the companies to form or join a regional transmission entity.[30]

FERC again voiced concerns about the exclusionary use of transmission and generation in *American Electric Power/Central and Southwest*, which combined two geographically separate utilities with large transmission systems and generation portfolios in a "dumbbell" fashion. Opponents alleged— in an expanded version of *Ohio Edison/Centerior*—that the merged company could strategically operate their transmission systems in conjunction with generation to foreclose competing generators from transmission markets. Mechanisms for foreclosing rivals included: operating generation to create transmission constraints; curtailing transactions through the use of transmission loading relief (for reliability purposes); or misrepresenting the amount of available transmission capacity. In remedying the likely anticompetitive effects of the merger, FERC required and accepted a number of conditions, including: quarterly independent market monitoring reports; conditions on availability and priority of transmission service; and turnover of transmission control to an RTO.[31]

The decisions in *Ohio Edison/Centerior* and *American Electric Power/Central and SouthWest* made two major contributions to the network access debate in electricity. First, the cases forced the Commission to clearly articulate a unilateral exclusion (i.e., vertical) theory of competitive harm for the first time in a merger case. This basic vertical problem was never articulated clearly in FERC's generic rulemakings that addressed the access problem. A second contribution of *Ohio Edison/Centerior* and *American Electric Power/Central and Southwest* was an implicit acknowledgement of the inherent limitations on the open access rules, thus paving the way for more effective remedies for the access problem.

It is probably safe to say that had the antitrust agencies found either the *Ohio Edison/Centerior* or *American Electric Power/Central and SouthWest* mergers to be problematic, a consent decree would likely have required divestiture of generation to eliminate any incentive for the merging companies to engage in exclusionary practices.[32] In dealing with the pervasive problems of market power in the industry today, policymakers may well be forced into either generic or case-specific (e.g., in merger proceedings) divestiture requirements.

Implementation issues and the success of access

Regulatory policy in the U.S. has favored a conduct-based solution to network access in electricity transmission. But the incremental approach forced upon FERC over the last several years might well reveal that forced access has been more costly than the structural reforms not pursued. No empirical work to date supports this assessment, but growing questions about the efficacy of conduct-based approaches emphasize the need for further work in this area.

The compulsory access approach in electricity is explained by a number of factors. Among the more important was a distinctly conservative reading of any authority under the FPA to require divestiture of generation. FERC also considered the high economic and political costs associated with massive restructuring. Jurisdictional issues relating to generation would have forced a difficult (if not impossible) consensus between federal and state regulatory authorities, enabled only through Congressional action.[33] Finally, in continuing to go down the forced access road over time—even while continuing to admit serious flaws and gaps in the access system—the Commission understandably needed to defend its policy choice in practice.[34] Thus, there was a strong incentive for the Commission to cite the rigors of open access in adjudicating merger and vertical restraints-type cases that followed Order No. 888.

A number of factors can slow or stymie the implementation of access regimes: new technologies that may reduce the severity of efficiency losses related to poor access; legal challenges that slow the implementation process; politically-charged issues that frustrate the development and implementation of coherent access policy; and protracted compliance with access initiatives because of failure to mandate unpopular policies. Most of these issues have arisen in the electricity industry. One exception has been the failure of technologies that would allow competitors to bypass the network to reach the end user directly. Distributed generation, which serves consumers on-site, is a potential example. Ironically, diffusion of this technology has suffered because transmission owners resist interconnecting generators to the grid for the purposes of selling back at times of lower demand.

There have been a number of legal challenges to FERC's access initiatives. For example, in *Northern States Power v. FERC* a lower court addressed whether FERC could require a public utility under Order No. 888 to curtail transmission to wholesale customers on a comparable basis with its retail customers when the utility experiences constraints on its transmission system.[35] Northern States Power (NSP) argued that such curtailment would detrimentally affect retail customers who had no other alternative for the purchase electricity service. Compliance would force NSP to violate state regulatory laws that embodied retail customers' implicit guarantee of bundled sales without curtailment of service in exchange for NSP's exclusive grant to sell to retail customers in a franchised service area. FERC's answer to NSP's dilemma was that the federal tariff must prevail under the supremacy clause, but the court found that FERC had transgressed its Congressional authority which limits the Commission's jurisdiction to interstate transactions.[36] In *New York et al. v. Federal Energy Regulatory Commission*, the lower court disagreed with the Commission's assertion of jurisdiction in Order No. 888 over unbundled retail transmission. The Supreme Court overturned the lower court's decision on the basis that the nature of the national grid effectively made unbundled retail transmission FERC-jurisdictional.[37]

Transmission access has also been slowed by a number of issues that prevent broader penetration or more coherent policy development. One example is a balkanized system of state and federal jurisdiction which disables FERC from directly ordering transmission expansion or siting transmission facilities needed to relieve congestion. The Commission has also had trouble developing coherent regional siting policies because of lack of state/federal coordination. State opposition to the Commission's SMD also demonstrates state/federal friction.[38] Reliability issues will likely slow progress on access. Outages in California and in the Midwest in 1998 through 2001 raised concerns about the relationship between reliability and changed commercial incentives resulting from access and more competitive markets. The massive, cascading outage in the eastern part of the country in August of 2003 punctuated the problem. Here, reliability is not only a symptom of changed markets in the era of access, but also a potential contributor to the access problem. In the first case, reliability has arguably faltered in the face of greater diversity of market participants (all with differing commercial incentives), more intensive and different uses of the grid, and gradually deteriorating investment in transmission infrastructure. On the other hand, it is widely alleged that vertically integrated utilities have denied rivals access to the transmission network under the guise of reliability. This problem is exacerbated by command-and-control type reliability policies administered outside the rubric of the compulsory access regime and by jurisdictional problems that prevent effective solutions.

Finally, protracted compliance has been a prominent feature of network access in electricity, particularly in regard to RTOs. This stems directly from the Commission's choice not to mandate RTOs. Lack of a strong mandate with clearly defined punitive measures in the event of non-compliance created predictable delay, since relinquishing control over bottleneck transmission facilities (which allows the leverage of market power into complementary generation markets) runs counter to rational seller incentives. As a result, only a few regions of the country (e.g., California, New England, New York, and Pennsylvania/New Jersey/Maryland) have taken significant steps toward forming RTOs that meet the Commission requirements.

In sum, a number of factors have heavily influenced the implementation of transmission access in the U.S. industry. Many of these problems are virtually intractable, as in the case of jurisdiction over transmission siting and voluntary compliance with access policies. Many of these problems could be effectively addressed through coherent legislation that augmented or changed FERC's statutory authority. But Congress declined the opportunity in the 2003 Energy Bill, leaving open the question of how—absent a mid-course correction to a structural access approach—the Commission will continue to make progress on the linchpin of competitive market development in the electricity industry.

Success of network access

Despite ongoing friction in promoting network access in electricity transmission, compulsory access initiatives have not failed to produce results. Whereas wholesale markets were virtually nonexistent 25 years ago, they have become hugely important in the process of delivering electricity to all types of users. What are the metrics for assessing the success of network access in electricity? Longer term decreases in prices to residential, commercial, and industrial consumers may be one indicator, but studies that disaggregate the effects of access policies on other determinants of prices (e.g., generation and transmission cost differentials, weather, capacity utilization, etc.) are lacking. Empirical assessments of market integration (i.e., as indicated by lower regional price differentials that are not accounted for by transmission costs or constraints) may shed some light on the effect of access policies on expanding regional markets.

The costs and benefits of access in electricity have been intensively studied. Many would argue that, on the whole, access has produced tangible benefits in the form of lower prices and consumer choice.[39] Critics might argue that while access has likely produced benefits, the indicators of success are—without very careful and sophisticated economic analysis—difficult to disaggregate from the many other factors that influence electricity prices and other variables. Either way, given the continuing challenge of promoting access in electricity, policy makers will increasingly demand evidence that links policy initiatives to tangible benefits.

Notes

1 Vice-president and Senior Research Fellow, American Antitrust Institute.
2 In states that have implemented retail "access," consumers have their choice of generation supplier and so that component of the price may or may not be bundled with the components provided by the local utility.
3 16 U.S.C. §824(b).
4 Wholesale markets exist within the three major network grids that emerged in the U.S.—the Eastern Interconnect, the Western Interconnect, and Texas.
5 See *United States v. Otter Tail Power Co.*, 410 U.S. 366 (1973).
6 W. E. Kovacic, "The antitrust law and economics of essential facilities in public utility regulation," in *Economic Innovations in Public Utility Regulation*, M. A. Crew (ed.), Boston: Kluwer, 1992, p.1.
7 Kovacic, op cit., p. 3.
8 Customers include retail and wholesale, and services include the so-called point-to-point (i.e., delivery of power from point A to point B) versus network (i.e., delivery of power to any point on the system).
9 There are a number of load pockets in U.S. electricity markets, including areas in Nevada, the Midwest, and the Northeast.
10 FERC has implicitly acknowledged that some electricity markets will remain

uncompetitive in its recent proposal to standardize electricity market design by instituting must-offer and bid-cap requirements for certain generators.

11 Online. Available HTTP: <http://thomas.loc.gov/cgi-bin/query/F?c108:1:./temp/~c108Ck7FoE:e511493> (accessed June 14, 2004).

12 See generally, Standardization of Generator Interconnection Agreements and Procedures, Order No. 2003, 104 FERC ¶61,103 (2003), and Order No. 2003-A, 104 FERC ¶61,220 (2004).

13 Online. Available HTTP: <http://www.eia.doe.gov/cneaf/electricity/chg_stru_update/chapter5.html#tech> (accessed June 14, 2004).

14 At the wholesale level, these products include capacity (a reservation-based product), energy (a usage-based product), and the ancillary services necessary to balance and manage electricity supply and demand (e.g., losses, load-following, energy balance).

15 16 U.S.C. §2601.

16 Many of these utilities chose to buy out their contracts instead of continuing to pay high avoided costs.

17 16 U.S.C. §§824j(a) and 16 U.S.C. §§824k(a).

18 See generally, Inquiry Concerning the Commission's Pricing Policy for Transmission Services Provided by Public Utilities Under the Federal Power Act, FERC Stats. & Regs. ¶31,005 (1994).

19 American Electric Power Service Corporation, 67 FERC ¶61,168 (1994), p. 61,490.

20 See generally, Promoting Wholesale Competition Through Open Access Non-Discrimination Transmission Services by Public Utilities; Recovery of Stranded Costs by Public Utilities and Transmitting Utilities, Order No. 888, 76 FERC ¶61,009 (1996) and 76 FERC ¶61,347 (1996); Order on Rehearing, Order No. 888-A, 79 FERC ¶61,182 (1997); Order on Rehearing, Order No. 888-B, 81 FERC ¶61,248, (1997); and Order on Rehearing, Order No. 888-C, 82 FERC ¶61,046 (1998).

21 See generally, Open Access Same-Time Information System (Formerly Real-Time Information Network) and Standards of Conduct, Order No. 889, FERC Stats. & Regs., Regulations Preambles 1991–96 ¶31,035 (1996); Order on Rehearing, Order No. 889-A, FERC Stats. & Regs., Regulations Preambles 1996–2000 ¶31,049 (1997); and Federal Energy Regulatory Commission, Order on Rehearing, Order No. 889-B, 81 FERC ¶61,253 (1997).

22 Wisconsin Public Power Inc., 83 FERC ¶61, 198 (1998).

23 See generally, Regional Transmission Organizations, Order No. 2000, 81 FERC ¶61, 285 (2000) and Order on Rehearing, Order No. 2000-A 90 FERC ¶FERC 61,201 (2000).

24 FERC set forth minimum characteristics (e.g., independence, scope) and minimum functions (e.g., tariff administration, congestion management, market monitoring, planning, and expansion) for acceptable RTOs.

25 Competition at the transmission network level can occur when there is more than one possible path to move power from point A to point B.

26 See generally, Standards of Conduct for Transmission Providers, Order 2004, 105 FERC ¶61,248 (2004) and Order 2004-A, 107 FERC ¶61,032 (2004).

27 See generally, Standardization of Generator Interconnection Agreements and Procedures, Order 2003, 104 FERC ¶61,103 (2003) and Order 2003-A, 104 FERC ¶61,220 (2004).

28 See generally, *U.S. v. Rochester Gas & Electric Corporation*, No. 97-CV-6294T (W.D.N.Y. February 17, 1998). In this case, Rochester Gas & Electric discouraged the University of Rochester from building a cogeneration plant by offering a low rate for service and other non-related benefits. The Department of Justice sued for violation of Section 1 of the Sherman Act.

29 Ohio Edison, *et al.*, 81 FERC ¶61,110 (1997), pp. 2–3.

30 The Commission stated that the formation of an ISO would attract new entrants into the market, facilitate the implementation of efficient transmission pricing and thereby expand the effective scope of the geographic market.

31 See generally, American Electric Power Company and Central and Southwest Corporation (Opinion 442), 90 FERC ¶61,242 (2000).

32 The Department of Justice in the merger of San Diego Gas & Electric and Southern California Gas did in fact require divestiture of a large amount of fossil-steam generation. This merger, however, raised vertical issues relating to generation and gas transportation, not electric transmission. Even so, FERC used conduct-based remedies in conditioning its approval of the merger. The remedies imposed by the two agencies were not incompatible.

33 We note in this regard that FERC never directly ordered divestiture in a merger proceeding. Rather, it conditioned its own approval of mergers in some cases on the merging parties' compliance with *state* requirements to divest or on acceptance of offered divestiture commitments.

34 The access regime did not apply to the significant portion of transmission utilities utilized to serve retail demand (i.e., "native load") obligations.

35 *Northern States Power Company v. Federal Energy Regulatory Commission*, No. 98–3000 (8th Cir. 1999).

36 On remand, the Commission argued that curtailing service to wholesale customers before retail customers meant that the former were receiving a lower quality of service and should therefore pay lower rates, but in the end, NSP saw no need to impose discriminatory curtailments.

37 *New York v. FERC*, 535 U.S. 1 (2002).

38 Whether the competitive problems related to network access will be lessened by market standardization remains to be seen. Economic and physical characteristics of electricity markets vary widely from one region of the U.S. to another and these differences make for different degrees of market competitiveness, ease of entry, and conduct of market participants. FERC appears amenable to considering regional differences in implementing standardized markets.

39 See generally, C. Winston, "U.S. industry adjustment to economic deregulation," *Journal of Economic Perspectives* 12, 1998, pp. 89–100; P. L. Joskow, "Restructuring, competition and regulatory reform in the U.S. electricity sector," *Journal of Economic Perspectives* 11, 1997, pp. 119–38; T. Klitgaard and R. Reddy, "Lowering electricity prices through deregulation," Federal Reserve Bank of New York, *Current Issues in Economics and Finance*, December 2000; S. Borenstein and J. Bushnell, "Electricity restructuring: deregulation or reregulation?" Competition Policy Center, Institute for Business and Economic Research, Working Paper No. CPC00–014, Berkeley, California: University of California, Berkeley, February 2000; I. Vogelsang, "Network utilities in the U.S.—sector reforms without privatization," CESifo Working Paper No. 1142, 2004; and A. N. Kleit and D. Terrell, "Measuring potential efficiency gains

from deregulation of electricity generation: a Bayesian approach," *Review of Economics and Statistics* 83, 2001, pp. 523–30; P. L. Joskow, "Deregulation and regulatory reform in the U.S. electric power sector," in *Deregulation of Network Industries: What's Next,* S. Peltzman and C. Winston (eds), Washington, D.C.: AEI-Brookings Joint Center for Regulatory Studies, 2000, pp. 135–6. See also, online. Available HTTP: <http://www.epsa.org/forms/documents/Document FormPublic/view?id=34790000000F> (accessed June 14, 2004).

Case 3

Natural gas pipelines

Richard P. O'Neill[1]

Introduction

Much of federal economic regulation in the U.S. covers transmission net-works—natural gas, electricity, telecommunications, railroads, and high-ways. These networks are highways for moving people, goods, messages, and energy. The markets for network services range from some that are nearly competitive to others that are seen and operated essentially as public goods. High entry barriers, high sunk costs, scale economies, exter-nalities, and eminent domain have led governments to regulate or own most of these networks. At the same time, firms use networks to compete in other markets, most of which are much more competitive.

This paper focuses on the governance of the transmission networks for natural gas. These networks are distinctive because they combine the following features: (1) they transmit a uniform commodity by displace-ment (unlike, say, roads or telecommunications, where each delivery is discrete); (2) they are in large part privately owned (unlike most highways or waterways); (3) they are oligopolies rather than monopolies (unlike most distribution systems); (4) there is little or no on-site storage of the commodity (unlike coal piles and oil tanks); and (5) they use eminent domain to acquire land for network expansion (creating an immediate public interest). Together, these features create a distinctive set of regula-tory (or governance) problems.

The federal laws regulating natural gas networks date mostly from the 1930s against the backdrop of franchised monopolies. This seemed rea-sonable at the time, since federal regulation was meant to supplement state-level regulation of preexisting, monopoly distribution companies. These laws regulate prices. Over time, contract (tariff) rates have come to be set using original-cost-of-service concepts. Entry and exit are regulated via licenses, franchises and certificates. In addition, the utilities were par-tially protected against the antitrust laws by regulatory preemption—the State Action Doctrine.

The monopoly franchise model was never entirely appropriate for gas transmission. Many companies were involved from the beginning, although competition among them was minor and, to some extent, often discouraged by regulation until recently. With the growth of open access transmission and competition to supply gas, the oligopolistic reality has become ever more important. But, despite a great proliferation of theory on regulating monopolies (and deregulating competitive markets), there is today no simple coherent theory for regulating network oligopolies. Historically, primitive communication and control systems may have encouraged vertical integration in the natural gas and other industries. Today, communications technology has evolved so that vertical integration is no longer as important for efficiency—and may create bad incentives leading to inefficiencies in the commodity markets trading on these networks.

Since the early 1980s, the Federal Energy Regulatory Commission (Commission) has worked to unbundle network service from the commodity and rely more on market forces and incentives (generally supported by the President, Congress and the courts). The result has been more flexibility and greater reliance on contracts, information, and market rules. This chapter describes the framework in which the Commission has been working. The governance framework includes rules to unbundle network services from commodities and trading rules for both transmission capacity and the commodity itself. Short term network services with a backstop regulated tariff can allow for greater choice and flexibility. With the lack of storage, information must be available quickly and electronically for both network and commodity trading. Open group governance plays a major role in setting rules and resolving complaints. Equity and efficiency are served by making no captive customers worse off during the transition.

In the remainder of the chapter, we shall examine more specifically what will be needed for good regulation of the natural gas and electric transmission grids in the future. The following sections review approaches to modern public utility regulation, the laws, regulation and history of these markets, current structure, and an approach to governance of these industries.

Gas regulation in the U.S.

In the early years of the twentieth century, the gas industry had a very similar structure to the electric industry. Most gas was manufactured locally from coal and fed into local distribution systems. Gas companies were regulated at the local or state level. With the discovery and development of natural gas, first near, large markets (for instance in Appalachia) and then, as an adjunct to the oil business in the Southwest, long haul transportation became an increasingly important part of the business. Pipelines began to link the Southwest with the Midwest. A series of Supreme Court decisions declared that neither the producing state nor the consuming state could regulate the interstate pipelines (which, in

Table II.3.1 Chronology: natural gas use and regulation

Period	Development
Pre-1900	• Manufactured gas • Gas competes with electricity for lighting
1900 to early 1930s	• Metallurgical advances permit development of pipelines to transport Appalachian and Southwest gas • First large-diameter gas pipeline from Texas to Chicago (1931), followed by development of interstate gas transportation system
Mid-1930s to 1970s	• Public Utility Holding Company Act (1935) broke up large, powerful trusts that controlled the nation's gas and electric distribution networks • Natural Gas Act (1938) brought federal regulation to interstate gas. • Phillips decision (1954) required sales of resale jurisdiction to apply to wellhead prices • Natural Gas Policy Act (1978) started deregulation • Powerplant and Industrial Fuel Use Act (1978) limited the use of gas for industrial and utility purposes
1980s to the present	• Fuel Use Act repealed • Natural Gas Wellhead Decontrol Act (1989) mandated full wellhead decontrol by 1993 • FERC Order 636 (1992) requires interstate gas pipeline companies to unbundled their sales and transportation services and provide open access to transportation • FERC Order 637 (2000) clarifies the implementation of Order 636

those days, formed a very sparse grid that conformed much more to a franchised monopoly theory of the business than today's grid does).

In 1938, to close this "regulatory gap," Congress passed the Natural Gas Act and brought Federal regulation to interstate gas commerce. Again, regulation could trump antitrust law. In 1954, the *Phillips* decision, a literal reading of the law by the Supreme Court that had no empirical or theoretical rationale, required sales for resale jurisdiction to apply to well-head prices. A series of political blunders blocked Congressional repeal of the unfortunate court decision. The system of price and contract regulation, once implemented, created entitlements that made it politically more difficult to correct. From the early 1960s to the mid-1980s, interstate natural gas prices were set and translated to city gate by the Federal Power Commission (now the Federal Energy Regulation Commission), creating vertical bilateral monopolies and balkanized quasi-franchised markets.

The 1970s saw serious inflation and artificial shortages in interstate natural gas markets, leading to a very negative view of public utility commissions. Many natural gas policies wrongly anticipated long term shortages and rising prices. Instead of introducing market forces to ration supply and bring incentives to the markets, efforts were put in administrative curtailment schemes. High inflation exposed the shortcomings of original cost-of-service (OCOS) regulation. Purchase gas adjustment (PGA) clauses began in the early 1970s as a way to let the pipeline's sales rates track forecasts of increasing regulated wellhead prices without revisiting the rest of its costs. The quid pro quo was a general rate case every three years. From then until the early 1990s, general debates about each pipeline's costs and prices took place every three years.

The Natural Gas Policy Act of 1978 (NGPA) started to deregulate gas as a commodity and ended the rigid separation of interstate and intrastate markets. The NGPA and the Commission's success with open access led Congress to push the use of market forces even further. The Natural Gas Wellhead Decontrol Act of 1987 mandated full wellhead decontrol by 1993 and urged non-discriminatory open access to improve the competitive structure of gas markets. The transition to open access for the natural gas transmission network and greater commodity competition started in the mid-1980s. In 1983, the first signs of a visible spot market (that is, a market with generally available published prices) began to appear. With the advent of spot markets, players looked for places to buy and sell gas. The concept of market centers or hubs developed, first in the production area, then downstream. In late 1985, the Commission issued Order 436 authorizing voluntary open access on pipelines. By late 1986, only one company had accepted the invitation. In 1987, with further Commission encouragement, most pipelines applied for open access, but their compliance with many details was weak and piecemeal. This meant that gas commodity markets were not as competitive as they could have been.

In 1987, the Commission removed price controls on Transwestern's commodity sales service because it lacked market power. Its largest customer walked away. Since then, the Commission has granted market-based rates when the seller lacks market power, that is, when the customer has good alternatives, some possibly regulated. This success lead the Commission to grant market-based rates to sellers of many regulated products and services in the gas, electric, and oil markets. In 1987, a Commission staff paper suggested incorporating auction techniques as a part of the ratemaking process. In 1988, the New York Merchantile Exchange (NYMEX) had proposed a futures market, originally with deliveries at Katy, TX, but finally settling on the Henry Hub in Erath, LA. Many argued it could not work or would distort the market. It is now accepted by many as the basis for pricing in longer term contracts.

In 1988, the Commission required gas pipelines to establish Electronic Bulletin Boards (EBBs) for posting information on affiliated transactions. In Order 636, the Commission required capacity release information and auctions on pipeline EBBs—a precursor to Internet trading. In 1993, the Gas Industry Standards Board (GISB) was established. In the early 1990s, visible spot markets developed in downstream markets near potential market centers such as Chicago, Illinois, Niagara, New York, and Kern River, California. This led some producers, pipelines, and distributors to ask the Commission to take a market-oriented (as compared with a pipeline-by-pipeline) approach to production area rates and tariff conditions.[2] Without a generic market approach, pipelines are faced with the classic "prisoner's dilemma game"—if all play all can benefit, but without all playing it does not work.

One major problem the Commission faced was how to allocate pipeline service efficiently. Even partial competition for gas as a commodity made it important to give transportation to those who most valued it. But OCOS rate-making provided no way for price signals to ration capacity. The Commission considered several approaches to the problem during the late 1980s.

In 1991, the Commission proposed a rule that became Order 636. Order 636 dealt comprehensively with the problems of Order 436 by mandating unbundling, continuing the transition to the era of open access and commodity competition. Issued in 1992, Order 636 supported and encouraged market center development to simplify transactions and enhance opportunities for additional network efficiencies through better use of capacity. The players and the dynamics of the markets will largely determine the exact directions in which the market develops. Order 636 mandated a "release" or secondary market in capacity rights. This program was much more flexible than the earlier experiments, but contained safeguards to prevent abuse.

Under Order No. 636, the natural gas industry has developed a strong second generation of natural gas markets. The short-term market has evolved from monthly deals (now called base load) to trading for a day or less. Gas markets are more competitive, more efficient and more reliable than ever before. If gains from competition are to continue, rules and institutions must now adapt further, offering faster trading at lower cost and letting small buyers and sellers trade in the market.

Almost all observers of the natural gas industry now believe that the structural changes were necessary, perhaps overdue, and that significant benefits have been realized. Actual costs caused by Orders 436 and 636 were minimal, but the reformation process made costs already in the system more visible. Further, to mitigate the impact of cost shifts, Order 636 tried to effect a transition to more efficient markets using essentially a no-losers test. Open access lowered prices to consumers. Although transitions can be problematic, consumers have generally benefited greatly during the transition to open access. From 1985 to 1995, residential prices fell 20 percent in real terms reversing a decade-long upward trend. Since average consumption per household also fell 8 percent, average gas bills were 27 percent lower. This happened during a time when overall consumption was increasing. The general consensus is that the benefits of open access seem large.[3]

Until the winter of 1995–96, gas prices were about as volatile as the most volatile seen for other commodities. During the winter of 1995–96, gas prices were more volatile than those for most commodities. This volatility has implications for regulation. Volatility represents risk, which also represents cost. To the extent that volatility is artificially high (for instance, because of a lack of retail access and real-time pricing), it adds needless costs to the system. In an extreme case, the need to ration supplies is handled administratively, most likely under NGPA curtailment categories. Also, the short term market value of both gas and (especially) pipeline capacity tends to be concentrated into occasional, brief peak periods. As a result, any market power problems are likely to be found during such short periods of stress, and even a short run market power problem during such periods can lead to substantial abuse, discourage entry and lead to more concentrated markets.

In the 1990s, the Commission considered two other forms of "incentive regulation": indexing and negotiated rates. The Commission now uses an indexing scheme for pipeline and transmission rates and has invited gas pipelines to propose new incentive schemes that fit under very general parameters. The biggest obstacle to incentive programs is the lack of good information to measure and reward results. Incentives to avoid detrimental behavior on the networks are necessary.

The Commission has also adopted a policy that lets natural gas pipelines negotiate rates with customers, provided that the customer always has the option of a backstop service available at OCOS rates. This lets pipelines tailor rate structures to the needs of individual customers without exercising market power. The process must also consider the incentives generated by negotiated rates such as rates based on commodity price differences. Building on the Order No. 636 framework, a new natural gas industry is emerged. In 2000, Order 637 farther clarified the market-oriented rules. By 2002, the Order 637 compliance process was completed.

Market structure

Historically, many services remain regulated by law long after competition could discipline prices. Regulation itself sometimes becomes a bar to competition. This can be seen in industries such as trucking. Even after competitive forces begin to affect an industry, regulatory inertia tends to favor incumbents over entrants in a number of subtle ways. The ownership pattern of natural gas networks is unusual. First, this industry is, for the most part, privately owned and has been for many years. Until recently, in most parts of the world, similar networks have been or still are state-owned (as are the American water and highway networks). Second, these industries are not owned by a single monopolist, but by a group of companies. Most other countries are considerably smaller than the United States, and privately owned networks tend to be monopolies (as most distributors are in the United States). Thus, the United States faces a problem largely unknown in other countries: how to govern a transportation network owned by an oligopoly of private and public firms. Further, largely due to historical market development, commodity markets may be highly concentrated locally, and vertically integrated.

The oligopoly nature of the natural gas and electric markets is complicated. In natural gas, long haul pipelines do not have geographic franchises. As a result, most face competition in some markets, either from other pipelines following similar routes, from pipelines that connect to different supply sources or markets, or from local distribution companies through storage strategies. In some cases, a fairly large number of pipelines may compete in a given market, and the result may be essentially competitive. At the same time, most pipelines serve some markets in which they are the sole supplier or hold a dominant position. Any given pipeline is likely to range simultaneously from a monopolist in some markets to a nearly competitive firm in other markets to providing complementary services to other pipelines.

Two additional factors make the situation even more complex. First, there is a secondary market for pipeline capacity, where the sellers consist of all the rights-holders on the pipeline. This adds a layer of competition in short term markets. Second, shippers may also exercise market power. This is especially likely near the extremities of the system where transmission service can resemble a bilateral monopoly. In some markets with multiple pipelines, some shippers have more market power than the network operators.

Economic theory is much better at handling competitive and monopoly industries than it is at handling oligopolies. However, even the theories of oligopoly that exist may offer misleading guidance for these industries, with their odd juxtapositions of competition and market power. On the other hand, the mix of competitive and non-competitive parts of the network can be useful. In some cases, it is possible to tie allowable price changes in captive markets to those a company experiences in competitive markets, as the Commission has done for some oil pipelines.

The strategic importance of storage

Natural gas differs from other displacement networks in that customers on-site storage. In contrast, most other commodities from grain to metals to coal to oil can be stored on site. The basic similarity in the role of storage in the gas industry is an important point. Natural gas is stored, in depleted reservoirs, in other underground formations such as salt caverns, in liquefied natural gas storage tanks and, to some extent, by packing the compressible fluid in the pipeline system itself. However, none of these forms of storage (except, arguably, line pack) is normally located at or near the point of consumption. So, stored gas must move through the network to reach customers.

Risk

Any long term construction project is risky. But investments in displacement networks are likely to be exceptionally risky. As the commodities delivered by displacement networks become more and more subject to competition and as secondary markets develop for transmission rights, the value of transmission can become exceptionally volatile. Transmission rights become an option to buy or sell a commodity in one place instead of another. At any given time, that option is worth the difference in spot prices between the two places, not embedded costs. Over the long term, transmission rights become tools for managing the price risk of the underlying commodity, since they prevent network congestion from affecting the price one pays or receives for the product.

Unfortunately, risk management had little place in the traditional way that both companies and regulators have operated. Credit ratings implicitly included the utilities' ability to pass on costs to customers, thus increasing the potential for and magnitude of the stranded cost problems and the credit crisis. As noted earlier, both companies and regulators believed in their ability to forecast the future, despite the clear evidence that getting a forecast right was equivalent to winning the lottery. They also believed (less publicly, but more practically) that the regulated company's market power would always allow them to make good any forecasting problems later. If the market value of capacity was too low, the company could simply act as a monopolist and raise prices. Or if the value was too high, the regulator could impose binding price caps and find some way to ration the capacity (perhaps to those who had held the rights before).

The difficulty of grafting a reasonable approach to risk onto a traditional regulatory regime is severe. Compared with the precision and elaboration of thinking about risk in other industries, the concept of putting a company "at risk" is both vague (e.g., What does it mean? How much risk? Under what conditions? With what loopholes?) and unsophisticated (What risk is being managed? At what price? For what purpose?). The assumptions behind today's regulatory tools avoid important institutional uncertainty, long term and dynamic issues. Consequently, these important issues such as risk/reward tradeoffs are often left to unstructured side discussions. Later, after costs are sunk, they are revisited under the vague constructs of the "compact," "prudence," and "used and useful."

Governance institutions

Both private and public institutions operate and oversee markets (see Table II.3.2). The New York Stock Exchange (NYSE) is a private institution that makes rules for membership and trading. The Securities Exchange Commission (SEC), in turn, oversees the NYSE. The Commodities Futures Trading Commission oversees future exchanges. These institutions have rules and audit standards for information disclosure. Governance—rules, regulations, and mores—is unavoidable in civilized human society, and for good reason. Not understanding their role was a contributing factor in recent market problems in California.

Energy displacement network regulation

North American energy markets range from those that are highly competitive to monopolies. Much economic regulation is devoted to networks and markets that are connected physically by a transmission network. These networks require long, narrow stretches of property rights. Often, obtaining property rights to the corridor requires condemnation of private property and environmental impacts or externalities in the surrounding area. This process alone creates a public interest and barriers to entry. The sunk costs, natural monopoly and public good aspects of the industries add to the need for governance structures. "Free market" advocates call for deregulation but ignore eminent domain questions and often call on antitrust laws to work a 'competitive' magic that is hard to understand. On the other side, many want these markets to be managed

Table II.3.2 Private and public institutions overseeing markets

Auction	Private institution	Government institution	Law
Stock	New York Stock Exchange	Securities and Exchange Commission	Securities and Exchange Act
Futures	New York Mercantile Exchange	Commodities Futures Trading Commission	Commodity Futures Trading Commission Act
SO_2 allowances	Chicago Board of Trade	Environmental Protection Agency	Clean Air Act
Spectrum	None	Federal Communications Commission	Federal Communications Commission Authorization Act
Transmission capacity	Pipelines/ utilities	Federal Energy Regulatory Commission	Federal Power Act Natural Gas Act

publicly for a greater good that includes subsidizing certain groups and actively promoting environmental causes. Without strong governance of the network, the potential competitive efficiency of the commodity market may be compromised.

The search for new approaches to regulation is a worldwide phenomenon. The approach, advocated here, relies more heavily on the game theory and transaction cost schools because the learning from these schools has been underemployed. Important concepts that get more attention are information, incentives, institutions, and choice. At the same time, forecasting models, continuing *ex post* allocation of sunk costs, and rules that limit choices need less emphasis.

In many ways the biggest problem is a transition in how to think about the industry. Competition ideas started out as heresy for many in the natural gas industry. Transition from OCOS to Network Oligopoly Regulation (NOR) is like the transition from the physics of Newton to the physics of Einstein. Newtonian physics works well except at the extremes—the atomic and cosmic scales. The atomic scale is similar to short term markets. Short term markets move too quickly to be disciplined by any traditional cost-of-service concept. The cosmic scale is similar to long term markets. Long term markets require more attention to contracts for cost-allocation signed before costs are sunk rather than after the fact.

Although friction is usually omitted from basic physics, engineers are made painfully aware of friction, thermal losses and constraints. In practice, reducing friction is important for efficiency improvements. Reducing transaction costs in markets is often the key to making markets both more efficient and more competitive. When current trends are combined with new policies for greater gas use, painting an accurate picture today of natural gas and electric markets in five or ten years should be no easier than it has been for the last 20 or 30 years. This means that the continuing design and development of efficient institutions should be the most important task of regulatory bodies.

Regulatory approaches need to recognize the huge sunk cost and interdependence of the transmission network and rethink basic and long accepted paradigms. Economic topologies of networks need to be better understood. Market power in the network will not be uniform. Sub network types such as webs and radials need to be identified and analyzed. Analysis and regulation of sub network webs may require different approaches from the bulk transfer or radial links that interconnect the grids. The extremities and interior of the network may require separate analysis and regulation. Isolated areas in the network may have market power. Managing the pockets of high market power in the network is critical for efficiency and fairness.

Governance structures focus on giving market participants most affected by the rules the opportunity to make the rules in a fair and open structure. In regulating assets with natural monopoly characteristics, *ex ante* competition and better specified contracts can be used to help foster efficiency. *Ex post* prudence, interpretation of a vague regulatory "compact" and cost allocation invite unnecessary criticism with the benefit of hindsight, and a destabilizing effect on long term investment.

With additional choice, good, timely information is critical for good decisions. To take advantage of the information revolution, better information, communication, and control systems are needed. Better monitoring prevents and detects some unwanted behavior.

The case-by-case approach must give way to a regional market approach. Introducing effective competition on the network and effective regulation of the network is not a simple process of sitting back and watching, but a careful step-by-step process, with new institutional arrangements involving industry players in a more cooperative atmosphere. In the commodity market, it is necessary to unbundle network service from the commodity trading. In the new environment of network oligopolies, neither the concepts from franchised, regulated monopoly nor those from perfectly competitive markets are directly applicable. A blend of competition and cooperation is necessary to achieve the greatest benefit. Fostering or forcing, if necessary, cooperation in the operation of the network is essential.

There are a number of changed imperatives for regulation. The first is focusing on regulating the network assets and services. Network assets have sunk natural monopoly characteristics. To the extent possible, create an *ex ante* approval process with a well-specific contract. A second imperative is not forcing network competition where cooperation is necessary for the network to work efficiently. A third is creating management incentives for the network that are compatible with policy objectives, for example protection of captive customers and efficient use. In other words, reward good management, not just capital investment. A fourth objective is avoiding tying non-network service that can be competitive to network services. It is an invitation to be mischievous and distort the market. Economies of scope arguments must be quantified and documented, not asserted. Fifth is focusing regulation on bad behavior (while rewarding good behavior) and establishing good institutions and incentives for competition to work. In other words, let players be rewarded for lower costs or higher quality. Finally, good governance structures for strong oligopoly markets are not well understood. Command-and-control, cost-of-service regulation is fading quickly in many markets. Laissez-faire approaches create more opportunity for behavior with negative effects on other players and society as a whole. A middle ground is evolving.

What should future policy be toward transmission networks? OCOS regulation is no longer appropriate because it is no longer effective. The paradigm for regulatory policy must shift to creating robust institutions that allow for many possible changes in market conditions and rely on more decentralized decision-making. This is largely uncharted territory.

Market-based regulation or the governance of oligopolies is missing from much of the academic theory of regulation, since it is a relatively new phenomenon. Deregulation is certainly one option, more of an external force coming from legislative or executive bodies than an internal regulatory initiative. On the empirical front, there is evidence that tight oligopolies are likely to outperform regulated monopolies. In any case, there must be considerable flexibility in rate structures to create meaningful incentives for the firms and their customers to behave efficiently.

Institutional design

Highly structured markets exist side-by-side with highly unstructured markets. Highly structured markets, including the stock and commodity exchanges, are overseen by commissions. Central electric power auctions operated by Independent System Operators (ISOs) are an example of structured trading. The government auctions such things as debt instruments and the electromagnetic spectrum under very structured rules. Trading institutions need rules, governance structures, and public oversight. When concentrated markets are emerging from decades of regulation, trading institutions and oversight become very important.

Regulatory tools are also being redesigned. Players are allowed to bargain, but all too often the bargains are subject to a later, *ex post*, regulatory review that strips much of the meaning away from the bargain. *Ex ante* prudence makes more sense than "gotcha" or *ex post* prudence. Profitability is tied to the firm's efficiency which includes quality service for its customers.

Competitive market forces will substitute for many activities that were traditionally heavily regulated. However, this can only be effective if regulation is replaced by institutions that foster effective competition. To allow the market to continue to develop, regulation must ensure that the market is fair and open to all who can benefit from it. Such openness in markets runs counter to the understanding and interests of many parties accustomed to a regulated monopoly model of the industry.

Notes

1 Chief Economic Advisor, Office of Markets, Tariffs and Rates, Federal Energy Regulatory Commission.
2 See Federal Energy Regulatory Commission, *Request of Transco Gas Pipeline for Technical Conference*, in RM91–11, November 5, 1992.
3 See generally, R. Crandall and J. Ellig, *Economic Deregulation and Customer Choice: Lessons for the Electric Industry*, Fairfax, Virginia: Center for Market Processes, George Mason University, 1997 and C. Winston, "Economic deregulation: days of reckoning for microeconomists," *Journal of Economic Literature* 31, 1993, pp. 1263–89.

References

Alger, D. R., O'Neill, R. P., and Toman, M. A., "Gas transportation rate design and the use of auctions to allocate capacity," Washington, D.C.: Federal Energy Regulatory Commission, July 1987.

Bonbright, J. C., Danielsen, A. L., and Kamerschen, D. R., *Principles of Public Utility Rates*, Arlington, Virginia: Public Utility Reports, 1988.

Harunuzzaman, M. and Costello, K., *State Commission Regulation of Self-Dealing Power Transactions*, Columbus, Ohio: National Regulatory Research Institute, January 1996.

Hogan, W. W., *Firm Natural Gas Transportation: A Priority Capacity Allocation Model*, Cambridge, Massachusetts: Putnam, Hayes and Bartlett Inc., 1989.

Indicators of Energy Efficiency, An International Comparison, Washington, D.C.: Energy Information Administration, July 1990.

Johnson, P., *The Birth of the Modern*, New York: Harper Collins, 1991.

Joskow, P., "Asset specificity and the structure of vertical relationships: empirical evidence," *Journal of Law, Economics, and Organization*, 4, 1988, pp. 95–117.

Joskow, P. and Schmalensee, R., *Markets for Power*, Cambridge, Massachusetts: MIT Press, 1983.

Littlechild, S. C. "A game-theoretic approach to public utility pricing," *Western Economic Journal* 8, 1970, pp. 162–6.

McAfee, R. P. and McMillan, J., "Analyzing the airways auction," *Journal of Economic Perspectives* 10, 1996, pp. 159–75.

MacAvoy, P. W. and Noll, R., "Relative prices on regulated transactions of natural gas pipelines," *Bell Journal of Economics* 4, 1973, pp. 212–34.

MacAvoy, P. W. and Pindyk, R., "Alternative regulatory policies for dealing with natural gas storage," *Bell Journal of Economics* 4, 1973, pp. 454–98.

MacAvoy, P. W., Spulber, D. F., and Stangle, B. E., "Is competitive entry free? Bypass and partial deregulation in natural gas markets," *Yale Journal on Regulation* 6, 1989, pp. 209–47.

McCabe, K., Rassenti, S. and Smith, V. L., "An experimental examination of competition and 'smart' markets on natural gas pipeline networks," Technical Report, Washington, D.C.: Federal Energy Regulatory Commission, July 1988.

McMillan, J., "Selling spectrum rights," *Journal of Economic Perspectives* 8, 1994, pp. 145–62.

Newberry, D. M., *Privatization, Restructuring, and Regulation of Network Utilities*, Cambridge, Massachusetts: MIT Press, 2002.

O'Neill, R. P., "Overall integration of rate design," *Efficient Rate Design for Natural Gas Pipelines*, Washington, D.C.: Federal Energy Regulatory Commission, Office of Economic Policy, September 1989.

O'Neill, R. P. and Stewart, W. R., "Auctions with incentives for fair and efficient pricing of public utility services," Discussion Paper, Federal Energy Regulatory Commission, Washington, D.C., March 1990.

O'Neill, R. P. and Whitmore, C. S., "Benchmark Regulation," Discussion Paper, Washington, D.C.: Federal Energy Regulatory Commission, August 1994.

O'Neill, R. P. and Whitmore, C. S., "Network oligopoly regulation: an approach to electric federalism," in *Regulating Regional Power Systems*, C. J. Andrews (ed.), Westport, Connecticut: Quorum Books, 1995.

O'Neill, R. P., Willard, M., Wilkins, B., and Pike, R., "A mathematical programming model for allocation of natural gas," *Operations Research* 27, September–October 1979, pp. 857–73.

Phillips, C. F., Jr., *The Regulation of Public Utilities: Theory and Practice*, Arlington, Virginia: Public Utility Reports, 1988.

Rose, K., *An Economic and Legal Perspective on Electric Utility Transition Costs*, Columbus, Ohio: National Regulatory Research Institute, July 1996.

Rothkopf, M. H., Kahn, E. P., Teisberg, T. J., Eto, J., and Notaf, J. M., *Designing PURPA Power Purchase Auctions: Theory and Practice*, Berkeley, California: Lawrence Berkeley Laboratory, August 1987.

Spulber, D. F., *Regulation and Markets*, Cambridge, Massachusetts: MIT Press, 1989.

Spulber, D. F., "Market microstructure and intermediation," *Journal of Economic Perspectives* 10, 1996, pp. 135–52.

Taccardi, R., Rodgers, L., and O'Neill, R. P., "An assessment of forecasts of the crude oil and natural gas," Working Paper, Washington, D.C.: Energy Information Administration, September 1985.

Vickery, W., "Counterspeculation, auctions, and competitive sealed tenders," *Journal of Finance* 16, 1961, pp. 8–37.

Wirick, D. W., Lawton, R. W., and Burns, R., *Information Risk in Emerging Utility Markets: The Role of Commission-Sponsored Audits*, Columbus, Ohio: National Regulatory Research Institute, March 1996.

Case 4

Local telecommunications

Jonathan L. Rubin[1]

Introduction

Competition in local telecommunications services represents the last of a three-part transition in the telephone industry in the United States from monopoly to competition. The first two stages established competitive markets in telephone equipment and in interexchange services (i.e., long distance). The transition to competition in these markets involved the relatively straightforward task of providing new competitive entrants with access on one end of the local exchange network or the other: Competitors in the long distance market required access to the local exchange central office switch; Competitors in the telephone equipment market required access to the local exchange network on either the subscribers' end (in the case of terminal equipment) or on the central office end (in the case of switching or routing equipment). In either case, the local loop between the central office and the subscriber—the so-called "last mile"— was the "bottleneck;" Competition in equipment and long distance was largely a matter of compelling access to the monopolists' local loop.

But what of the local network itself? If the local loop is the bottleneck, what kind of "network access" is needed to open this last segment of the system to competition? What should a competitive local exchange market look like? In this chapter, I describe the answers to these questions provided by Congress in the form of the pro-competitive statutory scheme for local exchange services established in the Telecommunications Act of 1996,[2] its implementation by the Federal Communications Commission (FCC), and some of the difficulties faced by this ambitious legislative initiative.

The rest of the chapter is organized as follows. The first section presents a brief history of U.S. telephony, followed by a description of the structure of the local exchange market. Section 3 describes the 1996 Act, including a discussion of the FCC's three attempts to implement its provisions relating to mandated access, and its rules relating to access terms. Section 4 contains a brief discussion of the progress made under the Act toward a competitive local exchange market, and Section 5 sets forth brief concluding remarks.

Historical background

On account of Alexander Graham Bell's patents on the telephone, the first of which was granted in 1876, the Bell Telephone Company enjoyed an initial temporary monopoly in telephony. Upon the expiration of the crucial Bell patents in 1893–94, however, multiple independent local exchange competitors began to spring up almost immediately, and by 1910 independent phone companies had nearly 3 million subscribers, as many as the Bell Company. Re-joining the company in 1907, Theodore Newton Vail[3] launched a major re-organization of Bell's affiliated local exchange companies, its long distance operations, and its research and engineering activities, unifying them as a single, interconnected system that was to be known as the Bell System. Vail vigorously promoted the idea of telephony as a "natural monopoly," claiming that no collection of separate companies could provide the service of a unified system, and adopting the corporate credo, "One Policy, One System, Universal Service."

To implement his vision, Vail oversaw the aggressive acquisition of independent phone companies and a controlling interest in the telegraph giant Western Union, and isolated unaffiliated exchanges by refusing them interconnection. In the company's 1910 Annual Report, Vail opined that "[e]ffective, aggressive competition, and regulation and control are inconsistent with each other, and cannot be had at the same time." In the "Vail Compromise" of 1910, AT&T was granted a monopoly in long distance in exchange for price regulation in both long distance and local services. The following year, Congress placed telephone companies providing interstate communications under the jurisdiction of the Interstate Commerce Commission (ICC) (albeit without the extensive tariff and regulatory oversight exerted by the ICC over railroads), and required them to provide service at request at just, reasonable, and non-discriminatory rates.[4] At the same time, the regulation of intrastate communications was delegated to the state utility commissions, extant in most states by 1915. Vail's strategy was successful, and agreeing to regulation of the firm, by then known as the American Telephone & Telegraph Company (AT&T), led to the creation of the largest company—and the largest monopoly—in the world. The jurisdictional separation between inter- and intrastate telephone regulation continues to this day.[5]

The Bell System's aggressive acquisition of telephone companies and the refusal of its long lines division to interconnect with unaffiliated exchanges brought it to the attention of the antitrust authorities. In July 1913, the government filed an antitrust suit focusing on its interconnection and acquisition policies in Oregon. Antitrust sentiment was strong in the nation at the time, and the Postmaster General was advocating nationalization of the telephone system, so AT&T settled the case in a letter from its vice president Nathan C. Kingsbury. The letter came to be known as the Kingsbury Commitment, in which AT&T agreed to dispose of its interest in Western Union, permit independent companies limited interconnection with its long lines network, and refrain from acquisition of additional telephone properties without prior ICC approval. In effect, the Kingsbury Commitment locked-in AT&T's dominance in local and interexchange markets.

AT&T argued that the large capital demands of a telephone network combined with minor or even negligible marginal costs meant that telephony was a natural monopoly, and that it should be permitted to further develop the Bell System as a unified network under solitary management.[6] The belief that a telephone network represents a natural monopoly held sway as recently as the early 1990s. Further expansion of the Bell System, however, required relief from the antimerger provisions of the Clayton Act.[7] The Willis-Graham Act of 1921[8] carved out an antitrust exemption to allow the continued development of the Bell System. Between 1921 and 1934, the ICC approved 271 of AT&T's 274 acquisition requests, giving the Bell System control of 80 percent of the local exchange services and all of the interexchange services in the nation.[9]

With the passage of the Communications Act of 1934 ("the 1934 Act"),[10] oversight of the Bell System was transferred to the newly established FCC. The 1934 Act echoed the Mann-Elkins Act by assigning interstate regulation to the FCC and regulation of the local Bell Operating Companies (BOCs) to the state public utility commissions. AT&T became a fully regulated monopoly.

The beginning of the end of the Bell monopoly came in the 1960s, when the FCC began to deregulate the telephone equipment market.[11] At the same time, Microwave Communications, Inc. (the predecessor of MCI Communications Corporation, or MCI) requested approval for a point-to-point link between Chicago and St. Louis. The decision to grant permission to MCI to establish point-to-point private line service[12] resulted in a deluge of applications to provide specialized common carrier services, including MCI's applications to provide specialized common carrier service to more than 100 cities.[13]

Through its control of the BOCs, AT&T frustrated the introduction of competition into the long distance and equipment markets. In November, 1974 the U.S. Department of Justice filed suit against the Bell System alleging sweeping violations of the antitrust laws. AT&T was accused of delaying or failing altogether to provide adequate local exchange interconnections to MCI and other carriers, refusing to sell terminal equipment, and maintaining a monopoly through equipment provisioning.[14] The proposed relief, "divestiture of the Bell operating companies from AT&T in a manner that would separate the local exchange functions of the operating companies from AT&T's interexchange, manufacturing and other functions,"[15] was fashioned to encourage competition in basic long distance services and equipment. The result of the divestiture was seven independent local exchange carriers (LECs) vested with collective dominion over local telephone services.[16] The regional Bell Operating Companies (RBOCs) continued as regulated monopolies in control of 164 local access and transport areas (LATAs).[17]

The local exchange market

The local exchange consists of numerous "elements:" One or more central switching offices that serve subscribers through local loops, "transports" between central offices, the port which provides the dial tone and connects the local loop to the central office switch, local network signaling facilities, information databases, routing hardware and software, and operator and information services. Natural monopoly never fit the equipment market, and its application to the market for interexchange services was clearly counterfactual once alternative long haul transmission modalities (e.g., microwave and satellite) became widely feasible. In at least some local exchanges, however, particularly in rural areas where "universal service" subsidies are still required, natural monopoly might still describe the economics of at least some elements of the local exchange.

Nonetheless, most assumptions underlying the natural monopoly view are now discredited. Regulation based on natural monopoly assumes that monopoly dead-weight loss exceeds the costs of regulation and a single, best technology is equally well-known by all existing or potential market participants, any of which will operate at the production-possibility frontier.[18] Natural monopoly also assumes that duplicate networks are always and everywhere inefficient. But competition in the local exchange market could come from numerous potential competitors, each employing a different technology. For example, intensive users who self-supply by establishing a private branch exchange (PBX) with access to one or more interexchange carriers (IXCs), by-pass the LECs. Self-suppliers can also use private, satellite-based very small aperture terminals (VSATs), which are just as effective in rural areas as in urban areas, and can join dispersed locations into an integrated network. Competitive access providers (CAPs), small firms offering large users by-pass access to IXCs, offer a niche service which competes at the edges of the local exchange. After passage of the 1996 Act, many CAPs expanded to provide "local dial tones," effectively becoming competitive local exchange carriers (CLECs).[19]

Substantial competition also comes from wireless technology. Initially, one cellular license went to the incumbent LEC (ILEC), and the other to the winner of a lottery, but in 1993 the FCC auctioned off as many as six licenses for personal communications services (PCS) in each area, and at least one license for special mobile radio service, all to compete directly with traditional wireline LECs. Similarly, cable television (originally known as "Community Antenna Television," or CATV) systems promise to compete with the ILECs.[20] To the extent that internet access is provided by cable-modem, satellite, or other alternatives to ILEC-provided dial-up access, voice-over internet will be an important competitor for local exchange traffic. Finally, the gas, electric, and water utilities, most of which already own suitable rights-of-way and many of which own extensive fiber optic networks, are uniquely poised to compete with LECs, especially in the upgrade of the last mile of the local loop to fiber optics. The competitive potential of these operators will be formidable in the years to come.[21]

Even given the deterioration of natural monopoly as a rationale for traditional regulation, however, the transition to competition in local telephone services remains fundamentally different than was the case for equipment or long distance services. Local exchange competitors require "network access" both in the sense of access *by* networks and access *to* networks. Competitors in the local segment could compete using entirely new, facilities-based networks that tie subscribers together or to subscribers on other networks. But competing networks also could be created by combining network elements of the ILECs with facilities owned by the competitor. To the extent that local network elements cannot be economically duplicated, a new entrant may need to share elements of an existing network to enable entry. Thus, the configuration of any competing network lies on a continuum between a separate, facilities-based parallel network (requiring access *by* the network to adjacent networks) and a network combining an ILEC's physical facilities with a competitor's own sales and billing functions (requiring access *to* the incumbent's network elements). Accommodating this range of configurations is the approach that Congress took in the Telecommunications Act of 1996.

The Telecommunications Act of 1996

In the 1996 Act, Congress substantially altered the regulatory regime of the 1934 Act. The Act put an end to the ILECs' state-protected monopolies and drastically altered the jurisdictional separation between interstate and intrastate regulation. To a large extent, the Act is a series of intra-industry compromises. For example, IXCs, such as AT&T and MCI, agreed to entry by the BOCs into the long distance market, but only if the IXCs could enter the local exchange markets. CATV companies agreed to let the LECs carry video programming, but only if CATV rates would be deregulated.

The Act provides for access to "unbundled network elements" (UNEs) by imposing special duties on the ILECs.[22] Congress appeared to be convinced from the outset that at least some elements of the local exchange were "essential facilities;" i.e., without mandated access to them, competition in the local exchange would not develop through the construction of duplicate facilities alone. Two different kinds of access issues arise under the approach adopted by the 1996 Act. The first is to determine the appropriate scope of access, i.e., which, if any, network elements cannot be duplicated economically by new entrants? The scope issue in turn depends on the balance between opening markets through mandated access on the one hand and the disincentives to build out facilities that must be shared with competitors on the other. Second, on what terms should ILECs be required to offer such access?

Scope of access to existing facilities

Congress was apparently fully cognizant of the interconnection difficulties faced by MCI and other IXCs seeking to enter the long distance market some 20 years earlier, and fearful of the power of incumbents to stifle or prevent competitive entry altogether. As one Senator put it, "Competition is the best regulator of the marketplace. But until that competition exists, until the markets are opened, monopoly-provided services must not be able to exploit the monopoly power to the consumers' disadvantage."[23]

The Act's access policy resides in §§251, 252 and 253, which allow entry by a "requesting telecommunications carrier" into the local exchange market by one or a combination of three possible methods. First, new entrants can build facilities, and request interconnection with the ILECs' existing networks. Second, new entrants can obtain one or more UNEs at cost-based prices "determined without reference to a rate-of-return or other rate-based proceeding."[24] Third, new entrants can purchase local exchange services at wholesale rates and resell them to their own customers.

Section 251, entitled "Interconnection," spells out the three key duties of the ILECs. Section 251(c)(2) requires any ILEC to interconnect with any requesting carrier for the transmission and routing of telephone exchange service and exchange access at "any technically feasible point within the carrier's network." Section 251(c)(3) requires any ILEC to provide access to UNEs at rates that are "just, reasonable, and nondiscriminatory," to permit an entrant to choose among them, and to combine them with its own facilities in any manner it sees fit. Section 251(c)(4) requires any ILEC to offer to resell at wholesale rates any telecommunications service it provides to subscribers who are not telecommunications carriers. Additional provisions require ILECs to co-locate the requesting carrier's equipment on premises[25] and to "negotiate in good faith ... the particular conditions of agreements" to fulfill their duties.[26]

The standard set forth in §251(d)(2)(B) requires the FCC to determine whether the failure to provide access to a network element would "impair the ability of the telecommunications carrier seeking access to provide the services that it seeks to offer," while §251(d)(2)(A) requires the Commission to determine whether access to elements that are proprietary in nature is "necessary." The FCC's attempts to implement this compound "necessary and impair" standard have been found wanting by the courts no less than three times, and as of this writing the FCC is still in the process of determining the appropriate rules to implement the scope of mandated access.

Section 252 of the Act establishes the procedures to be followed by ILECs and new entrants to reduce the requirements of §251 to binding interconnection agreements. The Act clearly expresses a preference for voluntarily negotiated agreements, subject to approval by the state regulatory authority, in which case the agreement need not comply with §§251(b) and (c), although it must be consistent with the public interest, convenience, and necessity. If the parties are unable to reach agreement through voluntary negotiations, §252(c) authorizes the state commissions to resolve disputes by arbitration, in which case all the conditions of §251 must be met. If the state commission fails to act, the agreement may be approved by the FCC. Parties aggrieved by the approval procedure may seek review in the appropriate federal district court.

Additional provisions of the Act impose on all LECs obligations not to prohibit or limit resale, to provide competing carriers with number portability, dialing parity, and access to poles, ducts, conduits, and rights-of-way, and to establish reciprocal compensation arrangements for the transport and termination of telecommunications.[27] Section 251(d)(1) directs the FCC to establish rules to implement the requirements of these provisions.

The first UNE implementation

Six months after passage of the Act, the FCC promulgated detailed implementing regulations. The FCC interpreted the "impairment" standard of §251(d)(2) to have been met "if the quality of the service the entrant can offer, absent access to the requested element, declines and/or the cost of providing the service rises."[28] The Commission also adopted Rule 319, which came to be known as the "all elements rule."[29] According to its interpretation of the "necessary and impair" standard, the FCC assumed authority to require incumbents to provide access to *all* of the basic network elements. New entrants could thus lease the entire network "platform," an arrangement that came to be known as UNE-P.[30] The FCC also adopted the so-called "pick and choose" rule, which required an ILEC to make available any interconnection or UNE provided under any approved agreement upon the same terms and conditions, without accepting the terms and conditions of the entire agreement.[31] The FCC also adopted rules[32] requiring all LECs to provide dialing parity to CLECs and IXCs,[33] and required the cost of numbering administration arrangements to be shared by all carriers on a competitively neutral basis.[34]

In *AT&T Corp. v. Iowa Utilities Board*,[35] the Supreme Court vacated the all-elements rule on the grounds that the FCC had failed to give any "substance to the 'necessary' and 'impair' requirements."[36] In determining impairment the Court held that elements available from sources outside the ILECs' network should have also been considered, and a mere increase in cost or decrease in service quality did not establish a "necessity" or an "impairment." The Court left intact the pick and choose rule, the Commission's definition of UNEs, and a rule requiring ILECs to make available certain combined services. The Court recognized that the effect of the Act was a substantial transfer of jurisdiction over local telecommunications from States to the federal government.[37]

Not surprisingly, the ILECs had argued that §251(d)(2) codified the essential facilities doctrine of antitrust theory, so that only 'bottleneck' elements unavailable elsewhere in the marketplace should be unbundled.[38] The majority declined to decide whether the Act required the FCC to apply that standard, or some other limiting standard, but did hold that the FCC should have applied *some* standard to determine the scope of its UNE rules. Justice Breyer's dissent disapproved of not only the all-elements rule, but also of the dramatic shift in regulatory oversight from the states to the FCC. With respect to the former, Justice Bryer said,

> [A]lthough the provision describing which elements must be unbundled does not explicitly refer to the analogous "essential facilities" doctrine (an antitrust doctrine that this Court has never adopted), the Act ... requires a convincing explanation of why facilities should be shared (or "unbundled") where a new entrant could compete effectively without the facility, or where practical alternatives to that facility are available.[39]

The second UNE implementation

In new unbundling rules, the FCC concluded that a proprietary network element is "necessary" if, given the availability of alternative elements outside the ILEC's network, lack of access to that element would, as a practical, economic, and operational matter, preclude a CLEC from providing the services it sought to offer. Lack of access would "impair" the ability of a CLEC to provide services if its ability was "materially diminished."[40] Noting that legislation expressly referring to essential facilities had been rejected by Congress in favor of the "necessary and impair" standard,[41] the FCC declined to read the essential facilities doctrine into §251(d)(2), finding that the Act plainly imposed on ILECs a broader duty to deal with competitors "not limited to situations in which the incumbent is misusing control of a unique facility to foreclose competition in a downstream market...."[42]

Under the newly interpreted standard, seven network elements would be unbundled on a national basis, subject to certain geographic and product market exceptions: (1) loops, (2) subloops, (3) network interface devices, (4) certain circuit switching, (5) interoffice transmission facilities,

(6) signaling and call-related databases, and (7) operations support systems. The new UNE rules excluded some circuit switches, as well as operator services and directory assistance. They also added additional elements, including high capacity loops, dark fiber, subloops, and packet switches in some circumstances. Moreover, the FCC required ILECs to combine UNEs for resale wherever technically feasible, and applied its unbundling rules uniformly to all elements in every market. In addition, the FCC promulgated rules requiring unbundled access to a new network element, the high frequency portion of the local loop.[43] The rules required the ILECs to make their local loops suitable for carrying high frequency digital transmissions and to lease the high frequency segment to CLECs to enable them to offer digital subscriber line (DSL) services.

In *United States Telecom Ass'n v. FCC*,[44] the D.C. Circuit Court vacated both the FCC's revised UNE rules as well as the *Line Sharing Order*. The court said "adding the adjective 'material' contributes nothing of any analytical or qualitative character" that could serve as a standard. The FCC's impairment standard was "so broad and unrooted in any analysis of the competing values at stake" that even the two non-universal mandates (for circuit switches and packet switches) would have to be vacated.[45] Noting that scholars had raised "very serious questions" about the essential facilities doctrine, the court suggested that the doctrine "may nonetheless offer useful concepts" when Congress has directed an agency to provide competitor access in a specific industry.[46] The circuit court also criticized the nation-wide applicability of the rules, which could make UNEs available to CLECs in markets where competitors did not suffer from any impairment.[47] Moreover, the broad scope of the FCC's interpretation of the "impair" standard led to access requirements that enabled the UNE-P arrangement, which the court perceived to be unfair to the ILECs.

The third UNE implementation

The *USTA I* decision sent the FCC back to the drawing board. On February 20, 2003, new rules were announced which abandoned the line sharing obligations and limited UNE-P to residential customers only.[48] In its 576-page *Remand Order*, the Commission struggled with the "impair" standard, attempting to strike the balance that the D.C. Circuit had found lacking between providing access to existing facilities sufficient to stimulate competition and imposing such broad UNE requirements that the ILECs would have a disincentive to invest in new infrastructure (particularly fiber-based transmission systems), and the CLECs would have a disincentive to invest in competitive facilities.[49]

Under the revised standard, a CLEC would be considered "impaired" when the "lack of access to an incumbent LEC network element poses a barrier or barriers to entry, including operational and economic barriers, that are likely to make entry into a market uneconomic."[50] Relevant barriers to entry include scale economies, sunk costs, first-mover advantages, and barriers within the control of the ILECs.[51]

To introduce "granularity" into its impairment analysis of UNEs, the Commission distinguished between three classes of customers: mass market, small and medium enterprise, and large enterprise customers.[52] Additional granularity was based on geographic distinctions which take "market-specific variations" into account.[53] The Commission developed provisional national rules that could vary by geography but authority was delegated to state commissions. Critics of this arrangement included the Chairman of the Commission, who maintained that delegating this granular analysis to the states could result in a patchwork of local versions of the UNE obligations.[54]

The FCC conducted separate "loop impairment analyses" based on the loop type and capacity levels and whether the loops serve mass market or enterprise market customers. For mass market, narrowband services, ILECs would be required to provide unbundled access on a national basis to copper loops and copper subloops and replacement fiber optic loops, and copper loops or subloops could not be retired without first receiving approval from the state public service commission.[55] ILECs need not afford access to fiber to the home and hybrid loops that employ packet switching and digital loop carrier (DLC) technology over the copper loop portion, although a narrowband channel would have to be made available, as would high capacity loops utilizing time division multiplexing (TDM), such as DS1s and DS3s.[56] With respect to line-sharing, the FCC would no longer require the high frequency portion of the loop to be made available as a UNE, and CLECs currently offering broadband services through line sharing would have three years to migrate to a new arrangement.[57]

In the enterprise market, dark (unused) fiber, DS1, and, on a limited basis, DS3 high-capacity loops must be unbundled, unless, according to specific findings by state public utility commissions, alternative facilities are available.[58] The alternative facilities that could act as "triggers" to overcome the national presumption of impairment include self-provisioning or alternative wholesale facilities.[59] No impairment is presumed without access to OCn "lit fiber."

With respect to interoffice transports, the FCC found that requesting carriers would not be impaired without access to unbundled OCn transport facilities, but would be impaired without access to dark fiber, DS3, or DS1 transports, subject to a granular route-based review by the states of the existence of triggers necessary to overcome the impairment presumption.[60] With respect to circuit switches, the FCC presumed no impairment for local circuit switches serving DS1 capacity and higher enterprise markets, but impairment for circuit switches serving mass market customers, primarily because of the cost of the "hot cut" process needed to switch mass market customers from one carrier to another, unless the state commissions determine otherwise in a particular locality. Moreover, the FCC directed the state commissions to initiate a batch cut migration process, unless they determine that competitive carriers would not be impaired without it.[61]

When a requesting carrier uses its own switches, unbundled access to the incumbents' signaling network and call-related databases would not be required, but would be when a CLEC purchases unbundled switching.[62] For services that qualify, ILECs would have to offer unbundled access to their operations support systems, such as pre-ordering, ordering, provisioning, maintenance and repair, and billing functions supported by an ILEC's database and information.[63] The FCC determined to revisit the pick and choose rule and the issue of intercarrier compensation.

In *United States Telecom Ass'n v. FCC*,[64] the D.C. Circuit Court of Appeals again vacated the FCC's unbundling rules. The court held that the Commission had no authority to subdelegate its §251(d)(2) responsibilities to determine whether CLECs are impaired without access to network elements to state commissions, which the court characterized as "outside" rather than "subordinate" parties, an arrangement that risks "policy drift."[65] The court did not accept the FCC's argument that the role of the states was limited to "fact finding," because the *Remand Order* "lets the states make crucial decisions regarding market definition and application of the FCC's general impairment standard to the specific circumstances of those markets, with FCC oversight neither timely nor assured."[66] Having invalidated the "(unlawful) innovation" of a "provisional national impairment finding from which state commissions could deviate,"[67] the court determined that the finding of national impairment for mass market switches[68] and certain dedicated transport elements[69] must be vacated. The court also vacated the Commission's decision that wireless carriers are impaired without access to unbundled transport.[70]

The court was also critical of the Commission's "barriers to entry" interpretation of the "impairment" standard, stating that in at least one respect its definition was "vague almost to the point of being empty."[71] For whom would entry be "uneconomic"? For *any* CLEC, regardless of efficiency, or for an "average" or a "representative" CLEC?

On the other hand, the *USTA II* court found that the FCC's refusal to order unbundling of the broadband capacity of hybrid loops, Fiber to the Home (FTTH), and line sharing was a permissible exercise of statutory authority and based on substantial evidence.[72] The court stayed its vacatur for 60 days, or the denial of a petition for rehearing, whichever came first. On April 13, 2004, the court stayed its mandate for an additional 45 days to give competitive carriers an opportunity to negotiate access agreements with the ILECs. As of this writing, neither the solicitor general nor the Commission has decided whether to seek an appeal of the D.C. Circuit court decision to the U.S. Supreme Court.

Terms of mandated access

The *First Report and Order* established a forward looking cost-based procedure for determining rates for UNEs known as "total element long run incremental cost," or TELRIC, a variant of total service long run incremental costs (TSLRIC), modified to apply to individual network elements. "Long run" refers to a period long enough so that all of the firm's costs become variable or avoidable, thus treating all capital expenditures as variable costs. TELRIC pricing requires an estimate of the cost of reconstructing a hypothetical network using the best available technology given the existing switch locations. Costs attributable to the network element, forward-looking costs of capital and depreciation expenses, and a markup to cover common costs not causally attributable to any single network element are included.[73] Despite the Act's preference for voluntarily negotiated access agreements, to avoid delay the FCC adopted TELRIC as guiding methodology for the states, together with "default proxies" for cases in which the cost studies called for by TELRIC are infeasible.

The FCC opted to calculate costs based on "the relationship between market-determined prices and forward-looking economic costs,"[74] reasoning that if forward-looking costs exceeded market prices, CLECs would not enter. In *Iowa Utilities Bd. v. FCC,*[75] the ILECs and other parties claimed that the TELRIC rules exceeded the FCC's interLATA jurisdiction, failed to allow incumbents to recover embedded costs (amounting to an unconstitutional "taking"), and introduced distortions which inhibited investment in competitive facilities or new technology. The court of appeals agreed that the FCC exceeded its jurisdiction by imposing pricing policies on state commissions, and vacated the TELRIC rules, staying its order pending an appeal to the U.S. Supreme Court.

The Supreme Court reversed and remanded the case, reasoning that since the Act gave jurisdiction to the FCC over "matters to which the 1996 Act applies,"[76] the Commission properly exercised its ancillary jurisdiction. On remand, the Eighth Circuit found that TELRIC fell short of the requirements of law because the Act required that rates be based on the "actual" rather than the "hypothetical" cost of providing the network element. The Supreme Court reversed again, reasoning that "the 'hypothetical' element is simply the element valued in terms of a piece of equipment an incumbent may not own."[77] Moreover, the court held that the FCC's rules for the state commissions "were reasonably within the pale of statutory possibility," and reinstated the TELRIC rules.

Despite the fact that TELRIC has survived judicial scrutiny, the various subsidies in telecommunications may render the TELRIC rules suboptimal. Moreover, unless an appropriate measure of risk is included in the pricing methodology, the TELRIC rules can have the effect of granting a free "real option" to CLECs to employ ILEC facilities or build their own, as they see fit.

A pricing methodology that passes judicial muster, however, is not necessarily economically optimal. An "optimal" pricing policy in this context would be one that satisfies a multiplicity of constraints. Setting prices too high would permit the ILECs to earn supra-competitive profits and discourage CLEC entry, defeating the purposes of the Act. Setting prices too low would encourage inefficient entry and discourage both ILECs and CLECs from making capital investments in infrastructure. Moreover, the imposition of the type of cross subsidies that have traditionally characterized telecommunications (and are expanded in the Act) is generally incompatible with a uniform pricing scheme and the goal of stimulating competition and driving prices toward their competitive levels. Uniform pricing rules can generate cream-skimming and incentives not to offer service to subsidized customers.

TELRIC rates adjust over time to reflect the most up-to-date technology. Since the value of even the most modern infrastructure will decline as soon as new technology is introduced, TELRIC rates will reflect the real costs of the incumbent's actual network only if the entire network is re-installed using the best available technology, and only momentarily, before any of the equipment is surpassed by newer technology.

Moreover, TELRIC rates are unrelated to embedded costs, so there is the possibility that capital investments made by an ILEC could be stranded, even though a proportional share of the depreciation of the value of equipment may be recovered. This is because the cost basis used to recover depreciation is related to the hypothetical best technology and not historical cost. New equipment may cost substantially less than existing equipment, and the depreciation allowance may not cover the actual costs incurred. However, TELRIC rates may also overcompensate for depreciation, depending on the particular circumstances, a result explained below.

The most vigorous objection to TELRIC has been the possibility that incumbents will fail to recover embedded costs. But TELRIC pricing can just as easily over-compensate an incumbent as under-compensate it, depending on the cost-savings of installing new equipment and the magnitude of remaining embedded costs.

A simple example illustrates how TELRIC-based prices are calculated, and how, in some circumstances, embedded costs may be stranded and in others may be over-recovered. Let v represent (short-run) variable costs, j joint and common costs, c the cost of capital, and d depreciation costs. Further, let TC be total forward-looking costs, EC embedded costs, and P the price. The subscript o represents old equipment and b represents the best available equipment. The TELRIC price using installed (i.e., old) equipment is $P_o = v_b + j_b + c_b + d_b$. The total, forward-looking cost of installed equipment, TC_o, is $TC_o = v_o + j_o + c_o + d_b$. In order for an ILEC to be compensated for its actual forward-looking costs for old equipment, condition P_o? TC_o, must be satisfied, or, what is the same thing, TELRIC ? TC_o. Calculating embedded costs as $EC = c_o + d_o$, this inequality becomes

$(v_b + j_b) - (v_o + j_o) + (c_b + d_b) - EC \geq 0$. Under the reasonable assumption that new equipment is cheaper to operate than old, $(v_b + j_d) - (v_o + j_o)$ will be negative. Thus, whether or not embedded costs will be recovered under TELRIC pricing depends on the relationship between the variable costs and depreciation allowances on the best equipment and the embedded costs of the actual equipment, in light of the cost savings of installing the best equipment. Very old existing equipment is liable to have quite low embedded costs, and in this case the age of the existing infrastructure will be the main determinant of whether historical costs will be recovered or stranded.

Economic inefficiency can result from either failing to invest in new, more efficient equipment, from over-compensating old equipment that should be replaced, or from too frequently updating infrastructure as new equipment becomes available. Clearly, constant updating of equipment so that the hypothetical best technology is always in place, aside from its practical impossibility, represents a waste of resources. The TELRIC method, despite being based on the best available technology, attempts to strike an appropriate balance and avoid inducing inefficiencies.

Another criticism of the TELRIC rules is that they now require incumbents to make decisions not only on the rates they charge customers, but also on rates to be charged to competitors. That is, TELRIC pricing has changed the rules under which substantial investments were initially made. Business decisions initially made under one rate-setting regime are now required to be executed under a different regime. However, as long as the change in regulatory regime is a one-off occurrence, this aspect of the new rules should have only a transitory deleterious effect.

A more serious criticism involves the interaction of TELRIC pricing and cross-subsidies. Among the pricing methodologies rejected by the Commission in favor of TELRIC was the efficient component pricing rule (ECPR). This rule sets the price of an input element equal to the input's direct per-user incremental costs plus the opportunity cost of the sale. This approach, advocated by the ILECs, was rejected because the FCC determined that prices set in this manner were inconsistent with the mandate of the Act that rates be set based on "cost."

Approaches to cost-based pricing fall into three broad categories, depending on whether they are based on historical or embedded costs, i.e., the book value of existing infrastructure, forward-looking costs irrespective of the actual historical costs, such as the TELRIC method, which is based on the most efficient available infrastructure, or forward-looking costs based on the actual existing infrastructure, such as the efficient component pricing rule. In connection with the Notice of Proposed Rule-Making (NPRM) which led to the First Report and Order, Economist William J. Baumol (with Professors Janusz Ordovr and Robert Willig) filed an affidavit with the FCC in which EPCR was rejected in favor of TELRIC. The FCC agreed, determining that EPCR, which depends on the retail prices charged for services, was inconsistent with the cost mandate of the

Act. EPCR sets the price of a UNE equal to the incremental cost of a UNE plus the incumbent's opportunity cost of providing the UNE to a competitor, with the latter determined by the amount the incumbent would have earned had it sold retail services using the UNE.

Interestingly, Professor Baumol, in a 1999 article,[78] disavowed TELRIC, claiming that the only competitive neutral pricing method is EPCR. By "competitively neutral," Baumol means a pricing method which favors neither the incumbent nor new entrants. He also claims that EPCR can achieve neutrality even in the presence of cross-subsidies and price discrimination. His change of heart has been enthusiastically received in some quarters as supporting the only approach capable of accommodating cross-subsidies.[79]

Another objection to TELRIC arises from the fact that the UNE rules give, in effect, a free real option to the CLECs to use existing infrastructure or to invest in new facilities, placing the risk of obsolescence entirely on the incumbents without compensating them for it. The FCC has apparently found some merit in this objection, since on the occasion of its February 20, 2003 announcement of new UNE rules the Commission also announced a revision to TELRIC pricing that will attempt to make a risk adjustment to the cost of capital, presumably to account for the technology-driven decline in rates implied by the TELRIC methodology.

A further objection to TELRIC is that it is based on the hypothetical full replacement of the network, so it may act to penalize efficient equipment up-grades by incumbents. When an ILEC invests in new equipment, it does so only when all the forward looking costs of the new equipment are lower than the short run costs of continuing to operate the existing equipment. Once having decided to make such an up-grade on an efficiency basis, it makes little sense to lower prices again as soon as even newer equipment becomes available, since it is likely that further replacement will not be efficient and will represent a waste of resources. One solution to this is to permit an acceleration of depreciation expense, front-loading it to reflect the rapid availability of new infrastructure and to increase the likelihood that TELRIC prices will properly compensate ILECs that invest in newer technology. This possibility is not addressed by existing TELRIC regulations.

Finally, some commentators object to TELRIC because it relies on the "omniscience" of regulators to set prices rather than on market forces. One critic who is particularly harsh on the FCC for its "arrogance" in assuming that they are better equipped than the market to set prices is Dr. Alfred Kahn.[80] According to Professor Kahn, the FCC has, in effect, said,"[W]hy should we bother with that messy, undependable competitive process, we can do it. We're smart enough. Why not, since we know what the price is going to be, we'll set it right away. It saves an awful lot of trouble."[81] One problem with this criticism, however, is that there is no existing market for unbundled elements of a local exchange, i.e., there is no market price. Moreover, to the extent the Act depends on negotiated prices, such terms are probably as close to "market prices" as are possible. Only when negotiations fail is TELRIC mandated as the method by which prices should be set by state regulators.

TELRIC is also "wrong" in Professor Kahn's view, because "no one will invest in the expectation of obtaining a price when the facilities are constructed that just covers the cost of capital and public utility rates of depreciation or obsolescence, knowing that the next day the return will fall below that level because of the dynamic [of] technology."[82] The Commission recognized this problem by modifying the TELRIC pricing rules in its *Remand Order* to more closely account for the risks of investing in network elements, and commencing a proceeding to inquire into further modifications.[83] Henceforth, carriers can propose UNE-specific costs of capital that reflect the unique risks pertaining to that element,[84] and may accelerate the depreciation rate to more accurately anticipate its decline in value.[85]

The progress towards local competition

One indicator of the difficulties posed by the pro-competitive access scheme embodied in the 1996 Act is the D.C. Circuit's reference at the close of *USTA II* to the FCC's "failure, after eight years, to develop lawful unbundling rules, and its apparent unwillingness to adhere to prior judicial rulings."[86] Given the novelty and complexity of the task, and the competing interests that shaped the legislative language, this criticism may not be entirely fair. Nonetheless, at least one author has suggested that a greater role for antitrust as a mechanism by which to introduce competition might have been preferable, not only by side-stepping the additional layer of regulation engendered by the 1996 Act but also by more narrowly defining the scope of the UNE rules based on judicial interpretations of the essential facilities doctrine and by providing a powerful incentive for ILECs not to disregard their duties to the CLECs.[87] The Supreme Court's decision in *Verizon Communications Inc. v. Trinko*,[88] however, appears to have foreclosed *any* role for the antitrust laws in the transition to competitive local exchange markets, so that progress hinges entirely on the 1996 Act and its interpretation by the FCC.

Since 1999, the Commission has collected statistics from ILECs and CLECs to assess the state of competition in the local markets.[89] Out of 182 million switched access lines reported, the CLECs' share as of June, 2003 was 26.8 million, or 14.7 percent, up from 4.3 percent as of December, 1999 and 9 percent as of June, 2001. Whether the CLECs' share of switched access lines eight years after passage of the Act represents success is difficult to judge in the abstract. It depends, in part, on the importance placed on facilities-based competition compared to resale or purchase of UNEs. It is noteworthy that the proportion of CLEC lines provided over CLEC-owned facilities has actually declined, from 33.2 percent in 1999 to

23.3 percent in 2003, while provisioning via UNEs has increased, from 23.9 percent to 58.5 percent over the same period.

Competition in the local market is skewed by the increase in the share of CLEC customer lines subscribed to by medium and large business, institutions, and governmental users. While the ILECs' share of the enterprise market has remained fairly steady at about 78 percent, enterprise customers have steadily increased from 41.1 percent of CLEC subscribers as of December, 1999 to 62 percent as of June, 2003, indicating that a certain degree of cream-skimming of the more lucrative enterprise market by CLECs is taking place.

On balance, the increase in the CLECs' share of switched lines appears to be accelerating, albeit skewed in favor of enterprise customers, although no metric can quantify whether the observed growth in CLEC-supplied lines is above or below what could reasonably have been expected when the Act was passed in 1996.

Conclusion

Unlike the introduction of competition into the long distance or equipment markets, entry by would-be competitors into the local market is substantially more complex. The local exchange transition does not depend on judicially imposed compliance with the antitrust laws. Instead, markets controlled by reluctant monopolists are to be pried open without direct appeal to known principles of antitrust law, with the unfortunate result that the transition has been sent into uncharted waters, untethered to any well-established jurisprudence of competition, left to be tossed about by torrents of litigation and regulatory uncertainty. Even after eight years under the Act, the rules for mandated access are not yet settled, and no precise evaluation of whether the Act has lived up to its promise is possible. Only future developments will determine whether the transition of the local exchange to competition will yield benefits to consumers that outweigh its costs.

Notes

1 Senior Research Fellow, American Antitrust Institute.
2 Pub. L. 104–104, 110 Stat. 56 (1996), codified at 47 U.S.C. et seq. (the "1996 Act," or simply, the "Act").
3 General Manager and President of AT&T, 1878–89 and 1907–19.
4 The Mann-Elkins Act, Ch. 309, §7, 36 Stat. 539, et seq. (1910).
5 See, for example, *Smith v. Illinois Bell Telephone Co.*, 282 U.S. 133 (1931) (invalidating rules of the Illinois Commerce Commission which failed to distinguish between telephone company property used for interstate and intrastate services), *Louisiana Public Service Commission v. FCC*, 476 U.S. 355 (1986) (the FCC does not have jurisdiction to preempt state depreciation regulations), *Competitive Telecommunications Association v. FCC*, 117 F.3d 1068 (8th Cir. 1997)

(vacating temporary regulations under the 1996 Act requiring contributions to the universal service subsidy in the form of intrastate—as opposed to inter-state—access charges), and *United States Telecom Association v. FCC*, 359 F.3d 554 (D.C. Cir. 2004) (vacating FCC Order sub-delegating to state utility commissions determinations related to unbundling certain network elements).

6   A natural monopoly is said to exist when a single firm operating at minimum efficient scale (MES) can supply the entire market demand for output at a lower per-unit cost than two or more firms operating at MES. In the single product case, it is sufficient that long run average costs are in decline over the entire range of market demand. In the multi-product case, economies of scale are neither sufficient nor necessary, but economies of scope, in which a single firm can produce the bundle of products at a lower average cost than two or more firms, is a sufficient condition. Economies of scale or scope are sufficient, but not necessary. The necessary condition is subadditivity of the long run average cost function for all levels of output equal to or greater than total market demand, which can pertain even in a region of rising total average costs (i.e., decreasing returns to scale). See W. J. Baumol, "On the proper cost test for natural monopoly in a multiproduct industry," *American Economic Review* 67, 1977, pp. 809–22.

7   Ch. 323, §7, 38. Stat. 731 (1914).

8   Ch. 20, 42 Stat. 27 (1921).

9   The Bell System eventually developed into a combination of the AT&T Long Lines Division (interexchange services), Western Electric, Inc. (telephone equipment), Bell Telephone Laboratories (research), and a network of 23 local Bell Operating Companies (BOCs).

10   Ch. 652, 48 Stat 1064, 1934, 47 U.S.C. §151, et seq., as amended.

11   See the Use of the Carterfone Device in Message Toll Telephone Service, 13 F.C.C.2d 420 (1968) and *North Carolina Utility Commission v. F.C.C.*, 552 F.2d 1036 (4th Cir. 1977).

12   Microwave Communications, Inc., 18 F.C.C.2d 953 (1969) and 21 F.C.C.2d 190 (1970).

13   Including foreign exchange (FX) and common control switching arrangements (CCSA), which require switching services from the BOC-controlled local exchanges, in contrast to point-to-point services, which do not. See *MCI Communications Corporation, et al. v. American Telephone and Telegraph Company* (MCI v. AT&T), 708 F.2d 1081 (7th Cir.) *cert. den.*, 464 U.S. 891 (1983).

14   See *United States v. American Telephone & Telegraph Co.* (AT&T II), 552 F.Supp. 131 (D.D.C. 1982), *aff'd sub nom.*, *Maryland v. United States*, 460 U.S. 1001 (1983).

15   Competitive Impact Statement, 47 Fed.Reg. 7170, at 7171 (1982).

16   These companies were the "Baby Bells," or regional Bell Operating Companies (RBOCs).

17   LATAs were designed to be "large enough to comprehend contiguous areas having common social and economic characteristics but not so large as to defeat the intent of the decree to separate the provision of intercity services from the provision of local exchange service." Competitive Impact Statement, op. cit., 7176, n. 14.

18   In the multi-product case, these assumptions apply to the product bundle.

19   CLECs are the new entrants into the local exchange market created by the

1996 Act, but the most successful of them have been established IXCs, such as AT&T and MCI.

20 However, most CATV operators have focused instead on high speed internet services, see R. G. Harris, and C. J. Kraft, "Meddling through: regulating local telephone competition in the United States," *Journal of Economic Perspectives* 11, 1997, p. 102.

21 It is interesting that Sprint, now part of MCI, started as SP Communications, the microwave communications subsidiary of Southern Pacific Railroad.

22 1996 Act, op. cit., §251(h)(2). The ILECs include the BOCs plus non-Bell LECs, such as GTE, Sprint, Frontier, and any other LEC which the FCC by rule determines should be treated as an ILEC.

23 Statement of Sen. Ernest F. Hollings, 141 Cong. Rec. S7889, at S7984 (daily edn), June 7, 1995.

24 1996 Act, op. cit., §252(d)(1)(A)(i).

25 Ibid., §251(c)(6).

26 Ibid., §251(c)(1).

27 Ibid., §251(b).

28 In re Implementation of the Local Competition Provisions in the Telecommunications Act of 1996 ("First Report & Order"), 11 FCC Rcd 15499, 15643 (1996), ¶285.

29 47 C.F.R., §51.319 (1996).

30 First Report and Order, op. cit., ¶328–40.

31 47 C.F.R., op. cit., §51.809.

32 See Implementation of the Local Competition Provisions of the Telecommunications Act of 1996, Second Report and Order ("Second Report and Order"), CC Docket No. 96-98, 11 FCC Rcd 19392, August 8, 1996.

33 1996 Act, op. cit., §251(b)(3); 47 C.F.R. §§51.205-51.215, op. cit.

34 1996 Act, op. cit., §251(e)(2), 47 C.F.R., op. cit., §52.17.

35 525 U.S. 366 (1999)("AT&T").

36 Ibid., 391.

37 Ibid., 378, n. 6.

38 Ibid., 388 (citation omitted).

39 Ibid., 428 (Breyer, J., concurring in part and dissenting in part) (citations omitted).

40 See Implementation of the Local Competition Provisions in the Telecommunications Act of 1996 ("Third Report & Order"), Third Report and Order and Fourth Notice of Proposed Rulemaking, 15 FCC Rcd 3696 and 3725, September 15, 1999, ¶51, amending 47 C.F.R. §§51.5, 51.317, and 51.319, 65 Fed.Reg. 2542 (January 18, 2000).

41 See 137 Cong. Rec. at S7058 (daily edn), June 5, 1991, (reading S. 1200, 102d Cong. §202, 1991).

42 Third Report and Order, op. cit., ¶60 (citations omitted).

43 In re the Matter of Deployment of Wireline Services Offering Advanced Telecommunications Capability and Implementation of the Local Competition Provisions of the Telecommunications Act of 1996, Third Report and Order in CC Docket No. 98-147 and Fourth Report and Order in CC Docket No. 96-98, 14 FCC Rcd 20912, December 9, 1999 ("Line Sharing Order").

44 290 F.3d 415 (D.C. Cir. 2002), *cert. den. sub. nom.*, *WorldCom, Inc. v. United Telecom Ass'n.* ("USTA I"), 123 S.Ct. 1571 (U.S. 2003 Mem.).

45 Ibid., 427–8.
46 Ibid., 428, fn. 4 (citation omitted).
47 Ibid., 422. The Commission had addressed the question of whether the Supreme Court decision in AT&T precluded its adoption of universal rules for each network element, and concluded that the opinion did not require it to determine on a state-by-state or market-by-market basis which unbundled elements are to be made available. See Third Report & Order, op. cit., ¶122.
48 Implementation of the Local Competition Provisions of the Telecommunications Act of 1996; Review of the Section 251 Unbundling Obligations of Incumbent Local Exchange Carriers; Deployment of Wireline Services Offering Advanced Telecommunications Capability, Report and Order and Order on Remand and Further Notice of Proposed Rulemaking, FCC Docket Nos. 96–98, 01–338, 98–147, August 21, 2003 ("Remand Order").
49 Ibid., ¶70 and ¶119.
50 Ibid., ¶84.
51 See, for example, ibid., ¶235.
52 Ibid., ¶124 and ¶128. Mass market customers include residential and very small business customers that primarily purchase "plain old telephone service" (POTS); Small and medium enterprises include business willing to sign term contracts and purchase packages of services; Large enterprises demand extensive, sophisticated packages of services.
53 Ibid., ¶130.
54 See dissenting statement of Chairman Michael K. Powell regarding the announcement of the *Remand Order*, in which the Chairman stated:

> The nation will now embark on 51 major state proceedings to evaluate what elements will be unbundled and made available to CLECs. These decisions will be litigated through 51 different federal district courts. These 51 cases will likely be decided in multiple ways—some upholding the state, some overturning the state and little chance of regulatory and legal harmony among them at the end of the day. These 51 district court cases are likely to be heard by 12 Federal Courts of Appeals—do we expect they will all rule similarly? If not, we will eventually be back in the [. . .] same [Supreme] Court that vacated our excessively permissive unbundling regime in 1999.

Online. Available HTTP: <http://hraunfoss.fcc.gov/edocs_public/attachmatch/DOC-231344A3.pdf> (accessed July 25, 2004).
55 Remand Order, op. cit., ¶271.
56 Ibid., ¶272–5.
57 Ibid., ¶255 and ¶264.
58 Ibid., ¶328.
59 Ibid., ¶329.
60 Ibid., ¶359.
61 Ibid., ¶486–90.
62 Ibid., ¶551. Such databases include the line information database, toll free calling database, number portability database, calling name database, operator services/directory assistance databases, and the advanced intelligent network database. The 911 databases are excluded from the rule.
63 Ibid., ¶563.
64 359 F.3d 334 (D.C. Cir. 2004) ("USTA II").

65 Ibid., 565–6.
66 Ibid., 567.
67 Ibid., 568.
68 Ibid., 571.
69 Ibid., 574.
70 Ibid., 578.
71 Ibid., 572.
72 Ibid., 585.
73 First Report and Order, op. cit., ¶677–80.
74 Ibid., ¶620.
75 120 F.3d 753 (8th Cir. 1997).
76 AT&T, op. cit., 380.
77 *Verizon Communications Inc. v. FCC*, 535 U.S. 467 502, (2002).
78 B. J. Baumol, "Having your cake: how to preserve universal-service cross subsidies while facilitating competitive entry," *Yale Journal on Regulation* 16, 1999, pp. 1–17.
79 See, for example, M. J. Doane, D. S. Sibley, and M. A. Williams, "Response: having your cake—how to preserve universal-service cross subsidies while facilitating competitive entry," 16, *Yale Journal on Regulation*, (1999), pp. 311–25.
80 See, for example, A. Kahn, *Telecom Deregulation: The Abominable TELRIC-BS*, speech before the Manhattan Institute for Policy Research, October 1, 2002. Online. Available HTTP: <http/www.manhattan-institute.org/html/kahn. htm> (accessed May 30, 2004).
81 Ibid., p. 7.
82 Ibid., p. 6.
83 Remand Order, op. cit., ¶676.
84 Ibid., ¶684.
85 Ibid., ¶690.
86 USTA II, op. cit., 595.
87 E. A. Nowicki, "Competition in the local telecommunications market: legislate or litigate?" *Harvard Journal of Law & Technology* 9, 1996, pp. 353–73.
88 540 U.S. 398, (2004).
89 See Federal Communications Commission, Industry Analysis and Technology Division, Wireline Competition Bureau, *Trends in Telephone Service*, May 2004. Online. Available HTTP: <http://www.fcc.gov/Bureaus/Common_Carrier/ Reports/FCC- State_Link/IAD/trend504.pdf> (accessed May 30, 2004).

Case 5

Long distance telecommunications

Michael D. Pelcovits[1]

Introduction

The long distance industry in the United States has undergone several major structural changes over the past fifty years. The industry was monopolized and later dominated by the vertically-integrated AT&T monopoly for much of the twentieth century. Competitors entered some market segments in the 1960s, but faced significant problems competing with AT&T, until the 1984 divestiture of the integrated Bell System. Competition flourished for much of the past twenty years. In the last three or four years, the industry has undergone another major restructuring as the local Bell companies have been allowed to provide long distance service. This has been accompanied by a shift of the policymakers' focus to competition in the local market, and in the market for integrated local and long distance service.

Regulation and antitrust law have played major roles in the long distance industry over this entire period. While initially hostile to competition, the Federal Communications Commission (FCC), and later the Courts, moved aggressively to wedge open the market. This led to a long period where regulators attempted to impose interconnection requirements on the Bell System. In 1984, these efforts were supplanted by antitrust action that broke apart the Bell System and eliminated the need for the types of conduct regulation practiced ineffectually for so many years. Clearly, this industry provides a very rich and varied history, from which much can be learned about how competition policy functions in the United States.

History of access

Prior to the 1950s AT&T enjoyed a monopoly on long distance service in the United States. AT&T provided long distance service connecting the networks and subscribers of all of the local telephone companies. In most of the country, local telephone service was provided by AT&T's wholly-owned subsidiaries. A small minority of customers (approximately 20 percent nationwide) were served by unaffiliated, independent telephone companies.

Long distance service was provided over copper wires, which had to be run across the country. This created significant economies of scale in the industry. Advancements in microwave technology made during the Second World War, however, altered the scale economies of the business, and made it possible for very large customers to build their own systems. In the *Above 890 Decision* in 1959, the FCC responded to large customer demands for spectrum to operate their own systems and allowed them to obtain licenses to operate private systems. This initiated the competitive era in long distance telecommunications.

Over the 25 years following the *Above 890 Decision*, competition advanced very slowly in the long distance market. Following the success of private customers in obtaining microwave licenses, MCI applied to provide service on a common carrier basis in 1963. It took nearly ten years for MCI to obtain regulatory approval and construct its system before it initiated service in 1972. It took another six years (1978) before MCI was able to provide switched (direct dial) service. During this period, on account of all of the legal and regulatory obstacles to competition erected by AT&T and the FCC, MCI earned the well-deserved reputation of a "law firm with an antenna on top." During the period 1978 through 1983, MCI, SPCC (later acquired by Sprint), and other common carriers struggled to take about 10 percent of the market from AT&T, in spite of inferior access to the local exchange bottleneck. Table II.5.1 summarizes the major events during this period.

During the 1970s and early 1980s the Justice Department pursued an antitrust case against AT&T, alleging various anticompetitive acts in the long distance and other telecommunications markets. The case was settled

Table II.5.1 The long road to competition in long distance

Year	Event
1956	Above 890 Inquiry began into private long distance microwave licenses
1959	Above 890 Order grants private microwave licenses
1963	MCI application filed at FCC
1969	MCI Order approves application for Chicago–St. Louis private line service
1971	Specialized Common Carrier Decision allows competition in specialized private line service
1973	MCI files complaint against Bell companies for failure to interconnect
1974	FCC orders Bell companies to provide interconnection
1976	FCC orders MCI to cease providing switched services (Execunet I)
1977	Execunet I reversed by Court of Appeals
1978	Execunet II decision by Court of Appeals reaffirms right of MCI to offer switched service
1979	ENFIA tariff instituted for entrant's direct dial services
1980	Resale restrictions lifted from MTS/WATS services of ATT
1984	Divestiture of Bell System

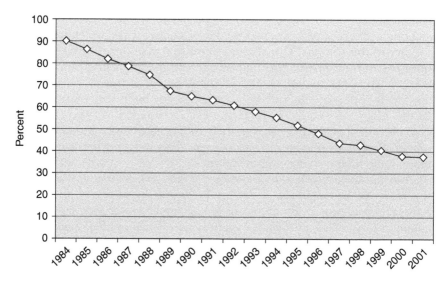

Figure II.5.1 AT&T's share of toll revenues, 1984–2001.

in 1982, when AT&T agreed to a divestiture that separated the local and long distance business. The Bell Operating Companies were divested from AT&T, and prohibited from offering interLATA long distance service, and required to provide "equal access" to other long distance providers. The restructuring of the industry eliminated anticompetitive incentives and behavior by the Bell companies in the interLATA long distance market, and without an artificial advantage, AT&T saw its dominance erode steadily over the next fifteen years, as shown in Figure II.5.1.[2]

The divestiture of AT&T did not eliminate all competition problems in the long distance market, because the Bell companies were still allowed to provide intraLATA toll service.[3] The Bell companies tried mightily to hold on to this business (worth about $12 billion in 1984), and refused to provide equal access to competitors for as long as possible. This meant that customers had to dial extra digits to place intraLATA toll calls on any carrier other than the local phone company, which essentially foreclosed very active competition in this market. Some states ordered equal access in the early 1990s, but it was not until the 1996 Telecommunications Act was implemented by the FCC (and then upheld in the Supreme Court in 1999) that the equal access process was completed. The result of this process can be seen in Table II.5.2, which shows the Bell companies' toll revenues during the post-Divestiture period.

Table II.5.2 Local exchange carrier toll revenue by year (1984–2001)

Year	Revenue (billions of dollars)
1984	12401
1985	12185
1986	12873
1987	13736
1988	15113
1989	14840
1990	14690
1991	14115
1992	13615
1993	13757
1994	13375
1995	11332
1996	11248
1997	10765
1998	10659
1999	9458
2000	9066
2001	8597

Source: Federal Communications Commission, *Trends in Telephone Service*, Table 10.7, May 2002

Key issues in access

Gerald Brock explains that there were three barriers to entry in the long distance market of the 1950s.[4] The first was the regulatory barriers established by FCC through its jurisdiction over radio frequency and licensing requirements for common carriers. The second was the interconnection restrictions imposed by AT&T. The third was the economies of scale in microwave transmission. Another factor that also played a major role was the pricing response of AT&T to competition.

The FCC's responsibility for spectrum allocation required it to determine initially whether the microwave frequencies could accommodate traffic from multiple licensees. The FCC decided that there was room in the spectrum for multiple providers, and thus allowed private carriers to provide services that were in direct competition with AT&T's common carrier services. Eventually, the FCC had to confront broader issues of competition policy, as it considered applications by common carriers to provide a broader range of services. The greatest obstacle faced by competitors was to convince the FCC (and state regulators) that the elaborate system of cross-subsidies built into telephone rates would either survive or could be modified to handle competition. This issue came to a head when MCI attempted to expand service from private lines to direct dialed (Message Telecommunications Service, or MTS) long distance. The FCC

supported AT&T's efforts to prevent MTS competition, but was overturned by the Court of Appeals, which let the competition genie out of
the bottle in 1978. Controversy over pricing and interconnection issues
continued at the FCC for several years but came to an abrupt halt with the
divestiture of AT&T in 1984.

Long distance competition would have been limited to service for very
large customers, if the entrants were not able to interconnect with the
local phone companies. Local telephone networks are subject to massive
economies of scale and scope, and therefore a long distance company
without interconnection rights would only have been able to serve the customers that it could connect to directly. (Economies of scale in the long
distance market were also a significant barrier to entry, except in the
densest markets. Competition would also have foundered if the FCC had
not mandated resale requirements on AT&T.) The *Specialized Common
Carrier Decision* issued by the FCC in 1971 ordered that the incumbent carriers "permit interconnection or leased channel arrangements on reasonable terms and conditions to be negotiated with the new carriers." The
actual process of interconnection involved abundant opportunities for
sabotage by AT&T, and required intense regulatory and legal intervention
(including a successful antitrust suit by MCI), before competitors could
implement a profitable business model.

The most enduring and notorious interconnection disputes related to
the method used for connecting a dial up call to a competitive long distance carrier. Prior to divestiture, the connections used by the new
entrants were identical to an ordinary business line, rather than the
higher-quality, trunk-side connection used by AT&T. These connections
were noisier, required customers to dial extra digits, and made it difficult
for the entrants to bill accurately for the length of calls. To compensate
for these inferior connections, the entrants were given a discount off the
supposed payments made by AT&T to the local operating companies. But
even this issue was shrouded in controversy, because the flow of payments
between the different Bell System subsidiaries was so complex and convo-
luted. Notwithstanding these handicaps, the new entrants were able to
make a dent in some parts of the long distance market.

AT&T responded to competition in the private line market immediately with a new tariff, Telpak, which offered large discounts on bulk
private line purchases. Later on, AT&T introduced geographical deaver-
aged prices for the first time, which were aimed at lowering prices along
the routes where they faced competition, and raising prices elsewhere.
These tariffs were subject to lengthy contests at the FCC and also became
a major focus of predatory pricing claims before the Courts. Although
commendable as a full employment act for economists, the proceedings
did not provide much certainty or clarity to the market.

The barriers to entry in this market were powerful and self-reinforcing.
The FCC and AT&T imposed substantial financial costs and enormous delay

on the entrants to the point that the future of competition was very much in doubt throughout the 1960s and 1970s. Although MCI and SPCC started to turn the corner and increase revenues substantially in the early 1980s, it is difficult to tell how successful they would have been absent divestiture.

Regulation and structural separation

The long distance industry provides an excellent test case of the effectiveness of structural separation compared to regulation. Prior to 1984, the industry was embroiled in intense and complex regulatory and legal battles over access issues. The issues were never resolved satisfactorily and competition was limited to some private line markets and to direct dial customers who were willing to purchase an inferior service at a lower price. By contrast, within a short time after divestiture, the vast majority of customers had equal access to all long distance carriers. The access method ordered by the Court and the FCC (requiring customers to pre-subscribed to their long distance carrier of choice) and the ease and low costs associated with changing carriers, encouraged hundreds of companies to enter the long distance market within a very short period of time.[5] AT&T began the post-divestiture period with more than a 90 percent share of the long distance market, and lost market share steadily over the past fifteen years to reach a 34 percent share in the year 2001.

The line of business restrictions imposed on the regional Bell Operating Companies (RBOCs) was the key to making divestiture work. The theory of the Modified Final Judgment (MFJ) was that the RBOCs would lose the incentive to discriminate against any long distance company, because they would no longer have any financial interest in this line of business. The theory proved to be correct. There were no allegations of an RBOC purposely providing preferential treatment to AT&T or any other long distance company, except when they received some exemptions to the line of business restrictions.

The intraLATA toll market was a different story. The Divestiture Decree did not rule on whether entry or equal access was required in this market. Therefore, until the Telecommunications Act was passed in 1996, regulations governing this market were set by the state commissions. Some state commissions did not allow intraLATA competition for several years after divestiture, because of the concern that the RBOCs needed subsidies from intraLATA toll to keep local rates low. Almost all states allowed the RBOCs to retain a monopoly on pre-subscription to intraLATA toll to help insulate them from competition. And even where one-plus pre-subscription was ordered by the state commission, the implementation was bogged down for years, repeating the pre-divestiture experience with interstate long distance. IntraLATA equal access did not become widespread until the Telecommunications Act ordered it on a nationwide basis within three years of passage of the Act.

Measures of success

Long distance rates have fallen dramatically since divestiture. The Consumer Price Index (CPI) for interstate toll service, which potentially *underestimates* the actual decline in rates, shows rates falling in real terms by 68 percent between 1984 and 2003. Other studies that look at the change in average revenue per minute paid by long distance customers showed even greater declines in long distance prices.[6] As mentioned above, during the same period, AT&T's market share fell abruptly from over 90 percent, while the number and type of new entrants proliferated.[7]

This does not imply that all economists regard divestiture as a successful policy intervention that led to robust competition in the long distance market. According to some economists, the post-divestiture long distance market was characterized by a collusive oligopoly of AT&T, MCI and Sprint, which were able to maintain high prices and high margins especially in residential long distance markets.[8] These economists argue that the decline in long distance prices is fully explained by declines in per minute access charges, and that indeed long distance carriers did not even pass on their full access reductions. These claims were made in the course of proceedings where the Bell companies were applying for the authority to enter the long distance market. The Bell companies, and the economists they hired, argued that substantial barriers to entry existed in the long distance market. They also argued that the Bell companies, which were restricted from competing in this market by the Divestiture Decree, were uniquely positioned to enter and compete for customers in the long distance market.

The Telecommunications Act of 1996 created a process that the Bell companies could follow to enter the long distance market. In exchange for opening their local telephone markets to competition, the Bells were allowed to enter the long distance market (on a state-by-state basis). This process has now been completed and the Bell companies have been authorized to enter the long distance market nationwide.

The Bell companies have taken market share away rapidly from the long distance companies' share very quickly. For example, Verizon reports

Table II.5.3 Verizon long distance penetration

Year	Quarter	Penetration (percent)
2002	4	28
2003	1	30
	2	35
	3	39
	4	41

Source: Online. Available HTTP: <http://investor.verizon.com/news/20040205/>, Slide 13 (accessed July 20, 2004).

its long distance penetration rate of 41 percent, as of the fourth quarter in 2003 (see Table II.5.3).[9] Also, subscribers' appetite for bundles of telecommunications services (e.g., local, long distance, DSL) has grown enormously. Verizon reports that in 2003, 47.9 percent of its customers purchased bundles, compared to 21.6 percent in 2001.[10]

Conclusion

Competition in the long distance industry would not have been possible over the last 50 years without regulatory and legal intervention. The divestiture of AT&T, and the quarantine of the local Bell company monopolies, permitted the new entrants to increase their market share rapidly and eroded the market power of AT&T. The structure of this industry, however, is undergoing massive change, with the reentry of the Bell companies in the market. All of the major telecommunications carriers are integrating backward or forward into local and long distance markets, and the nexus of competition has shifted to bundled offerings. Whether this bundled service market will be competitive depends upon how technology, law, and regulation affect the barriers to entry in the local market.

Notes

1 Principal, Microeconomic Consulting and Research Associates (MiCRA), Inc.
2 Figure II.5.1 data taken from Federal Communications Commission, *Trends in Telephone Service*, May 2002, Table 10.8. Online. Available HTTP: <http://www.fcc.gov/Bureaus/Common_Carrier/Reports/FCC-State_Link/IAD/trend502.pdf> (accessed June 15, 2004).
3 The Divestiture Decree defined the Local Access and Transport Areas (LATA) as the areas within which the Bell companies were allowed to carry calls. The portion of the U.S. served by the Bell companies was divided into 162 LATAs. In less populated areas, the LATAs covered very large geographic areas—up to an entire state. In more densely populated areas, the LATAs included large metropolitan areas, including many nearby suburbs and more rural areas. For example, the New York Metro LATA included all of New York City, Long Island, and Westchester County.
4 G. W Brock, *The Telecommunications Industry: The Dynamics of Market Structure*, Cambridge, Massachusetts: Harvard University Press, 1981, p. 198.
5 By the end of 1985, 256 carrier identification codes were assigned. *Trends in Telephone Service*, Washington, D.C.: Federal Communications Commission, May 2002, Table 10.5. Online. Available HTTP: <http://www.fcc.gov/Bureaus/Common_Carrier/Reports/FCC-State_Link/IAD/trend502.pdf> (accessed June 15, 2004). Although individual carriers sometimes hold more than one code, the number of carriers is unlikely to have been below 200.
6 See generally, R. E. Hall, *Long Distance: Public Benefits From Increased Competition*, Menlo Park, California: Applied Economic Partners, October 1993.
7 Several long distance carriers built nationwide long distance networks and

competed across-the-board for all types of customers. Hundreds of other companies entered the market as resellers using a variety of marketing approaches. One surprisingly effective means of entry was to offer service on a "dial-around" basis, whereby customers were encouraged to select a carrier on a call-by-call basis rather than through pre-subscription.

8 See generally, P. W. MacAvoy, *The Failure of Antitrust and Regulation to Establish Competition in Long-Distance Telephone Service,* Cambridge, Massachusetts: MIT Press and AEI Press, 1996.

9 See generally, Verizon, RBC Capital Markets Telecommunications Conference, Banff, Alberta, February 5, 2004, Slide 13. Online. Available HTTP: <http://investor.verizon.com/news/20040205/> (accessed July 20, 2004).

10 Ibid.

Case 6

Broadband

Richard M. Brunell[1]

Should cable television companies be required to open their cable networks for unaffiliated Internet service providers (ISPs) to offer residential high speed Internet service ("broadband") over cable lines? The debate over this question has been simmering for several years before the Federal Communications Commission (FCC), and elsewhere, but remains unresolved.[2]

High speed, "always-on" Internet access has been dubbed the "third generation internet."[3] By allowing transfer speeds hundreds of times faster than "narrowband" or "dial-up" access, broadband not only enhances the functionality of existing Internet services, but promises a vast array of new services enabled by increased bandwidth, such as video-on-demand, telemedicine, full-featured software applications, and long distance learning, among other things.[4] Congress made broadband deployment a national priority in the Telecommunications Act of 1996,[5] and even the presidential candidates in the 2004 campaign noted its importance.[6] It is estimated that high speed Internet access is available to approximately 80 percent of all households in the U.S.,[7] although only 20 percent of all households actually subscribed to broadband service as of year-end 2003.[8]

Since its commercial introduction around 1998, broadband has been principally available from cable operators over their hybrid fiber-coaxial cables in the form of "cable modem" service, which now accounts for approximately two-thirds of all broadband lines.[9] Broadband is also available in many locations from local exchange carriers (telephone companies) over copper telephone lines in the form of digital subscriber line (DSL) service, which accounts for approximately one-third of all broadband lines.[10] Other technologies for providing broadband include terrestrial fixed wireless, satellite, WIFI, and broadband over power lines, although these technologies currently have quite limited applicability, and their competitive future significance is uncertain at best.[11]

The open-access movement

The "open-access" movement began soon after residential cable modem service was commercially introduced. At the time, cable operators offered, or planned to offer, cable modem service exclusively through Excite@Home, which was owned by a consortium of cable operators, or Road Runner, which was controlled by Time Warner. A coalition of ISPs, local exchange carriers, consumer activists, and others (led by America Online prior to its merger with Time Warner) sought to condition AT&T's acquisition of TCI (then the nation's largest cable operator) on AT&T providing "open" or "equal" access to unaffiliated ISPs over TCI's high-speed cable lines. Open-access advocates contended that the merged entity would seek to maintain exclusive control over high speed transport through its Excite@Home affiliate or otherwise discriminate against unaffiliated ISPs.[12] They argued that the success of the "narrowband" Internet was premised on the availability of non-discriminatory access over telephone lines.[13] And some, particularly local exchange carriers, maintained that "regulatory parity" dictated open access because incumbent local exchange carriers had to provide such access when offering DSL broadband service.[14]

The FCC declined to impose an open-access requirement on AT&T, apparently satisfied with the company's commitment that it would not deny any customer the ability to access the Internet content or portal of his or her choice.[15] The Commission noted that other methods of providing high speed Internet access were emerging and that it would monitor broadband deployment closely.[16] A subsequent FCC staff report urged the Commission to continue its policy of "vigilant restraint," concluding that applying "prophylactic" open-access measures to the "nascent" broadband industry "would be unsound public policy that could have the unintended effect of impeding the rapid development of this industry."[17] The Commission continued its "hands off" broadband policy in approving AT&T's subsequent acquisition of MediaOne,[18] and Comcast's acquisition of AT&T Broadband.[19] Open-access advocates had some successes at the local level, when certain franchise authorities imposed open-access requirements on AT&T in connection with its acquisitions of TCI or MediaOne. But these successes were short lived, as the courts found such requirements preempted by federal law.[20]

In 2002, the FCC dealt a blow to open-access advocates when it issued a ruling declaring that cable modem service was not subject to common carrier regulation as a "telecommunications service" under Title II of the Communications Act, including the common carrier requirements of non-discriminatory access.[21] Rather, the Commission concluded that cable modem service was an interstate "information service," and that the transmission component of cable modem service was not a "telecommunications service" but merely "telecommunications."[22] At the same time, the FCC acknowledged that as an interstate information service, cable modem service was at least potentially subject to the Commission's less stringent ancillary jurisdiction under Title I of the Communications Act, and the Commission sought comment on whether it could or should impose some type of access requirement under its Title I authority.[23] In a decision currently on appeal in the Supreme Court, the Ninth Circuit reversed the FCC's ruling on cable modem transport, reaffirming the court's prior determination that the transmission element of cable modem service *is* a "telecommunications service" subject to common carrier regulation under Title II.[24] Even so, the Commission could forbear from applying common carrier requirements, and it had indicated it would do so if reversed by the Ninth Circuit.[25] In short, the regulatory treatment of cable modem service remains unsettled, and the Commission is evidently in no hurry to regulate or resolve the legal or policy questions surrounding open access.

While so far declining to impose an open-access requirement on cable operators, the Commission has proposed liberalizing the regulatory treatment of local exchange carriers that offer DSL service.[26] The Commission previously imposed open-access requirements on local exchange carriers' DSL offerings for the benefit of unaffiliated ISPs under its *Computer Inquiry* rules.[27] However, those requirements may be lifted as a result of the Commission's new "tentative conclusions" that high speed broadband service over telephone lines, like cable modem service, is an "information service" and does not contain a "telecommunications service" element.[28]

AOL/Time Warner merger

The high-water mark of the broadband open-access movement was reached with the AOL/Time Warner merger, when the Federal Trade Commission imposed (by consent order) a "multiple" access requirement as a condition of approving the merger. Specifically, Time Warner was required to make available at least three non-affiliated ISPs on its cable systems and to negotiate access agreements in good faith with other ISPs, subject to certain constraints.[29] The FTC's grounds for imposing the access requirement are not entirely transparent. The Commission recited that residential broadband Internet access service is a relevant market (distinct from narrowband access), which would become substantially more concentrated due to the combination of Time Warner's controlling interest in Road Runner with AOL's broadband service over non-cable broadband transmission facilities (i.e. DSL). According to the FTC, because of AOL's installed base of narrowband subscribers, it was "positioned and likely to become the leading provider of broadband Internet access as well."[30] But the multiple-access requirement appears designed not so much to remedy the loss in horizontal competition (or, more accurately, potential competition) between AOL and Road Runner, but rather to address Time Warner's incentives to exclude unaffiliated ISP rivals from its cable systems, which arguably did not materially change as a result of the merger.[31] The FCC's decision on the merger, which it approved subject to certain additional conditions discussed below, focused more directly on the foreclosure issue.

The FCC found that the merged company would have the ability and incentive to discriminate against unaffiliated ISPs based on Time Warner's "natural inclination to maximize the value of its cable network by converting its captive base of Time Warner cable customers into customers of ISPs affiliated with the merged firm" and AOL's incentive to ensure that its narrowband subscribers that migrate to broadband do not select a competing high speed ISP.[32] The FCC did not see DSL as sufficiently available in Time Warner service areas to constrain the merged firm, "at least in the short term."[33] The FCC rejected Time Warner's argument that it had an incentive to permit unaffiliated ISPs to interconnect with its cable network (and was willing to do so voluntarily) to encourage the adoption of "open access" by other cable operators, who controlled the other 80 percent of cable subscribers nationwide to which AOL needed access. On the contrary, the FCC concluded that AOL Time Warner—with its leading brand among ISPs and the largest library of proprietary content in the world at its disposal—would be able to secure access to other cable systems and would do so regardless of whether it discriminated against unaffiliated ISPs on its own platform.[34] The FCC has subsequently indicated that *AOL/Time Warner* should not be considered a precedent for cable open access generally because it involved a "unique combination of services, facilities, and content."[35]

The terms of the debate

The debate over broadband open access centers largely on three issues—whether cable operators are likely to engage in monopoly leveraging, whether open access promotes or hinders investment and innovation, and whether cable operators should be regulated like telephone companies offering DSL broadband service.[36]

Monopoly leveraging

The principal argument offered in support of a mandatory access requirement is a "monopoly leveraging" or "essential facilities" argument which posits that cable lines are effectively a "bottleneck" facility to which cable operators have the incentive and ability to limit access in order to gain market power or obtain an advantage in complementary markets, primarily the ISP market. ISPs can provide many functions beyond the connection to the Internet itself. Many also provide customer support, ancillary web-surfing functions such as caching and server-based filtering, and services such as e-mail, chat rooms, news groups, web hosting, content aggregation, and other services.[37] Beyond the ISP market, the concern is that cable operators may discriminate in the distribution of all kinds of broadband content, from streaming video that may compete with their core cable business, to unaffiliated e-commerce websites.[38] Competition in the

ISP market thus is valued not only for its direct effect on prices, quality, and innovation in that market, but for its indirect effect in preventing discrimination in content and services available on the Internet. Indeed, many of the advocates of open access, perhaps fearing that the ISP access battle cannot be won, have shifted to arguing that the FCC should impose a "network neutrality" regime, which would directly bar all broadband Internet service providers from discriminating against applications, content or devices that consumers may wish to use or access on the Internet.[39]

As the FCC has noted, "it is technically feasible for a cable operator to deny access to unaffiliated content, or to relegate unaffiliated content to the 'slow lane' of its residential high-speed Internet access service. . . ."[40] However, whether cable operators have the *economic* ability to limit access to unaffiliated content or ISPs depends critically on whether they have substantial market power in the local markets for broadband Internet transport ("last mile" access), or whether telephone companies' DSL lines are a satisfactory substitute for reaching broadband consumers. Both the Federal Trade Commission (FTC) and FCC in *AOL/Time Warner* apparently concluded that, because of its limited availability, DSL is not an adequate substitute.[41] Moreover, the high switching cost for consumers where both cable modem and DSL are available tends to reinforce cable operators' (and perhaps DSL providers') market power.[42]

Cable operators' *incentive* to "discriminate" against unaffiliated ISPs or unaffiliated broadband content depends on a variety of factors. It has been argued that cable operators have an incentive to make available as broad an array of content as consumers desire in order to increase usage of their high speed lines.[43] This argument is based on the standard Chicago School argument that an integrated monopolist can only earn a "single" monopoly profit and hence has no incentive to monopolize a complementary market. Open-access advocates have challenged this argument on theoretical and empirical grounds. In theory, the owner of a bottleneck facility may well be able to gain additional profits by restricting access to its facility if the complementary product is not always a complement (as is the case with ISPs or broadband content that can be delivered over other platforms) and if the restriction increases the demand for the bottleneck owner's complementary product (for example by preventing upstream competitors from reaching or maintaining minimum viable scale).[44] Or, the cable operator might provide favored or exclusive access even to an unaffiliated ISP or content provider in exchange for additional compensation.[45] Moreover, a cable operator may be able to discriminate in favor of affiliated content without losing any broadband sales if the discrimination is not detectable by consumers. Or, a cable operator may limit ISP access in order to engage in price discrimination.[46]

In practice, most cable systems offer only one, affiliated broadband Internet access service, although there are notable exceptions.[47] Indeed, the cable industry argued that it has "moved with remarkable speed to provide their customers with a choice of ISPs despite the enormous technical difficulties and costs involved," making a mandatory access requirement unnecessary.[48] Open-access advocates contend that the industry has moved slowly and partially in the direction of multiple access, largely as a result of government pressure. Moreover, the "multiple access" that has been offered has been criticized as merely a "rebranding" exercise, in which the cable operator retains the technical ability to discriminate against unaffiliated content and applications.[49] Cable operators, whether or not offering multiple ISPs, apparently have placed certain limits on the applications available to subscribers, although it is disputed whether these limits are anticompetitive.[50]

Innovation and investment

The second argument offered in support of open access is that such a requirement preserves the "end-to-end" architecture of the Internet, which is said to be a source of its tremendous innovativeness. According to Professors Lemley and Lessig, the end-to-end design principle "counsels that the 'intelligence' in a network should be located at the top of a layered system—at its 'ends,' where users put information and applications onto the network. The communications protocols themselves (the 'pipes' through which information flows) should be as simple and general as possible."[51] Implicit in this design is the principle of nondiscrimination among applications, which has been a hallmark of the telephone network on which the Internet was built.[52] According to Lemley and Lessig, the Internet has enabled extraordinary innovation because of its open nature: potential innovators know that their inventions that use the Internet will be used if useful. Permitting cable operators to restrict broadband Internet access violates the end-to-end principle, and thereby is likely to retard innovation.[53] According to Lemley and Lessig, even if cable operators do not actually discriminate against any particular application, the mere threat of discrimination increases the risk that potential innovators must take into account and thus chills innovation.[54]

The flip side of the end-to-end innovation argument is the claim that "forced" access will reduce the returns earned by cable operators on their infrastructure investments and thereby reduce their incentives to develop the infrastructure in the first place. Concomitantly, it is argued that mandatory access will reduce the incentives of ISPs to develop alternative platforms to cable broadband. This standard "property rights" critique of mandatory access requirements is at least facially plausible in the context of an infrastructure that is still in the process of being built, and was one of the cable industry's principal arguments at the outset of the open-access debate.[55] Even now, after "very substantial broadband cable investment (in the form of updated cable plant) has ... taken place," the cable industry maintains that the investment incentives argument retains force because some systems remain to be upgraded and "it is the systems and subscribers that have not yet been updated to broadband that, as a logical matter, promise the lowest returns on investment."[56] Moreover, the industry maintains that the "growing use of broadband service will require continuous investment in smaller nodes in order to maintain quality of service standards."[57]

The incentives issue cannot be resolved by simply not regulating the price of access, as some have suggested,[58] because, if the cable operator is free to charge whatever it wants, it may set the price so high to effectively deny access.[59] Nor can the issue of reduced incentives be resolved by allowing cable operators to charge the full "monopoly price" for broadband transport, without allowance for lost profits on affiliated content, even if such a price could be feasibly calculated. First, limiting cable companies' profits available from complementary markets reduces their investment incentives, particularly if profits are reduced on services already provided by the cable company (e.g., video programming). Second, a single "monopoly price" for access may not maximize cable companies' profits in the market for broadband transport.[60] Nonetheless, a relatively permissive pricing scheme should at least significantly mitigate any incentives concern.

In any event, recognizing that open access may reduce cable companies' incentives to invest does not mean that the incentives will be insufficient to induce them to complete the upgrade of their cable systems. Indeed, it is widely recognized that the cable industry's principal motive to upgrade the companies' cable plants has not been to offer broadband Internet service, but rather to improve their video offerings to compete with direct broadcast satellite,[61] or to offer telephone service.[62] By all accounts, the incremental cost of upgrading a cable system for broadband Internet access, once it has been upgraded for increased bandwidth generally, is not substantial.[63] Moreover, it hardly seems plausible that an open-access requirement would lead cable operators to refrain from making the ongoing investments necessary to maintain service quality as usage increases, particularly in the face of competition from DSL.[64] Finally, one might be willing to accept a slower deployment of broadband facilities as a cost of open access if innovation in the long run would be advanced.[65]

Regulatory parity and DSL open access

Open-access advocates originally argued that regulatory consistency favored an open-access requirement on cable operators since incumbent telephone companies had to make their DSL lines available to unaffiliated ISPs on an open and non-discriminatory basis.[66] The telephone companies strongly endorsed this view, opening up a regulatory food fight between the two industries.[67] Subsequently, the telephone companies have taken the argument a step further and argued that if open-access requirements are *not* going to be applied to cable operators, then regulatory parity dictates that such requirements be eliminated for DSL services offered over telephone lines, a move that the FCC is now considering. Indeed, the telephone companies maintain that the justification for mandatory access is much weaker for DSL than for cable broadband because cable dominates the broadband market, and the telephone companies have no video services to protect. Moreover, the phone companies point to the fact that they will have to spend as much as $200 billion to replace copper wires with end-to-end fiber optic transmission facilities to match the capabilities of existing cable networks, which they say cannot be justified under a "one-sided regulatory regime."[68]

The cable industry has maintained that asymmetric broadband regulation is justified and that DSL open-access rules should not be lifted for several reasons.[69] First, cable companies contend that, even though cable has two-thirds of the broadband market on a national basis, telephone DSL facilities are still a bottleneck for reaching most business customers and for many residential areas where cable broadband is not available.[70] Second, the cable industry argues that telephone companies' interest in preventing "cannibalization" of their narrowband and "second line" revenues limits their incentive to speed the deployment of DSL and provide access to competing DSL providers.[71] Third, the cable industry argues that telephone company incentives to invest will not be lessened because the price for access can properly take into account the costs and risks of investments made to upgrade wireline facilities for broadband, including "fiber-to-the-curb investments."[72] Moreover, telephone companies have other incentives to upgrade their facilities, including cost savings on voice and narrowband services, and competition from cable operators.[73] Finally, the cable industry argues that the wireline infrastructure on which DSL is offered was paid for by ratepayers under a regulatory regime that shielded incumbent local exchange carriers from competition, whereas the cable industry has spent billions of "private risk capital" on its facilities with no guarantee of earnings.[74]

Complaints that the cable industry is engaged in rank hypocrisy are easy to understand, particularly when cable companies contend that DSL lines are bottlenecks *because* ISPs lack access to cable broadband.[75] While there are certain plausible reasons not to deregulate access to DSL lines regardless of the cable broadband regulatory regime (namely, eliminating DSL open access would upset settled expectations[76] and DSL open access may promote competition in local telephone service[77]), the cable industry's attempt to justify asymmetric regulation is strained at best. The incentive and ability of cable operators and telephone companies to restrict access seems comparable. Both platforms have similar incentives to limit certain applications (e.g., streaming video over cable; IP telephony over

DSL) and favor affiliated ISPs and content. And, absent regulation, both platforms have similar abilities to do so. In many areas, only one or the other is available; and where both are available, switching costs and other factors give each a degree of market power, as evidenced by the relatively high prices for retail broadband service and the fact that competition from DSL has not spurred most cable operators to offer multiple ISPs. Moreover, the cost of open access, in terms of the potential incentive effect on investment and the cost of implementation, also seems comparable. As for the legacy of rate regulation of telephone service as a justification for DSL open access, it can similarly be argued that much of the cable infrastructure was built under the monopoly protection of *de facto* exclusive local franchises and "paid for" by cable rate payers.[78]

Versions of cable open access

Open-access advocates have proposed three principal models for cable modem open access: a "network neutrality" model, the *AOL/Time Warner* multiple ISP access regime, and a model based on the *Computer Inquiries* unbundling requirements, which currently applies to DSL.

"Network neutrality"

Many open-access advocates are apparently willing to concede cable operator exclusivity over broadband Internet access as long as cable operator ISPs are required to maintain neutrality as to content, applications, and services available from the Internet. Thus, a coalition of online content companies, consumer groups, and consumer electronics manufacturers has proposed a rule that would prohibit a broadband network operator from, "on a discriminatory or unreasonable basis, interfer[ing] with or impair[ing] subscribers' ability to use their broadband service to access lawful Internet content or services, use applications or services in connection with their broadband service, or attach nonharmful devices to the network."[79] A network neutrality regime would permit broadband operators to impose usage limitations necessary for network administration and to prevent harm to the network or other users.[80] But the limitations could not be based on "inter-network criteria," such as IP address, domain name, cookie information, TCP port, and so forth.[81] Thus, for example, a network operator would be free to limit a customer's bandwidth usage generally, but could not prohibit particular bandwidth-intensive uses.[82]

One problem with the network neutrality model—and any direct prohibition of content discrimination as an alternative to ISP open access—is that it ignores the value of independent ISPs. The advent of cable broadband has led to a dramatic decline in the number of ISPs, and even the largest independent ISPs may not survive without access to cable facilities, except perhaps as web portals.[83] The demise of the independent ISP may involve a significant social loss; some have suggested that "[t]hese small, entrepreneurial enterprises play a critical role in facilitating deployment, expanding adoption by the public and servicing niche markets."[84]

Indeed, one of the values of ISPs is that they can provide certain forms of content "discrimination" that may be desired by consumers. A good example is caching (local storage) of web content. Caching of web content on ISP servers permits faster downloads of that content. It would be highly objectionable if caching were used by an ISP to favor certain content if consumers had no choice in ISP.[85] However, some consumers may prefer such caching, either because they prefer the content that is favored, or perhaps they are willing to tolerate it in exchange for lower rates, just as some consumers subscribe to "free" ISPs that bombard them with advertising. Similarly, server-based filtering of content may be desired by some consumers, but could not be tolerated if undertaken by a sole broadband ISP.[86] ISPs may also provide other kinds of preferential treatment for their content "partners," such as exclusive links on their home pages, which might be acceptable in a multiple ISP environment, but which raises troubling questions if consumers have no choice of ISP.

By the same token, if consumers do have a choice of ISP, content discrimination is of less concern. Thus, for example, in *AOL/Time Warner*, the FCC declined to impose any requirement that AOL (as an ISP) refrain from discriminating against unaffiliated content providers because consumers would have a choice of ISPs on the Time Warner cable platform. Although the FCC noted that there was some evidence that AOL sought to limit its members' access to unaffiliated content on the web, [87] the Commission concluded that the requirement that Time Warner provide access to multiple ISPs on its cable systems would largely mitigate its incentive and ability to withhold unaffiliated content from AOL subscribers.[88] Another factor favoring ISP open access as a remedy for content discrimination is that ISP open access arguably would be more "structural" and less intrusive than a network neutrality regime insofar as it allowed regulators to focus on a small number of interconnection arrangements with ISPs, rather than the cable operator's conduct toward the entire universe of potential broadband content.[89]

The FTC multiple ISP access model

As noted above, the FTC required Time Warner to make available at least three non-affiliated ISPs on its cable systems and to negotiate access agreements with other ISPs, subject to certain constraints.[90] Time Warner's initial agreement was with Earthlink, which was approved by the FTC prior to the consent order and was the model for the other ISP agreements Time Warner was required to enter. Alternatively, under a most-favored-nations clause required by the FTC, unaffiliated ISPs that entered into agreements with Time Warner would be entitled to the same terms that AOL might obtain in its ISP agreements with other cable operators.[91]

While the FTC's role in fashioning the terms of the Earthlink agreement apparently has not been publicly reported, and it is unclear to what extent, if any, Time Warner's arrangement with its affiliated Road Runner service served as a model for the Earthlink agreement, the regulatory task undertaken by the FTC was rather simple: potentially difficult issues of pricing and the terms of access were left to the parties to negotiate, subject to the background requirement that an agreement had to be reached.[92] AOL's position as an ISP seeking access on other cable systems served as a backstop template. However, the FTC order did specify certain non-discrimination terms. Time Warner was: prohibited from "interfer[ing] in any way, directly or indirectly," with content passed along the bandwidth contracted for by the ISP;[93] required to provide the same physical connection point to unaffiliated ISPs that it provided to its affiliated ISPs;[94] and was required to provide the same service levels and network monitoring flow data to unaffiliated ISPs that it provided to its affiliated ISPs.[95] The FCC added certain conditions strengthening the non-discrimination provisions.[96]

The Time Warner arrangements with ISPs are described by the FCC and Time Warner "as a kind of partnership" "in which the [unaffiliated] ISP and cable operator ... offer an integrated Internet service to consumers and both retain a direct interest in providing the service to the consumer."[97] Time Warner analogizes the business model to that of a pay cable service and a cable operator, in which each share the revenue from each subscriber.[98] This multiple access model has been criticized for precisely this reason, because the "partnership" may give too much control to the cable operator. Indeed, as noted above, some critics maintain that the *AOL/Time Warner* model involves ISPs merely "rebranding" the service provided by the cable operator. According to one report, under the multiple access regime adopted by Time Warner and other cable operators, the ISP does not even provide any physical link to the Internet backbone; rather, the link is provided by Time Warner.[99] According to this report, the "end result of this rebranding scenario is that multiple ISPs offer the same Internet connection and restricted services as a single ISP" provided by the cable operator."[100]

Computer II unbundling

Some open-access proponents[101] advocate the application of the unbundling requirements of the FCC's *Computer II* rules.[102] Those rules simply require that carriers that own common carrier transmission facilities and provide "enhanced services" (now "information services") must acquire transmission capacity pursuant to tariff and give competing enhanced service providers access to their facilities under the same rates, terms and conditions.[103] Such a regime seemingly offers more liberal access than the *AOL/Time Warner* model in that it potentially allows for unlimited access, while *AOL/Time Warner* allows for limits on access based on capacity constraints, technical limitations, and broadband business considerations.[104] However, any model of ISP access would have to take technical limitations into account; multiple access may be all that is feasible. Moreover, the *Computer II* access regime appears to have the same drawback as the *AOL/Time Warner* model in that it permits the cable operator to impose limits on how the network is used, provided the limits are imposed on the affiliated and unaffiliated ISPs alike. The cable operator may retain substantial control over the connection to the ISP. Furthermore, determining the terms of access might still be difficult. While the cable operator's arrangement with its affiliated ISP might be a useful basis for determining the physical interconnection terms for competing ISPs, such non-arm's-length dealing hardly seems a reasonable basis for establishing the price of access and other financial terms.

Conclusion

The lack of consensus in the broadband open-access debate does not reflect a fundamental disagreement about the relevant policy goals. Although there is some question as to the value of ISP competition over the same platform, there seems to be little dispute over the goal of promoting competition, diversity and innovation in the content and services available from the broadband Internet. And there seems to be a consensus that an "open" or "free" Internet is an essential ingredient in achieving this goal. Indeed, the chairman of the FCC has lauded the openness of the Internet, noting that "ensuring that consumers can obtain and use the content, applications and devices they want is critical to unlocking the vast potential of the broadband Internet."[105]

The debate over open access is principally over the extent to which cable broadband operators (or other platform owners), in the absence of regulation, are likely to limit that openness, and discriminate in the distribution of broadband content. According to Chairman Powell, while "[a] few troubling restrictions have appeared in broadband service plan agreements," the "case for government imposed regulations regarding the use or provision of broadband content, applications and devices is unconvincing and speculative."[106] Contrariwise, open-access advocates focus on the instances where restrictions have been imposed, and the chilling effect on innovation from the mere potential for discrimination. The empirical evidence is somewhat clouded by the fact the FCC's scrutiny may be responsible for inhibiting cable operators from restricting access. Ironically, the FCC's endless "watchful waiting" approach may have a certain logic, as it encourages the cable broadband providers to operate their networks in a neutral fashion, while deferring regulation until the broadband networks are built out and the risk of impairing investment incentives is minimized.

Notes

1 Roger Williams University (rbrunell@rwu.edu).
2 See generally Inquiry Concerning High-Speed Access to the Internet Over Cable and Other Facilities, Internet Over Cable Declaratory Ruling, Appropriate Regulatory Treatment for Broadband Access to the Internet Over Cable Facilities, 17 FCC Rcd. 4798 (2002) (Declaratory Ruling and Notice of Proposed Rulemaking) (*"Cable Modem NPRM"*).
3 F. Barr, S. Cohen, P. Cowhey, B. DeLong, M. Kleeman, J. Zysman, "Access and innovation policy for the third-generation internet," *Telecommunications Policy* 24, 2000, p. 489.
4 See Barr *et al.*, op. cit., p. 493; Applications for Consent to Transfer of Control of Licenses and Section 214 Authorization by Time Warner, Inc. and America Online, 16 FCC Rcd. 6547, 6575 ¶69 (2001) (*"FCC AOL/Time Warner Merger Order"*). The FCC observes that high speed "applications so completely change the experience of using the Internet that the difference can be likened to the contrast between looking at a still photograph and watching a movie." Ibid. According to the International Telecommunication Union, "the term broadband typically describes recent Internet connections that range from 5 times to 2000 times faster than earlier Internet dial-up technologies." International Telecommunication Union, Birth of Broadband—Frequently Asked Questions, September 2003. Online. Available HTTP: <http://www.itu.int/osg/spu/publications/birthofbroadband/faq-en.html> (accessed June 4, 2004). The FCC presently defines "high speed" services as involving the ability to send or receive information at speeds higher than 200 kbps (while a standard dial-up connection allows transfer speeds of up to 56 kbps). See Inquiry Concerning Deployment of Advanced Telecommunications Capability to All Americans in a Reasonable and Timely Fashion, and Possible Steps to Accelerate Such Deployment Pursuant to Section 706 of the Telecommunications Act of 1996, 17 FCC Rcd. 2844, 2850–51 ¶9 (2002) (Third Report) (*"Third 706 Report"*).
5 Telecommunications Act of 1996, Pub. L. No. 104–104, 110 Stat. 56, Title VII, § 706(a) (1996) (providing that the Federal Communications Commission and each state public utility commission "shall encourage the deployment on a reasonable and timely basis of advanced telecommunications capability to all Americans").
6 See President George W. Bush, Remarks at the American Association of Community Colleges Annual Convention, Minneapolis Convention Center, Minneapolis, Minnesota, April 26, 2004. Online. Available HTTP: <http://www.whitehouse.gov/news/releases/2004/04/20040426–6.html> (accessed June 4, 2004); J. Darman, "Broadband in every pot: how high-speed internet access became an issue in campaign 2004," *Newsweek*, May 14, 2004. Online. Available HTTP: <http://www.msnbc.msn.com/id/4980129/site/newsweek/> (accessed June 4, 2004).
7 *Cable Modem NPRM*, op. cit., 4803 ¶9 (noting that industry analysts estimated

high speed service was then available to 75–80 percent of households via DSL or cable modem service).

8 See Jupitermedia Corp., Press Release, *Jupiter Research Reports U.S. Broadband Adoption Surpassed 20 Million U.S. Households in 2003 and Will Grow to 46 Million by 2008*, January 29, 2004. Online. Available HTTP: <http://www.jupitermedia.com/corporate/releases/04.01.29-newjupresearch.html> (accessed June 4, 2004). The U.S. ranks eleventh worldwide in broadband usage, with a penetration rate less than one-third that of Korea, the world leader. See *International Telecommunication Union, ITV Internet Reports: Birth Of Broadband*, Executive Summary, Figure 1, 2003, Online. Available HTTP: <http://www.itu.int/osg/spu/publications/sales/birthofbroadband/BoBexecsumm.pdf> (accessed June 4, 2004).

9 See Federal Communications Commission, Wireline Competition Bureau, *High-Speed Services for Internet Access: Status as of June 30, 2003*, Washington, D.C.: Federal Communications Commission, December 2003, Table 5.

10 Ibid.

11 See *Cable Modem NPRM*, op. cit., 4803–4804 ¶9 (noting that analysts estimated that technologies other than DSL and cable modem accounted for only about 3 percent of all broadband customers).

12 See, for example, America Online, Inc., Comments, In re Joint Application of AT&T Corp. and Tele-Communications, Inc. for Transfer of Control to AT&T of Licenses and Authorizations Held by TCI and Its Affiliates or Subsidiaries, CS Docket 98–178, p. 15 (October 29, 1998).

13 Ibid., p. 17.

14 See Ameritech, Inc., Reply Comments, In re Joint Application of AT&T Corp. and Tele-Communications, Inc. for Transfer of Control to AT&T of Licenses and Authorizations Held by TCI and Its Affiliates or Subsidiaries, CS Docket 98–178, p. 7 (November 13, 1998).

15 See Applications for Consent to the Transfer of Control of Licenses and Section 214 Authorizations from Tele-Communications, Inc., Transferor, to AT&T, Transferee, 14 FCC Rcd. 3160, 3207 ¶96 (1999) ("*FCC AT&T/TCI Merger Order*").

16 Ibid. The Commission also observed that the open-access issues were independent of the merger. Ibid. In its first annual statutory review of broadband deployment, issued at about the same time as the AT&T/TCI Merger Order, the Commission similarly found no warrant to take action on the issue because "the record, while sparse, suggests that multiple methods of increasing bandwidth are or soon will be made available to a broad range of customers." Inquiry Concerning Deployment of Advanced Telecommunications Capability to All Americans in a Reasonable and Timely Fashion, and Possible Steps to Accelerate Such Deployment Pursuant to Section 706 of the Telecommunications Act of 1996, 14 FCC Rcd. 2398, 2449 ¶101 (1999) (First Report).

17 D. A. Lathen, *Broadband Today: A Staff Report to William E. Kennard, Chairman Federal Communications Commission, on Industry Monitoring Sessions Convened by the Cable Services Bureau*, October 1999, pp. 15, 44. Online. Available HTTP: <http://www.fcc.gov/Bureaus/Cable/Reports/broadbandtoday.pdf> (accessed July 20, 2004).

18 In approving AT&T's acquisition of MediaOne in 2000 without imposing any

ISP access conditions, the FCC relied in part on AT&T's "voluntary" commitment to open its cable modem platform in the future to unaffiliated ISPs. See Applications for Transfer of Control of Licenses and Section 214 Authorizations from MediaOne Group, Inc., Transferor, to AT&T Corp., Transferee, 15 FCC Rcd. 9816, 9870 ¶121 (2000). The Justice Department had required AT&T, with its majority control over Excite@Home, then the largest residential broadband provider, to divest MediaOne's interest in Road Runner, then the second largest residential broadband provider. See Proposed Final Judgment and Competitive Impact Statement; *United States v. AT&T Corp. and MediaOne Group, Inc.*, 65 Fed. Reg. 38584 (June 21, 2000). The competitive harm was not simply the increase in horizontal concentration, but the vertical concern that "[b]y exploiting its 'gatekeeper' position in the residential broadband content market, AT&T could make it less profitable for unaffiliated content providers to invest in the creation of attractive broadband content, and reduce competition and restrict output in that market." Ibid., 38588.

19 Application for Consent to the Transfer of Control of Licenses from Comcast Corporation and AT&T Corp., Transferors, to AT&T Comcast Corp., Transferee, 17 FCC Rcd. 23,246 (2002) (*"FCC AT&T/Comcast Merger Order"*).

20 See *AT&T Corp. v. City of Portland*, 216 F.3d 871 (9th Cir. 2000), reversing 43 F. Supp. 2d 1146 (D. Or. 1999); see also *MediaOne Group, Inc. v. County of Henrico*, 257 F.3d 356 (4th Cir. 2001) (holding that cable modem platform is a "telecommunications facility" as to which the Communications Act forbids franchise authority from requiring access as a condition of franchise transfer). According to the Ninth Circuit in *AT&T v. Portland*, cable modem service could not be regulated by a franchise authority because it is not a "cable service;" rather, it is an interstate "information service," the transmission component of which is a "telecommunications service," subject to common carriage regulation by the FCC. 216 F.3d 878.

21 *Cable Modem NPRM*, op. cit., 4820–4832 ¶¶34–59.

22 Ibid., 4823 ¶¶39, 40. The Commission recognized that its ruling on cable modem transport conflicted with the Ninth Circuit's *AT&T v. Portland* decision (see n. 20) but claimed that the Ninth Circuit's decision to the contrary was essentially dicta, made without benefit of the FCC's briefing on the matter. Ibid., 4831 ¶58.

23 The Commission would face substantial hurdles in imposing an access requirement under its Title I authority. As the Commission stated, its "authority pursuant to Title I . . . is not 'unrestrained' and may only be exercised provided such action is 'necessary to ensure the achievement of the Commission's statutory responsibilities.'" *Cable Modem NPRM*, op. cit., 4841 ¶75 (quoting *F.C.C. v. Midwest Video Corp.*, 440 U.S. 689, 706 (1979)). Not surprisingly, the cable industry maintains that the FCC lacks a legal basis to impose a multiple access requirement under its ancillary jurisdiction. See National Cable & Telecomm. Ass'n, Comments, Cable Modem NPRM, CS Docket 02–52, pp. 5–13 (June 17, 2002); see also J. B. Speta, "FCC authority to regulate the internet: creating it and limiting it," *Loy. U. Chi. L. J.* 35, 2003, p. 24 (questioning how regulation of Internet service was necessary to protect common carrier, broadcast or cable regulation).

24 *Brand X Internet Services v. F.C.C.*, 345 F.3d 1120, 1132 (9th Cir. 2003), cert.

granted, *National Cable and Telecommunications Assn v. Brand X Internet Services*, 2004 U.S. LEXIS 7981 (December 3, 2004).

25 To forbear under §10 of the Communications Act, the Commission would have to find that telecommunications regulation is not necessary to prevent discrimination or protect consumers and that forbearance is in the public interest. See 47 U.S.C. § 160. Recognizing the possibility that it might be reversed by the Ninth Circuit, the Commission ruled that to the extent that cable modem service may be subject to telecommunications service classification, it "tentatively conclude[d] that . . . forbearance would be justified" because, *inter alia*, "cable modem service is still in its early stages; supply and demand are still evolving; and several rival networks providing residential high-speed Internet access are still developing." *Cable Modem NPRM*, op. cit., 4847 ¶95.

26 See Appropriate Framework for Broadband Access to the Internet over Wireline Facilities, 17 FCC Rcd. 3019 (2002) (Notice of Proposed Rulemaking) ("*Wireline Broadband NPRM*").

27 See, for example, Deployment of Wireline Services Offering Advanced Telecommunications Capability, 13 FCC Rcd. 24,011, 24,029 ¶35 (1998) (Memorandum Opinion and Order, and Notice of Proposed Rulemaking). In addition, the Commission had also required incumbent local exchange carriers to make certain of their facilities available for competing local exchange carriers to offer DSL service under Section 251 of the Telecommunications Act (ibid., 24,017–18 ¶11).

28 *Wireline Broadband NPRM*, op. cit., 3032–33 ¶¶24, 25. To the extent that the Ninth Circuit's *Brand X* decision stands (see n. 24), the Commission would presumably need to at least reconsider its tentative conclusion that DSL transport is merely telecommunications, not a telecommunications service. The Commission has also recently eliminated many of the DSL unbundling requirements under Section 251 of the Telecommunications Act. See Review of the Section 251 Unbundling Obligations of Incumbent Local Exchange Carriers, 18 FCC Rcd. 16,978, 16,991 (2003) (Report and Order and Order on Remand and Further Notice of Proposed Rulemaking), aff'd in rel. part, *United States Telecom Assoc. v. Federal Communications Commission*, 359 F.3d 554 (D.C. Cir. 2004). And very recently the Commission lifted DSL unbundling requirements as to the Bell Operating Companies under Section 271 of the Act. See Petition for Forbearance of the Verizon Telephone Companies, 2004 FCC LEXIS 6098 (Memorandum Opinion and Order).

29 America Online, Inc. and Time Warner, Inc., 2001 FTC LEXIS 44, *15 (Decision and Order April 17, 2001) ("*FTC AOL/Time Warner Consent Order*"). The details of the AOL Time Warner consent order are discussed in the text *infra*.

30 America Online, Inc. and Time Warner, Inc., 2001 FTC LEXIS 44, *4 ¶8 (Complaint December 14, 2000) ("*FTC AOL/Time Warner Complaint*").

31 The merger did increase AOL/Time Warner's incentive to discriminate against non-cable broadband *platforms* (i.e. DSL) in areas in which its cable holdings are located. Accordingly, the FTC required Time Warner to market its DSL service in areas where it offers cable modem service on the same terms as it markets DSL service elsewhere. *FTC AOL/Time Warner Consent Order*, op. cit., *36–37 ¶IV.

32 *FCC AOL/Time Warner Merger Order*, op. cit., 6585 ¶86. The FCC noted that the merged company would have the incentive to restrict access to its affiliated ISP because, as an initial matter, "it would receive two revenue streams (ISP service and transmission) from subscribers to its affiliated ISP service, but only one revenue stream (transmission) from subscribers to unaffiliated ISPs." (Ibid., n. 271). Of course, this conclusion depends on the assumption that the charge for transmission could not compensate for the loss in ISP service revenues.

33 Ibid., 6583–84 ¶84 and 6586 ¶87 n. 274 (noting that "one analyst estimate[d] that less than 50% of households have access to DSL due to distance and network limitations").

34 Ibid., 6587 ¶90. Events indicate that the FCC was not terribly prescient in that AOL had great difficulty in securing broadband agreements with other cable operators. At this point, AOL has essentially stopped selling high speed Internet access under its own brand. J. Angwin, "AOL, Covad set marketing deal," *Wall Street Journal*, March 11, 2004, p. B4.

35 *FCC AT&T/Comcast Merger Order*, op. cit., 23, 299–300 ¶135. The FCC also sought to backtrack from AOL/Time Warner by asserting that it did not mandate that Time Warner provide access, rather it merely "supplemented an unaffiliated ISP access condition imposed by the FTC by requiring that, if AOL Time Warner provided such access voluntarily or otherwise, it must do so on non-discriminatory terms." Ibid.

36 First amendment and media-diversity considerations are also important issues but are not addressed here. See, for example, *American Civil Liberties Union, No Competition: How Monopoly Control of the Broadband Internet Threatens Free Speech*, 2002, p. 7 ("Internet access is not just any business; it involves the sacred role of making available to citizens a forum for speech and self-expression—a forum that is perhaps the most valuable new civic institution to appear in the United States in the past century."). Online. Available HTTP: <http://www.aclu.org/Files/OpenFile.cfm?id=10519> (accesssed June 4, 2004).

37 See *Cable Modem NPRM*, op. cit., 4805–06 ¶10.

38 See Barr *et al.*, op. cit., p. 512 (closed access will permit "the creation of a cyber-marketplace which systematically favors the providers of content, services or transactions who have a privileged financial relationship with the monopoly owner of the infrastructure which supports the cyber-marketplace"); see also Amazon.com Holdings, Inc., Comments, Cable Modem NPRM, CS Docket No. 02–52, p. 4, (June 17, 2002), (favoring open-access requirement to protect "freedom to choose among Internet-based information, products and services").

39 See, for example, T. Wu and L. Lessig, Ex Parte Submission, Cable Modem NPRM, CS Docket No. 02–52, (August 22, 2003). Details of this proposal are discussed in the text *infra*.

40 *Cable Modem NPRM*, op. cit., 4845 ¶87.

41 The FTC noted that "DSL service is available only to a portion of residences that have local telephone service, primarily because of technical constraints." *FTC AOL/Time Warner Complaint*, op. cit., *6 ¶11; see also *FCC AOL/Time Warner Merger Order*, op. cit., 6583–84 ¶84 (FCC's analysis). DSL generally does not work beyond 18,000 feet of the telephone carrier's central office,

does not work on lines that were upgraded for voice transmission, and is incompatible with digital loop carrier technology that has been employed in large parts of the Southeast, although these limitations may be overcome in the future. See *Third 706 Report*, op. cit., 2880–81 ¶¶86–87. DSL was estimated to be available to about 45 percent of U.S. homes at the end of 2001 (ibid., 2866 ¶51). But *cf.* Verizon, Broadband Competition: Recent Developments, Ex Parte Submission, Petition for Forbearance of the Verizon Telephone Companies, CC Docket No. 01–338, p. 2 (March 26, 2004) (claiming that DSL is available to about 75–80 percent of the homes passed by the Bell companies). According to one study, 38 percent of residential customers who reside in areas where broadband is available have access solely to cable modem service. See State of California, Comments, Cable Modem NPRM, CS Docket No. 02–52, pp. 3–4 (June 17, 2002) (citing study). Gerry Faulhaber, formerly the FCC's chief economist, calls DSL "a stopgap measure designed to squeeze yet more life out of the copper twisted pair" "whose days are likely numbered." G. R. Faulhaber, "Broadband deployment: is policy in the way?" in *Broadband: Should We Regulate High-Speed Internet Access?* R. W. Crandall and J. H. Alleman (eds), 2002, pp. 236–7; see also SBC Communications, Inc., Reply Comments, Cable Modem NPRM, CS Docket 02–52, p. 13 (August 6, 2002) (describing DSL as a "transitional technology with limited reach and bandwidth capabilities").

42 See Barr *et al.*, op. cit., pp. 502–5 (finding switching costs, including installation and equipment costs, to be "substantial"); see also Amazon.com Holdings, Inc., Comments, op. cit., pp. 5–6 (citing "tremendous friction for a consumer to move among available broadband technologies," such as "sunk equipment costs, start-up hassles, etc."). Another factor tending to enhance cable operators' broadband market power is their ability to bundle video services with broadband and telephony, which cannot be matched by telephone companies offering DSL. See Barr *et al.*, op. cit., p. 504. But see A. Latour, "Bells join race to offer TV," *Wall Street Journal*, April 29, 2004, p. B1 (describing efforts by Bell companies to offer video, including marketing arrangements with satellite-TV companies and plans to install fiber-optic lines).

43 See generally J. B. Speta, "The vertical dimension of open access," *U. Colo. L. Rev.* 71, 2000, p. 994 (positing that "the demand for broadband internet access will be characterized by indirect network externalities, in which consumer demand for internet access will significantly increase with a wider variety of services available over the broadband platform."). According to Speta, cable operators even have an incentive to allow ISPs to provide streaming video that would compete with their video offerings because they can make up for lost cable video revenue with additional broadband revenue. Ibid., p. 1005.

44 See D. L. Rubinfeld and H. J. Singer, "Open access to broadband networks: a case study of the AOL/Time Warner merger," *Berkeley. Tech. L. J.* 16, 2001, pp. 664–70 (integrated provider will engage in content discrimination if the loss in broadband access revenues from customers that demand the withheld content is exceeded by additional content and advertising revenue from increased demand for affiliated content); see also D. W. Carlton, "A general analysis of exclusionary conduct and refusal to deal—why Aspen and Kodak are misguided," *Antitrust Law Journal* 68, 2001, p. 659 (describing profitable

foreclosure strategies); see generally J. Farrell and P. J. Weiser, "Modularity, vertical integration, and open access policies: towards a convergence of antitrust and regulation in the internet age," *Harv. J. L. & Tech.* 17, 2003, p. 85 (describing menu of exceptions to monopolist's incentive to promote competitive complementary market, including monopolist's incompetence).

45 Amazon points out that "[a]lthough it is easy to see, for example, how an ISP that has an online automobile advertising service may be reluctant to allow consumers easy access to competing services, it is just as likely that the ISP would accept compensation from another party in order to impede consumer access to yet another party's services." Amazon.com Holdings, Inc., Comments, op. cit., p. 6.

46 Opponents of open access have offered "pro-competitive" rationales for cable's exclusive bundling of ISP service, such as quality assurance. See T. W. Hazlett and G. Bittlingmayer, "The political economy of cable 'open access,'" *Stan. Tech. L. Rev.* 2003, ¶¶88–91. According to Hazlett and Bittlingmayer, the efficiency of exclusive bundling is demonstrated by the fact that the leading cable overbuilder, which presumably lacks market power, bundles transport and ISP service. Ibid., ¶88.

47 See *Cable Modem NPRM,* op. cit., 4812 ¶20. Time Warner Cable now offers Earthlink (plus its own Road Runner) broadband service on a national basis, as well as a number of regional ISPs. See, for example, Time Warner Cable, *Overview: Cable Modem Services.* Online. Available HTTP: <http://www3.twcnyc. com/NASApp/CS/ContentServer?pagename=twcnyc/internet&mysect=internet/overview> (accessed June 4, 2004). Comcast, in addition to its proprietary high speed service, offered Earthlink and other unaffiliated ISPs in Seattle and New England, United Online on systems in Indianapolis and Nashville, and had agreements to offer AOL and MSN broadband nationwide. See *FCC AT&T/Comcast Merger Order,* op. cit., 23,296–97 ¶130. Certain other MSOs have conducted or announced trials for offering multiple ISPs. See *Cable Modem NPRM,* op. cit., 4818–19 ¶28.

48 AT&T Corp., Reply Comments, Cable Modem NPRM, CS Docket No. 02–52, p. 9 (August 6, 2002); see also AOL Time Warner Inc., Comments, Cable Modem NPRM, CS Docket No. 02–52, p. 24 (June 17, 2002) ("As long as marketplace forces continue progress towards . . . multiple ISP choice on a reasonable and timely basis, embarking upon the huge regulatory undertaking that would be required to implement new mandatory multiple ISP access regulations would be premature and unnecessary"). But see AT&T Corp., Comments, Wireline Broadband NPRM, CC Docket No. 02–33, p. 51 (May 3, 2002) (arguing that open access is necessary for telephone companies in part because "multiple ISP access over cable remains in its infancy and is available only in very limited areas"). Of course, if multiple access is being adopted by the industry voluntarily, one wonders why the industry protests so much.

49 See American Civil Liberties Union, op. cit., p. 7; see also discussion in the text *infra.*

50 For example, at least in the past, cable ISPs have placed limits on customers' use of streaming video, operating a server, and use of a home network. See J. H. Saltzer, "*Open access" is Just the Tip of the Iceberg,* October 22, 1999. Online. Available HTTP: <http://web.mit.edu/Saltzer/www/publications/openaccess.html> (accessed June 4, 2004). A survey of broadband operators' policies

and architecture in 2002 showed that broadband operators disfavored certain applications and usage, such as home networking, peer-to-peer applications and home telecommuting (virtual private networks), and that "cable operators tended to impose far more restrictions on usage than do DSL operators." T. Wu, "Network neutrality, broadband discrimination," *J. Telecomm. & High Tech. L.* 2, 2003, p. 157. The High Tech Broadband Coalition, a coalition of trade groups that does not presently favor an open-access requirement for cable, has noted "troubling restrictions imposed by certain cable ISPs" on subscribers' use of the network, including restrictions on virtual private networks, running servers, offering web hosting, and use of "excessive" bandwidth. High Tech Broadband Coalition, Comments, Cable Modem NPRM, CS Docket No. 02–52, pp. 10–13 (June 17, 2002). The cable industry contends that these limits are "reasonable attempts to prevent individual customers from imposing excessive burdens on the system to the detriment of other residential customers." National Cable and Telecommunications Ass'n, Reply Comments, Cable Modem NPRM, CS Docket No. 02–52, p. 12 (August 6, 2002); see also *Cable Modem NPRM*, op. cit., 4845 ¶87 (stating that "although it is technically feasible for a cable operator to deny access to unaffiliated content, or to relegate unaffiliated content to the 'slow lane' of its residential high-speed Internet access service, we are unaware of a single allegation that a cable operator has done so").

51 M. A. Lemley and L. Lessig, "The end of end-to-end: preserving the architecture of the internet in the broadband era," *UCLA L. Rev.* 48, 2001, pp. 930–1.

52 Ibid., p. 931. See also Barr *et al.*, op. cit., p. 494 ("America's remarkable success in promoting the internet revolution owes a major debt to determined regulatory action that encouraged all aspects of network openness and interconnection").

53 The FTC adopted this theme in its approval of the AOL/Time Warner Merger Order. According to then-Chairman Pitofsky, "In the broad sense, our concern was that the merger of these two powerful companies would deny to competitors access to this amazing new broadband technology. . . . This order is intended to ensure that this new medium, characterized by openness, diversity and freedom, will not be closed down as a result of this merger." Federal Trade Commission, Press Release, *FTC Approves AOL/Time Warner Merger With Conditions*, December 14, 2000. Online. Available HTTP: <http://www.ftc.gov/opa/2000/12/aol.htm> (accessed June 4, 2004).

54 Lemley and Lessig, op. cit., pp. 944–5.

55 See, for example, B. M. Owen and G. L. Rosston, Cable Modems, Access and Investment Incentives p. ii, Ex Parte Submission of National Cable Television Ass'n, Inquiry Concerning Deployment of Advanced Telecommunications Capability to All Americans in a Reasonable and Timely Fashion, and Possible Steps to Accelerate Such Deployment Pursuant to Section 706 of the Telecommunications Act of 1996, CC Docket No. 98–146 (December 10, 1998) ("[E]ven the threat, much less the actuality, of government regulation, such as the mandatory unbundling proposed by AOL and others, will chill the appetites of investors and reduce the pace of telecommunications infrastructure construction"). The FCC seemed moved by this argument. See, for example, Lathen, op. cit., p. 45 ("Mandated access also could reduce the

financial incentives and the build-out capital for cable companies to make the large investments necessary to upgrade their systems").

56 B. M. Owen, Forced Access to Broadband Cable ¶40, Comments of National Cable & Telecomm. Ass'n, Cable Modem NPRM, CS Docket 02–52 (June 17, 2002). According to the NCTA, cable system upgrades were nearly 85 percent complete by year-end 2003. See National Cable & Telecommunications Ass'n, 2003 Year-End Industry Overview pp. 2, 5 (also noting that 85 percent of homes passed by cable had access to cable broadband). Online. Available HTTP: <http://www.ncta.com/pdf_files/Overview.pdf> (accessed June 4, 2004).

57 Owen, op. cit., ¶40.

58 See Lemley and Lessig, op. cit., p. 959 ("It is possible to grant sufficient incentives by letting cable companies set the appropriate price to consumers for the use of the wires themselves.").

59 Similarly, insofar as the cable operator is restricted to charging no more than it charges its affiliated ISP, the cable operator may be able to manipulate its internal transfer price to squeeze out unaffiliated ISPs.

60 Jerry Hausman suggests that the "likely decrease in profits" from an open-access regime "occurs because of the very fixed (and sunk) costs of providing [ISP] services, which means that downstream perfect competition cannot hold. Also, given diverse consumer preferences, the importance of advertising revenue to Internet service provider profitability, and the possibility of price discrimination, given the individual addressability of the Internet, I expect that the tying strategy employed by the cable industry may yield higher profits than a non-exclusive bundling strategy." J. A. Hausman, Investment and Consumer Welfare in Broadband Internet Access p. 4, Comments of America Online, Inc., In re Joint Application of AT&T Corp. and Tele-Communications, Inc. for Transfer of Control to AT&T of Licenses and Authorizations Held by TCI and Its Affiliates or Subsidiaries, CS Docket 98–178 (January 13, 1999).

61 Faulhaber argues that "[t]he impetus for the costly upgrade to digital systems was not broadband; it was competitive pressure from DBS satellite, an alternative video delivery system that promised far higher quality and far more channels than the old analog cable systems could deliver.... To meet this competitive threat, cable systems were pressed to invest heavily in system upgrades of their systems to digital; fortunately for broadband customers, this digital upgrade, required for cable to compete in the video marketplace, made the provision of high speed access to the Internet a very inexpensive add-on to the new systems." Faulhaber, op. cit., pp. 232–3; see also Affidavit of Jeffrey M. King ¶5, Reply Comments of AOL Time Warner Inc., Cable Modem NPRM, CS Docket No. 02–52 (August 6, 2002) (CEO of Road Runner attests that Time Warner's "reasons for upgrading had nothing to do with cable-modem service. Rather, the driving forces behind the upgrade were increased channel capacity, better picture quality, and enhanced reliability").

62 See J. K. MacKie-Mason, *Investment in Cable Broadband Infrastructure: Open Access is Not an Obstacle*, November 5, 1999, pp. 18–21 (discussing AT&T's plans to offer telephone services over its cable systems). Online. Available HTTP: <http://www-personal.umich.edu/~jmm/papers/broadband.pdf> (accessed June 4, 2004).

63 Upgrading cable facilities to increase the bandwidth "allow[s] operators to increase channel capacity for video and other downstream services, as well as the capacity to maintain reliable two-way activated systems," such as telephony and Internet service. Annual Assessment of the Status of Competition in Markets for the Delivery of Video Programming, 13 FCC Rcd. 24,284, 24,305 ¶38 (1998) (Fifth Annual Report). Hazlett and Bittlingmayer argue that cable companies have devoted far too little of their increased bandwidth to broadband services—only 6 MHz (one video channel) for downstream traffic, which is less than 1 percent of available spectrum on a 750 MHz cable system. Hazlett and Bittlingmayer, op. cit., ¶¶22–5. They maintain that the reason cable operators are "starving broadband access" is that the companies fear regulatory "appropriation," namely that regulators will impose common carrier requirements such as open access. Ibid., ¶¶27–35.

64 Faulhaber maintains that open-access requirements for DSL have not slowed the roll out of DSL, as "the regional Bells are deploying broadband as fast as they can as a competitive necessity..." Faulhaber, op. cit., p. 241. But see Hazlett and Bittlingmayer, op. cit., ¶¶77–87 (suggesting that the poor showing of DSL versus cable modem is due in part to telephone open-access rules). MacKie-Mason cites the experience in Canada as a similar counter-example, observing (in 1999) that the Canadians were way ahead of U.S. cable operators in broadband facilities deployment despite the Canadian government's announcement in 1996 that open access would be required. Mackie-Mason, op. cit., p. 27. Yet, the example might be questioned in light of subsequent events because while Canada has maintained its lead over the U.S. in broadband deployment and penetration, see International Telecommunication Union, op. cit., Fig. 1 (showing that as of 2002, broadband penetration in Canada was third highest in the world, and more than 60 percent greater than in the U.S., per one hundred inhabitants), cable companies' implementation of third-party Internet access service in Canada has been long delayed. See Canadian Radio-television and Telecommunications Commission, *Report to the Governor in Council, Status of Competition in Canadian Telecommunications Market*, November 2003, §4.4(d). Online. Available HTTP: <http://www.crtc.gc.ca/eng/publications/reports/PolicyMonitoring/2003/gic2003.htm?Print=True#44> (accessed June 4, 2004).

65 See Lemley and Lessig, op. cit., p. 960.

66 See, for example, ibid., pp. 927–8 ("there is no justification in law or policy for giving cable operators special treatment").

67 See, for example, Ameritech, Inc., Reply Comments, op. cit., p. 7 ("AT&T must be required to provide access to its 'last mile' infrastructure to the same extent as other advanced broadband competitors, including incumbent LECs"); Bell Atlantic, Reply Comments, In re Joint Application of AT&T Corp. and Tele-Communications, Inc. for Transfer of Control to AT&T of Licenses and Authorizations Held by TCI and Its Affiliates or Subsidiaries, CS Docket 98–178, p. 2 (November 13, 1998) ("The TCI cable systems are 'bottlenecks' to the same extent as those of incumbent LECs, and there is no reason that they should be treated any differently").

68 See, for example, SBC Communications Inc., Reply Comments, Wireline Broadband NPRM, CC Docket 02–33, pp. 15–16 (July 1, 2002).

69 While the National Cable & Telecommunications Association and certain

cable companies (including Comcast) have formally taken "no position" as to whether DSL service should remain subject to unbundling regulation, the NCTA maintains that there are sufficient differences between cable and DSL to justify not regulating cable even if DSL remains regulated. See National Cable & Telecommunications Ass'n, Reply Comments, Cable Modem NPRM, CC Docket No. 02–52, pp. 16–17 (August 6, 2002).

70 See, for example, AT&T Corp., Reply Comments, Wireline Broadband NPRM, CC Docket No. 02–33, pp. 43–8 (July 1, 2002). According to the Californian PUC, 45 percent of California residents that live in locales with broadband capability have DSL service as their only broadband option. State of California, Comments, Wireline Broadband NPRM, CC Docket No. 02–33, p. 35 (May 3, 2002). But *cf.* Verizon, Ex Parte Submission, op. cit., pp. 24–5 (citing JP Morgan study that purportedly shows that only 5 percent of U.S. households were able to get DSL but not cable modem service).

71 See Declaration of R. D. Willig ¶33, Comments of AT&T Corp., Wireline Broadband NPRM, CC Docket No. 02–33, (May 3, 2002). As with cable broadband, DSL does not require a second line for telephone (voice) service. Apparently, telephone company margins for DSL are less than for narrowband plus a second line. The FCC staff has noted that telephone companies were slow to introduce DSL "for concern that it would negatively impact their other lines of business." Lathen, op. cit., p. 27.

72 See Willig, op. cit., ¶76 (maintaining that "properly set TELRIC-based rates – which, by definition, reflect a risk-adjusted, competitive market return – will not discourage any efficient investment."). Of course, the TELRIC (total element long run incremental cost) rate-setting methodology used by the FCC has long been attacked by the Bells as providing inadequate returns, and by definition lowers the returns over those that would prevail in an unregulated market, as Willig recognizes. Ibid., ¶81.

73 Willig argues, "With rare and trivial exceptions . . . the loop investments needed to enable both current and next-generation broadband services are independently justified by the cost savings that the incumbent LECs will realize in providing voice and other narrowband services." Ibid., ¶87. He also maintains that experience belies the telephone industry's incentives argument, as incumbent LECs have made substantial investments to upgrade their facilities to provide DSL notwithstanding their obligations to provide access at TELRIC-based rates. Ibid., ¶93.

74 See National Cable & Telecommunications Ass'n, Comments, Cable Modem NPRM, CS Docket No. 02–52, p. 40 (June 17, 2002); see also AOL Time Warner Inc., Reply Comments, Wireline Broadband NPRM, CC Docket No. 02–33, p. 11 (July 1, 2002) ("Having deployed their wireline facilities with regulated ratepayer dollars, the ILECs should not now be permitted to deprive the public of the competitive benefits flowing from new and innovative broadband information services provided over their common carrier facilities"). The cable industry also maintains that the existing rate regulation of local telephone service, but not cable television, justifies different treatment because of the potential for cross subsidization of the unregulated service. See, for example, National Cable & Telecommunications Ass'n, Reply Comments, Cable Modem NPRM op. cit., p. 37.

75 AT&T argued that cable broadband was not a realistic alternative to DSL lines

for unaffiliated ISPs because "multiple ISP access over cable remains in its infancy and is available only in very limited areas." AT&T Corp., Comments, Wireline Broadband NPRM, CC Docket No. 02–33, p. 51 (May 3, 2002). SBC calls AT&T's argument "a feat of stunning hypocrisy and opportunism." SBC Communications Inc., Reply Comments, Wireline Broadband NPRM, CC Docket No. 02–33, p. 5 (July 1, 2002).

76 See High Tech Broadband Coalition, Reply Comments, Wireline Broadband NPRM, CC Docket No. 02–33, p. 7 (July 1, 2002) (arguing that "the expectancy interests and sunk investment of unaffiliated ISPs and the reliance of their customers on uninterrupted service warrant continuation of the existing [access] requirement").

77 The policy of promoting facilities-based competition in local phone service may be furthered by a requirement that incumbent local exchange carriers open their DSL lines to competing local exchange carriers, as the FCC originally determined. See Deployment of Wireline Services Offering Advanced Telecomm. Capability and Implementation of the Local Competition Provisions of the Telecomm. Act of 1996, 14 FCC Rcd. 20,912, 20,928, ¶25 (1999), rev'd by *United States Telecom Association, Inc. v. F.C.C.*, 290 F.3d 415, 429 (D.C. Cir. 2002). And it may be that line sharing afforded to competing local exchange carriers effectively would be available to ISPs. See J. Speta, "Handicapping the race for the last mile? A critique of open access rules for broadband platforms," *Yale J. Reg.* 17, 2000, pp. 68–9 (noting that ISP could set up affiliated telecommunications carrier). However, this argument for asymmetric regulation of DSL seems rather weak in light of the FCC's moves towards abandoning telephone companies' DSL line-sharing obligations. See discussion at note 28.

78 Moreover, it cannot reasonably be argued that the $60 billion in so-called "private risk capital" spent to upgrade cable systems since the 1996 Telecommunications Act was invested based on the expectation that cable modem service would be unregulated, because those investments would have been made in any event. See *supra* nn. 61, 62. Indeed, a number of cable operators upgraded their systems under "social contracts" approved by the Commission under which the operators agreed to make upgrades in exchange for being given substantial flexibility in setting rates for new video services. See, for example, Social Contract for Time Warner, 11 FCC Rcd. 2788 (1995) (Time Warner required to spend $4 billion to rebuild and upgrade all of its cable systems within five years); see generally Annual Assessment of the Status of Competition in the Market for the Delivery of Video Programming, 17 FCC Rcd. 1244, 1261–62 ¶33 (2002) (Eighth Annual Report) (describing social contracts with Time Warner, AT&T, Comcast and Cox).

79 Coalition of Broadband Users and Innovators, Ex Parte Submission, Cable Modem NPRM, CS Docket No. 02–52, p. 12 (July 17, 2003). The coalition includes companies such as Microsoft, Disney, Yahoo!, and Amazon.com, as well as consumer groups such as the Media Access Project and the Alliance for Public Technology.

80 Ibid. (contending that proposed rule would not prohibit provider from "managing its broadband network in a technically efficient manner or from implementing reasonable measures to prevent unlawful conduct").

81 See Wu and Lessig, op. cit., p. 14.

82 Michael Powell, the chairman of the FCC, has endorsed the *principle* of network neutrality, or "Internet freedoms," including the freedom of consumers to access their choice of legal content, to run applications of their choice, to attach any devices they choose to the connection in their homes, and to receive meaningful information regarding their service plans. M. K. Powell, *Preserving Internet Freedom: Guiding Principles for the Industry*, Remarks at the Silicon Flatirons Symposium p. 5, February 8, 2004. Online. Available HTTP: <http://hraunfoss.fcc.gov/edocs_public/attachmatch/DOC-243556A1.pdf> (accessed June 4, 2004). However, Powell maintains that cable operators should and do *voluntarily* adhere to these "freedoms." Ibid., p. 3. Compare High Tech Broadband Coalition Comments, op. cit., pp. 7–8 (proposing voluntary "connectivity principles" similar to Powell's "Internet freedoms.").

83 See J. Shiver, Jr., "ISPs to get crack at cable broadband," *Los Angeles Times*, October 7, 2003, p. C1 (noting that the shift to broadband and cable dominance had slashed the number of ISPs from more than 5,000 in 2000 to about 1,500). See also J. Angwin, "Speed kills: the traditional companies that sell Internet connections are struggling to survive the broadband revolution," *Wall Street Journal*, May 19, 2003, p. R10 (noting that America Online and MSN "have essentially thrown in the towel, saying they are no longer focused on selling broadband," but rather are promoting a "bring your own access" product that offers their online content without Internet access).

84 Consumer Federation of America, *et al.*, Comments, Cable Modem NPRM, CS Docket No. 02–52, p. 27 (June 18, 2002) (accusing the FCC of "shocking ignorance" of the importance of ISPs to the "Internet ecology"). See also Lemley and Lessig, op. cit., p. 944 (maintaining that "[o]ne should not think of ISPs as providing a fixed and immutable set of services," and that, in the future, "ISPs could be potential vertical competitors to access providers who could provide competitive packages of content, differently optimized caching servers, different mixes of customer support, or advanced Internet services"); Willig, op. cit., ¶¶73–4 (maintaining that "[i]t was the [independent] ISPs...that have been the leaders in developing the technologies and programs that make the 'Internet' what it is today," and that "ISPs can be likewise expected to take the lead in developing unique broadband services").

85 But see High Tech Broadband Coalition Comments, op. cit., p. 8 (maintaining that "ISPs should be permitted to provide enhanced access to their own content, through, e.g. caching").

86 Server-based filtering may be used by families to protect their children from certain content deemed harmful and may be more effective than software-based filtering. See Consumer Federation of America, *et al.*, op. cit., p. 32 (discussing server-based filtering).

87 The FCC cited the example of AOL requiring that content appearing on its websites have only a limited number of hyperlinks to unaffiliated content. See *FCC AOL/Timer Warner Merger Order*, op. cit., 6594 ¶106.

88 Ibid., 6594–95 ¶107. *Cf.* Amazon.com, Inc., Ex Parte Submission, Cable Modem NPRM, CS Docket No. 02–52, p. 9 (December 2, 2002) (proposing rule barring cable broadband operator from impairing consumer's access to any Internet content, unless the cable operator opened its network to three or more unaffiliated ISPs).

89 Professor Wu favors a network neutrality regime over ISP open access as the preferred solution to the issue of content discrimination, for two reasons. See Wu, op. cit., p. 146. First, he maintains that an ISP open-access model threatens to preclude certain vertical relationships that may in fact enhance network neutrality. For example, he suggests that quality of service guarantees, which may be necessary to ensure neutrality in the use of the network between data and non-data applications, may not be possible under ISP open access, since such guarantees can only be provided by the network operator. Ibid., p. 149. Second, Wu argues that "[c]ompetition among ISPs does not necessarily mean that broadband operators will simply retreat to acting as passive carriers in the last mile." Ibid. While it is certainly possible that certain integrative efficiencies are sacrificed when a network is designed to ensure open access to multiple competitors, it is not obvious that is the case with ISP access to cable broadband given the available technology, including the technology to allow multiple ISPs to provide quality of service guarantees. See, for example, Columbia Telecomm. Corp., *Technological Analysis of Open Access and Cable Television Systems*, December 2001, p. 30 (noting that DOCSIS 1.1 allows for quality of service capability with multiple ISPs). Online. Available HTTP: <http://www.aclu.org/Files/OpenFile.cfm?id=13680> (accessed June 4, 2004). Moreover, the point of multiple ISP access is not that all ISPs will remain content neutral, but that competition among ISPs will ensure that consumer choice will drive the market.

90 Time Warner was only permitted to decline to enter into agreements with additional ISPs "based on cable broadband capacity constraints, other cable broadband technical limitations, or cable broadband business considerations," provided that "such determinations are made without discrimination on the basis of affiliation" and "are not based, in whole or in part, on the impact or potential impact on" Time Warner's ISPs. *FTC AOL/Time Warner Consent Order*, op. cit., *33–34 ¶II.E. The ability of Time Warner to deny access based on "cable broadband business considerations" may be a rather large loophole.

91 Ibid., *29–30 ¶II.C.1.

92 Absent the advance agreement with Earthlink, presumably the FTC would not have approved the transaction. As an incentive for the roll out of Earthlink, Time Warner was required to actually make available Earthlink to its cable subscribers before it made AOL's broadband ISP service available. Ibid., *24–25 ¶II.A.1. And if Time Warner failed to enter into two additional ISP agreements within 90 days of offering AOL, a monitor trustee was permitted to do so on the company's behalf. Ibid., *26–29 ¶¶II.A.3, II.B.2.

93 Ibid., *35 ¶III.A.

94 Ibid., *35 ¶III.B.

95 Ibid., *30–31 ¶¶II.C.2, 3. At the same time, Time Warner was permitted to "impose rates, terms, or conditions based on cable broadband capacity constraints, other cable broadband technical limitations, or cable broadband business considerations" provided that such determinations are made without discrimination on the basis of affiliation. Ibid., ¶II.E.

96 These additional conditions required Time Warner to: (a) allow customers to select a participating ISP by a method that does not discriminate in favor of Time Warner's affiliates; (b) permit each participating ISP to determine the

contents of its subscribers' first screen; (c) permit each ISP to have a direct billing arrangement with the customer; and (d) not discriminate in terms of technical performance. *FCC AOL/Time Warner Merger Order*, op. cit., 6600–02 ¶126.

97 *Cable Modem NPRM*, op. cit., 4831 ¶52 (internal quotations omitted).

98 AOL Time Warner Inc., Comments, Cable Modem NPRM, op. cit., pp. 19–20.

99 See Columbia Telecomm. Corp., op. cit., p. 21.

100 Ibid., p. 22.

101 See, for example, Earthlink, Comments, Cable Modem NPRM, CS Docket No. 02–52 (June 17, 2002).

102 See Amendment of Section 64.702 of the Commission's Rules and Regulations (Second Computer Inquiry), 77 FCC 2d 384 (1980), aff'd, *Computer & Communications Industry Ass'n, Inc. v. F.C.C.*, 693 F.2d 198 (D.C. Cir. 1982).

103 Ibid., 474–475 ¶231. These rules did not apply to the pre-divestiture AT&T (and GTE), which were subject to structural separation requirements that limited their ability to offer enhanced services at all. In *Computer III*, and subsequent proceedings, the Commission lifted the structural separation requirement on the Bell Operating Companies in favor of similar unbundling rules requiring them to provide network interconnection to competitive enhanced service providers that is comparatively efficient to the interconnection that their own enhanced service operation enjoys. See Amendment of Section 64.702 of the Commission's Rules and Regulations (Third Computer Inquiry), 104 FCC 2d 958, 1019 ¶112 (1987).

104 See also *Cable Modem NPRM*, op. cit., 4831 ¶55 (stating that "AOL Time Warner is determining on an individual basis whether to deal with particular ISPs and is in each case deciding the terms on which it will deal with any particular ISP").

105 Powell, op. cit., pp. 3 and 6 (noting that the "possibilities [for consumer empowerment] arise from the Internet's open architecture" and that "Internet Freedom...promotes innovation by giving developers and service providers confidence they can develop broadband applications that consumers and run as designed").

106 Ibid., p. 4.

Case 7

Automated teller machines

Donald I. Baker[1]

Overview of the ATM industry

Convenience has long been recognized as the cornerstone of the retail banking industry; and concerns about convenience and competitive imbalance led to an elaborate patchwork of government regulation over where a bank "branch" could be deployed. In the process, the Federal Government deferred to the states, and a national bank could only deploy a "branch" if and where a state-chartered bank could do so.[2] The policy idea was "competitive equality," which became a byword for limiting competition. Interstate banking was generally barred. Because the government also limited the interest that banks could pay (or were prohibited from paying) to their depositors, competition was centered on location and convenience—and the bricks, mortar, and brass that went with it.[3]

Automated teller machines (ATMs) arrived on this balkanized banking scene in the early 1970s, as a way of allowing consumers round-the-clock access to cash and banking services in many more locations. This technological threat to the whole idea of "competitive equality" was highly uncongenial to much of an industry that was surely over-invested in bricks, mortar, and brass. For 25 years prior to 1996, the political and legal battles raged over whether an ATM should be treated as a "branch" and hence subject to all kinds of often baroque restrictions over where it could be deployed.[4] In addition, out of fear of competitive disruption, a considerable number of states passed in the 1970s what came to be called "compulsory sharing laws"—which obliged a bank deploying an ATM to share it with any other bank in the state.[5]

In the 1980s, the idea of ATM *networks* became fashionable in the banking industry; and a great many of these were created as joint ventures under such forgettable logos as "Plus," "Pulse," "MoneyStation," "NYCE," "Cirrus," "Owl," "Yankee24," and "Star." Under the typical network arrangement, each member was obliged to mark its cards and ATMs with the network logo, and each ATM owner was obliged to allow other network members' cardholders to access to its ATMs in return for an interchange fee (which was set by the network and paid by the card-issuing bank to the ATM owner). In some areas there were competing ATM networks with different members and in others there was only a single system. Over time, there tended to be consolidations which have generally resulted in a single dominant network being the norm (New England, Pennsylvania, and Texas are all clear examples of such consolidation at work).

The normal ATM network tends to be a fairly sparse organization, with the facilities owned and operated by others. Its members issue the cards and own the ATMs, communications carriers provide the wireline links, and a third party data processor normally provides the switching under contract. Thus the network emerges as the owner of the logo (which may sometimes be an important asset), collector of fees from members, advertiser and promoter of the network service, and rulemaker for network operations. In the latter role, the network will establish (1) highly technical rules on such subjects as response times, logo display and data capture, and (2) economic-driven rules on interchange terms, switching fees, bypass transactions, and similar subjects. These rules can generate serious disputes and antitrust litigation with noisy minorities of network members.

Approaches to access

The normal shared ATM network tends to be dominated by the larger banks that contribute the majority of the cards, traffic, and ATMs to the network. This dominance can be reflected in weighted voting (e.g., based on cards or transactions), permanent seats on the board, shareholding, or various veto rights.[6] The larger banks still generally want to have smaller banks as part of the network, because of correspondent banking relationships and the fact that the participation of the smaller banks adds incremental traffic and value to the network. Thus, the "network access" issues have tended to be about *the terms of access and usage*, rather than access per se.

The network logo tends to be a key part of the equation. It is the key to an ATM owner's access to a larger card base, and key to a card-issuer's ability to offer depositors and potential depositors more flexible banking access. Some larger networks heavily promoted their logos to enhance their value and encourage usage and acceptance (but none of this has approached the scale of promotion and value seen in the big Visa and MasterCard credit card networks).

Most of the ATM networks limited membership to federally-insured depository institutions (commercial banks, thrift institutions, credit unions); and the regional networks tended to limit membership to those institutions operating offices in the region. The justifications were largely based on "free rider" concerns: those who founded the network and incurred the up-front costs did not care to give access to out-of-area banks or non-bank sellers of what they regarded as competitive products. With the advent of widespread interstate banking in the 1990s, the potential geographic access issues have largely disappeared. The "non-traditional financial enterprises" issue has largely been settled by threats of antitrust boycott claims, which the networks have not thought worth bearing the cost of defending. The principal public example is a case called *Household Bank FSB v. Cirrus System, Inc.*, filed in the Northern District of Illinois in 1987; as a consequence, the network admitted a finance company and the case was dropped. Other networks seem to have done the same thing. In sum, access questions and disputes based on eligibility for membership seem to have declined (while remaining important in the credit card area).

In recent years, we have seen a large growth of essentially unbranded ATMs in convenience stores, supermarkets, gas stations, and other heavy traffic locations. These are generally owned by (1) the owner of the site (e.g., the store), or (2) an ATM-owning entrepreneur who generates income from interchange fees and surcharges. The bank-controlled networks seem to have allowed these independent, non-bank ATM owners to have access to the networks as long as they were "sponsored" by a network member bank which guaranteed the non-member's obligations. This whole system of entrepreneurial ATMs seems to have grown up incrementally, and is competitively interesting since it must divert at least some traffic from member-owned ATMs.

In the earlier years, there were some "access" disputes over whether an ATM network could deny membership to an institution that was a member of a competing network. The two national networks (Plus and Cirrus) had exclusivity rules and competed for members. Those who favored exclusivity rules argued that there was real competition at the "network" level which would be enhanced by having the networks compete for members, and their members compete for depositors based on offering more comprehensive ATM coverage in the relevant region(s). The counter-argument was that an ATM network was just a big electronic clearing house, and that the only real competition was at the "member" level—where the banks competed for depositors and ATM sites and transactions. After the Justice Department declined in 1983 to give Pulse (the major Texas network) a Business Review clearance for its exclusivity rule, that network abandoned the rule and allowed the members of the competing MPACT network to join; the result was a very dominant regional network, which ceased to be a source of differentiation among Texas banks.[7] This pattern was generally followed in other parts of the country where there had been competing regional networks (most notably in Pennsylvania and New England).

There is definitely a "tipping" phenomenon present in ATM networks. An ATM-deploying bank makes its decision to deploy additional ATMs largely in terms of (1) its own efforts to compete for depositors (which it can do by offering preferential access for "on us" ATM transactions), and

(2) the number of "foreign" transactions that it can attract at its ATMs. The ATM business has a high proportion of fixed costs and the network whose members have the larger card bases is clearly more attractive. (The institution that forced the issue in Texas discussed in the last paragraph was a thrift which was a major deployer of ATMs without a large card base of its own, and was counting on "foreign" transactions from multiple network sources for its revenues.)

Another impetus to the "monopoly utility" solution were the "compulsory sharing" statutes enacted in various states in the early years.[8] These were especially popular in so-called "unit banking" states where branch banking was prohibited (e.g., Illinois, Nebraska, Iowa, Texas, Colorado); and the small banks were concerned that the bigger banks would use ATMs to invade protected local enclaves and gain special competitive advantages. Accordingly, these statutes generally provided that an ATM deployer had to share access to its machines with any similar type institutions in the state; thus commercial banks had to share with each other but not with credit unions and thrifts, and vice versa. The Justice Department attacked these laws strongly, stating that, "The major difficulty with mandated sharing is that it undercuts in advance any incentive to innovate, creating a 'free rider' problem with respect to initial risk taking."[9]

Probably the most serious "access" questions have arisen in connection with third party data processors.[10] A smaller bank will generally use such a processor to (1) authorize and process card transactions, and (2) program (drive) its ATMs. Many (but not all) larger banks have traditionally performed these functions internally, and hence are less dependent on third party processors (TPPs). In the early 1990s, the Pennsylvania-centered MAC network adopted a policy of refusing all access to its network for TPPs; if a member did not perform its card authorization and ATM driving functions internally, then it had to use the network's own data processing arm to perform these functions. Regardless of whether labeled a "tie-in" or a "denial of reasonable access," this policy represented a serious antitrust problem when imposed by a dominant network. The Justice Department treated it as an illegal tie-in between "regional ATM network access" and "ATM processing"; and the practice was prohibited in a consent decree.[11] Since then (based on the best available information) no other network has tried to restrict TPPs so long as they could meet the network's technical standards.

Related are rules and disputes relating to the routing of transactions.[12] Where the card-issuer and the ATM owner both belong to more than one network, there are alternative ways that the transaction can be routed back to the card-issuer. This sets up a potential conflict, since the ATM owner collects a network-set interchange fee while the card-issuer pays both an interchange fee and a switching fee set by the network. The ATM owner (who would normally control the routing) would naturally opt for the "high interchange fee" network. In response, various networks have enacted rules that allow the card-issuer to direct the routing, or require low cost routing by the ATM owner.

Because these ATM networks serve institutions of hugely different scale and methods of operations, access-related conflicts can arise in seemingly small situations. For example, large banks with substantial branch and ATM coverage in a region will normally compete for depositors by offering "free" access for "on us" transactions at the bank's own ATMs. Meanwhile, the large bank will charge its own depositors a "foreign fee" on their monthly statements for a transaction at the ATMs of other network members, and it will also often surcharge any "foreign" transaction at its own machines. This type of competition puts a small bank at a serious disadvantage, because it has fewer of its own ATMs on which to offer "free" transactions and its cardholders are generally more dependent on "foreign" network transactions than the big bank is.

In at least one case, a group of smaller banks put together a "free reciprocity" sub-network, in which each member agreed to treat their partners' cardholder transactions as if they were "on us" transactions and hence "free" of surcharges. The small bank partners still felt that they had to remain part of the dominant regional network run by the larger banks, in order to get reasonable coverage for their depositors and "foreign" transaction volume for their ATMs. The network leaders were apparently not pleased with the reciprocity system of their smaller rivals and threatened to prohibit this cooperative effort as an improper discrimination under the network rules. Ultimately those who controlled the network decided to let this experiment go forward.

Conclusion

The ATM network industry may be an area where we have seen *too much access* and too little "network" level competition for institutional participation and transactions. Certainly, many of the original ATM pioneers saw the new devices as a source of product differentiation and competitive advantage in an industry where many avenues of potential competition were blunted by anti-competitive regulations based on populist politics and concerns about bank solvency. As it turned out, the ATM business turned out to be very different from credit cards—where different brands were vigorously promoted, competition existed at both the "network" and the "member" levels, and access disputes abounded in the antitrust courts.[13]

The ATM network business largely evolved to a "public utility" model in which card-issuers and consumers came to regard ATM access as being almost universal, rather than as a source of product differentiation. ATMs were generally tied to depository accounts and the commercial banks that dominated most of the shared networks followed antitrust advice and did not seek to exclude thrift institutions.[14] Because there was less competitive advantage from participating as compared with credit card networks, there was less reason for a network to accept the risks and costs of litigating an antitrust boycott suit in order to keep anyone out; and thus litigated disputes over ATM access were few and have become virtually unknown. It is an open question whether less universal access and more product differentiation would have produced a better competitive result— but my suspicion is that it would have.[15]

Notes

1 Senior Partner, Baker & Miller, PLLC, Washington, D.C.
2 See *First National Bank of Plant City. v. Dickinson*, 396 U.S. 122 (1969) (night depository treated and armored car each treated as a "branch" to avoid a national bank gaining a competitive advantage vis-à-vis Florida banks).
3 This was very much the central analytical point reflected in the Supreme Court's celebrated decisions in *United States v. Philadelphia National Bank*, 374 U.S. 321 (1963), and its progeny.
4 See D. Baker and R. Brandel, *The Law of Electronic Funds Transfer Systems* (Revised edn 2002), ¶25.02 (*EFT Law*), discussing *inter alia, Independent Bankers Assn of America v. Smith*, 534 F.2d 921 (D.C. Cir. 1975), *cert. den.* 429 U.S. 862 (1976).
5 *EFT Law*, op. cit., ¶25.03.
6 Most of the shared networks were organized as non-profit cooperatives, but a few were normal business corporations owned by a smaller group of larger banks, or even a single bank that franchised the network service.
7 See letter from Assistant Attorney General William F. Baxter to Donald I. Baker, August 3, 1983 and discussion in *EFT Law* ¶25.03[3][a].
8 *EFT Law*, op. cit., ¶25.03[4].
9 U.S. Department of Justice Antitrust Division, *Policy Statement on Sharing to the National Commission on Electronic Fund Transfers*, 1977.
10 *EFT Law*, op. cit., ¶24.07[3][a].
11 See *United States v. Electronic Payments Services, Inc.*, No. 94–208 (D.Del. 1994) (consent decree), 59 Fed.Reg. 24,711 (May 12, 1994). The defendant in that case was a for-profit network with its own substantial data processing operation.
12 *EFT Law*, op. cit., ¶24.07[3][b].
13 See generally *EFT Law*, op. cit., ¶24.02, 24.03, and 24.07[1], discussing *SCFCILC, Inc. v. Visa USA*, 36 F.3d 958 (10th Cir. 1994) and numerous other cases.
14 In 1977, the Justice Department had brought two cases to eliminate regional automated clearing house rules that excluded thrift institutions from membership. See *U.S. v. California Automated Clearing House Assn.*, No. 77–1643-LTL (D. Cal. 1977) and *U.S. v. Rocky Mountain Automated Clearing House Assn*, No. 77–391 (D. Colo. 1977).
15 See generally D. Baker, "Compulsory access to network joint ventures under the Sherman Act: Rules or Roulette?" *Utah Law. Rev.*, 1993, pp. 999–1019.

Case 8

Internet browsers

Norman Hawker[1]

Introduction

Internet or Web browsers serve as one of the most important, if not the most important, ways to access the Internet. Text, multimedia, and other types of information all pass through the browser as they make way their way across the Internet to and from a personal computer. The browser not only sends and receives data, it also renders the text into legible pages, displays multimedia as movies or music, and draws images on the computer screen. Thus, the browser is not only a conduit through which data flows, but also an application capable of manipulating the data. The browser also serves as a platform for other applications. Developers can write applications to run on the browser just as they can write applications to run on operating systems such as Windows or Unix. To some extent, all three functions of the browser, conduit, application, and platform, raise access issues.

Overview of the industry and history of access

The Internet dates back to the 1960s where it began as an attempt by the Pentagon to develop a communications system that would continue to work even if an enemy attack knocked out parts of the network.[2] When the Internet went online in the 1970s, e-mail delivery between university and government researchers served as its primary function. By some accounts, e-mail remains the most popular use of the Internet. Eventually, however, researchers developed various ways to transfer entire files over the Internet. Using technologies such as "File Transfer Protocol," or FTP, it became possible for researchers in Berkley and Ann Arbor to share not only messages but also raw data, images, and entire documents.

And so it was that Tim Berners-Lee, while working at European Laboratory for Particle Physics ("CERN") in 1989, proposed the development of what later became the World Wide Web.[3] The proposal received approval fourteen months later, and Berners-Lee created the first web browser in 1990.[4]

The World Wide Web constituted a revolutionary development in many respects, not the least of which was to "link" different documents on different computers together using the Internet.[5] Although Apple Computer had demonstrated the concept of "linking" documents with HyperCard in the 1980s,[6] Berners-Lee moved this concept to an entirely new level by enabling linking over an enormous variety of types of documents over the Internet. Users could effortlessly "browse" information, including images and sounds, over the entire globe simply by clicking on a link. From the beginning, then, the web browser was about access.

Berners-Lee created the first web browser using NeXTStep, a graphical version UNIX which has evolved into Apple Computer's Mac OS X, but, as Berners-Lee has pointed out, the "dream behind the Web is of a common information space" and the realization of that dream required web browsers for other operating systems.[7] With the essential web technologies in the public domain, numerous projects arose to create web browsers for a wide variety of platforms.

The introduction of Mosaic in 1993 eclipsed all the other browser projects.[8] Developed by Marc Andreessen, an undergraduate student, while working for the National Center for Supercomputing Applications (NCSA) at the University of Illinois at Urbana-Champaign (UIUC). Originally designed for the X-Windows Unix platform, Andreessen and his colleagues at NCSA quickly developed versions for the Macintosh and Microsoft Windows platforms. Mosaic was the first browser to render graphics and text on the same page.[9] In addition, and perhaps more importantly, Andreessen and his colleagues provided 24 hour support for Mosaic and made it easy to install. Mosaic quickly became the dominant browser on the Internet.

In the spring of 1994, Andreessen graduated and went to Silicon Valley where he formed what became Netscape Corp. (UIUC refused to relinquish its rights to the Mosaic name).[10] Within the first year and a half of Netscape's existence, its browser had achieved an installed base of 65 million users.[11]

In its infancy, the web browser allowed users of the client computer where the browser was installed to view data stored on another computer, the server, provided the data had been formatted using Hypertext Markup Language (HTML). But it quickly became apparent that the browser was not limited to "browsing" data. The browser could transfer data to and from the client and server computers, enabling the user to run programs on the server. In addition to running applications on remote servers, the web browser offered a platform for running applications on the user's computer. As a platform for running applications, the web browser competed with the operating system.

The potential for the web browser to compete with the operating system was not lost on Microsoft, which quickly moved to bring its own browser to market in July 1995.[12] The courts ultimately found that many of

the aggressive tactics used by Microsoft to enter the browser market constituted an illegal maintenance of its operating system monopoly,[13] but the
Court of Appeals rejected the finding that Microsoft had attempted to
monopolize the browser market.[14]

Statistics vary considerably depending on the source, but it appears that
Microsoft's market share quickly grew from 16 percent of the market in
early 1996 to roughly 40 percent two years later.[15] In the same period of
time, Netscape's market fell from 80 percent to 45 percent.[16] By mid to
late 1998, Microsoft surpassed Netscape.[17] Today, estimates of Microsoft's
market share range as high as 96 percent.[18]

Netscape reacted to Microsoft's entry into the market by copying
Microsoft's strategy of giving away the browser for free and releasing the
source code to the public.[19] AOL subsequently acquired Netscape, and
then merged with Time Warner. After the recent settlement of
AOL/Time Warner's antitrust lawsuit against Microsoft, AOL/Time
Warner ended its support of the Netscape development, leaving the future
development of the Netscape browser in doubt.[20] Nonetheless, by releasing the source code to the public, Netscape placed development of its
browser into the hands of so-called "open source" developers, and they
may continue to develop the noncommercial versions the browser, the
most popular of which is known as Mozilla.[21]

As previously noted, both Netscape's and Microsoft's browser
descended from the Mosaic browser. Further development of Mosaic by
the NCSA ceased in January 1997.[22] Other browsers have entered the
market as niche players based on non-Mosaic source code. Apple Computers, for example, recently introduced its Safari browser, which is limited to
the Mac OS X operating system.[23] Opera is perhaps the most prominent of
these niche players, having been developed as a "faster" alternative to
Microsoft's Internet Explorer and Netscape's Navigator.[24] Opera is also
unusual in that it does not give away its browser for free.

Key issues in access

The browser is the gateway through which nearly all of the data on the
web must pass.[25] Consequently, the browser presents several access issues.
These include not only the user's ability to access websites, but more
importantly the ability of competing web servers and applications to interoperate or work with the browser. Finally, if Microsoft exploits its monopoly power in the browser market, the issue of whether competing
operating systems will continue to have access to the browser may arise.
This last concern may have taken on a new urgency with Microsoft's
decision to stop development of its browser as an application separate
from the Windows operating system.[26]

As to the first concern, that users will not be able to access the websites
they want, some evidence exists that this has begun. Users of the Opera

browser, for example, may have been denied access to websites on Microsoft's MSN website.[27] Apple's Safari browser users cannot access some online banking and music download websites.[28] But the problem goes back to the original Netscape browser and its decision to introduce frames on web pages, a departure from the HTML standards set by World Wide Web Consortium ("W3C"). Netscape and Microsoft both have attempted to add their own proprietary standards to the open standards of HTML. To some extent this was justified by the W3C's slow adoption rate of HTML enhancements, but to some extent both Netscape and Microsoft attempted to "embrace and extend" HTML so as to hinder competing browsers. Whatever the motive, the result has been that some browsers recognized HTML code that other do not.

This leads to the second access concern, interoperability. The issue of interoperability operates at more than one level. Related to the first concern, website developers need access to the browser. Website developers need to know how their pages will render or look with a given browser. This goes beyond making sure that a picture fills the top half of the page or that all of the text can be read in the browser window. Websites increasingly offer much more than text and graphics. For example, websites can deliver music either by enabling the user to download a file to her own computer or by "streaming" the music so that it is played by the browser rather than being permanently retained on the user's computer. Given the ubiquity of Microsoft's browser, most website developers who want to stream music will likely choose from the streaming technologies that are supported by Microsoft's browser.

Of course, this means that the developers of streaming technologies must also have access to the browser. Microsoft competes in this streaming market with its Windows Media format, and it has at least two methods at its disposal to disadvantage its rivals. First, for the browser to play streamed music it must run a small application or "plug-in" written for the browser, and if Microsoft were to deny its rivals access to the Application Programming Interface(s) they need to write the plug-ins, then their formats would not play in the browser. It might be possible to work around this by having the browser launch a separate or standalone application to play the streamed music, but even this comparatively cumbersome method would, of course, require some interoperability between the browser and the standalone application.

Alternatively, Microsoft could disadvantage rival formats by failing to distribute the required plug-ins with the browser. This would simply repeat the pattern Microsoft imposed on original equipment manufacturers (OEMs) by requiring them to distribute their PCs without Netscape installed. Granted, users could download and install the plug-ins for rival formats themselves, but if the market for music technology shares the network characteristics of the browser and operating system markets, the ubiquity of the pre-installed Windows Media plug-in will win out over whatever technical or quality advantages rival formats may offer.

Nor is the problem limited to software installed on the end user's computer. If the website developer wants to process private information, such as credit card numbers, it must be sure that its website uses an encryption technology compatible with the encryption technology of the browser. With its monopoly status in browsers, Microsoft could essentially "force" website developers to choose its "next-generation secure computing base"[29] technology over that of rival security technology by virtue of the network effects present in information technology. Microsoft has not yet shipped its next-generation secure computing base, but if and when this technology is installed in the browser, the technology will become ubiquitous. If Microsoft also removes the existing encryption technologies from the browser, then Microsoft's next-generation secure computing base would be the only ubiquitous encryption technology. Users might be able to install competing technologies, but if a website developer wanted to ensure that his website worked for all consumers, he would have to use Microsoft's next-generation secure computing base.

This networking effect has ramifications beyond the website developer and the vendor of competing encryption technology since the technology requires interaction between the consumer's web browser and the web developer's server. The most popular web server is an open source product, Apache, but commercial vendors including Netscape and Microsoft sell web servers. Unless Microsoft were to license its next-generation secure computing base to the open source community and its other competitors in the web server market, website developers would be required to purchase Microsoft's web servers.

The legal issues surrounding the browser remain underdeveloped and untested. The United States Department of Justice successfully challenged Microsoft's bundling of the browser system as an attempt to maintain its operating system monopoly, but lost the attempted monopolization of the browser market claim when the Court of Appeals ruled on the grounds that the browser market had not been properly defined.[30] Access to the browser, as opposed to the operating system, was not directly at issue. Microsoft's apparent plans to abandon development of its browser for competing operating systems[31] and the potential that Microsoft's current browser monopoly has for the development of websites that utilize Microsoft's proprietary technologies once again raises the specter of the browser as a tool for monopoly maintenance. Yet neither the settlement with the Department of Justice and the settling states nor the Final Judgment entered by the District Court at the conclusion of the trial by the litigating states required Microsoft to make the browser available for competing operating systems.[32] It seems unlikely that a court would order such a remedy in a future case.

Despite much discussion of the importance of access to the application programming interfaces (APIs), the Court of Appeals rule on whether Microsoft had violated the antitrust laws by failing to disclose them on a timely basis to Netscape. Nonetheless, both the settlement and the Final Judgment require Microsoft to disclose some of the operating system APIs. Section III.D of the Final Judgment, for example, requires disclosure of the operating system APIs used by "Microsoft Middleware to interoperate with a Windows Operating System Product." Any inference that this might create a legal obligation for Microsoft to disclose the browser APIs now that the browser will only be developed as part of the operating system is negated by the fact that Section VI.U of the Final Judgment gives Microsoft sole discretion to define what source code constitutes part of the "Windows Operating System Product."

Does the browser constitute an essential facility? The answer depends on how one approaches the browser. For most purposes, the answer would have to be no. The basic elements of an essential facilities claim are: (1) control of the essential facility by a monopolist; (2) a competitor's inability practically or reasonably to duplicate the essential facility; (3) the denial of the use of the facility to a competitor; and (4) the feasibility of providing the facility.[33]

The presence of alternative browsers, including open source browsers such as Mozilla that are available free of charge, probably dooms most access claims until such time as Microsoft's proprietary extensions of the HTML and other Internet standards make it impractical to access websites using any other browser.

If, however, one views the browser as a distribution device, then developers of rival internet technologies may be able to make out an essential facilities claim. The characteristic of the browser which is "essential" and which Microsoft's rivals cannot "practically or reasonable duplicate" is ubiquity. The District Courts in both the government's and Sun Microsystems' antitrust cases understood the importance of networking effects and initially fashioned remedies tailored to deal with this problem. The District Court in Sun's case showed unusual sensitivity to this issue in granting a preliminary injunction requiring Microsoft to install Sun's Java technology.[34] The preliminary injunction, however, has been stayed by the Court of Appeals for the Fourth Circuit while it considers the case.[35] Similarly, the Court of Appeals for the District of Columbia displayed some ambivalence about the merits of network effects in the operating systems market.[36]

In conclusion, although the browser presents a range of access problems, to date nothing has been done to address the problems. This, of course, begs the question of what should be done.

Approaches to the problem

Thus far, nothing has been done to address any of the problems of browser access. This is not to say that nothing has been attempted. The District Court in the government's antitrust lawsuit originally ordered

Microsoft to spin off its browser, along with other applications software, into a separate company. This might have alleviated the threat that competing operating systems would lose access to the browser. Without the burden of maintaining the Windows operating system monopoly, an independent browser company would have an incentive to make its browser widely available across multiple platforms. One could argue that the browser company might choose to reduce its costs by writing its browser only for the Windows platform, but given the disproportionate use of Unix and the Macintosh operating systems on the Internet, it seems unlikely that an independent browser developer would want to cede those markets to a competitor. The District Court's remedy, however, was vacated on appeal and nothing in the Final Judgment addresses the problems of browser access.

Spinning off the browser into a separate company might have ensured access by website developers. Without the burden of supporting Microsoft's other goals, a browser developer should have an incentive to make its browser work with as many websites as possible. To do otherwise might encourage consumers to try another browser. As Netscape's experience before the advent of Microsoft's browser shows, a browser developer will also have an incentive to introduce proprietary features unique to its browser to enhance the network effects. By itself, the introduction of proprietary features does not impair access by website developers, since the proprietary features can work for the browser developer's benefit only if website developers use those features. If one assumes that the monopoly status of Microsoft's browser would continue after it was no longer bundled with Windows, then the access issue becomes moot for website developers. If, however, competition were to break out in the browser market, each browser might incorporate its own proprietary features in order to create network effects. A website developer could take advantage of the proprietary feature of any given web browser only at the risk of making his website inaccessible to consumers using a competing browser. It is, of course, possible that in a competitive browser market some or all browser developers would compete on the basis of their ability to implement open standards. Given a multiplicity of proprietary standards and competitive pressure to perform well at implementing open standards, the end result could be a stifling of proprietary standards unless or until the market tipped in favor of one developer's browser.

For developers of web servers and other software that must interact with the browser, the success of a separate browser company at alleviating the problems of access would depend on whether the browser company also competed in these other software markets. While a browser-only company, regardless of whether it has a monopoly in the browser market, has incentives to make its browser with as wide a range of complementary software as possible, a browser company that also developed complementary software would also have incentives to use its browser to promote the sale of its complementary products. It is difficult to predict how this would play out in a competitive browser market place, but a browser company with a monopoly would almost certainly attempt to leverage its browser monopoly into other markets.[37] Consequently, a separate browser company might not alleviate the problem of software developer access.

Given the existence of network effects, the browser monopolist does not have to make his software incompatible with complementary software developed by his competitors. Instead, he can rely on the general proposition that "ubiquity beats quality" in information technology. For example, Microsoft does not have to make its browsers incompatible with competing multimedia formats from companies such as Apple and RealNetworks. If Microsoft only includes its own Windows Media plug-in with the browser, then consumers would have to download plug-ins from Apple and RealNetworks to play multimedia in these alternative formats. This may not seem like a major burden for Apple and RealNetworks, but a website developer could be assured that her multimedia content would work on everyone's computer only if she used Microsoft's Windows Media format. If, for example, she chose to use Apple's QuickTime format for her multimedia, she would also have to develop some way of installing Apple's QuickTime plug-in software on the computers of visitors' website.

A similar problem exists for the developers of web server technology. Microsoft does not have to make its browser incompatible with Netscape's server software. If Microsoft implements a proprietary technology in its browsers that interacts with the web server, competing web server developers could not take advantage of that feature of the browser. Website developers who wanted to use that browser features would have to purchase their web servers from Microsoft.[38] Competing developers of web servers may be able to write combinations of plug-ins and server side software that duplicates the functionality of Microsoft's features, but these competitors cannot duplicate the ubiquity of Microsoft's implementation of the features. Consequently, separating the operating system and Microsoft's other software into two separate companies would not ensure the access that software developers need.

What Microsoft's competitors need access to, i.e., the essential facility, is not the communication protocols, APIs, etc., to enable their web servers, plug-ins, etc., to work with the browser. The number and quality of open source web browsers would easily allow any Microsoft competitor to develop a browser compatible with whatever technology it offered in competition with Microsoft. What the competitors need access to is the ubiquity of distribution that comes with being incorporated into the browser.

The appropriate method of regulation, therefore, is to treat the browser as a common carrier for competing technologies that implement the same functionalties. Judge Motz recognized the same role played by the operating system in giving Microsoft ubiquitous distribution of middleware.[39] And Judge Motz appropriately ordered Microsoft to carry Sun's middleware with the Windows operating system. Judge Motz's preliminary injunction has been stayed pending an appeal by Microsoft,[40] but if the Fourth Circuit upholds the preliminary injunction, it may pave the way for the adoption of similar "must carry" injunctions for the browser.

Notes

1 Associate Professor of Strategy, Law and Ethics, Haworth College of Business, Western Michigan University and AAI Research Fellow.
2 See B. M. Leiner, V. G. Cerf, D. D. Clark, R. E. Kahn, L. Kleinrock, D. C. Lynch, J. Postal, L. G. Roberts, and S. Wolff, *A Brief History of the Internet*, Internet Society, August 4, 2000. Online. Available HTTP: <http://www.isoc.org/internet/history/brief.shtml> (accessed August 11, 2002); V. G. Cerf, *A Brief History of the Internet and Related Networks*, Internet Society, November 18, 2001. Online. Available HTTP: <http://www.isoc.org/internet/history/cerf.shtml> (accessed August 11, 2002); R. X. Cringely, *Nerds 2.0.1*. Online. Available HTTP: <http://www.pbs.org/opb/nerds2.0.1/index.html> (accessed August 11, 2002); R. H. Zakon, *Hobbes' Internet Timeline*, 2002. Online. Available HTTP: <http://www.zakon.org/robert/internet/timeline/> (access August 11, 2002); R. Davila, *History & Development of the Internet*, San Antonio Public Library. Online. Available HTTP: <http://www.sat.lib.tx.us/Displays/itintro.htm> (accessed August 11, 2002); W. Howe, *A Brief History of the Internet*, 2001. Online. HTTP: <http://www.walthowe.com/navnet/history.html> (accessed August 11, 2002); D. Kristula, *The History of the Internet*, 1997. Online. Available HTTP: <http://www.davesite.com/webstation/net-history.shtml> (accessed August 11, 2002); R. T. Griffiths, *History of the Internet, Internet for Historians (and Just About Everyone Else)*, Universiteit Leiden, 2001. Online. Available HTTP: <http://www.let.leidenuniv.nl/history/ivh/frame_theorie.html> (accessed August 11, 2002).
3 T. Berners-Lee, *Information Management: A Proposal*, 1989. A copy of the original proposal with some commentary is available on the Internet. T. Berners-Lee, *The Original Proposal of the WWW, Htmlized*, 1998. Online. Available HTTP: <http://www.w3.org/History/1989/proposal.html> (accessed August 11, 2002); see also T. Berners-Lee, *The World Wide Web: A Very Short Personal History*. Online. Available HTTP: <http://www.w3.org/People/Berners-Lee/ShortHistory> (accessed August 11, 2002); R. Cailliau, *A Little History of the World Wide Web: From 1945 to 1995*, 1995. Online. Available HTTP: <http://www.w3.org/History.html> (accessed August 11, 2002).
4 T. Berners-Lee, *The WorldWideWeb Browser*. Online. Available HTTP: <http://www.w3.org/People/Berners-Lee/WorldWideWeb.html> (accessed August 11, 2002).
5 It seems appropriate, therefore, that the oldest surviving web page is the definition for "link." See *Hypertext Links*, 1990. Online. Available HTTP: <http://www.w3.org/History/19921103-hypertext/hypertext/WWW/Link.html> (accessed August 11, 2002); see also R. Cailliau, op. cit.
6 See L. Kahney, "Hypercard: what could have been," *Wired News*, 2002. Online.

Available HTTP: <http://www.wired.com/news/mac/0,2125,54370,00.html> (accessed August 14, 2002).

7 T. Berners-Lee, *The World Wide Web: A Very Short Personal History*, op. cit.

8 The NCSA's website states that it introduced Mosaic in 1992, *About NCSA*, 2002. Online. Available HTTP: <http://www.ncsa.uiuc.edu/About/NCSA/> (accessed August 14, 2002); but Mosaic is not identified as one of the known projects by the W3 project at CERN in the fall of 1992, *WWW Software Products*, 1992. Online. Available HTTP: <http://www.w3.org/History/19921103-hypertext/hypertext/WWW/Status.html> (accessed August 14, 2002). While development on Mosaic may have begun in 1992 (R. X. Cringley, op. cit., Nerds 2.0.1—A Human Face), it appears to have made its first appearance outside the University of Illinois in 1993. See R. Cailliau, The History of the Internet, Chapter Two, Universiteit Leiden, 2001. Online. Available HTTP: <http://www.let.leidenuniv.nl/history/ivh/chap2.htm> (accessed August 11, 2002); W. Howe, op. cit.; T. Berners-Lee, *Frequently Asked Questions by the Press*. Online. Available HTTP: <http://www.w3.org/People/Berners-Lee/FAQ. html> (accessed August 14, 2002).

9 T. Berners-Lee, *"Frequently Asked Questions by the Press,"* op. cit.

10 R. X. Cringely, op. cit., Nerds 2.0.1—A Human Face.

11 Ibid.

12 *United States v. Microsoft Corp.*, 84 F. Supp. 2d 9, 14 (D.D.C. 1999). Ironically, Microsoft created Internet Explorer by licensing the source code for Mosaic. B. Wilson, *Browser History: Internet Explorer*, 2002. Online. Available HTTP: <http://www.blooberry.com/indexdot/history/ie.htm> (accessed June 2, 2003).

13 See *United States v. Microsoft Corp.*, 253 F.2d 34, 58–78 (D.C. Cir. 2001).

14 Ibid., 80–5.

15 M. J. Thompson, *Behind the Numbers: Browser Market Share*, CNN.com, 1998. Online. Available HTTP: <http://www.cnn.com/TECH/computing/9810/08/browser.idg/> (accessed June 2, 2003); *Browser Market Share and Selected News Stories*, Conroy Hewitt and Associates, 1999. Online. Available HTTP: <http://www.web-imagination.com/wow/cha-share9810.html> (accessed June 2, 2003).

16 M. J. Thompson, op. cit.

17 *Browser Market Share by Vendor—Historical Trend*, Janco Associates, Inc., 2003. Online. Available HTTP: <http://www.psrinc.com/Browser/Trends.htm> (accessed June 2, 2003) (indicates that Microsoft had almost 60 percent of the market in April of 1998); R. Chandrasekaran and E. Corcoran, "Microsoft's web browser overtakes Netscape's," *Washington Post*, October 1, 1998, p. C08. See also D. Toft, *Netscape Browser Market Share Drops To 25%* 1999. Online. Available HTTP: <http://www.idg.net/idgns/1999/08/09/NetscapeBrowser-MarketShareDropsTo.shtml> (accessed June 2, 2003).

18 G. Johnston, *Data Shows Netscape Browser Usage Down to Just 3.4%*, 2002. Online. Available HTTP: <http://www.computerworld.com/developmenttopics/websitemgmt/story/0,10801,73850,00.html> (accessed June 2, 2003). See also C. Upsdell, *Browser News*, 2003. Online. Available HTTP: <http://www.upsdell.com/BrowserNews/stat.htm> (accessed June 2, 2003); *Microsoft's Internet Explorer Global Market Share is 95% According To Onestat.Com*, OnesStat.com, 2002. Online. Available HTTP: <http://www.onestat.com/html/aboutus_

pressbox15.html> (accessed June 2, 2003); T. Olavsrud, *IE Continues to Gain in Browser Wars*, 2002. Online. Available HTTP: <http://www.internetnews.com/dev-news/article.php/1557411> (accessed June 3, 2003). But see *Browser Market Share By Vendor—Historical Trend*, Janco Associates, Inc., 2003. Online. Available HTTP: <http://www.psrinc.com/Browser/Trends.htm (accessed June 2, 2003) (indicating a 65 percent market share for Microsoft and a 15 percent market share for AOL, which uses Microsoft's web browser, for a combined market share of 80 percent).

19 B. Wilson, *Browser History: Netscape*, 2002. Online. Available HTTP: <http://www.blooberry.com/indexdot/history/netscape.htm> (accessed June 2, 2003).

20 J. Bonné, *Microsoft Settles Browser Suit With AOL*, 2003. Online. Available HTTP: <http://msnbc.com/news/919691.asp?0dm=C11MT> (accessed June 2, 2003); D. Becker, *Is This the End of Netscape?* 2003. Online. Available HTTP: <http://news.com/2100–1032–1011356.html> (accessed June 2, 2003); *AOL Cuts Remaining Mozilla Hackers*, mozillaZine, 2003. Online. Available HTTP: <http://mozillazine.org/talkback.html?article=3422> (accessed August 14, 2003); D. Gillmor, "Silicon Valley view: AOL cuts ties, but browser project still may flourish," *The Seattle Times*, 2003. Online. Available HTTP: <http://seattle-times.nwsource.com/html/businesstechnology/2001374138_btgillmor04.html > (accessed August 14, 2003).

21 A. Leonard, *Resistance Really Was Futile*, Salon.com, 2003. Online. Available HTTP: <http://www.salon.com/tech/col/leon/2003/06/02/unholy_alliance/> (accessed June 3, 2003).

22 Brian Wilson, *Browser History: Mosaic*, 2002. Online. Available HTTP: <http://www.blooberry.com/indexdot/history/mosaic.htm> (accessed August 14, 2002).

23 P. Festa, *Welcome to the Browser Jungle*, Safari, 2003. Online. Available HTTP: <http://news.com/2100–1023–979583.html> (accessed June 2, 2003).

24 See B. Wilson, "Browser history: Opera," 2002. Online. Available HTTP: <http://www.blooberry.com/indexdot/history/opera.htm (accessed June 2, 2003).

25 It is possible to access web servers with other types of software for limited purposes. Some e-mail clients, for example, do this to display graphics and other information in messages. Yet most, if not all, of these e-mail clients launch a web browser if a user clicks on a link contained within the message.

26 E. Hansen, "Microsoft to abandon standalone IE," CNET News.com, 2003. Online. Available HTTP: <http://rss.com/2100–1032_3–1011859.html> (accessed June 3, 2003); P. Festa, "Microsoft's browser play," CNET News.com, 2003. Online. Available HTTP: <http://news.com/2100–1032_3–1012943.html> (accessed June 4, 2003) (noting the possibility that Microsoft's browser "has gained such an overwhelming share of the market, as the de facto browsing standard, that Web surfers will be compelled to buy Windows—or upgrade Windows—in order to satisfactorily access important Web sites").

27 J. Lettice, "MSN deliberately breaks Opera's browser, claims company," *The Register*, 2003. Online. Available HTTP: <http://www.theregister.co.uk/content/6/29219.html> (accessed June 3, 2003); P. Festa, "Opera cries foul against MSN—again," CNET News.com, 2003. Online. Available HTTP:

<http://news.com/2100–1023–983500.html?tag=fd_top> (accessed June 2, 2003); J. Wilcox and S. Junnarkar, "MSN lockout stirs antitrust rumblings," CNET News.com, 2001. Online. Available HTTP: <http://news.com/2100–1023–274998.html> (accessed May 3, 2003) (noting that neither Mozilla nor Opera could access the MSN site); J. Watson, "New look MSN turns away non-MS lovers," *The Register*, 2001. Online. Available HTTP: <http://www.theregister.co.uk/content/6/22441.html> (accessed May 13, 2003).

28 "Fleet Bank: no plans to support safari," Mac News Network, 2003. Online. Available HTTP: <http://www.macnn.com/news/19959> (accessed August 12, 2003); "TD Waterhouse website lacks safari support," Mac News Network, 2003. Online. Available HTTP: <http://www.macnn.com/news/20125> (accessed August 12, 2003); M. Wendland, *BuyMusic Blocks Macs*, Mac-Mike.com, 2003. Online. Available HTTP: <http://www.mac-mike.com/archives/000244.html> (accessed August 12, 2003); see also R. Ford, *Macintosh Web Browser Future*, MacInTouch, 2003. Online. Available HTTP: <http://www.macintouch.com/browserfuture.html> (accessed August 14, 2003).

29 This is the security/digital rights management technology formerly known as "Palladium." R. Lemos, "What's in a name? Not palladium," CNET News.com, 2003. Online. Available HTTP: <http://news.com/2100–1001–982127.html> (last visited January 25, 2003).

30 *United States v. Microsoft Corp.*, op. cit.

31 See P. Festa, "Microsoft's browser play," op. cit.

32 As of this writing, the District Court's order remains on appeal.

33 *MCI Communications Corp. v. AT&T*, 708 F.2d 1081, 1132–33 (7th Cir. 1983).

34 *Sun Microsystems, Inc. v. Microsoft Corp.* (In re Microsoft Corp. Antitrust Litig.), 237 F. Supp. 2d 639 (D. Md. 2002).

35 *Sun Microsystems, Inc. v. Microsoft Corp.* (In re Microsoft Corp. Antitrust Litig.), 2003 U.S. App. LEXIS 1994 (4th Cir. 2003).

36 *United States v. Microsoft Corp.*, op. cit., 49–50.

37 In response to the single monopoly profit argument, one monopoly is never enough in information technology. First, all information technology monopolies depend on intellectual property law which, unlike other forms of property law, has expiration dates. Second, even though some expiration dates, especially copyright law, are generations away, all information technology monopolies are susceptible to reverse engineering. For example, Microsoft Office Suite monopoly depends on the inability of competing software to read and create Word, Excel, and PowerPoint files. With assistance from Sun Microsystems, the open-source movement has recently enjoyed some success at developing software that reads and writes files in these three critical formats. Not only do these open-source projects threaten Microsoft's monopoly in the Office Suite software, they also threaten the dominance of Microsoft's operating system since unlike Microsoft Office there are versions of the open source software for Linux, Solaris and other competing operating systems. To avoid these threats from reverse engineering, the firm must leverage monopolies in existing markets into complementary markets. Third, at least some, and perhaps all, information technology monopolies are subject to paradigm shifts. It was a paradigm shift away from desktop to internet computing that Microsoft sought

to avoid by entering the market with its own browser, and it was IBM's failure to recognize the paradigm shift from mainframe to desktop computing that cost IBM its monopoly. To avoid the threat of a paradigm shift, a firm must leverage its monopoly in existing information technology into new markets.

38 The same situation could occur in the market for web design tools. See D. Becker, "Microsoft aims higher with Web software," CNET News.com, 2003. Online. Available HTTP: <http://news.com/2100–1012_3–1015009.html> (accessed June 10, 2003).

39 *Sun Microsystems, Inc. v. Microsoft Corp.* (In re Microsoft Corp. Antitrust Litig.), 237 F. Supp. 2d 639, op cit., 644–50.

40 Sun Microsystems, Inc. v. Microsoft Corp. (In re Microsoft Corp. Antitrust Litig.), 2003 U.S. App. LEXIS 1994 (4th Cir. 2003).

Case 9

Internet-based airline and travel services

Albert A. Foer[1]

Introduction

Many competition issues that deal with access to a network revolve around whether a business should be able to participate in a network that happens to be owned or operated by dominant suppliers or competitors. Does a railroad, for instance, have a legal right to access to a uniquely located terminal that is controlled by its rivals?[2] This is the *opening* problem. Other issues arise after the principle of access has been accepted, when attention turns to the terms and conditions of access. How can fairness to all parties be assured? This can be called the *discrimination* problem. Still another set of issues has evolved with the coming of electronic commerce and the Internet. The creation in November, 1999, of Orbitz, a joint venture for the marketing of airline and other travel services, owned by five major airlines and encompassing as charter associates most of the remaining airline industry, illustrates this third pattern, in which incumbent producers (here, the airlines) who had previously competed against one another while supplying product (air transportation) to a separate distribution level (travel agencies, both brick-and-mortar and electronic), create a joint venture (Orbitz) to compete directly against new Internet-based distributors (Travelocity, Expedia, and others), as well as against what might be called legacy distributors (travel agents). We can name this the *inventory access* problem.

Comparable patterns have been reported for such industries as online music, digital movies, cosmetics, hotels, and foreign currency. In each situation, it appeared that the threat of Internet competition from independent companies induced incumbent companies competing against each other at a different level in the distributional chain to come together to withhold their critical inventory from the newcomer e-commerce competitors.[3] The recurrent problem wasn't that access to the Internet was denied, nor even that terms and conditions of access were discriminatory. Rather, the common problem appeared to be that competitors who were outside of the joint venture would be deprived of, or be put at a competitive disadvantage in obtaining, the very inventory that was necessary to achieve a successful business of product distribution through the Internet.[4]

The case of Orbitz must be understood in the context of the computerized reservation system (CRS) that had been developed by the airlines—the first significant networked industry infrastructure for electronic commerce. Network access problems arose almost immediately. Who would control the system? How many CRS networks would there be? What types of discrimination would or would not be permitted in terms of access to a CRS? The answers were provided by CRS rules that were eventually implemented by the now-defunct Civil Aeronautics Board in 1984 and revised by the Department of Transportation (DOT) in 1992, but these rules naturally did not cover the Internet, whose revolution had not yet arrived. By the time Orbitz came into existence, the Internet made it necessary for the airline industry to revisit network access issues that had already been, to a large extent, played out once before. The debate ended in January, 2004, when the DOT deregulated the CRS by deciding to allow the rules to terminate in accordance with their sunset provision.

It is, rather obviously, in the interest of the airlines to facilitate access for consumers to information about flight offerings, seat availability, and fares, in order to attract potential customers and to maximize the yield on seats sold. Traditionally, the airlines have provided consumers access to the air transportation network either directly (e.g., the consumer telephones to the airline and makes a reservation) or through travel agents who are intermediaries between a multitude of airlines and the consumer. With the advent of the Internet and of Internet-based travel agents in the 1990s, the major airlines determined to integrate vertically, as an industry, into the joint marketing of their inventory through their creation of Orbitz. The five owning airlines account for over 75 percent of domestic air transportation, and virtually every other airline is a charter associate of the joint venture—except for holdouts Southwest, JetBlue, and a few small low-fare airlines. The question facing both the DOT and the Department of Justice (DOJ) at the end of the twentieth century was: does this joint venture simply represent the arrival of a dynamic new entrant who will compete, to the benefit of consumers, against the other distributors of access to the air transportation network? Or, alternatively, will this movement to owner-dominated distribution likely foreclose the market to other ticket distributors and/or work to the detriment of consumers?[5]

Air transportation is a classic network industry.[6] The network consists primarily of airports that are nodes within an international system. The nodes are linked together in what are called city-pairs, but might better be described as airport-pairs, in that some cities host multiple airports or are within range to be served by multiple airports. The network more broadly construed includes transportation ties between origination/destination points, linkages from home, hotel, or office to and from airport, parallel baggage transportation, scheduling of flights, interconnections to accommodate air journeys that are not non-stop, and—our focus—a system for distributing tickets to allocate seats on scheduled flights.

If the network is most essentially the collection of all airport-pairs available for scheduled flights anywhere in the world, then the ticket distribution system represents the consumer's mode of gaining access to the network. In this chapter, we will see that ticket distribution within the U.S. has changed dramatically in the period since deregulation of air travel, and that the addition of the Internet as a method of ticket distribution has brought on more change of a revolutionary nature. We will also see that an industry-wide joint venture that includes most of the major air carriers—Orbitz—represented a significant competitive—and perhaps anti-competitive—threat to the portion of the industry that provides consumer access. Our treatment of the subject ends with the DOJ's decision not to intervene and the DOT's ultimate decision to eliminate the CRS rules.

Consumer access to the air transportation network

From the perspective of the consumer who wishes to travel from A to B, the initial options are generally plentiful and complex.[7] The complexity that faces the consumer results from many factors, but reflects important structural aspects of the air travel industry. The airlines have created "a vast array of price discrimination, going well beyond any other industry's patterns."[8] Choice is good, but according to a business text whose relevance to Orbitz will be made clear later on, "Choice, beyond a certain point, implies bewilderment. Hence the rise of the navigator."[9] Navigators operate in many businesses, performing an intermediary function between the seller and the buyer.[10] Navigators provide shortcuts through the maze of information and choices that are available. "Some navigators serve the interests of buyers by expanding and comparing the choices available. Others serve the interests of sellers by guiding buyers to the seller's products, preferably those with higher margins."[11] Whether navigators are primarily aligned with consumers or with the air carriers is a subtle question of major importance in the air transportation network. We will come back to this.

Consumers have two doorways into the air transportation network. They can purchase tickets (i.e., reserve seats on particular flights) directly from the air carrier or they can purchase indirectly through a navigator (that is, a travel agent, online or traditional) who provides access to a wide range of carriers.

In 1978, when deregulation was taking place, only 38 percent of tickets were booked by travel agents. Ten years later, travel agents booked 80 percent of tickets.[12] What intervened were (a) deregulation and (b) expanded computer capabilities, primarily the invention of the CRS. Deregulation brought with it a larger number of rival airlines per city-pair market,[13] and a new emphasis on price (compared to the pre-deregulation period, where "the urge for rivalry was artificially channeled into nonprice directions, such as airplane décor, youthful female cabin attendants, sumptuous meals, and a high frequency of flights"[14]). In addition, as a strategy responsive to the enhanced competitiveness of the industry, the major airlines developed hub-and-spoke networks, which in turn expanded the frequency and availability of service in most parts of the country, as well as the number of flight segments. Because of increased competitiveness, information needed by the consumer also became characterized by more frequent change. As the quantity and complexity of travel information expanded, so did the need for travel agents—expert intermediaries who could help the consumer navigate most efficiently to the desired destination.

In the early 1970s, travel agents had to rely on the telephone and on paper copies of the Official Airline Guide and other manuals to obtain information on flights and fares and to book reservations for their customers. In the late 1970s, there was an effort, under protection of antitrust immunity granted by the federal government, to create a single industrywide CRS. Competitive pressures led, however, to the development of multiple CRS networks. Today, there are four, Sabre, Galileo, Amadeus, and Worldspan, collectively also known as the Global Distribution Systems or GDS.[15] Typically, a travel agency would affiliate with one CRS, and pay it fees. Typically, too, each airline affiliated with all CRSs, and paid fees to the CRSs (which the airlines criticized as too high, even though there was for many years a significant airline ownership of some of the CRSs). In 1988, American Airlines owned Sabre, which had the leading market share of over 43 percent of bookings.[16] With travel agents becoming the predominant source of fare information, reservations, and ticketing, and virtually all of them relying on airline-owned CRSs (but each affiliating, generally, with only one CRS), it became imperative from a public perspective that CRSs would operate in an independent, neutral way. From each individual airline's perspective, however, the travel agent sells the airline's product and is an integral part of its marketing and distribution system.[17] An airline that owned a CRS therefore wanted to be able to take full advantage of the potentials for using the technology to drive business in its own direction. Thus, a tension was built into the system over the question: who should control the information that facilitates access to the network?

A series of studies demonstrated that the ownership of the CRSs by the major carriers gave them competitive advantages that had anticompetitive aspects. Most importantly for present purposes, the airlines were systematically using CRSs to bias the information given to consumers and to facilitate incentive plans for travel agents.[18] Consequently, the now-deceased Civil Aeronautics Board (CAB), in its last major action, issued regulations as early as 1984 that reduced the most glaring bias problems.[19] Under the CRS rules, an airline that owned 5 percent or more of a CRS

was required to furnish information about its own fares, flight information, and availability to all other CRSs on a nondiscriminatory basis.
Although the DOT, successor to the CAB, had been reviewing the CRS
rules for many years, it never made them applicable to the Internet.[20]

The Internet (and also the invention of the electronic ticket in 1995)
made feasible several important structural changes in the industry. Individual airlines found that they could sell their own tickets directly to the
consumer on their websites. This had at least two substantial advantages:
avoiding having to pay a commission to a travel agent and being able to
offer last-minute or other strategic discounts in order to fill up planes that
would otherwise fly with empty seats. (Increasingly sophisticated yield
management techniques expanded the airlines' ability to forecast the
implications of selling different seats at different prices at different times,
i.e., to price-discriminate more efficiently.) In addition, web sales enabled
each airline to deal directly with its customers in a more efficient way (i.e.,
without the intervention of a trained and salaried person) that also
reduced the likelihood that an independent travel agent would sell the
customer an alternative airline's ticket. One of Southwest's achievements
was to demonstrate the power of selling through its own website rather
than through distribution agents.

The second major structural change was the advent of the Internet-
based travel agency, including Travelocity and Expedia among others. It
was estimated in 2003 that approximately 15 percent of air travel reservations are made through such agencies and this percentage is predicted to
climb steeply. (Of the 15 percent, about 58 percent is sold directly by the
airline websites and 42 percent by third-party sites.) These e-commerce
systems allow the consumer to go online at any time of the day or night,
compare the various routes and terms for traveling from A to B, book a
reservation and obtain a ticket (or an e-ticket). The consumer benefits
from not having to spend time visiting a travel agent and avoiding any bias
that a travel agent might have, due to commissions[21] or over-rides paid by
the airlines.[22] The difference from working with an airline directly is that
the consumer can see most of the options offered by all the airlines at the
same time and in a relatively unbiased light,[23] and can select the one that
seems most appropriate.[24]

All of these developments reduced the airlines' reliance on brick-and-
mortar travel agents.[25]

About independent navigators: the quality of access to a network

With the Internet increasingly important, the airlines began to see a
benefit in reducing the role of travel agents. More or less in unison
around the time that Orbitz was being prepared and soon after its launch,
they repeatedly reduced the commissions that they would agree to pay to
travel agents (eventually reaching zero), with the result that thousands of

agents went out of business and those remaining tended to adopt service fees that made them less desirable to deal with from the consumer's perspective.[26]

Prior to the Internet, the airlines depended heavily on travel agents, to whom they paid commissions for bookings. Where possible, airlines attempted to bias the agents to represent their own perspective rather than the consumer's, by use of rigged CRS screens (prior to regulatory intervention), commissions, and special over-rides and incentives. The typical agent in effect had two masters, the airlines from whom compensation was obtained, and the consumer, whose repeat business depended on the consumer's sense that he or she was being well-served by the agent. Once the consumer had access to the Internet, new and more independent navigators (such as Travelocity and Expedia) came into existence with a more clearly consumer-aligned mission. This is not to say that there are absolutely no elements of bias in the Internet presentation, but that by making all relevant information more easily accessible to the consumer, the ability of the consumer to make an informed, objective decision was increased.

This process is described in more generic terms in *Blown to Bits*, a book whose authors were two senior vice presidents of The Boston Consulting Group (BCG), the organization hired by the airlines to create Orbitz. Their analysis is worth understanding before we turn our attention to what the Boston Consulting Group designed as the answer of a "legacy industry" to the rise of independent e-commerce navigators. The authors, Philip Evans and Thomas Wurster, focus on what they call the revolutionary process of "deconstruction," which they define as the dismantling and reformulation of traditional business structures, resulting from the new economics of information.[27] Deconstruction gives rise to navigators, who "lower the cost of search, increase its comprehensiveness, and align the search process more closely with the interests of the buyer."[28] Navigators pose a critical challenge to traditional sellers because they tend to be aligned with consumers rather than with sellers.

> As their reach goes up [i.e., as navigators' number of customers increases through internal growth and mergers], their affiliation to sellers loosens, which provides a further advantage in competing for buyers.[29] Some navigators get ahead of the others, cross the threshold of critical mass, and then march toward positions of monopoly in their respective search domains. Winner takes all. Armed with superior reach, a high level of consumer affiliation and trust, and equivalent richness ..., that navigator is advantaged in navigation against both retailers and suppliers. Retailers are demoted to the physical role of distributor. Suppliers see their business commoditized, or at least forced to compete on product-specific characteristics such as cost, technology, and features. Much of the value potential of the business is drained off.[30]

What should a company or an industry do when its business is challenged by a navigator? The BCG authors make numerous references to the airline industry, so it is probably no coincidence that their prescription appears to be so relevant to the germination of a joint venture that could keep essential inventory out of the hands of air service navigators like Expedia and Travelocity. The authors suggest several lines of defense for a challenged industry, perhaps the most relevant being this:

> [P]revent the new navigators from achieving critical mass.[31] Suppliers and retailers are the source of the information on product features, price, and availability that the new navigators need. So simply refuse to make that information available.[32] [But this is not so easy, Evans and Wurster admit.]

> Unless the selling business is highly concentrated, it is unlikely that the navigator's ability to achieve critical mass will depend on the availability of data from any one source. Therefore, while it is undoubtedly in the interests of all sellers *collectively*, it is not in the interests of any one seller *individually* to deny its own data to the navigator.[33]

When sellers act collectively to influence the essential terms of trade, they are usually called a cartel and subjected to antitrust scrutiny. The BCG authors offer no comment on whether a collective decision would be illegal or run the risk of being designated a cartel, but they suggest another line of defense with regard to which they reflect a counseling attitude that can be described as even more irresponsible. They suggest that an incumbent firm could "embrace customer affiliation and try to become an advantaged navigator,"[34] e.g., by going into direct competition with the navigator. But, the advice continues, do *not* truly align yourself with the consumer:

> Perhaps, provide comprehensive but not necessarily comparable data on one's own products and those of direct competitors, and slightly bias the presentation through the ordering of alternatives and the occasional emphasis, or omission. ... Conceal from the consumer the navigator service's supplier affiliation. ... The theory is that such a navigator may not be ideal for the seller, but is preferable to the independent alternative, and might suffice to deny to the latter critical mass.[35]

Could the authors have been thinking about something like Orbitz? They note that the strategy "worked for American Airlines' Sabre system, where American was able to bias presentation of a comprehensive flight listing by giving its own offering slightly more richness and greater prominence."[36] This statement, offered without any suggestion of possible legal impropriety, is accompanied by an extraordinary little footnote at the back of the book: "American Airlines was eventually forced by industry and governmental pressure to stop the practice of presenting schedule information to favor its own flights."[37] (It strikes me as disingenuous that the authors fail to suggest that the CRS rules that emerged to stop this type of display bias were undertaken pursuant to Section 411 of the Federal Aviation Act, specifically to prevent unfair methods of competition and deceptive practices in air transportation and the sale of air transportation.[38]) Back in their main text, the authors identify two (and only two) problems with their advice, neither relating to a possible antitrust issue. One is particularly interesting, however: they recognize that the incumbent's own navigator product is likely to be inferior from the customer's point of view (because of skepticism about its objectivity) to that provided by an independent third party.[39] In many industries, they say, the incumbents would have to worry about the long term defensibility of a weakly biased navigator. But "[I]n the airline customer [sic] reservations system (CRS) business, the staggering complexity of the data-processing requirements proved a lasting barrier to new entrants."[40] If Orbitz were to knock out the independent navigators, one could infer it might well be protected against later new entry, particularly if the network effects result in "winner take all."

This analysis of the role of navigators, using examples from the airlines' experience with computer reservation systems and written by the management consulting firm that was hired by the airlines to design Orbitz, has the appearance of a blueprint for a collective plan to withhold essential inventory (information regarding the lowest priced fares) from new (and perhaps still unprofitable) independent navigator companies, in order to keep them from reaching critical mass.

When should regulators act?

In June 2001, Orbitz was launched to compete against both the traditional travel agents and the newer Internet agents and to force CRSs to reduce booking fees.[41] Within six months, Orbitz had reportedly become the equal of Travelocity and Expedia, despite the fact that it had taken the latter each around five years to attain their market shares. Normally, a new competitor is a plus for consumers, but certain aspects of the Orbitz entry raise questions about the nature of network industries in which the owners of mission-critical information are able to withhold it from competitors. Believing that Orbitz gained its foothold by anticompetitive means, a variety of consumer advocacy organizations[42] supported the competitors of Orbitz in seeking antitrust or regulatory modification of its structure.

As noted, Orbitz is a joint venture of the five major airlines (American, United, Delta, Northwest, and Continental—representing over 75 percent of the market) and includes as affiliates virtually all airlines other than Southwest, JetBlue, and a few other low-fare carriers. Among the justifications offered for their investment in Orbitz was the airlines' desire to build a favorable alternative to what they perceived as the non-competitive, expensive CRS booking structure (Orbitz operates through the Worldspan CRS, which was then owned by affiliates of Delta, Northwest, and American airlines, who are partners in Orbitz). Orbitz also offered the airlines a guarantee of neutrality.

The arrival of Orbitz had been announced sufficiently far in advance of its launch that both the Department of Transportation and the Department of Justice had opportunity to evaluate it and take action, if they chose to. This is not unusual in the case of network businesses, which require substantial advance planning and negotiations with multiple participants. A venture like Orbitz acts prudently in exploring government reaction before large sums are invested. Both relevant federal agencies were on notice of widespread concern about the plan for Orbitz; Senate hearings were even held in July, 2000.[43]

Like many other critics, the American Antitrust Institute (AAI) focused on two specific aspects of the joint venture ascertainable through a reading of the agreement between Orbitz and its charter associates. First, it noted that a most favored nations provision (MFN) assured Orbitz that its affiliated airlines would not enter into deals with other travel agents that they would not also make available to Orbitz. This permitted Orbitz to market itself as the one-stop shopping destination providing the lowest fares of anyone in the industry (no one could offer lower!). It also had the potential of undermining the incentives for airlines to make special secret deals with competitors of Orbitz, that in the past would have increased the amount of price competition in the industry.[44] As Adkinson and Lenard have written,

> The MFN provision of the Associate Agreement raises clear competitive problems and is likely to reduce competition in fare-setting and online ticket distribution. There is a serious risk that the MFN will inhibit selective or camouflaged discounting of fares, including discounting by members who feel forced to join to avoid discrimination.[45]

Second, Orbitz' contract with affiliates contained incentives (as well as a pervasive but informal understanding, reflected in various Orbitz marketing pronouncements) that seemed likely to ensure that the airlines' lowest fares would go exclusively to Orbitz, despite clear language in the Associate Agreement stating that there is no agreement as to exclusivity. The Associate Agreement nonetheless requires affiliated airlines to provide annual "in-kind promotions" of a certain minimum value to Orbitz. This obligation can be satisfied in a variety of ways, such as placing the Orbitz brand in ads, which have a cost to the affiliated airline, or can be satisfied by providing exclusive fares (fares available only on the Orbitz site) or semi-exclusive fares (available only on the Orbitz site or the airline's own site). Until some time in 2002, opponents of Orbitz were reporting that the lowest fares of the Orbitz airline group were in fact going *only* to Orbitz. Orbitz denied this, emphasizing that its affiliates are free to provide web fares to both Orbitz and others, and saying that online competitors are obtaining web fares.[46] Sabre countered by saying,

> In recent months, *some* of the Orbitz carriers have started to provide *some* web fares to a select few of the independent agents. However, those carriers that do have deals to provide web fares to independent sites have evidently reserved discretion to deny to others the same fares Orbitz gets because of the continued prevalence of a large number of instances where Orbitz, and Orbitz alone, possesses web fares on all five Orbitz owners and often, on any of them. And Orbitz has now confirmed that it has *ten year contracts* with its owners that, among other things, guarantee Orbitz access to all these web fares.[47]

Competitors and consumers made sure that the two relevant regulatory agencies were aware of all this. But their case against Orbitz rested on predictions of what would likely happen after Orbitz was up and running. At what point, if any, should the government intervene?

Antitrust and public policy issues

In its early analysis the AAI suggested that there were four types of antitrust issues presented by the Orbitz joint venture. First, if low fares were to be withheld from competing distributors, this might constitute an illegal group boycott by the owners of the joint venture. Second, the failure of the CRS rules to cover the Internet re-opened the door for anticompetitive discrimination by the owners of Orbitz, which had previously been precluded by the DOT after substantial experience of the effects of biased information in the CRS arena. Third, the joint venture seemed too inclusive, including virtually the entire industry, possibly eliminating the existence of multiple competing access points. And fourth, there was need to be assured that the new information flows would not be used to facilitate tacit collusion.[48]

Concerns about tacit collusion and over-inclusiveness gradually faded from discussion as criticism of Orbitz came to focus increasingly on the MFN clause and the incentives for exclusivity. A fifth issue emerged somewhat later, questioning whether the joint venture was a monopsonistic device, a buyers' cartel aimed at pressing below the competitive level the price that airlines would pay to online ticket distributors.[49] Although pressed at various times by competitors of Orbitz, there is little indication in the public record that it was taken seriously by either DOJ or DOT.

On April 13, 2001, the U.S. Department of Transportation notified Orbitz that it would not prevent Orbitz from beginning operations. DOT's letter recognized the anticompetitive potential of the joint venture, but concluded that it would be premature to act.[50] Rather, Orbitz would be required to report on its own operations six months after the launch so that DOT could keep an eye on its actual behavior.

In a meeting with high level Antitrust Division officials on May 22, 2001, the AAI and representatives of 25 consumer groups argued that, despite the DOT position, the Justice Department should take action prior to the launching of Orbitz. The type of behavior that was most in question, we argued, related to the exclusive availability on Orbitz of the airline industry's lowest fares. Web fares (referring to discounts offered exclusively to those who purchase tickets on the Internet) include the last-minute bargain prices that an airline uses to fill empty seats, but they also include special discounts, such as Delta's "online discount" of 5 percent on most shuttle fares that were then being promoted. This discount category, which Orbitz had argued would be *de minimus*, was ignored by DOT, but we argued that it was perceptibly growing and could become quite large. (This is in fact what later happened.) In answer to the claim of Orbitz that its joint venture agreement did not compel these lowest fares to be sold exclusively through Orbitz, we recognized that the documents had been well-lawyered so as to say explicitly that there would be no exclusivity, but we said the question should be whether this extraordinary venture of virtually the entire industry is so replete with incentives to keep the lowest fares in Orbitz that exclusivity is indeed what is both intended and likely to occur.

DOT's letter to Orbitz said that DOT would be concerned if "Orbitz substantially reduces charter associate carriers' incentive to make their lowest fares (including web fares) available through other online travel agencies," and that it will monitor developments closely. DOT also said, "We have serious concerns about incentives toward exclusivity, however limited." But DOT was prepared to reserve judgment until it could see how things would work out.

We told the Justice Department that in our view, either Orbitz expected the joint venture to be the exclusive source for the lowest fares or it did not. If it did not, let Orbitz enter into an agreement with the government that would assure the government, consumers, and competitors that exclusivity will not occur. Let Orbitz agree to act as if the CRS rules applied to the Internet by having its five owning carriers agree that any information they provide to Orbitz would also be provided to other distributors on commercially reasonable and non-discriminatory terms.[51] If Orbitz refused to enter into such an agreement, we said, then this should be taken as evidence of the anticompetitive nature of the joint venture.

We further argued that the type of harm that Orbitz is capable of doing may not later be remediable, from a public perspective. Suppose Orbitz does market itself successfully as the only website with the lowest airfares, and that this draws a substantial part of the market away from other distributors. What, realistically, could be done about this at a later date? And how quickly could anything be done, given the drawn-out nature of antitrust enforcement and the airlines' political influence? Travelocity and Expedia reportedly were only on the edge of profitability, after five years of operating history, despite Orbitz' depiction of them as entrenched incumbents. If Orbitz were to succeed dramatically because of its unique relationship with the carriers, it could force one or both of the incumbents out of the market, by denying them critical mass, as suggested by *Blown to Bits*. Possibly, with difficulty, such a victimized company could win an antitrust case for monetary damages, but that would not likely restore it as a realistic competitor, especially if network effects were to give Orbitz a large advantage. So what could the government do at that later point in time? It could do later, we argued, only what it can do before Orbitz is officially launched, *viz.*, require that any fares made available to Orbitz also be made available to other ticket distributors or eliminate the MFN and the provisions incentivizing exclusivity. The question about this remedy at some later date, after the competitive damage is done, will be whether a badly wounded competitor can be restored to health.

So we argued to the Justice Department. But DOJ took no action. This illustrates a problem—or others could argue, a strength—that is inherent in the American antitrust process, where law enforcement decision-makers are loathe to make predictions for which, naturally, there will be little solid evidence that can be expected to persuade a court to issue an injunction. On the other hand, an administrative agency like the DOT, with a more broadly defined mission of protecting the public interest, might arguably act more aggressively on the basis of its industry expertise, which tends to be credited by courts. The difficulty is that administrative agencies that have substantial industry expertise generally also have close ties to the regulated industry (if they are not indeed captured by it, as a substantial literature suggests is not unusual), and may be reluctant to take an action that the stronger elements within the industry oppose.

The path to deregulation

After six months of operation, and still without DOT action to extend the CRS rules to the Internet, Orbitz presented its report to the DOT, as required by the DOT letter. As opponents had predicted, it concluded that Orbitz was working positive wonders both for the industry and for consumers and there would be no reason to change its structure or operation. Others, of course, were less sanguine. Sabre, for instance, filed comments with the DOT that included the following points.[52] First, in November, 2001, Orbitz surpassed Expedia to become the number two travel website in terms of airline bookings. Second, as of March 20, 2002, none of the five airline owners of Orbitz paid "base commissions" to U.S. travel agents, but all five appear to continue to pay Orbitz the "transaction fees" that Orbitz is guaranteed pursuant to the Orbitz airline participation agreement. This discrimination would be forbidden under the CRS rules if they applied to the Internet. Third, the owners of Orbitz have made available to Orbitz—and only to Orbitz—wave after wave of Web fares, often for discounts across all or much of their entire network of flights.[53] Fourth, smaller and low-fare carriers do much more poorly at Orbitz than at Travelocity or Expedia. Fifth, in December, 2001, Orbitz initiated a $5 transaction fee for all tickets purchased on its site.[54] Finally, Travelocity and, reputedly, Expedia have been forced to shift their focus away from the sale of scheduled air to the sale of other products, such as hotels, package vacations, and cruises.[55] In short, Sabre asserted that all of the anticompetitive evils warned against before Orbitz was launched have in fact occurred within the first year of operation.[56]

Half a year later, in November, 2002, the National Commission to Ensure Consumer Information and Choice in the Airline Industry issued its final report, concluding, among other things, that the MFN provision was not necessary and that the government should seriously consider compelling its elimination. A year later, on July 31, 2003, however, the Antitrust Division announced that it had closed its investigation of Orbitz. In an unusual statement,[57] Assistant Attorney General Hewitt Pate explained that during its three-year investigation, the Division had sought to understand whether the MFN provision would reduce competition for discount airline fares.

> The available empirical evidence, however, did not show that the MFN has resulted in a reduction in discount fares.... Although average web-only fares have increased since Orbitz began offering its service, the evidence indicates this is the result of a change in the nature and composition of web-only fares.... The Division's investigation showed that the volume of web-only fares offered has increased dramatically— six-fold in less than a year—since Orbitz began its service. Because there are so many more of the newer type of web fares, which are not as deeply discounted as the distressed inventory fares, it is not surprising that average web fares have increased. And, as noted above, the average of all domestic airfares decreased over this time period.... The Division's investigation also showed that participating carriers continue to compete through their own websites.... Finally, many low cost carriers, including Southwest, Jet Blue, ATA, and Air Tran, did not become charter associates, and therefore Orbitz creates no disincentive for these carriers to offer low fares. Moreover, in the markets they serve, the low cost carriers exert pressure on Orbitz owners and charter associates to offer more competitive fares.

To some extent, this missed the point. Even critics of Orbitz recognized that its entry would likely increase the incidence of discount fares. The question was, would Orbitz take advantage of its ownership structure in order to drive competitors out of the market—after which it could raise fares? More to this point, Pate said that

> The evidence gathered in the Division's investigation showed that while Orbitz initially grew rapidly, its growth leveled off after several months. Not only has Orbitz not achieved a dominant position, it has remained the third largest online travel agency for over a year. The Department of Transportation reported in December 2002 that Orbitz had 24 percent of online ticket sales. Rival sites have continued to grow in airline ticket revenues and other revenues. Notwithstanding the MFN, rival websites continue to compete aggressively against Orbitz and have been able to obtain access to many web-only fares. As for the incentives to offer fares exclusively on Orbitz, our investigation revealed that few, if any, such exclusives were ever employed, and the likely future effect of this provision appears trivial.

In other words, the Antitrust Division concluded, predictions that Orbitz would use its control over the lowest airfares as a weapon of exclusion in order to gain dominance had not been borne out during the period after the launch. Orbitz had gained a solid foothold in the electronic ticket distribution market, but had neither gained dominance nor appeared about to do so. What remained unclear, the AAI said in its own press release, was whether (a) DOJ's prediction that Orbitz would not be a winner who takes all would turn about to be correct or whether (b) Orbitz had pulled its punches during the period it was monitored. Would its behavior change now that the investigation was closed? [58]

Six more months went by while DOT's CRS rulemaking continued.[59] The Bush Administration, committed to a pro-business philosophy of minimal regulation, decided after prolonged consultations involving the White House, not to extend the CRS rules to the Internet, but rather to eliminate the rules entirely.[60] An episode that began with the question of government intervention to assure network access ended, after significant changes in technology and business practices, in government apparently stepping back to let the market operate more freely.

Some observations

What lessons might the Orbitz case hold for network access? Ownership of a producer network may create opportunities and incentives for withholding critical inventory from intermediaries, to maximize owners' control over access to the network. This can be arranged through formal or informal, total or partial exclusionary agreements. Antitrust analysis must look to the whole picture, going beyond the words on a paper, to understand the dynamics of exclusion.[61]

Consideration of access to a network should include a focus on the motivation and incentives of the intermediaries who make access available to consumers. The Internet has made it possible for independent navigators to align themselves closely with consumers, by providing objective information facilitating consumer decisions that will predictably reduce the profits of the incumbents. Orbitz may have to appear, in its early years, as an independent navigator, in order to compete against other independent navigators. But if it were to use the competitive advantage of exclusive access to low fares to successfully gain industry dominance, it could be predicted that those who control Orbitz, i.e. the five largest carriers, would find ways to skew its operation in their favor.[62]

In terms of remedies, the Orbitz story illustrates that tried and tested fair-access remedies may need to be adjusted to account for developments on the Internet. The CRS rules against discrimination in the provision of information by CRS owners could have assured that Orbitz would play on a level playing field, had the rules been revised in a timely way to apply to the Internet.

Antitrust, too, could have been utilized without great risk. A strong argument can be made that eliminating the MFN provision would have facilitated more discounting for consumers, without jeopardizing the joint venture. Would Orbitz have gone to court to preserve the MFN, had DOJ made this the target of a limited attack? This would have thrown the venture into question and no doubt delayed it. But should a prosecutor use the threat of litigation in order to compel an agreement to drop a clause in a joint venture agreement? Is the litigation mentality appropriate to this type of situation or should the antitrust prosecutor be playing more of a policy role?

This aspect of the Orbitz experience also suggests that a future-oriented rulemaking approach, by an expert administrative agency, may or may not have advantages over dependence on antitrust enforcement, when the threatened harms have not yet materialized in a substantial way that can unquestionably be demonstrated in court. The advantages are theoretically present, but there must be a will to act. Here, both the DOT and the DOJ seemed to recognize risks of allowing Orbitz to proceed unchanged, but neither was willing to take action based on predictions. Of course, not acting was also based on a prediction, namely that the benefits of non-intervention would outweigh any competitive harm that would occur prior to imposition of a later, effective remedy. Now, it remains to be seen whether post-hoc remedies will be needed or invoked and, if so, whether they will come in time to make a difference.

As we go to press, it appears that Orbitz' growth has reached a plateau and that the feared tipping of the ticket distribution industry is not about to occur. Assuming the initial fears were legitimate, why then did the industry not tip? It would appear that the advantages of one-stop shopping were overestimated, perhaps because consumers found that they could so easily shop around electronically. (Today there is even a website that consolidates a wide variety of electronic travel options—www.SideStep.com.) But at least equally important, the huge potential advantage of Orbitz having exclusive access to the lowest fares was not maintained for long, in that the distribution sector responded—when the federal agencies were not intervening beyond the investigation stage—by making deals with the airlines for their content on terms that were essentially set by Orbitz.

One way to look at this whole episode, in retrospect, is to view it not so much as a collective effort by the airlines to create the dominant air travel reservation service, as to use the threat of Orbitz to force the CRSs, travel agencies, and online agencies to negotiate lower fees for the airlines.[63] This was achieved. In the battle for the consumer's dollar, the middle was drained. It is generally understood that the third-party sale of airline reservations, while driving transactions, is no longer the lucrative part of the reservation business. Profitability now resides with the package transactions, the hotel deals, and the cruise deals that the distribution industry increasingly promote.

Finally, we should note the role of antitrust monitoring in a rapidly evolving industry. The mere fact of an investigation usually has some impact on whomever is being investigated. It would be worth determining whether the Orbitz case may be one in which an antitrust investigation caused the airlines to pull their competitive punches. Left alone, perhaps Orbitz would have accomplished what its critics feared: quick domination of electronic travel through exclusive control over low-price fares. Or perhaps not.

In the context of a network industry, where it is unknown whether there will be a winner-takes-all (or even a winner-takes-most) outcome, investigation can be a safe, even a wise low cost/low risk strategy for the government, provided there is a commitment and ability to take further action if justified. For the Orbitz joint venture, this strategy allowed a newcomer to compete; kept public policy options open; facilitated fact gathering and analysis; and postponed more serious action until experience threw greater light on the likelihood of various predictions of competitive harm being correct. Meanwhile, however, the absence of further government action probably resulted in the distribution sector having to cave in to the collective fee-cutting strategy of the airlines, a strategy which, had it been naked rather than masked through the joint venture, would have likely been viewed as violating the Sherman Act. Having closed the investigation, it should remain incumbent on the Antitrust Division to monitor developments and be prepared to take swift action if the no-harm predictions need re-evaluation. All the more so in that the intensive focus on Orbitz led, ultimately, to DOT's decision to deregulate the CRS system.

Notes

1 President, American Antitrust Institute. AAI has been a critic of the Orbitz joint venture on antitrust grounds. Among contributors to the AAI have been the Sabre Corporation and Southwest Airlines.

2 See the first access case to be decided by the Supreme Court, *U.S. v. Terminal Railroad Association of St. Louis*, 224 U.S. 383 (1912).

3 See materials relating to the Workshop on Supplier Internet Joint Ventures sponsored by the American Antitrust Institute and the National Consumers League, September 26, 2002. Online. Available HTTP: <http://www. antitrustinstitute.org/recent2/204.cfm> (accessed June 16, 2004). See generally, A. A. Foer, "E-commerce meets antitrust: a primer," *Journal of Public Policy & Marketing* 20, 2001, pp. 51–63.

4 An important but little-noted case illustrating this pattern was brought by the FTC in 1998. A Chrysler dealership in Kellogg, Idaho, created a website where consumers in Idaho and nearby states could shop for cars from the comfort of their homes. A group of rival dealers responded by forming an association and collectively threatening that they would refuse to sell certain Chrysler vehicles and would limit their warranty service unless Chrylser changed its allocation system to disadvantage dealers that sold large quantities of vehicles outside their local geographic areas. In effect, this was an attempted group boycott of Chrysler. The FTC obtained a settlement that stopped the practice. FTC, Fair Allocation System, Inc.: Analysis to Aid Public Comment, 63 Fed.Reg. 43182 (1998).

5 A considerable amount of information relating to these questions may be found on the website of the National Commission to Ensure Consumer Information and Choice in the Airline Industry at http://www.ncecic. dot.gov/. The Commission was established under U.S. Public Law 106–181, the Wendell H. Ford Aviation Investment and Reform Act for the 21st Century, which became law April 5, 2000. The Commission's final report was issued on November 10, 2002. Online. Available HTTP: <http://www.ncecic. dot.gov/ncecic/reports/execsum.pdf> (accessed June 16, 2004).

6 In their fourth edition of *The Antitrust Revolution*, Kwoka and White inaugurate a section on network issues. See J. E. Kwoka, Jr. and L. J. White (eds), *The Antitrust Revolution*, New York: Oxford University Press, 2004, pp. 414–27.

7 If the distance is under about 150 miles, it typically makes sense to travel by car, bus, or perhaps train. While these usually remain options for longer distances, the appeal of air transportation with its great advantage of speed obviously grows with the distance to be covered. Focusing on air travel, the consumer is met by what can be a complicated, indeed bewildering, menu of alternatives for traveling from A to B, involving numerous tradeoffs in price and convenience. The lowest fare may entail making reservations a month or more in advance and routing through one or more intermediary airports. Or it may entail flying to C, located near B, and renting a car to complete the trip. Additional choices may include, e.g., whether to fly first class or economy, whether to fly on a well-known national airline or a low-cost, new-entrant airline or a regional carrier, whether to stay at the destination over a weekend, and whether to redeem frequent flyer awards that may be available.

8 W. G. Shepherd, "Airlines," in *The Structure of American Industry*, W. Adams and

J. Brock (eds), 10th edn, Upper Saddle River, N.J.: Prentice Hall, 2001, p. 213. This takes advantage of the recognition that different consumers have different elasticities of demand (most importantly, the difference between business and leisure travelers), that seats have a different value depending on when they are purchased (the airline is advantaged if it can sell off unoccupied seats at the last minute, even at a steeply discounted price), and that government policy facilitates price discrimination. For legitimate "safety" reasons, the FAA requires travelers to show their identification to the check-in agent. This turns out to be a perfect device to promote the airlines' maximization of the use of price discrimination, since it prevents the re-selling of tickets.

9 P. Evans and T. S. Wurster, *Blown to Bits, How the New Economics of Information Transforms Strategy*, Boston: Harvard Business School Press, 2000, p. 64.

10 Ibid., p. 104 "(In some instances, navigation may be a business in its own right (the Yellow Pages, a personal shopper, or an independent financial adviser). Often, it is a function within a business (the White Pages, a salesperson, or a stockbroker)."

11 Ibid., p. 105.

12 Transportation Research Board, National Research Council, *Winds of Change: Domestic Air Transport Since Deregulation*, Washington, D.C.: National Research Council, 1991, p. 152; Transportation Research Board, National Research Council, *Entry and Competition in the U.S. Airline Industry: Issues and Opportunities*, Washington, D.C.: National Academy Press, 1999, p. 125.

13 At the outset of deregulation, only about 20 percent of city-pair markets had three or more competitors; this share grew to 40 percent by 1991. See Transportation Research Board, National Research Council, *Entry and Competition in the U.S. Airline Industry*, op. cit., p. 2.

14 Shepherd, op. cit., p. 200.

15 This piece of history demonstrates the difficulty in predicting whether a particular network, in its infancy, will have a "winner-take-all" character. Clearly, the GDS industry could sustain competing networks.

16 Transportation Research Board, National Research Council, *Winds of Change*, op. cit., p. 151, Table 4–1 (Apollo (dominated by United) controlled 28 percent of bookings. Sabre is now independent).

17 *Entry and Competition*, op. cit., p. 125.

18 For example, "By determining the order in which carriers' flights show up on a travel agent's computer screen, an airline reservation system can influence the distribution of demand among airlines. For example, in response to a request for a 3:00 P.M. flight, the Apollo system [owned by United] would show a 1:00 P.M. United flight prior to showing a 3:00 P.M. flight of its competitors." W. K. Viscusi, J. M. Vernon, and J. E. Harrington, Jr., *Economics of Regulation and Antitrust*, 2nd edn, Cambridge, Massachusetts: MIT Press, 1998, p. 593.

19 In 1992, before many sales were made on the Internet, DOT amended the regulations to prohibit CRS-owing carriers from withholding from competitors fare and other data they provided to their own system, as long as the competing system offered commercially reasonable terms. 57 Fed.Reg. 43780 (September 22, 1992).

20 The CRS Rules are found at 14 CFR. Part 255. The DOT extended the life of the current rules until March 31, 2003, and then until January 31, 2004. In November, 2003, Amadeus petitioned DOT to further extend the rules or to

eliminate the sunset date entirely. (Docket No. 03–16469.) The DOT ultimately allowed the rules to lapse. 69 Fed.Reg 976 (January 7, 2004).

21 An agent might be biased in favor of suggesting more expensive flights, to maximize commissions earned—if commissions are being paid. Standard (base) commissions were generally eliminated in 2002.

22 Individual airlines can attempt to influence the agent by paying additional commissions or providing other incentives above the base commission.

23 Both brick-and-mortar travel agents and Internet agents are subject to the bias of commission overrides, although one could overstate the importance of this. All retailers are aware that not all inventory carries the same profit margin. The combination of competition and reputation (common knowledge of the potential bias) can often protect consumers adequately. Orbitz has criticized its competitors as being biased, pointing out that, unlike Travelocity and Expedia, it does not permit advertising. This policy has its own competitive drawbacks, however, in that start-up and fringe airlines do not have the ability to advertise on Orbitz or to promote through temporary commission overrides.

24 For example, if a consumer calls United Airlines about a flight from Washington Reagan to Chicago O'Hare, the operator is not likely to suggest a cheaper United flight from BWI to Midway, and certainly won't call attention to a competitor's flight. An Internet travel agent can automatically make such alternatives obvious.

25 For a description of the ways in which ticket distribution has changed over time, see Statement of Michael Levine before the National Commission to Ensure Consumer Information and Choice in the Airline Industry, July 26, 2002. Online. Available HTTP: <http://www.ncecic.dot.gov/ncecic/hearings/levine-testimony.pdf> (accessed June 16, 2004).

26 See AAI letter to the Secretary of Transportation raising questions about the airlines' imposition of a cap on commissions for international flights, November 16, 1998. Online. Available HTTP: <http://www.antitrustinstitute.org/recent/13.cfm> (accessed June 16, 2004). Also see Sarah F. Hall d/b/a *Travel Specialists v. United Air Lines, Inc., et al.*, No. 7:00-CV-123-BR, U.S. Dist. Ct., Eastern District of N. Carolina, Southern Div., Order granting summary judgment to defendant airlines in class action claiming changes in terms of commission were act of illegal conspiracy, and also alleging that Orbitz was established to divert commissions from travel agents. (Decided in October, 2003.) The class of 25000 travel agents had claimed damages of $17 billion, before trebling.

27 Evans and Wurster, op. cit., p. 39.

28 Ibid., p. 151.

29 [Author's note:] Travel agents were historically the agents of the airlines, not of their consumer customers. In recent years, they have come increasingly to represent the consumer. Travelocity is part of Sabre, Inc., which was once owned by American Airlines, but is now an independent company. Expedia, although once part of Microsoft, was independent of airlines from birth. An independent navigator does not worry about the profitability of the airlines, but rather builds up the largest possible body of consumers who will repeatedly use the site, thereby generating fees (via commissions) for the site.

30 Evans and Wurster, op. cit., p. 135. For example, electronic navigators make it

easy for a consumer to find the lowest applicable fare, whereas the airlines presumably want to sell the highest fare the consumer is willing to accept. Electronic navigators make it easy to find alternative routes from nearby airports, which might be cheaper for the consumer, whereas the airlines would presumably prefer that the consumer's search would be limited to the precise city-pair the consumer is initially focused on.

31 [Author's note:] Most Internet-based navigators lose money for a number of years as they expand their network, making them particularly vulnerable to aggressive strategies during the phase when they are trying to achieve a critical mass.

32 Evans and Wurster, op. cit., p. 138.

33 Ibid., p. 140.

34 Ibid., p. 141.

35 Ibid., p. 142.

36 Ibid.

37 Ibid., p. 241, at n. 4. The footnote also points out that the CRS rules "eliminated a competitive advantage for the airline but also eliminated a competitive *disadvantage* for SABRE. Since SABRE the navigator is now a business twice as valuable as AA the airline, the shareholders probably benefited." SABRE is today independent of American Airlines.

38 49 USC 41712. *United Airlines v. CAB*, 766 F.2d 1107 (7th Circ. 1985).

39 Evans and Wurster, op. cit., p. 142.

40 Ibid., p.143. The second possible problem with their advice, reported by the authors, is that sellers acting to protect their own businesses from commoditization, might happily commoditize each other's.

41 A useful description of Orbitz may be found in W. F. Adkinson, Jr., and T. M. Lenard, "Orbitz: an antitrust assessment," *Antitrust* 16, 2002, pp. 76–83.

42 See, for example, "Twenty-five consumer groups ask justice to modify Orbitz launch vehicle," May 22, 2001. Online. Available HTTP: <http://www. antitrustinstitute.org/recent/121.cfm> (accessed June 16, 2004).

43 The American Antitrust Institute provided comments to the DOT and DOJ in September, 2000. Online, Available HTTP: <http://www.antitrustinstitute. org/recent/85.pdf> (accessed June 16, 2004).

44 This point was emphasized in Senate testimony of Alfred Kahn, the 'godfather of airline deregulation.' Dr. Kahn summarizes his oral testimony in the AAI submission to DOT. Online. Available HTTP: <http://www.antitrustinstitute. org/recent/85.pdf> (accessed June 16, 2004).

45 Adkinson and Lenard, op. cit. Evans and Wurster, op. cit. Sabre's Executive Vice President and General Counsel, David A. Schwarte, testified to the National Commission to Ensure Consumer Information and Choice in the Airline Industry, June 12, 2002, p. 8 that "The 'clandestine deals' by the big five on Travelocity and Expedia that were commonplace before Orbitz, and played a special role in the competitive process, have slowed substantially." Online. Available HTTP: <http://www.ncecic.dot.gov/ncecic/hearings/sabre_ testimony.pdf> (accessed June 16, 2004).

46 See testimony of G. Doernhoefer, Vice President of Orbitz, before the National Commission to Ensure Consumer Information and Choice in the Airline Industry, June 26, 2002, p. 8. Online. Available HTTP: <http://www. ncecic.dot.gov/ncecic/hearings/orbitz.pdf> (accessed June 16, 2004).

47 Schwarte, op. cit., n. 44.

48 We are not aware, for example, of any informational firewall between Orbitz and its airline owners, who control its board of directors, regarding fare offerings by rival airlines.

49 This theory focuses on the role of the airlines as unhappy buyers of what they claimed were monopoly-priced CRS services. In order to drive down CRS prices, the airlines first established a supplier-based joint venture that was expected to operate at a loss. The airlines, subsidizing the venture, would then drive huge volumes through it by providing exclusive access to discount fares. Once market power was established, independent travel agencies and CRSs would be forced to reduce their fees to the airlines, if they wanted access to discount fares. Meanwhile, fees would be charged to consumers in order to offset the operating loss. Evidence cited for this interpretation includes the Orbitz scheme of declining "transaction fees" to be paid by airlines and the one-third rebate of the Worldspan booking fee to the Orbitz owners/participants that was agreed to in late 1999—long before Orbitz had any operating history to show what the true costs of selling airline tickets would be for Orbitz. In other words, according to this argument, the owners agreed on an artificial price point that they would pay Orbitz, but the fee was so low, in comparison to Orbitz' costs, that Orbitz was forced to adopt a $5 service fee for consumers within six months of operation. If this was the strategy, it apparently succeeded, in that fees paid to independent agencies and CRS's reportedly have been reduced to the point that profitability must now be attained through sale of other travel services rather than air reservations. The author cannot suggest whether group buying power was abused in a way that might have violated the antitrust laws, which in any event are not favorably disposed toward claims of monopsonistic abuse. Had the airlines simply joined together to negotiate lower CRS fees, price fixing would have been more apparent.

50 On April 4, 2001, sixteen consumer and antitrust advocacy groups had written to Secretary of Transportation Norman Mineta urging him to block Orbitz. Online. Available HTTP: <http://www.antitrustinstitute.org/recent/113.cfm> (accessed June 16, 2004). Twenty-three Attorneys General had slightly earlier endorsed a letter underscoring "certain striking features in the Orbitz scheme that may produce negative consequences outweighing any benefits to consumers." The Attorneys General called on the DOT to apply its computer reservation rules to the Internet (thereby covering Orbitz) and raised the potential of separate state-based antitrust action. Ibid.

51 In retrospect, this remedy, also proposed by the State Attorneys General in their letter to DOT, could be criticized as amounting to a MFN for everyone, with the same potential anticompetitive outcome of eliminating the special ('clandestine') deals that keep the competitive pot boiling. Perhaps the better remedy would have been to ban the Orbitz MFN and the provisions that promote exclusivity.

52 In Re Advance Notice of Proposed Rulemaking Computer Reservation System Regulation, Docket Nos. OST-2002–11577–25 and OST-1997–2881–272 (March 28, 2002).

53 The DOT letter to Orbitz had been based, in part, on statements by Orbitz that web fares would represent only "one-tenth of one percent" of the fares on offer. SABRE offered comparisons of screen shots by Orbitz, Travelocity, and

Expedia, which showed that as much as 72 percent of the first ten options presented by Orbitz in response to a total of ten requests for service were web-only fares. Whether Orbitz' earlier statements were intentionally false we cannot say, but in Orbitz' defense, it would seem likely that the well-known problems of the travel industry after September 11, 2001, caused a higher level of discounting than would have been predicted.

54 The AAI called this to the attention of the Justice Department, arguing that the service fee amounts to a form of price fixing, in that the fee produces a uniform price increase by virtually the entire industry for a class of consumers. March 8, 2002. Online. Available HTTP: <http://www.antitrustinstitute. org/recent2/176.cfm> (accessed June 16, 2004) (DOJ did not comment.) Travelocity and Expedia say they did not (with a few exceptions) charge fees to consumers. It appeared that Orbitz could charge a fee without losing out to Travelocity and Expedia because it was able to show consumers discounts that are so deep (and unavailable to other ticket distributors) that $5 will not deter the consumer. The fee did not show on the screen as part of the price, until after the consumer was ready to make the purchase.

55 Meanwhile, all indications are that website booking of air travel is on the steep increase. Delta has reported that ticket sales over their website grew 60 percent in 2001, representing more than 10 percent of their total ticket sales. U.S. Airways reported that it now sells about 25 percent of its tickets through all online channels, of which about 12.5 percent are through its own website. *Aviation Daily*, January 30, 2002, p. 6. By one measure, airline websites held 11 of the top 15 positions among all websites. *Airline Financial News*, February 18, 2002.

56 Another travel agency, American Express, described its perspective this way in July, 2002: "Business and leisure travelers who choose to work with American Express cannot easily and efficiently get information and access to the lowest fares needed to run their businesses or visit friends and family. Economy conscious travelers must now book outside their preferred booking programs and locations, and book directly on an airline owned distribution system such as Orbitz if they are sure they have researched all avenues pertaining to lowest airfares. Because of this trend, agencies that have serviced individuals such as these in the past will see reduced or negative customer growth and their earnings will decline further. In turn, the number of agency locations will be reduced and the traveler will have fewer options when booking their travel. When the number of choices a consumer has is reduced, it is typical that the cost to the consumer rises."

57 Online. Available HTTP: <http://www.usdoj.gov/atr/public/press_releases/ 2003/201208.htm> (accessed June 16, 2004). Generally, no details are given when an Antitrust Division investigation is closed. The AAI, which has had a major objective of increasing the transparency in antitrust enforcement, praised the Division for issuing this statement. Online. Available HTTP: <http://www.antitrustinstitute.org/recent2/258.cfm> (accessed June 16, 2004). See W. S. Grimes, "Transparency in federal antitrust enforcement," *Buffalo L. Rev.* 51, 2003, pp. 937–93.

58 Online. Available HTTP: <http://www.antitrustinstitute.org/recent2/ 258.cfm> (accessed June 16, 2004).

59 The CRS rule, which was originally scheduled to terminate in 1990 and has

been responsible no doubt for the death of many trees, was going through a revision process in which the DOT most recently asked open-ended questions like, should regulation continue? Advocates of deregulation pointed to the fact that the CRSs are no longer (for the most part) owned by airlines and that the Internet has substantially changed the nature of competition in this market. For example, according to a filing by Sabre, McDonalds concluded that it does not need a traditional travel agent, but instead will use Orbitz (which bypasses the CRSs and connects directly with the largest airlines) for its travel needs. Sabre argued that this demonstrated that CRSs are no longer necessary to sell airline tickets to business travelers. Sabre also cited data showing that price competition in booking fees among the CRSs reflects the leverage of airlines, rather than any market power of CRSs. Opposition of Sabre, Inc., to Amadeus' Petition to Eliminate the CRS Rules' January 31, 2004, Sunset, In the Matter of Computer Reservation System (CRS) Regulation: Statements of General Policy, Docket No. OST- 03–16469 *et al.* (November 11, 2003). AAI comments in the DOT rulemaking called for a deregulatory approach, premised on elimi- nation of airline ownership of distribution facilities (except for the airlines' own websites and call-up units) but also tempered by elements of regulation such as continuing controls over screen bias and caps on duration of contracts between CRSs and travel agents, and a new form of mandatory sharing of information on all airlines' routes and schedules. Comments of the AAI to the FCC Regarding Computer Reservation Systems, Docket No. 97–2881 (March 16, 2003). Online Available HTTP: <http://www.antitrustinstitute.org/ recent2/239.cfm> (accessed June 16, 2004). AAI said the following concerning Orbitz and the CRS rulemaking:

> Orbitz has from its inception been under close scrutiny by both the DOT and the DOJ. It would not be unreasonable to assume that it may be pulling some of its strategic punches in light of this scrutiny. Although some of the airlines have recently reached agreements with certain travel agents to provide them with web fares, the potential for exclusivity and favoritism remains. We believe that Orbitz should be required to compete with CRSs and other travel agents on a level playing field, and the best way to assure that would be to require that the airlines sell Orbitz to investors from outside the industry, much as Worldspan has announced it is doing, and to reject the MFN clause.
>
> The fact that Orbitz operates on the Internet should not be a distinguish- ing factor for regulatory purposes. Whatever rules apply to other CRSs and travel agents should apply equally to Orbitz. All the more, because if Orbitz can obtain sufficient airline information directly so that it can bypass other CRSs, it would become a combination travel agency and CRS, owned entirely by the airlines, thereby raising all the old questions of ownership to a new degree.

60 DOT concluded that there was no need for a CRS Rule and that the old rule would be allowed to terminate on January 31, 2004. 69 FR 976 (January 7, 2004).
61 See W. K. Tom, D. A. Balto, and N. W. Averitt, "Anticompetitive aspects of market-share discounts and other incentives to exclusive dealing," *Antitrust Law Journal* 67, 2000, pp. 615–39.

62 In late 2003, Orbitz announced that it was attempting to make an initial public offering (IPO), so that ownership will not rest exclusively with the five airlines. However, there is no indication that actual control will change. This raises an interesting question about the fiduciary obligation to the public shareholders when the controlling owners have their own corporate interests at stake in Orbitz' decisions. As noted by Business Week, Dec. 17, 2003, in T. J. Mullaney, "Is Orbitz' IPO worth a flyer?": "the airlines that own this company—and are getting the benefit of those huge commission cuts—are pulling nearly all of their money out just as it goes public, although they do plan to retain 66 percent ownership and 95 percent voting control after the IPO.... Even after the airlines cash out their initial investment in Orbitz, they'll have the same strategy: to use it (through their retained majority stake) primarily as a lever to push rivals to lower commissions and pay higher fees for air tickets."

63 Ibid., n. 49.

Case 10

Online music

Harry First[1]

Introduction

Perhaps no industry has been more fundamentally challenged by the growth of the Internet and its related technologies than the recorded music industry. For most industries, the Internet mainly provides a new, albeit potentially far more efficient, channel of distribution. For the recording industry, however, the Internet has challenged the basic product the industry makes and the way it does business. The recording industry has mostly bundled prerecorded music into packages ("albums"); the Internet offers consumers the opportunity to unbundle music and choose only the songs they want to hear. The recording industry has maintained tight control over which artists get to distribute their work to the public; the Internet offers the opportunity for artists to deliver music directly to consumers. The recording industry has created the end-product on which songs are sold (music on CDs, tape, and vinyl records); computer software and hardware allows consumers to capture recorded music on the media of their choice. The recording industry has owned the copyrights to the music they sell; computer software and Internet connections allow consumers to obtain music for free, in seeming disregard for copyright protection and the economic interests of the copyright holders.

The initial response of the recording industry to some of the challenges posed by the Internet was the creation of two joint ventures, pressplay and MusicNet, to distribute music online. Producer joint ventures to control Internet distribution are not unique to the recording industry (the airline, hotel, and motion picture industries have also started such ventures), but the recording industry joint ventures dealt with some particularly challenging issues of antitrust, copyright, and innovation policy. When the online music joint ventures were announced, they appeared to offer more competition and significant efficiency benefits, creating new entrants with a new product in a new market. Given the concentrated nature of the prerecorded music industry, however, and the ability of the record companies to control the licensing of their music to online music distributors, it was also clear that the joint ventures deserved closer antitrust scrutiny. Indeed, the Department of Justice and the European Commission opened investigations of the two ventures even before the ventures began their operations.

Two and one-half years later the Department of Justice announced that it had closed its investigation because its "theoretical concerns ultimately were not supported by the evidence."[2] However appropriate this decision might be as a matter of enforcement policy, however, the Department's explanation focused only on the ventures' licensing practices and sheds little light on the appropriate analysis of the ventures' formation.

The thesis of this chapter is that the formation of these producer joint ventures was not justified by any efficiencies and that their formation was anticompetitive. More broadly, this chapter argues that the brief history of this industry demonstrates the danger to competition posed when the producers of essential inputs in a concentrated market join together to control downstream distribution, a danger exacerbated in this industry, involving, as it does, the distribution of intellectual property products.

The chapter begins with a description of the business and legal environment in which the joint ventures were formed and then traces how both have developed since the ventures' formation. The chapter then provides an analysis of whether the formation of the two joint ventures violated Section 1 of the Sherman Act. The chapter concludes with some observations regarding record industry joint ventures in today's rapidly changing market for the distribution of online music.

The online music business

Prerecorded music distribution

Sales of prerecorded music are substantial. Over the decade 1993–2002, the value of prerecorded music sales in the United States ranged between $10 billion and $14.5 billion annually.[3] Sales generally increased each year during that period, until 2001.[4] Although sales declined in 2001 and again in 2002, sales in 2002 were still higher than they were in every year from 1993 through 1998 and the decline may be reversing.[5] The cause of the sales decline, however, is the subject of some controversy.[6]

In 2002 there were five major companies (often referred to as "distributors") that manufactured prerecorded music produced by "labels" that they own. These five companies accounted for approximately 83 percent of U.S. album sales in 2002 (as they did in 2001).[7] The five companies were Universal Music Group (UMG), with 28.9 percent of sales in 2002,[8] Warner-Elektra-Atlantic Corporation, with 15.9 percent,[9] Sony Music Entertainment, with 15.7 percent,[10] BMG Music, with 14.8 percent,[11] and EMI Music Distribution, with 8.4 percent.[12] Warner was traditionally the market leader until UMG's 1998 acquisition of Polygram, which had been the sixth major distributor; UMG has led the market every year since that acquisition. At the time the joint ventures were announced, four of the five major distributors were owned by larger companies, each with substantial media and entertainment interests (respectively, Vivendi, AOL/Time Warner, Sony, and Bertelsmann), but the industry's ownership structure has not been stable. In 2000 Warner and EMI had attempted to merge their music businesses, but abandoned the effort after antitrust opposition from the European Commission.[13] In November 2003 Bertelsmann and Sony announced a merger of their music companies and Warner announced the sale of its music business to a group of private investors (rejecting a higher offer from EMI and after failing to reach a merger agreement with BMG).[14] Under the U.S. Department of Justice/Federal Trade Commission Merger Guidelines, the industry would have been viewed as moderately to highly concentrated when the joint ventures were announced.[15]

The major distributors are vertically integrated through manufacturing and wholesaling. Through their "labels" these companies contract with recording artists to record music. The labels oversee production of the recording and develop promotional plans; the distribution companies handle wholesale distribution and engage in various, often extensive, promotional efforts. These promotional efforts include securing television appearances for the artists, radio play for the music, and the payment of (sometimes extensive) fees to retail outlets to promote the records.

Retail distribution is done through a variety of channels. The three main channels are "traditional" retailers that specialize in the sale of pre-recorded music (such as Tower Records), general merchandise discount retailers that do not specialize (such as Wal-Mart), and electronics discounters (such as Best Buy). Retail distribution is also done through record clubs, which distribute their records by mail order; some of the major distributors have ownership interests in these clubs (for example, Columbia House, the largest club, is jointly owned by Sony and Time Warner). Retailers generally sell all or most genres of prerecorded music and do not limit their sales to music sold by any one particular distributor or record on any particular label.

The growth and spread of the Internet has expanded retail distribution channels. Internet distribution offers some obvious efficiencies in comparison with traditional brick-and-mortar retail distribution (centralized inventorying, no retail stores, fewer personnel). The first step in taking advantage of these efficiencies came when new retailers, such as Amazon and CDnow, began selling prerecorded music on the Internet; this led traditional music retailers (such as Tower) to start their own Internet sales sites. These Internet sites, however, still sold the same product that is sold through physical stores, which then needed to be physically delivered to consumers by mail.

The Internet, however, provides the opportunity to distribute prerecorded music in a form that is substantially different from music sold in physical stores, or even through Internet retail sites.[16] Prerecorded music in digital format can readily be transmitted via the Internet (and subsequently listened to, stored, and replayed), divorced from the physical medium in which it was originally embodied. Freed from the need for distribution of a physical medium, the original prerecorded package can also be untied and the music distributed in different combinations (most obviously, by single songs). The channels for this type of prerecorded music distribution bear more resemblance to applications program software than they do to physical stores (these channels relying, for example, on critical software technologies for file compression and transmission). These new distribution channels can be thought of as "distribution platforms," to distinguish them from physical stores and Internet sales sites.

The legal environment

Copyright protection

Prerecorded music is protected by copyright. Copyright law provides protection to the underlying "musical work" (the song) and to the "sound recording" (the sound of the song).[17] Different parties generally own different rights; music publishers and/or songwriters generally control the musical works while the record companies or the recording artists generally control the sound recording right.[18]

The owner of the copyright in the musical work has the right to control its public performance, distribution, and reproduction.[19] Absent the copyright owner's permission, a song cannot be performed in public (for example, by broadcasting it over the radio). Once the song is recorded, however, the reproduction and distribution rights are subject to a statutory compulsory license (the "mechanical license") which permits other performers to reproduce and distribute the song on payment of a prescribed fee.[20]

The owner of the copyright in the sound recording has only a reproduction and distribution right, but not a performance right.[21] That is, the copyright holder can prevent others from reproducing and distributing the particular recording of a song, but cannot prevent others from publicly performing the recording (say, by broadcasting it over the radio).

Internet transmission of music in digital formats potentially involves both the public performance and the reproduction of the copyrighted works. Congress has altered the general copyright statute, however, to take account of what it believed were the special problems raised by digital distribution.

For musical works, Congress in 1995 extended the compulsory mechanical license to include the digital distribution of musical works by "digital phonorecord delivery" (DPD).[22] Under this provision, the Internet transmission of a song that is downloaded to a computer creates a DPD, thereby requiring the payment of a compulsory license fee.[23] The performance right for musical works, however, was unaffected by the 1995 statute. Internet transmission of music to the public, even when received by someone who is listening at home, is a public performance for which permission is needed from the owner of the copyright in the musical work.[24]

The 1995 statute also created a new public performance right for sound recordings that are performed by a "digital audio transmission."[25] The new performance right distinguishes between interactive and noninteractive transmission services. Interactive services allow recipients to choose the music they want to hear; noninteractive services more closely resemble radio broadcasting, where the transmitter chooses the music that is transmitted.[26] For certain noninteractive transmission services the statute provides for a compulsory license (with fees to be set by the Librarian of Congress).[27] For interactive transmission services, however, permission of the owner of the copyright in the sound recording is required.

The sound recording reproduction and distribution rights are unchanged in the digital environment. Permission of the owner of the copyright in the sound recording is still required for making and distributing copies of sound recordings that are transmitted digitally.

File sharing

A rather remarkable convergence of complementary technologies and products has led to a situation where music listeners can share and copy substantial amounts of prerecorded music without paying royalties to any of the owners of the copyrights in the music or the sound recordings. These technologies include the growth of the Internet itself, the development of faster modems and broadband connections to the Internet, the increased dispersion of personal computers with ever-increasing disk storage space, and the development and dispersion of CD-ROM drives and software that enable users to copy ("burn") digital files to CDs.

Particularly critical to the growth of free sharing of prerecorded music has been the development of file compression technology and of software enabling users to share these files. File compression technology began in 1987 when the Moving Picture Experts Group set a standard file format for the storage of audio recordings in a digital format called MPEG-1 layer 3, abbreviated as MP3.[28] Compressing songs into smaller files first enabled users to "rip" songs from CDs and then allowed them to transmit those files over the Internet much more quickly, either by email or other file transfer protocol.[29]

Software enabling users to share files easily emerged in 1999 when Shawn Fanning developed the "MusicShare" software which was offered on the Napster website. This software enabled a user: (1) to list MP3 files stored on the user's computer hard drive that the user was willing to make available to other Napster users for copying; (2) to search for MP3 music files stored on other users' computers; and (3) to connect with a host user and download a copy of the contents of an MP3 file from one computer to the other over the Internet, "peer-to-peer."[30] Napster proved extremely popular, eventually attracting an estimated 50 million users.

Copyright holders sued Napster in 1999 for contributory and vicarious copyright infringement, successfully concluding the litigation in 2002 and shutting Napster down.[31] Despite the Court of Appeals' complete rejection of a variety of copyright defenses asserted by Napster, and the uncontested nature of the infringement of the reproduction and distribution rights by users of Napster, and, indeed, the demise of Napster, file sharing services continued to operate and copyright holders continued to litigate against them.[32]

The most popular file sharing software currently in use is KaZaA. KaZaA is based on "FastTrack" software, which, unlike Napster, does not create a centralized database that a single firm monitors or controls.[33] KaZaA's usage has now far surpassed Napster at its peak.[34] Between its creation in April 2000 until September 2003, for example, nearly 280 million copies had been downloaded, with approximately 2.5 million new downloads a week.[35] Only somewhat less popular have been file sharing software programs based on "Gnutella," an open-source peer-to-peer platform that is even less centralized than the FastTrack network.[36] By September 2003 nearly 125 million copies of the two main file sharing platforms using Gnutella (Morpheus and LimeWire) had been downloaded.[37]

Copyright litigation against these file sharing platforms has not been as successful as the litigation against Napster. Sued by both the music and motion picture industries, file sharing software companies that offer software based on FastTrack and Gnutella have so far been successful in asserting that their decentralized design frees them from contributory or vicarious copyright infringement, the grounds relied on by the Ninth Circuit in finding that Napster violated the copyright laws.[38]

The inability to shut down the distributors of file sharing software has led the industry to focus directly on the consumers who actually engage in downloading and uploading copyrighted music. Beginning at the end of 2002, the industry first sought names from Internet service providers of heavy music sharers.[39] The industry then filed suits against four students who ran file sharing systems at three universities.[40] Four months after the settlement of those suits, the industry filed copyright infringement suits against 261 individuals across the country who allegedly had more than 1,000 songs each on their personal computers.[41] This litigation approach has proved to be controversial, and its deterrent effects are as yet unknown, but the industry has continued its effort to sue individual consumers who share substantial amounts of music.[42]

Online music ventures

There are three somewhat different platforms for the distribution of music on the Internet: file-sharing services, webcasters, and interactive music services. File-sharing services provide downloading and burning; noninteractive services (webcasters or "Internet radio") transmit a stream of music to consumers via the Internet, allowing consumers to choose from an array of music formats that is much larger than is available on over-the-air radio but which cannot be downloaded and replayed; interactive music services offer varying combinations of streams of music, downloading, and burning.

The recording industry's initial efforts to enter the online music business came in December 2001 in the form of two joint ventures, pressplay and MusicNet, which were interactive subscription services that provided online music for a monthly fee.[43] Pressplay was owned by UMG and Sony, the first and third largest sellers of prerecorded music in physical form, with approximately 42 percent of that market. MusicNet was approximately 60 percent-owned by Warner, BMG, and EMI, the second, fourth, and fifth largest sellers of prerecorded music in physical form, with approximately 41 percent of that market.[44] RealNetworks, a developer of media playing software and an Internet content distributor, owned approximately 40 percent of the MusicNet venture.[45]

Each of the two joint ventures, as originally structured, held licenses for music only from its parent companies.[46] This meant that consumers who wanted access to all the music controlled by the five largest distributors would need to subscribe to both services. The two ventures also differed in the services they offered. Both restricted the number of songs that could be streamed, but with different amounts. Both services offered "tethered" downloads (downloads of songs that expired once the subscription was ended or had other types of restrictions that prevented sharing), but of different numbers of songs. Only pressplay offered "burning" of songs to CDs (at an additional cost).[47] Both services charged the same monthly fee ($9.95).

Consumer reaction to the original offerings was "tepid," with the two ventures reportedly having only 100,000 subscribers combined by mid-2002.[48] In fact, AOL, a part-owner of MusicNet, did not even distribute MusicNet when it was originally launched, apparently because the service was so poorly received.[49]

By the end of 2002, however, the joint ventures had changed in important ways. First, each of the music companies agreed to license their "non-affiliated" joint ventures (these agreements were announced virtually simultaneously by the online ventures). Second, both of the joint ventures loosened restrictions on the number of songs that could be streamed. Third, MusicNet, as distributed through AOL, began offering burning of individual songs.[50]

By the end of 2002 there was also a substantial independently-owned online music service in operation, called Rhapsody, offered by Listen.com. Listen.com was founded in 1998, but its efforts to secure licenses from the five major distributors "began to flower only after the labels themselves decided to move toward online distribution ventures."[51] By July 2002 Rhapsody announced that it had signed agreements with all five distributors (UMG, the largest distributor, being the last to agree).[52] Although initial agreements with the major distributors did not permit Rhapsody to offer burning of songs to CDs, by the end of 2002, four of the five major companies had agreed to allow Rhapsody to offer burning (Sony had not).

Online music continued to evolve in 2003. Four new independently-owned ventures entered the market. The most significant was Apple Computer, which began an online music service (iTunes Music Store) offering individual songs, as well as albums, for downloading, rather than offering a monthly music subscription service (the former has come to be known as the "a la carte" approach, the latter as the "all you can eat" approach).[53] It was the first service to offer downloading without a monthly subscription fee, although it was initially available only to users of Apple computers. Its attractiveness was greatly enhanced by the marketing of a complementary digital music player (the iPod) for storing and playing digital music files. After Apple's entry, and following Apple's business approach, BuyMusic.com began a service offering individual song and album downloads similar to Apple's but available on Windows PCs.[54] The third new entrant was MusicNow, owned by FullAudio and primarily distributed online through Clear Channel Communications (a Phoenix, Arizona, radio broadcaster), which entered with a monthly subscription service oriented toward "older adults."[55] It offered streaming, tethered downloads, and burning (although, at least at the beginning, Sony had not licensed any burning from its catalogue); by the end of the year it was also offering individual songs for downloading.[56] The fourth new entrant to offer individual songs was MusicMatch, which had been distributing music player software and Internet radio.[57]

In addition to new entry, there were two major structural changes in the online music business in 2003. RealNetworks, a minority owner of MusicNet (along with three of the five major record distributors), purchased Rhapsody, the major independent online service.[58] At about the same time, Roxio, a digital media technology company which had previously acquired Napster's assets, agreed to buy substantially all of pressplay, the joint venture owned by UMG and Sony.[59] Roxio's announced intention was to "build a reborn Napster service," using pressplay's infrastructure and licensing agreements and the Napster brand name, but without the peer to peer file sharing aspect.[60] Although both Sony and UMG will each have a director on Roxio's board, and will be entitled to substantial income from the new Napster service, nevertheless, the sale appeared to constitute an important change in the two companies' approach to online music.[61]

In 2004 Wal-Mart began a per song online music service, pricing its songs at 88 cents, below the "standard" 99 cents price of other competitors.[62] A group of music retailers (Best Buy Co., Tower Records, Hastings Entertainment Inc., Trans World Entertainment Corp., Virgin Entertainment Group Inc., and Wherehouse Music Inc.) which had announced the formation of a consortium to develop an online music subscription service, failed to launch their service,[63] but one of their members, Virgin, did enter on its own in late 2004 with a subscription and a per song download service.[64] Sony, having sold its interest in pressplay, began a new download service in spring 2004, launched along with the introduction of its own portable music player.[65] Viacom's MTV Networks entered at the same time by acquiring MusicMatch.[66] Finally, Microsoft made its entry in September 2004, with a beta release of a per song service, available through its MSN website as well as directly through its Media Player, which comes bundled with its Windows operating system.[67]

Although there is no publicly available information on the number of subscribers for each of the subscription services, it was reported that by early 2003 approximately 300,000 people subscribed to all the services in total (creating revenues of approximately $25 million).[68] Apple's per-song service received substantial initial use, selling more than 17 million songs in its first six months.[69] In terms of numbers of songs, the new Napster claims to have about 500,000 songs, MusicNet about 400,000, Rhapsody and BuyMusic about 300,000, and Apple and MusicMatch in excess of 200,000.[70]

Some convergence on pricing appears to have occurred. For the monthly subscription services, there is a fee of about $10 for access to a pool of all the songs on the service (allowing unlimited streaming and tethered downloads that expire when the subscription expires). The charge for downloading is approximately 99 cents a song (Apple), although at one time Rhapsody ran a promotional "sale" at 49 cents each, BuyMusic is charging variable amounts, and Wal-Mart launched its new service with a price of 88 cents per song; albums generally are sold for about $10.[71] Published estimates of the royalty paid to the record companies for downloads vary from 65 to 80 cents; costs for streaming paid to the record companies are estimated to be between two-tenths of a cent and a penny for each song to which a subscriber listens (although there is a monthly guarantee for streaming of about $5.00).[72] There are also additional fees that must be paid to those who hold the rights in the musical works.[73] There are still numerous variations in the rights that consumers get, in terms of numbers of downloads, burning, and sharing with other computers; these rights can vary by song as well as by Internet music service.

This is not to say that these pricing plans are the only ones possible. There is still some uncertainty about whether most consumers in the future will move completely to the online world, with no desire to maintain "hard copies" of music, in which case the current monthly fee might be considered to be too low.[74] Music companies (or the online services) may engage in differential pricing depending on whether a song is a "hot" release or part of the back catalogue.[75] Nevertheless, as Rob Glaser, the chief executive of RealNetworks, chairman of MusicNet, and (subsequently) owner of the Rhapsody online service, said in March 2003, "Everyone doesn't agree on everything, but everyone agrees on enough things that we can start putting products in the market."[76]

Antitrust analysis of online music joint ventures

Market definition

Markets are defined on the basis of substitutability by consumers and producers. That is, markets are made up of a set of products that consumers believe to be reasonably good substitutes in use and that producers of other, even of slightly different, products cannot readily make. Whether consumers or producers are likely to make substitutions can often be determined by the extent to which sellers of a set of products could raise their price by a small amount and not lose so many customers, or attract so many sellers of close substitutes into producing the product, that the price rise would be unprofitable.

Prerecorded music can, of course, be listened to ("consumed") in a variety of ways. Although the music is all the same no matter how it is listened to, each channel of distribution provides the buyer with a somewhat different product and experience. Music delivered in physical form has different characteristics than music that is broadcast over the air, although users certainly switch between the two. Similarly, music that is delivered digitally over the Internet has different characteristics than music delivered in the physical medium of a CD. And music delivered digitally over the Internet also varies by the different type of platform on which it is distributed, whether by free file sharing services, by webcasters, or by online interactive music services.

The closest substitutes for the product sold by online music services are free file sharing services and physical CDs. Although the streams of music that many of the online music services provide are similar to the service provided by webcasting, copyright law keeps webcasting and "interactive" services separate by product characteristics. Consumers who want their online music "on demand" can only select among various online music service offerings.

What about consumers who want to download or burn music? If the sellers of online music raised their price by some "small but significant and nontransitory" amount, would these consumers switch to free file sharing services? Using the Merger Guidelines' five percent test,[77] that would mean a nickel increase in the price of downloaded track, based on current market prices. Although we can't say for certain what would happen, an educated guess would be that the hypothetical monopolist could make such an increase stick. Both Napster and Rhapsody have experimented with prices that were more than a nickel below 99 cents per track (75 cents and 49 cents, respectively) and both have raised their prices back to 99 cents without losing so many sales as to make the increase unprofitable.[78] Indeed, the fact that sellers of music online can price their product positively without losing all their customers to zero-priced file sharing services is indication in itself that there is separate consumer demand for a legal music service, a demand which increased dramatically during 2003, despite the continued existence of free file sharing services.

Similarly, the hypothetical monopolist of online music could raise its price by a nickel a track without losing so much business to physical CDs as to make the price rise unprofitable. For one, songs come in a bundle on a CD, so a CD will not be a substitute for a consumer who wants only a particular song. For consumers who want to buy an entire album, the general online price is about $10; an increase to $10.50 would not likely cause consumers to switch to physical CDs, which are generally priced at around $14.

At the same time, there is little doubt that the availability of free music has constrained the pricing of online music sellers. Presumably, the greater the difference between the price of lawfully obtained music and the zero price of infringing music, the more willing consumers will be to substitute free file sharing for priced online music (unless the industry can increase the cost of free music by increasing the enforcement risk). Indeed, the industry's willingness to continue financing litigation against consumer-infringers shows that the recording industry views undeterred infringement as a competitive threat. Similarly, it is apparent that the retail price of physical CDs constrains the pricing power of sellers of online music and that, at least for now, sellers of online music have kept their prices below the average per track price of a physical CD.[79]

Paradoxically, perhaps, the argument for taking account of free file sharing is stronger in 2004 than it was in 2001 when the joint ventures were launched. The argument is stronger because in 2001 it looked as though the industry might be successful in suppressing pirated music; by mid-2003 the ability to stop file sharing services through litigation was in substantial doubt, forcing the industry to proceed against direct infringers, an easier legal case but a harder enforcement target. This is paradoxical, because the revenues from online music services were increasing substantially at the same time as the campaign to stop infringement was looking more problematic. Free file sharing may be a continuing competitive threat, but that has not prevented priced online music from flourishing as a product for which consumers are willing to pay.

The idea that market power can exist while still being subject to some constraint is not a surprising one, of course. More than sixty years ago Learned Hand observed that Alcoa's pricing power was constrained by imports and substitute metals, but that within these constraints Alcoa still had substantial power over price.[80] More recently, Microsoft's monopoly power in the operating systems market was somewhat constrained by competition from pirated software, but that was hardly reason to ignore the substantial power that it could and did exercise even subject to that constraint.[81]

Competitive effects of joint ventures

Joint ventures, like any other form of integration, offer efficiency benefits and pose competitive risks. Joint ventures allow firms to pool capital and spread risk. They may permit firms to achieve economies of scale or scope which reduce the cost of the product, or to bring products to market more quickly, or to combine different capabilities in a way that none of the individual firms would be able to do.[82] Joint ventures involving intellectual property can provide additional benefits. Intellectual property rights can be fragmented and conflicting. Making effective use of these rights often requires some degree of joint effort (pooling) so that rights can be combined in a way that will allow a product to be produced and will clear conflicting claims. Although the need for pools and collective action has long been acknowledged for patent rights, copyrights can be subject to the same problems, as, indeed, the splintering of rights in the music industry demonstrates.[83]

Joint ventures also have their anticompetitive risks. The primary structural risk comes from the fact that joint ventures often combine the efforts of actual or potential competitors. To the extent that the co-venturers might have produced the product individually, or one venturer might have produced the product while the other remained as a potential entrant, a joint venture ends competition between the co-venturers with regard to the output of the joint venture.[84] Joint ventures, by functioning as joint sales agencies, might allow the venturers to end interseller price competition and agree on price.[85] Joint ventures might also pose risks to competition at different levels of the production or distribution process. The co-venturers might withhold important inputs from competitors, or find other ways to raise their rivals' costs. The co-venturers might also use the joint venture to exchange information in ways that affect price in the markets in which the co-venturers continue to compete.

Forming the joint ventures

BMI's *guidance*

The case that would seem most directly on point with regard to the formation of the online music joint ventures is the Supreme Court's decision in
Broadcast Music, Inc. v. Columbia Broadcasting System, Inc.[86] That case
involved the licensing practices of ASCAP and BMI, the two major organizations in the United States that license performance rights to musical
works. ASCAP and BMI offered only a blanket license to all the music in
their repertories; neither offered licenses for the performance of individual musical works. The Supreme Court held that ASCAP and BMI's
joint licensing of performing rights was subject to a rule of reason analysis
under Section 1 of the Sherman Act. Even though the blanket license substantially reduced interseller price competition with regard to licensing
fees for individual music compositions, and could have been "literally"
viewed as price fixing, the Court required a fuller competitive analysis.
Central to its decision was the recognition of the integrative efficiency
benefits of the joint operation. The blanket license "is a different
product . . . of which the individual compositions are the raw material."
ASCAP and BMI "made a market" in which individual copyright owners
"are inherently unable to fully effectively compete."[87]

Thus *BMI* is both legally and factually relevant to an analysis of the
online music joint ventures. Legally, *BMI* underscores the importance of
considering the efficiency benefits of competitor collaborations, stressing
the need to allow for joint efforts among competitors where the joint
effort is necessary to produce the product (in that case, no individual
copyright holder could offer a blanket license). Factually, the conduct of
BMI and ASCAP shed light on the need for copyright holders to pool the
rights granted by the copyright laws in a way that economizes on what
would otherwise be the high transaction costs of numerous low value
licenses between individual users and the copyright owners.

BMI is generally assumed to be a critical case for justifying collaborative
behavior among competitors, with particular relevance to intellectual
property rights. What can easily be overlooked, however, is that *BMI* might
have some very different lessons to teach, once greater attention is paid to
institutional detail both for performing rights organizations and for
online music joint ventures. In fact, the development of online music may
show that *BMI* itself is now "wrong."

Fragmented rights and the need for pooling

ASCAP's formation dates back to a meeting in 1910 between Giacomo
Puccini and his U.S. publisher, at which Puccini mentioned the role
played by the Italian performing rights society in securing royalties for

composers (the performance right only entered U.S. law in 1897).[88] ASCAP was founded four years later. Its commercial and legal history since that time demonstrates a continuing effort by the music industry to capture revenues from each newly-emerging entertainment medium, from radio, to television, to motion pictures, to cable television, and now to the Internet.[89] The justifications for collective action in pursuing these revenues, however, as set out fifty years ago by Sigmund Timberg, the Justice Department lawyer responsible for the consent decree against ASCAP, have remained constant.[90] First is the "pragmatic plea of commercial necessity" which arises from the need of music users to obtain the right to perform the music in a sure and speedy way. Second is the need of a user to be assured that it has permission to perform the copyrighted work and will not be subject to conflicting claims of infringement. Third is the "helplessness of its individual members to enforce their rights," either because of the difficulty of detection or the high cost of litigation relative to the value of any single infringement.

Although each of these justifications involves transaction cost efficiencies, they do not necessarily justify the pooling and joint licensing of all performing rights in a single organization. For one, there is no reason why the need for collective enforcement of performance rights also means that these rights must be collectively licensed. Presumably, copyright holders could contract with a central agency to perform the policing function alone; this would capture the economies that flow from a single agent enforcing the rights of many holders more efficiently than each individual rights holder could.[91] In fact, the recording industry itself shows that the efficiency of joint enforcement of sound recording rights need not be connected to the pooling of rights. The industry's copyright infringement litigation against piracy has been led by a trade association vehicle, the Recording Industry Association of America, which does not engage in licensing.[92]

For another, the efficiency of collective licensing is related to the magnitude of the collective action faced by copyright holders and users. Performing rights ownership is highly fragmented. At the time the ASCAP decree was amended in 1950 there were 365 music publishers and 2040 participating composers and authors.[93] By contrast, approximately 80 percent of the sound recording rights critical for an online music venture were controlled by five companies.

Nor is it clear why the efficiency of using a collective agency to license rights necessarily requires that agency to offer these rights only on a pooled basis. Users may want to know where to go for copyright permissions, but that does not mean that they necessarily want to license all the rights that the collective has to offer. Put otherwise, ASCAP's refusal to offer a per song license makes the collective arrangement less efficient than it should be. Consumer welfare would be enhanced if the collective provided both the economies of offering the rights of numerous holders in one spot while still providing the licensee the ability to choose the rights that the licensee prefers. This was the choice that CBS wanted in *BMI*, of course.

In *BMI* the Court noted the ability of CBS to negotiate per song royalties directly with the copyright holder, but took this as proof of the efficiency of a blanket license rather than as an indication that efficiency could be enhanced if ASCAP were to offer both a blanket license and a per song license.[94] The Court's unwillingness to recognize the welfare loss from ASCAP's refusal to provide individual licenses may perhaps have been the result of its implicit assumption that performing rights societies could not easily operate in any way other than by a blanket license. As Sigmund Timberg wrote in 1954: "A blanket license covering ASCAP's total repertory is the price of avoiding industrial palsy in the entertainment world, says ASCAP, and thus far no important commercial user of ASCAP's music has contradicted this assertion for any length of time."[95]

Whatever the strength of this assumption when *BMI* was decided, the efficiency which justified the refusal to offer individual licenses likely no longer holds. In fact, the online music joint ventures help prove the point. Online music ventures began by only offering a "blanket license," that is, legal access to an entire pool of music for a single fee (the "all you can eat" model). Competition from free file sharing services showed, however, that consumers had a strong preference for per song consumption; indeed, consumers were rejecting even the smaller technological bundle of the "album" in favor of individual choices. Competition then forced the online ventures to recognize this demand and offer sales of individual songs in addition to a monthly subscription to the entire repertory of songs that the service wanted to offer. Apple was the first to recognize this consumer demand; others followed when it became apparent how strong that demand was.

Returning to the Court's decision in *BMI*, by allowing copyright holders to agree collectively not to offer single-use licenses, when such an offering would have increased consumer welfare, the Court may actually have retarded the development of competition on the price of performing rights licenses. In fact, whatever problems the performing rights organizations might have faced in the past in licensing individual compositions at competing prices, those technological problems have been reduced (if not eliminated) by the Internet itself and the development of distribution platforms which make such individual transactions economically feasible. Other copyright collectives, making use of the Internet, already offer both per use and blanket licenses, with per use royalties set by individual copyright holders.[96] Thus *BMI*, it turns out, is not as strong a case for collective action as is generally thought.[97] Far from offering strong justification for collective action by the record companies, *BMI* actually shrinks down to its underlying analytical approach: antitrust analysis must pay careful attention to the asserted efficiencies to see whether they are worth the cost of reduced competition.

Demand side economies and one-stop shopping

A major justification for the music joint ventures, at least at their inception, was thought to be consumer desire for one-stop shopping. An online music service could be that hoped-for "celestial jukebox," providing in one place all the music that exists in the world. This was thought possible on the supply side, perhaps because Internet distribution (in contrast to distribution in physical space) appeared to provide infinite economies of scale. This was thought desirable on the demand side because it would economize on consumer search costs. Similar claims have been made for other Internet producer joint ventures, such as Orbitz in the travel industry. As difficult as it may be to believe now, the claim for the efficiency of a single music site was a serious one in 2001.

Recall that one of the justifications for a performing rights organization is the need for users to gain "rapid and indemnified access" to copyrighted works, with assurance that they would not be subject to conflicting claims of infringement.[98] What better than a single source for licensing to achieve these aims?

Once again, however, the *BMI* case helps us see how weak this efficiency rationale actually is. One of the curious anomalies in the market for licensing performing rights is that there are three performing rights organizations in the United States, not just one.[99] ASCAP is the leading organization. BMI, the second largest organization, was formed in 1940 by broadcasters as a response to ASCAP's effort in 1939 to license broadcast networks for the first time, as well as ASCAP's simultaneous effort to raise its license fees for broadcast stations.[100] In 1941 the broadcasters boycotted ASCAP music and began broadcasting mostly Latin music. By late 1941 new licensing arrangements were agreed to between the broadcasters and ASCAP, "a peace of sorts."[101] BMI continued in operation, however, perhaps in an effort by the broadcasters to maintain some leverage over ASCAP in negotiating royalties.[102] Although BMI has historically had lower revenues than ASCAP and fewer songs in its repertory, its compositions now comprise about the same percentage of music performed in most venues as does ASCAP's.[103]

One particularly interesting point about the existence of the three separate performing rights organizations is that their repertories are mutually exclusive. Songs can be licensed only to one association at a time, and composers and publishers cannot belong to ASCAP and BMI at the same time. This means that users of music must take licenses from each of the organizations if they really want the "unplanned, rapid and indemnified access to any and all of the repertory of compositions," as the Court in *BMI* thought they would, unless they are willing (and able) to be more selective in the music that they perform.

The willingness of users to establish a competing performing rights organization, and the willingness of users to take licenses from more than one organization, indicates that the efficiencies from one-stop shopping may be small enough to be outweighed by the benefits that can flow from competition among different licensors of performing rights. Put otherwise, although some degree of collective action may be efficient, this does not tell us what the optimal size of the collective might be.

For online music joint ventures, the benefits of one-stop shopping are even weaker than they are for performing rights organizations. It is surely cheaper for a user to click to another site on the Internet for the music that he or she seeks than it is for a licensee of performing rights to deal with three performing rights organizations. Switching costs would be low even were the online music companies offering only a blanket license to an entire repertory (consumers might subscribe to two services, or switch at the end of a month's subscription). But switching costs are particularly low where consumers seek and can get individual songs; searching for a specific song on several websites does not seem like a particularly arduous task.

The other side of the equation is that multiple ventures offer the possibility of competition. This turns out to be true even in the performing rights organization context, where licensing fees negotiated with one organization can have an impact on the licensing fees of another.[104] The short history of online music shows that it is much more the case for online music ventures. Rather than a single platform, marketplace competition has produced a diversity of efforts to market online music, providing different services and different packages for selling online music. If we now had only a single platform, or the two industry joint ventures that we began with in 2001, consumers would never have received the benefits of this competition.

Applying BMI

The formation of pressplay and MusicNet in 2001 meant that the co-venturers in each of the ventures would not compete against each other by selling online music services. On a basic level this competition might have taken the form of the individual music companies selling music online at different prices (whether price was set for the entire repertory or on a per song basis). On a more important level, the competition might have taken the form of greater platform innovation, for example, offering music combined with different informational services, or offering music with different rights (e.g., full downloads).[105] These possibilities were apparent even in 2001, when the ventures were formed.

The joint ventures, of course, were still free to compete against each other (although, like the performing rights societies, they did so initially with mutually exclusive repertories), so price competition was not extinguished. Further, the venturers were still free to license their music to other online music ventures, again much as the copyright holders in

ASCAP and BMI, although it took a full year before all the music companies licensed any competitor outside the ventures.

BMI teaches us not to condemn collaborative arrangements on their face for "literal" price (or product) fixing. Even though each of the co-venturers could have produced the new product on its own (getting licenses from other companies for music they didn't control), and even though there are minimal demand side efficiencies from offering a single site (or two sites), there was also one obvious procompetitive effect from the joint ventures. Output in the online music market was expanded by the entry of the two ventures.

How to balance the prediction of competitive harm from the restriction of competition among the co-venturers against the reality of new entry? First there might be little to worry about if the two ventures themselves were not likely to have market power; in that case independent entry would not much matter. Assessing the ventures' market power would have been a somewhat difficult exercise in 2001, of course, given the unformed nature of the online music market when the ventures started, as well as the existence of competition from free file sharing services which provided at least some constraint on the ventures' price and product decisions. Nevertheless, there is one structural factor that would have led to a prediction that the ventures would have market power. Each venture brought together companies that controlled approximately 40 percent of the prerecorded music market; licenses to use this music are essential to an online music venture, in the sense that, for a lawful online music venture, there are no available substitutes. Using market shares of these inputs as a proxy for market shares in online distribution, the market would have looked very concentrated indeed.[106]

The joint venturers were, however, contractually free to license rivals in the online music market, thereby creating competition on price and product quality and diminishing their market power. But why would they do such a thing? All their incentives would have been not to license, or, at best, to license strategically, so as to disadvantage competitors. Firms in control of essential inputs do not usually want to help create competitors. Indeed, given the concentrated nature of the prerecorded music industry, the transparency of information in the industry, the extensive contacts that industry participants have with one another, and the economic interest each participant had in not cannibalizing physical CD sales, overt agreements not to license competing online music ventures would hardly have been necessary.[107] The prediction of tacit collusion regarding refusals to license other ventures, plus the prediction of less than vigorous competition in a two-firm online music market, would have led to the conclusion that anticompetitive effects from these joint ventures would be likely.

And yet, the record companies did license their music to others. Does that tell us that predictions of anticompetitive effects when the ventures

were formed would have been misguided and that the contractually unrestrained ability to license meant that the creation of these joint ventures
was not a competition problem? The answer to both parts of this question
should be no. The post-formation licensing behavior of the record companies has been the product of incentives, but of a particular sort. The
initial willingness to license Rhapsody came slowly and grudgingly, for
example, likely motivated more by a concern for antitrust liability than by
some desire to see competitors flourish, coming, as it did, at the same
time that the Department of Justice was investigating the ventures and as a
federal judge had expressed concern in open court about whether the
ventures would pass antitrust muster.[108] More importantly, subsequent
licensing may be explained by marketplace incentives arising from the
industry's inability to end consumer music piracy. To the industry's
dismay, it still faces competition from file sharing. In that environment,
exclusion of competitors by controlling the essential inputs is not possible.
A better business strategy, then, is to follow the one that applies in physical space, that is, sell to everyone.[109] It is no wonder that the owners of
pressplay decided to sell pressplay to RealNetworks, a firm that can more
effectively distribute digital music than pressplay could. As the CEO of
Sony Music was quoted as saying: "We want to be part of this space [digital
music distribution], but we don't feel that we, on a stand-alone basis, need
to dominate one platform."[110]

Prediction of anticompetitive effect is only one half of *BMI*. There is
still the fact that the joint ventures added new entrants to a nascent
market, providing consumers with choices that had not been in the marketplace. Would forbidding these joint ventures have meant less competition (lower output) than there would be if the ventures were allowed to
enter and compete, albeit imperfectly? Potential competition analysis
might answer this question, depending on what the plans were of any of
these firms to enter independently, or to threaten independent entry.[111]
But even if none of the record companies would have independently
entered, this does not mean that we would have been worse off without
the joint ventures. One important economic aspect of intellectual property is that, unlike physical property, its use by one party does not preclude simultaneous use by another. Without the joint ventures there
would have been no incentive to deny use of these intellectual property
rights to all other entrants. Even if the industry had succeeded in stopping
file sharing services and widespread consumer infringement, the huge
demand for digital music that these file sharing services uncovered would
have led the industry to try to sell its music over the Internet one way or
another. Whether digital music would have been provided by licensing
independent firms, or through vertical integration by individual record
companies, this demand would not have long gone unsatisfied.

Remedy

Suppose that the analysis of the formation of the joint ventures is correct in its assessment that the predicted anticompetitive effects outweighed the procompetitive justifications, what remedy would have been appropriate? The most obvious remedy, of course, would have been to enjoin the ventures from starting operations; or, subsequently, requiring the venturers to divest their ownership interests, leading, perhaps to the unwinding of the ventures. The co-venturers would then have been free to enter individually or to acquire sole control of one of the ventures. The injunctive provisions could have been limited to allow joint entry if market conditions changed sufficiently so that joint entry would no longer be anticompetitive.

An alternative to unwinding the venture might have been some form of non-discriminatory licensing under which the record companies would have been required to license other online music ventures on terms no less favorable than the terms under which they licensed their own joint ventures. Although this seems less drastic than divestiture, regulation of licensing might have ended up being more difficult to carry out and may have had unintended consequences on competition.[112] The record companies would have had little incentive to license other ventures on more favorable terms than the terms under which they license their own ventures, with the result being a homogenization of online offerings, a particularly unwanted outcome for a product in its early stages of development. Further, compulsory licensing often leads to further review of the terms of particular contracts. The incentives would be great for the joint venture participants to structure their agreements in a way that would disadvantage competing online music ventures (for example, by requiring the joint venture to pay high royalties for its music), or might simply prove unattractive to competitors (for example, by placing restrictions on burning). Review of such terms, however, would likely be a difficult process, as it has been for other compulsory licenses of copyrighted music.[113]

Here again, our experience with ASCAP and BMI should give us pause about the costs and benefits of such a decree. The ASCAP consent decree, entered in the original litigation in 1941, has been a continuing source of controversy. In recent years, the federal district court responsible for overseeing the decree has been required to decide on "reasonable fees" under the terms of the decree, and the court, the parties, and the Department of Justice have been required to continuously review the decree to keep it up to date.[114]

Conclusion

This chapter has argued that the appropriate analysis of the online music joint ventures, when announced in 2001, would have been to find that they were unreasonable restraints of trade in violation of Section 1 of the Sherman Act. This conclusion should have held even under the rule of reason inquiry mandated by *BMI*.

The joint ventures were made up of record companies that controlled approximately 80 percent of the non-substitutable inputs for a lawful online music service (that is, the licenses to the necessary sound recordings). This made it predictable that the ventures would diminish platform and price competition in the online music market, whether in the form of competition between the ventures or, more importantly, in the form of the competition that would likely have emerged if the record companies did not start joint ventures but instead licensed their music freely to independently owned online music providers. Although this predicted anticompetitive effect relies heavily on an ex ante view of the venturers' licensing incentives both with and without joint venture entry, particularly their incentives to license strategically, these anticompetitive effects still outweigh the very slight efficiency benefits from the joint ventures. As a closer comparison with the performing rights organizations involved in *BMI* shows, collective action in the online music industry was not necessary to produce an online music service and offered only the barest of demand-side benefits in the form of modest one-stop shopping. The appropriate remedy would have been to enjoin the operation of pressplay and MusicNet, requiring either divestiture or unwinding of the ventures.

As we know, however, the online music market has not turned out as predicted. The record company owners of pressplay have divested their interests. Licensing appears to be fairly open (although it is unclear what restrictions are being placed on various licensees) and there is a proliferation of offerings. However one might compute market shares at the moment, it would be doubtful that the market share held by MusicNet (the remaining joint venture) comes close to reflecting the shares its owners have in the wholesale market for prerecorded music. Ironically, time and the owners of the joint ventures have done the work of antitrust remedies, producing divestiture of ownership of one joint venture and full access to the essential inputs controlled by the co-venturers.

To what do we owe our good fortune? Surely it is to the inability of the music industry to control the widespread infringement of their copyrights. Whatever one thinks about the breadth of intellectual property rights today,[115] or about the extent to which such infringement adversely affects the incentives of those in the industry to create and distribute new music, one must acknowledge that the competition posed by unstoppable infringement changed the record companies' incentives with regard to providing digital music on the Internet. The foregoing antitrust analysis of the joint ventures was based on the assumption that the venturers controlled the essential inputs. When it became clear to them that they did not, they moved to a more efficient and more competitive strategy. The result has been the development of online music ventures and the increasing variety in the platforms on which this music is being distributed.

It may be that the wait-and-see approach to enforcement that the Justice Department followed was institutionally appropriate. This is an industry that is still in flux, based as it is on technologies that are still evolving, both in terms of the software platforms for delivering digital music and the hardware that is now being employed to store and transport digital music files. Still, there is no reason to believe that we have reached an equilibrium where we can comfortably leave online music to the dictates of marketplace competition, either. It is not likely that all the current sellers of online music will find the market profitable and it is still unclear what the optimal business model for delivering digital music over the Internet will be.[116] What is clear is that there is an underlying competition problem if control of the essential inputs returns to the hands of a concentrated production industry, and one which may become even more concentrated in the future.

The incentives to control distribution of music over the Internet remain. Care should be taken in the event that the markets shift once again and provide the music industry the ability to control the distribution of those inputs.

Notes

1 Professor of Law, New York University School of Law. I thank Peter Carstensen, Edward Cavanagh, Rochelle Dreyfuss, Rebecca Tushnet, and Diane Zimmerman, as well the participants at the Third Annual Loyola (Chicago) Antitrust Colloquium, for their very helpful comments on earlier drafts. I also thank Lee Bollinger, Idit Froim, and Daniel Hemli for their very valuable research assistance. This research was supported by the generosity of the Filomen and Max D'Agostino Research Fund at New York University.
2 Department of Justice Antitrust Division, *Statement Regarding the Closing of its Investigation into The Major Record Labels' pressplay and MusicNet Joint Ventures*, December 23, 2003, p. 4. Online. Available HTTP: <http://www.usdoj.gov/atr/public/press_releases/2003/201946.htm> (accessed June 17, 2004).
3 See *The Recording Industry Ass'n of America, 2002 Yearend Statistics.* Online. Available HTTP: <http://www.riaa.com/news/marketingdata/pdf/year_end_2002.pdf> (accessed June 17, 2004) (total dollar value of all shipments, net of returns; includes CDs, cassettes, LPs, music videos, and DVD video and audio; bulk of revenue is in CD sales). By comparison, in 2002 U.S. movie box office gross revenues were $9.5 billion and the U.S. video game industry had $10.3 billion in retail sales. See *U.S. Entertainment Industry: 2002 MPA Market Statistics*, an economic review by the Motion Picture Association. Online. Available HTTP: <http://www.mpaa.org/useconomicreview/2002/2002_Economic_Review.pdf (accessed June 17, 2004) and *The NPD Group Reports Annual 2002 U.S. Video Game Sales Break Record*, January 27, 2003. Online. Available HTTP: <http://www.npd.com/press/releases/press_030128a.htm (accessed June 17, 2004).

4 Ibid. There was a 2.5 percent drop in revenues between 1996 and 1997.

5 See E. Smith, "Music industry sounds upbeat as losses slow," *Wall Street Journal*, January 2, 2004, p. B1 (including sales by online services, 2003 sales only 0.8 percent less than 2002 sales; excluding online sales, sales in 2003 were 2.1 percent less than 2002).

6 See, for example, *Declining Music Sales: It's Not All Digital Downloading, Says The NPD Group*, June 5, 2003. Online. Available HTTP: <http://www.npd. com/press/releases/press_030605.htm> (accessed June 17, 2004) (based on consumer surveys, half of lost sales attributed to free file sharing; but 60 percent of music consumers with Internet access have not downloaded any music and sales to these consumers have also dropped; half of consumers aged 36 and over report that there is less music that they are interested in buying); Smith, op. cit. (strong sales in fourth quarter of 2003 included a number of hit albums, such as OutKast's "Speakerboxxx/The Love Below" and Norah Jones' "Come Away With Me").

7 See E. Christman, "UMVD expands market-share dominance," *Billboard*, January 18, 2003 (based on SoundScan data). The market share of the top five distributors was 83 percent in 2001 as well, see E. Christman, "UMVD marks 3rd straight year as top U.S. music distributor: UMVD leads in total, current album share," *Billboard*, January 26, 2002.

8 UMG's labels include A+M, Def Jam, Geffen, Island, MCA, Motown, Polydor, Universal, and Verve.

9 Warner's labels include Warner Brothers Records Inc., Atlantic Recording Corporation, Rhino Entertainment Company, and Elektra Entertainment Group, Inc.

10 Sony's labels include Columbia, Epic, WORK Group, C2, Nashville, Sony Classical, and Sony Wonder.

11 BMG's labels include RCA, Arista, BMG Classics, Windham Hill, and Bad Boy Entertainment.

12 EMI's labels include Capitol, Capitol Nashville, Blue Note, Angel Records, and EMI Latin.

13 See "Regulators sink EMI–Time Warner deal," *Wall Street Journal*, October 6, 2000.

14 See M. Lander, "Bertelsmann and Sony to join music units," *New York Times*, November 7, 2003, p. C1; E. Smith and C. Goldsmith, "Bronfman group wins Warner Music," *Wall Street Journal*, November 25, 2003, p. B4.

15 If the "independents" are considered as a single firm, the Herfindahl-Hirschman Index (HHI) is 1893; otherwise the HHI would be slightly over 1600. The federal enforcement agency Guidelines consider a market with an HHI above 1800 as "highly concentrated"; markets between 1000 and 1800 are considered "moderately concentrated." See United States Department of Justice and Federal Trade Commission, *Horizontal Merger Guidelines* §1.5. Based on these market shares, the Bertelsmann-Sony merger increases the HHI by more than 400 points, making the market highly concentrated.

16 See generally R. C. Picker, "Copyright as entry policy: the case of digital distribution," *Antitrust Bulletin* 47, 2002, p. 429 (discussing changes caused by online distribution).

17 See 17 U.S.C. §101 (sound recording is a work that results "from the fixation of a series of musical, spoken, or other sounds" which can be embodied in "material objects such as disks, tapes, or other phonorecords").

18 See Online. Available HTTP: <http://www.riaa.com/issues/licensing/howto.asp> (accessed June 17, 2004).

19 See 17 U.S.C. 106 (1), (3), (4).

20 See 17 U.S.C. §115. The Harry Fox Agency is the licensing agent for the copyright owners of most musical works (but not all), the copyrights to which are generally owned by music publishing companies, and most performers take mechanical licenses from the Harry Fox Agency rather than from the Copyright Office. See R. A. Reese, "Copyright and internet music transmissions: existing law, major controversies, possible solutions," *U. Miami L. Rev.* 55, 2001, p. 243 and n. 18.

21 See 17 U.S.C. 114 (a).

22 Digital Performance Right in Sound Recordings Act, Public Law 104–39.

23 See Reese, op. cit., pp. 243–4 and pp. 253–4. There is some question whether the DPD right applies to the retention in RAM of portions of a song transmitted over the Internet (which is typical of streaming software which buffers the transmission to allow for continuous reception).

24 Ibid., pp. 245–6 and p. 260. ASCAP and BMI contend that transmission for downloading also constitutes a public performance, even if the music is not audible during the transmission but only after the download.

25 17 USC §106 (6). The Digital Performance Right in Sound Recordings Act (DPRA) was subsequently amended in 1998 by the Digital Millennium Copyright Act (DMCA).

26 See 17 USC §114 (j) (defining an "interactive service" as one that "enables a member of the public to receive a transmission of a program specially created for the recipient, or on request, a transmission of a particular sound recording, whether or not as part of a program, which is selected by or on behalf of the recipient").

27 The statute places further restrictions on what webcasters operating under the compulsory license can do, including restrictions on the selections of sound recordings being transmitted (the "sound recording complement") and on the type of programming information provided. See 17 USC §114 (d)(2)(C).

28 See *A&M Records, Inc. v. Napster, Inc.*, 239 F.3d 1004, 1011 (9th Cir. 2001); M. Fagin, F. Pasquale, and K. Weatherall, "Beyond Napster: using antitrust law to advance and enhance online music distribution," *B.U. J. Sci. and Tech. L.* 8, 2002, p. 458 n.10. MP3 is not the only file compression technology, but it is apparently the most popular.

29 Ibid. For example, a three-minute song of 32 megabyte size could be compressed into an MP3 file of about three megabytes.

30 *A&M Records, Inc., v. Napster Inc.*, op. cit., 1012.

31 See *A&M Records, Inc., v. Napster Inc.*, op. cit., 1091 (affirming grant of preliminary injunction against Napster for contributory copyright infringement), 284 F.3d 1091 (9th Cir. 2002) (upholding order to shut down service). See also *UMG Recordings, Inc. v. MP3.com, Inc.*, 92 F. Supp. 2d 349 (S.D.N.Y. 2000) (defendant's service, allowing consumer-owners of CDs to access via the Internet copies of musical compositions recorded on those CDs, violated copyright laws where the actual stored and transmitted copies were made by defendant without authorization from copyright owners).

32 Litigation is also proceeding against services that enable users to search for music files. See, for example, *Arista Records Inc. v. MP3Board Inc.*, 2002 U.S.

Dist. LEXIS 16165 (S.D.N.Y. 2002) (suit seeking to enjoin operation of website that permits users to search the Internet for MP3 files; denying motions for summary judgment). The Napster brand was subsequently resuscitated by a new venture that acquired the assets of pressplay. Ibid. See infra text accompanying note 59.

33 For a description of the software, see *Metro-Goldwyn-Mayer Studios, Inc. v. Grokster, Ltd.*, 259 F.Supp. 2d 1029 (C.D. Cal. 2003), *aff'd*, 380 F.3d 1154 (9th Cir. 2004), *pet. cert. granted*, 73 USLW 3350 (Dec. 10, 2004) (No. 04–480); Fagin *et al.*, op. cit., p. 461.

34 See A. Harmon, "Music industry in global fight on web copies," *New York Times*, October 7, 2002, p. A1, A6 (nearly 3 million users of KaZaA Media Desktop software at any given time, roughly double Napster's usage at its peak).

35 See Online. Available HTTP: <http://download.com/3101-2001-0-1.html?tag=pop> (accessed October 3, 2003) (data compiled by CNET). For earlier figures, see, for example, R. Fixmer, "Showtime, Microsoft style," *New York Times*, September 26, 2002, p. G1 (reporting 2.7 million downloads for the week of September 15, 2002). By the summer of 2003 the number of downloads of KaZaA was five times the number of downloads of Napster. See K. J. Delaney, "KaZaA founder peddles software to speed file sharing," *Wall Street Journal*, September 8, 2003, p. B1. Not all downloads are for new users; some of these downloads are duplicates and upgrades. See S. Junnarkar, "'Honest thief' confronts music industry," CNET News.com. Online. Available HTTP: <http://news.com/2100-1023-985484.html> (accessed June 17, 2004).

36 For a description of the Gnutella technology, see *Metro-Goldwyn-Mayer Studios, Inc. v. Grokster, Ltd.*, op. cit., 1041 (users are connected through publicly available directories).

37 See Download.com, op. cit.

38 See *Metro-Goldwyn-Mayer Studios, Inc. v. Grokster, Ltd.*, op. cit., 1043 (defendants "are not significantly different from companies that sell home video recorders or copy machines, both of which can be and are used to infringe copyrights") (granting defendant software companies' motions for summary judgment relating to contributory and vicarious copyright liability).

39 The industry's initial efforts to use the provisions of the Digital Millennium Copyright Act to obtain from Internet service providers the names of alleged infringers was rejected in *Recording Indus. Ass'n of Am., Inc. v. Verizon Internet Services, Inc.*, 351 F.3D 1229 (D.C. Cir. 2003), *cert. denied*, 125 S.Ct. 309 (2004). For reaction to the initial effort to obtain names of alleged infringers, see D. K. Berman and A. W. Mathews, "Is the record industry about to bust your teenager?" *Wall Street Journal*, January 28, 2003, p. D1.

40 See A. Harmon, "Recording industry goes after students over music sharing," *New York Times*, April 23, 2003, p. A1.

41 See A. Harmon, "Suit settled for students downloading music online," *New York Times*, May 2, 2003, p. A22 (settlements ranged between $12000 and $17000 each; "billions of dollars" originally asked for in relief; "I don't believe I did anything wrong," said one of the students). N. Wingfield and E. Smith, "The high cost of sharing," *Wall Street Journal*, September 9, 2003, p. B1 (70 suits filed in New York).

42 For an argument that file sharing can be deterred by "a risk of jail or a fine," see J. Bernoff, "Can young file sharers be stopped? Yes!" Online. Available HTTP: <http://www.forrester.com/ER/Research/Brief/0,1317,17183,00. html#fig_1> (accessed June 17, 2004) (61 percent to 74 percent of downloaders between 12 and 22 would stop downloading; approximately 30 percent would stop if it took twice as long to download); E. Smith, "Music industry sounds upbeat as losses slow," *Wall Street Journal*, January 2, 2004, at B1 (reporting increased sales of music for 12 of 16 weeks after suits were filed; also reports that a series of hit albums were released during that period). See also J. Schwartz, "Music industry returns to court, altering tactics of file sharing," *New York Times*, January 22, 2004, p. C1 (filing suit against 532 alleged large-scale individual infringers); S. Hansell, "Crackdown on copyright abuse may send music traders into software underground," *New York Times*, September 9, 2003, p. C1 (discussing growth of software that masks users so that record industry cannot locate infringers).

43 Vivendi, the parent of UMG, had two pre-existing separate online ventures. One is EMusic, an MP3 subscription service acquired in 2001, which subsequently offered some UMG back catalogue for downloading. See J. Graham, "Pay-for-play music services mimic Napster," *The Journal News*, August 12, 2002, p. 4D. The other is MP3.com.

44 In 2003 Sony acquired a 4 percent stake in MusicNet in the form of a convertible note. See Reuters, "Sony backs rival MusicNet," CNET News.com, February 27, 2003. Online. Available HTTP: <http://news.com/ 2100–1027–990503.html> (accessed June 17, 2004) ("[T]he investment may also signal a shift in the alliances that span the music technology industry").

45 Zomba, which is part-owned by BMG, see www.hoovers.com, has a small ownership share in MusicNet.

46 Except for EMI, the smallest of the five major record companies, which licensed its music to its "non-affiliated" service, pressplay.

47 *Wall Street Journal*, op. cit., May 15, 2002.

48 See J. Borland, "Pressplay to offer unlimited downloads," CNET News.com, July 31, 2002. Online. Available HTTP: <http://news.com/2100-1023-947507. html?tag=fd_lede> (accessed June 17, 2004).

49 See J. Angwin and N. Wingfield, "AOL revamps music service, but it's costly," *Wall Street Journal*, February 26, 2003, p. D1.

50 See J. Angwin and N. Wingfield, op. cit., p. D1 ($17.95 to burn 10 songs, more than the cost of a CD in a store; quoting 15-year-old consumer complaining that the number of songs permitted "is not enough").

51 J. Borland, "Listen.com lands last big five label," CNET News.com, July 1, 2002.   Online.   Available   HTTP: <http://news.com/2100-1023-940841. html?tag=bplst> (accessed June 17, 2004).

52 Ibid.

53 See P. W. Tam and A. W. Mathews, "Apple polishes its music service," *Wall Street Journal*, April 14, 2003, p. B1.

54 See Bob Tedeschi, "Buy.com chief starts site to sell music downloads," *New York Times*, July 23, 2003, p. C4.

55 See   Press   Release,   February   17,   2003.   Online,   Available   HTTP: <http://www.fullaudio.com/pr.jsp?prDate=02172003>   (accessed   June   17, 2004).

56 See online. Available HTTP: <http://www.fullaudio.com/partners.jsp> (accessed June 17, 2004).

57 See Press Release, *MusicMatch Introduces 99 Cent Downloads for the PC*, September 29, 2003. Online. Available HTTP: <http://www.musicmatch.com/info/company/press/releases/?year=2003andrelease=13> (accessed June 17, 2004).

58 See D. Bank, "RealNetworks is launching its own online-music network," *Wall Street Journal*, May 28, 2003, p. B7. RealNetworks' chief executive, Rob Glaser, is chairman of MusicNet. See S. Hansell, "E-music sites settle on prices. It's a start," *New York Times*, March 3, 2003, p. C5.

59 See D. Clark and A. Wilde Mathews, "Roxio looks to resurrect Napster," *Wall Street Journal*, May 20, 2003, p. B7; N. Wingfield, "Roxio sells shares to revive Napster," *Wall Street Journal*, June 30, 2003, p. B5 (Roxio paid about $40 million to acquire pressplay).

60 See J. Borland, "Roxio taps Fanning for Napster take two," CNET News.com, February 24, 2003. Online. Available HTTP: <http://news.com/2100–1023–985748.html> (accessed June 17, 2004). At the time, Roxio only held a license from EMI, to offer downloads and burning.

61 See Clark and Mathews, op. cit., (pressplay was a "stepping stone" for finding new means to distribute music, according to CEO of Sony Music).

62 See "Wal-Mart opens online music store, undercutting competitors," *Wall Street Journal*, March 24, 2004, D2.

63 See N. Wingfield, "Retailers set internet music venture," *Wall Street Journal*, January 27, 2003; P. Patsuris, "Music chains raise the volume on downloads," *Forbes*, January 27, 2003. Online. Available HTTP: <http://www.forbes.com/2003/01/27/cx_pp_0127music.html> (accessed June 17, 2004); www.echo.com. The business plan of the service (called "Echo") included "kiosks" inside record stores to sell downloads or passes for downloads over the Internet. Echo's plans were said to be "on hold." See N. Wingfield, "Shakeout may mute some music-downloading services," *Wall Street Journal*, March 23, 2004, B1.

64 See N. Wingfield, "Virgin to launch online business to sell music," *Wall Street Journal*, September 27, 2004, B6.

65 See press release, "Sony Corporation of America will launch online music service in spring 2004," January 7, 2004. Online. Available HTTP: <http://news.sel.sony.com/pressrelease/print/4301> (accessed November 11, 2004). See also J. Schwartz and J. Markoff, "Power players; big names are jumping into the crowded online music field," *New York Times*, January 12, 2004, C1.

66 See "Viacom Inc.: MTV network plans launch of an online music service," *Wall Street Journal*, May 10, 2004, B6; K. J. Delaney, "Yahoo agrees to buy Musicmatch to take on Apple and Microsoft," *Wall Street Journal*, September 15, 2004, B10.

67 See press release, "MSN launches review release of music download service," September 1, 2004. Online. Available HTTP: <http://www.microsoft.com/presspass/press/2004/sept04/09-01MusicBetaLaunchPR.asp> (assessed November 11, 2004). See also N. Wingfield, "Online music's latest tune: Microsoft next week begins service to rival Apple's iTunes; Yahoo, MTV, Virgin Lurk, Too," *Wall Street Journal*, August 27, 2004, B1.

68 Angwin and Wingfield, op. cit. (Jupiter research estimate). See also J. Schwartz and J. Markoff, op. cit. (more than 300,000 total subscribers). Rhapsody reportedly had 250,000 subscribers in late 2003, see N. Wingfield and E. Smith, "With the web shaking up music, a free-for-all in online songs," *Wall Street Journal*, November 19, 2003, p. A1.

69 See Angwin and Wingfield, op. cit., See also A. Kover, "It's back. But can the new Napster survive?," *New York Times*, August 17, 2003, p. 4 (Apple sold 6.5 million songs in first three months).

70 See A. Harmon, "What price music? How your favorite song went on 99-cent special," *New York Times*, October 12, 2003, Section 2, p. 1. Rhapsody has more songs to listen to (385,000) than to purchase (275,000).

71 See, for example, Harmon, "What price music?" op. cit. For an earlier review of charges, see D. Pogue, "The internet as jukebox, at a price," *New York Times*, March 6, 2003, p. G1; W. Mossberg, "Rhapsody lets you burn cds online at 49 cents a song," *Wall Street Journal*, February 13, 2003, p. B1. For future developments in the pricing structure, see E. Smith, "Downloading music gets more expensive," *Wall Street Journal*, April 7, 2004, D1 ("affordable and straightforward pricing structure is already under pressure").

72 See Harmon, "What price music?" op. cit.; Hansell "Settle on prices," op. cit.

73 Although there is controversy over whether "buffering" of music that is being streamed to a computer user is a reproduction of the musical work, thereby implicating the compulsory mechanical license, see Reese op. cit., the online ventures paid what may be a one-time royalty to the Harry Fox Agency so as to get the ventures going. See A. Harmon, "Copyright hurdles confront selling of music on the internet," *New York Times*, September 23, 2002, p. C1 ($1 million up front payment by online music ventures to Harry Fox Agency, representing majority of music publishers); Interview with Nicholas Gordon, Esq., June 18, 2003.

74 See Hansell, "Settle on prices," op. cit., p. C5.

75 Ibid. Buy.com sells its songs at different prices; songs also have different rights of use, depending on the license from the record distributor. See Bob Tedischi, "Buy.com chief starts site to sell music downloads," *New York Times*, July 23, 2003, p. C4.

76 See Hansell, "Settle on prices," op. cit., p. C5.

77 See U.S. Department of Justice and Federal Trade Comm'n, *Horizontal Merger Guidelines* §1.11 (for market definition in merger cases, a 5 percent price increase lasting for the foreseeable future).

78 See Harmon, "What price music?" op. cit., p. 32. Rhapsody's sales more than tripled at the 49 cent price; Napster's increase in sales at 79 cents was not proportionally greater than the decrease in price.

79 Ibid. ("Ninety-nine cents is only slightly less than the cost of a song on a CD [given the usual price, around $14, and the usual number of tracks, around 12].")

80 See *United States v. Aluminum Co. of America*, 148 F.2d 416 (2d Cir. 1945).

81 See *United States v. Microsoft Corp.*, 84 F. Supp. 2d 9, 25 (D.D.C. 1999) (§58), *vacated and remanded on other grounds*, 253 F.3d 34 (D.C. Cir.), cert. denied, 534 U.S. 952 (2001).

82 See Federal Trade Comm'n and U.S. Department of Justice, *Antitrust Guidelines for Collaborations Among Competitors* §2.1.

83 See R. P. Merges, "Contracting into liability rules: intellectual property rights and collective rights organizations," *Calif. L. Rev.* 84, 1996, p. 1293; A. Harmon, "Copyright hurdles confront selling of music on the internet," *New York Times*, September 23, 2002, p. C1 (describing multiplicity of rights that need to be cleared to provide online music service).

84 See, for example, *United States v. Penn-Olin Chemical Co.*, 378 U.S. 1710 (1964) (joint venture may have eliminated potential competition from one of the co-venturers remaining on the fringe of the market and threatening entry).

85 See, for example, *Appalachian Coals, Inc. v. United States*, 288 U.S. 344 (1933) (joint sales agency for marketing coal; subject to rule of reason); *United States v. Columbia Pictures Indus., Inc.*, 507 F. Supp. 412 (S.D.N.Y. 1980) (joint venture of four motion picture companies to provide new pay television service; subject to per se rule), *aff'd*, 1981 U.S. App. LEXIS 21309 (2d Cir. 1981).

86 441 U.S. 1 (1979).

87 Ibid., pp. 22–3.

88 See B. Korman and I. F. Koenigsberg, "Performing rights in music and performing rights societies," *J. Copyright Soc. of the U.S.A.*, 1986, p. 350.

89 Ibid., pp. 337–42. The consent decree, originally entered in 1941, was amended in 2001 to cover "on-line music users" that publicly perform works via the Internet. See *United States v. ASCAP*, 2001–2 Trade Cas. (CCH) ¶73,474 (§II) (H) (second amended final judgment).

90 See S. Timberg, "The antitrust aspects of merchandizing modern music: the ASCAP consent judgment of 1950," *L. and Contemp. Probs.* 19, 1954, pp. 297–8.

91 See S. M. Besen, S. Kirby, and S. C. Salop, "An economic analysis of copyright collectives," *Va. L. Rev.* 78, 1992, p. 390 ("A premise of our analysis is that significant economies result from collective administration.").

92 See Online. Available HTTP: <http://www.riaa.com/about/default.asp> (accessed June 17, 2004) ("RIAA members create, manufacture and/or distribute approximately 90 percent of all legitimate sound recordings produced and sold in the United States").

93 See Timberg, op. cit., p. 313.

94 See 441 U.S. 1, op. cit., p. 21 and n. 35.

95 Timberg, op. cit., p. 297.

96 The Copyright Clearance Center licenses text reproduction and distribution rights on a per-use basis, with royalties set by copyright holders; it also offers a blanket license. See Online. Available HTTP: <http://www.copyright.com/Help/HelpApsFAQ.asp#5> (accessed June 17, 2004) (copyright holders set their own royalty fees; clearance center charges a uniform processing fee). Its willingness to offer these choices may be explained by the fact that, as in the music industry, holders of copyrights in written works face the difficult task of getting consumers to pay when piracy is cheap and easy.

97 The Department of Justice may be ready to question the continued vitality of *BMI* with regard to the refusal to offer per-song licenses. See Memorandum of the United States in Support of the Joint Motion to Enter Second Amended Final Judgment, *United States v. ASCAP*, p. 9 (S.D.N.Y., September 4, 2000) ("Technologies that allow rights holders and music users to easily and inexpensively monitor and track music usage are evolving rapidly. Eventually, as it becomes less and less costly to identify and report performances of compositions

and to obtain licenses for individual works or collections of works, these technologies may erode many of the justifications for collective licensing of
performance rights by PROs. The Department is continuing to investigate the
extent to which the growth of these technologies warrants additional changes
to the antitrust decrees against ASCAP and BMI, including the possibility that
the PROs should be prohibited from collectively licensing certain types of
users or performances"). Online. Available HTTP: <http://www.usdoj.gov/
atr/cases/f6300/6395.htm> (accessed June 17, 2004).

98 See 441 U.S., op. cit., p. 20.

99 This is unlike the situation in many other countries where there is only one
performing rights organization. For a description of performing rights societies outside the U.S., see R. Schulenberg, *Legal Aspects of the Music Industry*,
New York: Billboard Books, 1999.

100 At the time, ASCAP was estimated to control between 85 and 90 percent of
the music required by users such as broadcasters and dance halls. See *Buck v.
Swanson*, 33 F Supp 377, 386 (D. Nebr 1939).

101 Korman and Koenigsberg, op. cit., p. 351 n. 87.

102 See Besen, Kirby, and Salop, op cit., p. 402 (discussing the entry of BMI).

103 See Memorandum of the United States in Support of the Joint Motion to
Enter Second Amended Final Judgment, op. cit., n. 95, pp. 6–7 (ASCAP has
over 8 million songs in its repertory; BMI has 4 to 5 million). SESAC, the third
performing rights organization, was founded in 1930; its repertory, "once
limited to European and gospel music, has diversified to include today's most
popular music, including dance hits, rock classics, the best of Latina music,
the hottest jazz, the hippest country and the coolest contemporary Christian
music." See Online. Available HTTP: <http: //www.sesac.com/aboutsesac/
aboutmain.asp> (accessed June 17, 2004).

104 See *ASCAP v. Showtime/The Movie Channel, Inc.*, 912 F.2d 563, 594 (2d Cir.
1990) (ASCAP rate court proceeding; using fees negotiated with BMI as
benchmark for fees for ASCAP), discussed, Besen, Kirby, and Salop, op. cit.,
pp. 405–7.

105 See *Competitor Collaborations Guidelines*, op. cit., §2.2 (potential harm to
competition from increasing price or reducing quality of innovation below
what likely would prevail in the absence of the agreement).

106 *Competitor Collaborations Guidelines*, op. cit., §4.2. This would, at least, place the
ventures outside either of the Guidelines' safety zones (20 percent of the relevant market), §4.3 ("three independently controlled ventures" for research
ventures that require specialized assets to engage in competitive research).

107 The Department of Justice did consider in its investigation "whether the
major record labels used their joint ventures to suppress the growth of the
Internet as a means of promoting and distributing music, in order to protect
their present positions in the distribution of music on physical media, such as
CDs," but found that this fear did not materialize given the subsequent licensing of music by the venture participants. See Department of Justice, Closing
Statement, op. cit., pp. 3–4.

108 See In re Napster Inc. Copyright Litig., 191 F.Supp.2d 1087, 1108–09 (N.D.
Cal., 2002) (joint ventures "look bad, sound bad and smell bad"). Similarly,
the lack of a contractual restriction on licensing could very well have been the
product of careful antitrust counseling, given the importance of non-exclusive

licenses in *BMI*. See also *United States v. Columbia Pictures Indus., Inc.*, 507 F. Supp. 412 (S.D.N.Y. 1980) (granting to the joint venture a nine-month exclusive license of motion pictures, by motion picture co-venturers that controlled "one-half of the essential product of the industry," held to be per se unlawful group boycott), *aff'd*, 1981 U.S. App. LEXIS 21309 (2d Cir. 1981).

109 See Wingfield and Smith, "Free-for-all," op. cit., p. A1 ("For years, the major record labels balked at licensing their song catalogs to legitimate music sites, and most of them burdened the music with unwieldy technical safeguards that prevented consumers from recording songs onto CDs or transferring them to portable music players. Now, the labels have gone headlong in the other direction").

110 Clark and Matthews, op. cit.

111 For example, Sony subsequently announced its intention to enter independently. See J. Schwartz and J. Markoff, op. cit., p. C3.

112 *Compare* J. L. Harrison, "Online music: antitrust and copyright perspectives," *Antitrust Bull.* 47, 2002, pp. 488–9 (nondiscriminatory license requirement would be "effective response," although there are "complications" from such a requirement) *with* Fagin *et al.*, op. cit., pp. 522–7 (rejecting compulsory licensing as "least plausible" solution).

113 See Library of Congress, Copyright Office, Determination of Reasonable Rates and Terms for the Digital Performance of Sound Recordings and Ephemeral Recordings, 67 Fed. Reg. 45,240 (July 8, 2002) (reviewing report of the Copyright Arbitration Royalty Panel on rates and terms under the statutory compulsory license for webcasting; process began in 1998).

114 The Department of Justice, for example, has complained about the extent to which the per-program and per-segment licenses required under the consent decree have a real possibility of constraining ASCAP's market power by allowing users to substitute some of their music licensing needs away from ASCAP. See Memorandum of the United States in Support of the Joint Motion to Enter Second Amended Final Judgment, op. cit., p. 32 n.32. Section IX of the decree requires ASCAP to license at a "reasonable fee." See *United States v. ASCAP*, 2001–2 Trade Cas. (CCH) ¶73,474 (S.D.N.Y.) (second amended final judgment); this has sometimes required formal judicial findings. See, for example, *United States v. ASCAP*, 1999 U.S. Dist. LEXIS 7778 (S.D.N.Y. 1999) (local cable system operators). Korman and Koenigsberg, op. cit., p. 356 n.123, write that as of 1985 there had been no formal trial proceedings over the decree's requirement that fees be "reasonable," although users had employed court proceedings as a "context for negotiations ... often with the aid of the court."

115 See generally *Expanding the Boundaries of Intellectual Property: Innovation Policy for the Knowledge Society*, R. Dreyfuss, D. Zimmerman, and H. First (eds), Oxford: Oxford University Press, 2001.

116 See Wingfield and Smith, "Free-for-all," op. cit., at A1 (predicting that only three to six companies will be operating in the online music market by 2005).

Part III

Lessons learned and policy recommendations

Lessons learned and policy recommendations

Diana L. Moss[1]

The case studies included in Part II were selected to cover a broad range of industries and access scenarios. These experiences offer potentially valuable lessons for policymakers, some of which have already been learned over the course of many years. Many lessons will be relearned in different and novel situations because inertia and political resistance stifle new approaches. Here, policymakers proceed at the risk of underutilizing (or ignoring) important historical experience in applying compulsory access solutions to problems that call for vertical separation, in allowing network owners too much latitude in negotiating the terms and conditions of access, or in choosing remedies that reallocate rents among firms instead of helping the consumer. So, what the collective experience says about the perils of managing intervention in network access problems or in mismatching remedies and problems would—in an ideal world—steer policymakers away from proven ineffective solutions.

Part I posed a number of policy questions that would be useful to answer over the course of this volume:

- Under what circumstances does access to a network pose a competitive problem?
- What should be the timing of policy intervention?
- What should be the primary method of intervention?
- How should access be remedied?
- What should be the rules of access under a compulsory access regime?

This chapter attempts to cast light on these questions by drawing relevant comparisons and contrasts across the case studies and using them to formulate a number of observations and recommendations. These recommendations are not definitive. Indeed, the progressiveness of the network access debate and fluid nature of many network access scenarios require ongoing dialog and flexible policy responses. Thus, what follows are best viewed as tentative conclusions, based on much study but needing further scrutiny and testing.

When is access a competitive problem?

As a preliminary matter, intervention in network access situations is not without detractors. Opponents of "access" in cable, broadband, and rail-roads, for example, have put forward Chicago School theories as a defense for allowing owners of monopoly networks to operate unfettered or as a basis for the claim that mergers can not incrementally distort markets. But as the case studies demonstrate, these theories break down more often than not, and the competitive implications of network access arise with frequency, both in fledgling and mature networks. Lawrence Lessig puts the fundamental problem into perspective:

> The danger is discrimination engaged in by concentrated actors. . . .
> [W]hen there isn't a great deal of competition in access, when a small
> number of companies can set the rules for the whole system, then the
> dangers in discrimination return. When a few can make decisions
> about what types of innovation will be permitted, the innovation
> promised by an end-to-end architecture is lost.[2]

With Lessig's characterization in mind, what do the case studies say about when access is a competitive problem? Table III.1 lists a number of promi-nent case study features that bear on this question. They are general char-acterizations based on interpretation of the case study analyses.

Column 2 of Table III.1 indicates the degree of competition in each of the network markets studied in Part II. This competition can come from competing end-to-end networks, alternative distribution channels, or dif-ferent technologies. Three paradigmatic scenarios seem appropriate to characterize. One involves little or no competition in the network market. Alternatives to the network are severely (if not completely) limited. In these cases—freight railroads, electricity transmission, local telecommuni-cations, and long distance telecommunications (prior to the Modified Final Judgment (MFJ))—a bottleneck network is typically a monopoly. A second scenario involves moderate levels of competition at the network level where there exist alternative end-to-end networks or different tech-nologies. Gas pipelines are one example, in which there is competition to serve similar routes or from pipelines that connect to different supply sources. Broadband is another case that fits this description, in that it competes in some situations with DSL. Internet browser and ATM network markets also display more moderate levels of competition at the network level. These networks are typically oligopoly markets. A third sce-nario involves higher levels of competition in network markets, primarily because of competing end-to-end networks or alternative distribution channels. Most internet-based products and services fit this description, including airline and travel services and online music, which compete with traditional "bricks and mortar" distribution.[3]

Table III.1 Summary of key features across access cases

Case Study	Attributes							
	Competition in Network Market (1)	Vertical Integration? (2)	Competition in Complementary Markets (3)	Essential Facilities? (4)	Physical or Virtual (5)	Supply- or Demand-Side Economies (6)	Evidence/ Possibility of Tipping? (7)	Standards Important? (8)
Freight railroads	Low	Yes	Low–moderate (shipping)	Yes	Physical	Supply-side	No	Yes
Electricity transmission	Low	Yes	Low–moderate (generation)	Yes	Physical	Supply-side	No	Yes
Gas pipelines	Low–moderate	Yes	Low–moderate (shipping)	No	Physical	Supply-side	No	Yes
Local telecommunications	Low	Yes	Low–moderate (IntraLATA services)	Yes	Physical	Supply- and Demand-side	No	Yes
Long-distance telecommunications[a]	Low	Yes	Low (interLATA services)	Yes	Physical	Supply- and Demand-side	No	Yes
Broadband	Moderate	Yes	Low–moderate (Internet svc. provision)	No	Virtual	Supply- and Demand-side	Yes	Yes
ATMs	Moderate	Yes	Moderate (Banking)	No	Virtual	Demand-side	Yes	Yes
Internet browser	Low–moderate	Yes	Moderate (Applications)	No	Virtual	Demand-side	Yes	Yes
Internet-based airline and travel	Moderate–high	Yes	Moderate–high (Airlines)	No	Virtual	Demand-side	Yes	No
Online music	Moderate–high	Yes	Moderate–high (Recorded Music)	No	Virtual	Demand-side	Yes	No

Notes
[a] Prior to the MFJ.

Competition at the network level sheds some light on the conditions under which access is apt to be problematic. In general, the less competition at the network level, the fewer the options for a potential non-network market participant and the stronger the argument for mandated access. But other information shown in Table III.1 provides additional insight, such as the competitiveness of complementary markets into which network owners are integrated. It is not surprising that with *pervasive* vertical integration, the general level of competition observed in the network market is typically also found in the complementary market. With this in mind, three general types of network situations seem to emerge.

One situation ("Type 1") involves less competition in both the network and complementary markets. Such markets include freight rail, electricity transmission, gas pipelines, local telecommunications, and long-distance telecommunications. These industries involve a physical network that has, in most cases, been deemed an essential facility (e.g., in *Terminal Railroad, Otter Tail,* and *U.S. v. AT&T*)—a central finding for antitrust liability or a basis for requiring access on equal terms and conditions. As a result, the Type 1 examples have demonstrated histories of access problems and sometimes complex remedies for correcting them. These networks raise important standards issues and display both supply-side and demand-side economies. But because the latter effects are relatively weak, the markets are not particularly prone to tipping. Access scenarios that fit the Type 1 description will invariably create competitive problems and access policy should therefore be accordingly responsive.

A second type of network situation ("Type 2") involves network and complementary markets that are moderately competitive, including broadband, ATMs, and internet browsers. These are virtual networks that may display supply-side economies. But demand-side economies are relatively stronger, therefore increasing the probability of tipping. Standards issues have also arisen in these industries. Type 2 situations are potentially less problematic as indicated, for example, by the Federal Communication Commission's (FCC's) lighter handed approach to broadband and relatively early resolution of network issues in ATM networks. However, these network situations are still worthy of ongoing scrutiny, in order to anticipate changes that could produce competitive problems. A third access situation ("Type 3") involves network and complementary markets that can generally be considered competitive. In other respects, Type 3 situations are similar to Type 2, but do not exhibit strong demand-side economies or standardization issues. Internet-based services fit this description. Type 3 situations are unlikely to be problematic but, as in the second case, should be monitored in the appropriate policy forum.

We can make a number of observations about what some of the specific information in Table III.1 implies for access policy. These are particularly useful for identifying Type 1, 2, and 3 scenarios and for monitoring the latter two access situations, since proponents of access invariably run up against arguments that there are (or will soon be) changes in the Table III.1 parameters that obviate the need for intervention. First, virtually all of the problematic cases of access involve physical networks that are essential facilities in markets where there are low levels of competition. This stands in direct contrast to cases involving virtual networks in markets where tipping may be a concern, but in which competition is more robust. Higher levels of competition in markets involving virtual networks are not unusual. This is because for the most part, virtual networks do not display the natural monopoly characteristics (i.e., driven by scale economies) that many physical networks do. Moreover, many virtual networks reside on the internet, which has evolved over time as a competing channel of distribution. While policymakers should not rely entirely on the foregoing "physical v. virtual" distinction in deciding whether access is likely to be a competitive problem, it does have some general applicability.

Second, tipping is a risk only in networks that display demand-side economies. Strong network effects, for example, have tipped markets to a single branded ATM network in some parts of the country. One could also envision a tipping scenario in a competitive browser market if each browser incorporated proprietary features to create network effects. While physical networks and supply-side economies appear to be the most closely associated with essential facilities, it is not out of the question that tipping to a single firm or technology could produce an essential facility. Policymakers should be alert to the circumstances under which virtual networks have tipped in the past in deciding whether access issues pose competitive problems. Moreover, policy should anticipate the likely outcome if tipping actually occurs. If the market tips to the incumbent, for example, the winner obtains a monopoly and access is likely to be a more serious competitive problem. But if the market tips to an entrant, the winner may still face some competition from the incumbent.

Third, the wherewithal or "ability" to discriminate against or refuse to deal with rivals is made possible by the vertical integration that pervades the industries studied in Part II.[4] But exclusionary strategies are not easily executed without *both* the ability and the incentive to lessen competition. The case studies highlight the various exclusionary mechanisms that have been (or could be) used in network industries: exclusivity rules, refusals to provide service or providing higher priced or lower quality service, curtailing service for non-legitimate reasons, delaying interconnection, denying access to information that would ensure operability (e.g., browser-compatible applications or required "plug-ins"), discriminating in licensing inputs, MFN provisions that reduce incentives to sell to competing networks, and sharing sensitive competitive information with affiliates. So, while competitive issues involving unintegrated network ownership are possible (e.g., favoritism and bargaining), the weight of the evidence points strongly to vertical integration as a key indicator of potential competitive problems. Examining how various exclusionary mechanisms might emerge in novel and different situations is important, as well as how access policies (e.g., compulsory access) can be crafted to eliminate or prevent identified types of conduct.

Vertical integration also produces the incentive (i.e., profitability) to discriminate against or refuse to deal with rivals, which is generally greater if complementary markets are concentrated, with the vertically-integrated network owner possessing a large share.[5] The cases demonstrate that both geographic and product market issues are important in network industries. Constraints on physical networks can produce small, congested markets while legitimate questions are beginning to arise about the substitutability of internet-based services for traditional "bricks-and-mortar" distribution channels.[6] Policy analysis should be alert to the importance of market definition in evaluating competitive issues and the underlying economic, technological, and institutional parameters that affect the availability of access alternatives.

Fourth, standards development is an important component of the overall access picture. Standards govern (among other things) compatibility and interoperability, interconnection of complementary market rivals with the network, and competitively sensitive information disclosure. They can play a critical role in determining competitive outcomes in network industries. Minimum, voluntary, or unenforceable standards tend to be much less effective. As a result, standards are administered and enforced in many problematic access cases by external, independent, governmental or quasi-governmental bodies. For example, the absence of generator interconnection standards has until recently been a stumbling block. The prospect of proprietary HTML standards could hinder user access to websites since some browsers recognize proprietary codes while others do not. How standards are developed requires policy monitoring. Coordination (as opposed to atomistic competition) among firms in standard-setting may be socially beneficial, but only if it produces superior outcomes. As a result, tracking the development of standards in network industries should be an integral part of the policy monitoring process suggested for Type 2 and 3 access situations and in addressing Type 1 access problems.

Timing of policy intervention

The timing of intervention in access problems is a major issue in policy development. Consider, for example, the FCC's "wait and see" policies on broadband access, the Federal Energy Regulatory Commission's (FERC's) indecision on mandating RTOs, and DOJ's protracted investigations into internet-based joint ventures. The optimal time to intervene depends on complex and sometimes unknown factors such as technological change, network effects and tipping, competition in network and complementary markets, and the degree of risk aversion to competitive or consumer harm in the underlying commodity markets. Expectations about the timing of intervention can have a significant effect on decision-making, including entry, innovation, and other strategic variables. Moreover, expectations influence investors' decisions based on their perceptions of the relative riskiness of network versus non-network investments. Because of the importance of timing decisions and how they affect expectations, a high value is placed on estimates of when intervention can be expected.[7]

Another important consideration is that there is often a lag between the decision to intervene and when access remedies are actually in place, particularly in high profile cases involving protracted negotiations between stakeholders. Timing decisions, therefore, would ideally anticipate the incentives issues created by such gaps. One way to provide more certainty to market participants and investors is for policy makers to make clear the circumstances under which they will intervene to correct a network access problem. White papers or stakeholder workshops are possible mechanisms for revealing an agency's intervention "threshold." This would limit political jockeying and strategic positioning by market participants and assist investors in weighing the relative risks of investing in network projects.

There are a number of strategies that could govern the timing of intervention in access problems. One is to remedy the access problem early, a strategy that would apply in the Type 1 access situations identified in the previous section. Promoting competition in complementary markets in the presence of a bottleneck is important, so discrimination by the vertically-integrated network owner against competitors should be identified quickly and prosecuted early. Early intervention might also be appropriate when the competitive situation in network and/or complementary markets is precarious or when markets are in the formative stages of development. Inter-network competition is particularly important to preserve, as demonstrated by experiences in internet-based services and ATM networks, when exclusive agreements among the network owners or operators can diminish competition. Even in the event a single network ultimately legitimately prevails, promoting competition at the outset ensures that the survivor is more efficient, and not the winner because of anticompetitive conduct. However, it is particularly difficult to ascertain what type of access situation is likely to come about in the formative stages of network development. This may also be the time when intervention (e.g., mandatory access) will have the largest negative impact on a network-builder.

At the opposite end of the spectrum is a second possible timing strategy—the "wait and see" approach. While this approach has been misapplied in many cases, arguably to the detriment of competition and consumers, it may be justified in some situations. For example, technological change can create a dynamic access environment by introducing a relatively rapid succession of competing network technologies (e.g., cellular telephony vs. local or long distance telecommunications). In the hypothetical extreme, very rapid technological change could produce a "serial monopoly" phenomenon, or the periodic replacement of a monopoly network with the next generation of technology. Such a development potentially brings into question the need for *any* intervention, since market power is regularly created and destroyed. Because it is difficult for policymakers to operate in a fluid access environment, it is likely that a "wait and see" strategy may be the only feasible approach, unless it becomes apparent that a bottleneck (or even an essential facility) is developing, at which point intervention is important. Regulatory agencies in particular invest significant resources in regulating particular technological *systems*, changes in which pose significant challenges, in terms of redefining thresholds for intervention and dealing with industry pressure that can promote regulatory capture.

A third timing strategy is "active monitoring," a better approach in cases where there may be strong network effects and markets are prone to tipping. Such markets could ultimately produce an essential facility—a compelling reason for intervention. In some cases, network effects may be developing, so active monitoring to assist in determining if and when intervention is necessary might be preferable. Antitrust litigation is not the best venue in which to define the parameters of appropriate monitoring plans. Moreover, protracted investigations (which can inadvertently simulate monitoring) at the pre-prosecutorial level can chill pro-competitive actions and/or restrain anticompetitive behavior. A workable model may be the FTC's practice of convening stakeholder workshops on industries and competition issues. These workshops gather a wide variety of stakeholders having relevant expertise and interests, focus on specific issues, and ensure that competitive concerns are clearly articulated. This approach has the benefit of tracking changes in the industry and influencing access policy through an informal process. In general, regulatory agencies are well-equipped to monitor network markets since they have specialized staffs, significant institutional knowledge, and extensive experience with monitoring programs. Through these vehicles, private decision-makers gain a clearer perception of the concerns of public decision-makers.

Who should intervene?

What do the case studies suggest about who should intervene in network access problems? At the broadest level, the debate centers on whether antitrust or legislation and/or regulation should be the primary method of policy intervention.[8] The lines between regulatory and antitrust approaches are rarely clearly drawn, particularly in the context of today's mixed models of network organization which are candidates for regulatory oversight of the network and enforcement of competition laws in complementary markets. Generally, each type of intervention has advantages, depending on the access problem.

Federal and state legislative initiatives have an important role to play in fact finding and in educating the public about access issues because they are usually highly public and visible and attract the attention of a broad array of stakeholders. These efforts can be *ex ante*, in which the legislature plays an important role in brokering competing interests in the formative stages of the access debate. Conversely, legislative efforts can be *ex post*, whereby the legislature validates what antitrust or regulatory agencies have already attempted on an *ad hoc* basis. There have been many successful legislative approaches to network access. Common carrier legislation for telecommunications, for example was an early watershed in network access policy.

Legislation can be the primary method of intervention in access problems for a number of reasons. For example, if a regulatory agency lacks the statutory authority to remedy an access problem, legislation can change or grant such authority. Legislation is often needed in situations when antitrust intervention seems unlikely to remedy an access problem in a timely manner. Legislation and/or regulation can also take a more extensive approach to network access than would be available under the antitrust laws. For example, energy and telecommunications legislation contains broader policy objectives designed to "jump start" complementary markets, as opposed to curing a narrowly defined access problem. But many of these recent efforts have drawn criticism and challenge, signaling that legislative approaches are becoming increasingly unwieldy as network access problems grow more complex, varied, and widespread throughout the economy. If a legislative approach is favored to accomplish access policy objectives, policymakers should specifically articulate public interest goals and how multiple access objectives are intended to interrelate.[9]

Access issues involving unintegrated bottleneck networks, or integrated bottlenecks when compulsory access is the remedy of choice, are probably best addressed by regulatory agencies (when they possess adequate statutory authority). In general, regulators are better equipped to develop non-discriminatory service provisions and access pricing regimes. They also have a comparative advantage in fine-tuning existing regulations to reflect changing technology and market conditions, although experience in a number of venues reveals that regardless of the context, it is always likely to be a controversial issue. Regulatory agencies are also in the position of reviewing mergers under a broader "public interest" standard than the "no harm to competition" standard enforced under the antitrust laws. As a result, regulators sometimes use merger review as a generic means of promoting access by imposing more general access-promoting requirements—a practice that repels as many stakeholders as it attracts. When mergers do raise genuine network access issues, coordinated merger review between regulatory and antitrust agencies is important since the "cross-fertilization" that comes of shared experience can be a valuable part of the policy process. This is consistent with the more general view that antitrust has a comparative advantage in dealing with consolidation in industries with larger numbers of competitors than in situations where existing monopolists are realigning and reformulating their market positions.

Governmental antitrust litigation is better suited to solving access problems when it can respond reasonably quickly to identified harms in industries that do not involve pervasive bottleneck problems. These situations would include access problems in emerging network industries, where regulatory approaches would necessarily be less tailored and unwieldy, and when threatened harms of discriminatory access have not yet materialized. Recent experience in *Trinko*, however, paints a less-than-optimistic picture of antitrust enforcement when regulatory approaches (promulgated through legislation) are in place. At the time of this writing, the unanswered question, of course, is whether *Trinko* will set a precedent for antitrust enforcement in similar situations in other network industries.

Remedies

The case studies reveal a variety of remedies for network access problems. In some, no remedy was imposed in cases where one was arguably necessary (e.g., the Interstate Commerce Commission/Surface Transportation Board's approach to access in freight railroads). In other cases (e.g., online joint ventures), no remedy was necessary because no access problem ultimately developed. Policymakers often have imperfect information or face significant political or legal constraints in devising remedies for network access problems. As a result, more than one type of remedy is often needed to address access problems in the mixed models we see today. Moreover, "second-best" solutions are more likely to be the rule, rather than the exception.[10] Where there has been intervention, there are three major types of policy approaches: vertical separation, network expansion, and compulsory access. These approaches mandate certain practices or structural relationships that are expected to reduce or eliminate the access problem. But the suitability of various approaches to network access depends on a unique set of factors that may or may not be present or known.

Vertical separation removes the ownership or control link between a network and a complementary market asset(s) through divestiture of either, thus reducing or eliminating the ability or incentive for a vertically-integrated network owner to exclude rivals.[11] But facilitating a viable network sector after divestiture is a challenging task. Incentive issues associated with the operation of a divested network need to be resolved in order to maintain service quality, reliability, and safety.[12] If the network is divested, network services are generally subject to cost- or performance-based regulation and non-discriminatory service provisions. Among the case studies, the AT&T divestiture of the BOCs is the sole example of curing an access problem through divestiture, motivated largely by a long series of regulatory and antitrust battles that failed to stimulate competition in a monopolized long distance market.[13]

The suitability of vertical separation depends on a number of considerations. For example, the divestiture of complementary market assets requires identifying: the type and quantity of assets that should be divested, to whom the assets should be divested (e.g., incumbents or entrants), and time or other limitations on how long the network owner must stay out of complementary markets. It is important to note that technological developments and strong economies often provide powerful incentives for network owners to re-integrate after vertical separation. It may be necessary, therefore, to perform *ex post* monitoring and full-scale review after a certain period of time and to carefully specify the conditions (if any) under which a network owner can re-enter restricted markets. As a result, divesture is not often used because of political resistance and/or judicial reluctance or lack of conviction about "getting it right." Attempts to approximate divestiture have been used in electricity whereby vertically-integrated utilities have relinquished control over their transmission systems to independent entities.

Network expansion requirements focus on reducing the incentive and ability to engage in exclusionary behavior by requiring the network owner to upgrade or expand the network. This has the effect of broadening the scope of the geographic market, reducing market concentration, and therefore the likelihood of anticompetitive outcomes.[14] FERC's proposed Regional Transmission Organizations were essentially designed to accomplish this purpose.[15] Like vertical separation, however, network expansion is used infrequently to remedy access problems. It involves difficult decisions of how, when, and where to expand the network, who pays for expansion, ensuring that expansion is appropriately implemented, and what rules will determine who gets to use expanded capacity. Unless these issues are relatively easy to resolve, network expansion as a cure for access problems will remain a less-utilized mechanism.

Compulsory access is adopted frequently to cure access problems, both generically and in numerous merger cases. With some exceptions, antitrust rarely adopts compulsory access fixes because ongoing oversight and enforcement of access rules by an antitrust agency is not usually very efficient. Neither antitrust enforcers (who are generally litigators by profession) nor courts want their jobs to take on the characteristics of a regulatory agency. On the other hand, as we see from the case studies, involvement by regulatory agencies in administering access regimes in network markets is significant.[16] However, regulated access is not without its critics and challenges. An effective regime requires that policymakers know where scale economies are (or are likely to be) in the production chain and the magnitude of such economies. Others argue that while compulsory access is politically more palatable than divestiture, the incremental nature of many compulsory access regimes is costly. Rules of access also raise difficult price and non-price issues and require careful crafting, fine-tuning, and enforcement to discourage rent-seeking and strategic behavior.

A central goal of compulsory access regimes is that they provide for reasonable and nondiscriminatory access. This can be accomplished by unbundling the network service and complementary commodity prices, which reduces or eliminates the potential of cross-subsidy and improves price transparency. Price transparency allows consumers to shop among competing complementary product suppliers, thereby injecting competitive discipline into the market.[17] Nondiscriminatory access often requires the network owner(s) to provide service to rivals on a comparable basis (e.g., under the same terms and conditions it would provide "itself"). For example, the 1982 MFJ required that AT&T provide comparable exchange access with unbundled service elements. Access rules set forth in the 1996 Telecommunications Act focused, among other things, on local exchange competitors obtaining unbundled network elements at cost-based prices. Specific terms and conditions of nondiscriminatory access are often spelled out in *pro forma* tariffs or contracts, as in the case of FERC's Order Nos. 436 and 636 (natural gas) and Order No. 888 (electricity transmission).

As demonstrated by the case studies, there is also the risk that compulsory access will prove ineffective. Policymakers should therefore be alert to signs that other approaches to access should be tried. One is evidence of "incremental" access policy that is related to inadequate policy measures (as opposed to changes in underlying technology or market conditions). Another indicator is evidence that litigated antitrust battles have failed to solve access disputes or when significant levels of regulatory and legal intervention are likely to accompany a conduct-based solution. A third indicator may be evidence that network owners possess inadequate incentives to invest in network infrastructure.[18] In these situations other remedies, such as vertical separation, might be more appropriate.

Rules of access

With only one case study involving vertical separation as a remedy, we have at our disposal the many examples of compulsory access for drawing out useful ideas about how rules should be crafted in both generic access and merger proceedings.[19] When considering compulsory access as a remedy, policymakers should consider the practical aspects of compliance and dispute resolution. *Terminal Railroad* and *Otter Tail* demonstrated these issues when the courts passed off pricing and terms of access to regulators. But to ensure that compliance problems do not steer the courts away from certain remedies when they are appropriate, it may be useful for settlement orders to contain a defined process for dispute resolution and to implement a system for rapid challenge and authoritative review of decisions that hamper access.

Another question is whether access should be voluntary. The cases indicate numerous examples of failed voluntary access, only to be superseded eventually with mandatory access requirements. FERC's initial, unsuccessful voluntary access approach to gas pipelines was followed by mandated access requirements. We are aware of few (if any) problematic access scenarios that warrant a voluntary access approach. Stated a different way, it would seem that successful voluntary approaches do not get to the stage where government needs to craft a remedy, but by the time government intervention is needed, it is unlikely that a voluntary approach will be sufficient. Certainly, the presence of an essential facility and significant network owner interests in complementary markets would immediately rule in favor of mandatory access.[20]

The cases also illustrate the perils of allowing network owners and complementary market rivals to negotiate the prices and terms of access. The FCC's 1971 *Specialized Common Carrier Decision* requirements for negotiated interconnection of leased channel arrangements was part of a series of largely unsuccessful remedies that ultimately led to the MFJ. Negotiated outcomes are very likely to hamper the success of access since "give and take" presents many opportunities for delay and obstruction. Moreover, there is very likely to be asymmetric bargaining power in situations when the network owner has significant market power, thus leading to unsatisfactory negotiated access prices. Specific pricing methodology and *pro forma* tariffs generally promote faster and more successful access policy. But in their absence, prices will probably be easier to establish if non-price terms and conditions are relatively easy to agree to. Setting prices is also easier if there is a specific process for negotiating them and backstop arbitration is available in the event negotiations come to an impasse. Finally, establishing a time frame for arriving at mutually acceptable prices (with penalties in the event the time limit is exceeded) gives stakeholders an incentive to negotiate expeditiously.

Promoting the network owner's incentive to innovate is a controversial issue in crafting a compulsory access approach. For example, opponents of cable broadband access and TELRIC pricing at the local exchange level argued that forced access would reduce returns earned by the network owner, thus reducing incentives to develop new technologies. For networks not yet built, a policy of compulsory access might discourage the development of innovative network technologies or steer innovation toward network architectures that are less conducive to access problems. The risk in either case is that the expected returns from network development may be so low as to deter or reduce investment in the network. This is a particularly relevant concern for evolving markets and virtual networks.[21] Incentives to innovate are tightly tied to how access can be expected to be priced.[22] In practice, setting access prices involves a difficult balance that is hard to strike. Access prices that are too low encourage inefficient entry and weaken incentives to innovate. High access prices discourage efficient entry, while promoting monopoly returns to the network owner and welfare losses for consumers. Here, the cases offer relatively little to guide future policy. Access pricing is a heavily debated issue, but in practice has worked its way prominently to the top of the policy agenda only in telecommunications, where it has probably generated more controversy than agreement.

State and federal issues arise frequently in fashioning and implementing compulsory access initiatives. Many of the disputes over rules of access reveal themselves as protracted battles over regulatory authority (e.g., TELRIC pricing and authority over cable systems).[23] In some cases, state actions have eased the way for federal initiatives or greatly reduced the severity of network access problems. For example, retail electricity access mandates in a number of states required electric utilities to divest their generation to non-incumbent firms, thus easing the vertical integration problems that triggered intervention. But incremental policy approaches are often viewed negatively by the states. While these approaches may be indicative of a balkanized jurisdictional system, federal attempts to extend authority are often challenged as an encroachment on state jurisdiction. Conflicting federal and state policies on access have also created problems in telecommunications, broadband, and ATM networks. While there are no easy solutions for resolving jurisdictional problems, much more could be done at the outset of identified access controversies to gather stakeholders (including state and federal government) in generic proceedings or conferences, to scope out policy issues and to develop mutually consistent approaches.

Conclusions

Evaluating the success of access policy is a difficult task, complicated by the fact that the handling of access in many industries has evolved over a long period of time. How would one measure success? First, a decline in the number of antitrust complaints or formal regulatory filings seeking access could itself indicate an ameliorated situation—or it could indicate that the situation is so bad that outsiders have given up on seeking access. Evidence of more aggressive price competition—either through across-the-board reductions or regional discounting where competition prevails—could also suggest that an access problem has been dealt with in a pro-competitive manner. Or, if detected in conjunction with other strategies, it could reflect an anti-access strategy of exclusion, possibly amounting to predatory behavior. A third area in which to look for evidence of a successful access policy would be non-price competition, including the expansion of service offerings and quality improvements.

Finally, there may be evidence that complementary markets have become less concentrated or that formerly-balkanized markets have "integrated" over time (i.e., whereby regional price differences reflect transportation cost differentials, not discriminatory pricing). Our case studies reveal any number of these indicators, including the development of spot markets for gas pipelines, evidence of regional electricity and gas market integration, and increases in competitive long distance suppliers after the MFJ. It is important to note, however, that there is no simple formula for determining success that can substitute for careful empirical observation and a realistic judgment about how the marketplace is working.

In the process of evaluating the cases and key topics discussed in Parts I and II, it is clear that the relevant comparisons and contrasts across the cases can provide useful guidance for future access policy. Generally, the diversity of network access problems warrants a flexible approach (e.g., adjusting existing approaches to new problems) but should not sacrifice the general policy guidelines that flow from the cases. Some of the lessons learned from the cases were those expected at the outset. For example, competition should determine outcomes in network markets when those forces promote efficiency and consumer choice. This implies that multiple networks can legitimately prevail or that networks can coexist with alterative distribution channels and competing technologies.

Other recommendations, however, result from the holistic perspective offered by the case study approach. For example, certain circumstances signal situations where access is almost always likely to be a competitive problem. While vertical separation should be considered more frequently as a remedy in these situations, compulsory access approaches, if chosen, should be non-voluntary. Moreover, technological change and the ongoing market evolution may require a more active post-remedy role for antitrust than what has traditionally been used. It is also clear that there are relatively good indicators that compulsory access may not be working and that other policies should be considered. Finally, a challenge for policymakers will be to define the circumstances in which a bottleneck hampers competition in network industries. As the case studies demonstrate, essential facilities are a key component of the access problem and mandatory access has been a viable remedy for some abuses of essential facilities. But in the post-*Trinko* world, access policy must deal with an essential facilities antitrust doctrine that has been weakened, if not totally undermined.[24]

There are, of course, numerous case studies that could have been, but were not, included in this study. For example, international comparative law is bound to provide a broader framework, revealing additional insights. Emerging technologies will raise new problems and suggest new questions. As we go to press, for example, the FCC is being asked to approve regulations that will determine how digitally transmitted television content can be protected from copying. This raises questions (among others) about how firms can come together outside of the normal standard-setting process to propose standards for access and how firms and consumers gain access to needed technology and services, respectively—another arena in which the roles of intellectual property and antitrust must be sorted out. Thus, there are many fruitful avenues for research into additional topics or towards more focused examination of the observations and recommendations that come out of this study. Network access has provided, and will continue to provide, a rich area for policy study, one that offers real opportunities to build on past experience to improve and promote competition policy.

Note

1 Vice-president and Senior Research Fellow, American Antitrust Institute. I thank John Kwoka, Albert Foer, Donald Baker, Harry First, Richard Brunell, Lawrence White, Rudolph Peritz, Norman Hawker, Jonathan Rubin, Richard O'Neill, Peter Fox-Penner, and Michael Pelcovits for valuable review and comments on earlier drafts. I also thank participants in the Network Access Project workshops for their helpful insight and perspective.
2 Lawrence Lessig, *The Future of Ideas*, New York: Random House, 2001, p. 173.
3 Some internet-based alternatives may be more valuable to consumers, since they may offer the services of a "navigator" and the convenience of "one-stop shopping."
4 When there is more competition at the network level, leveraging market power to a second level is accomplished by diminishing rivals' competitive response (e.g., hindering access to critical inputs). Different exclusionary behaviors generate different economic analysis (not explored here) and are treated very differently in law and economics. Critiques of the "leveraging doctrine" can be found in S. F. Ross, *Principles of Antitrust Law*, Westbury, New York: Foundation Press, 1993; G. J. Werden, "The law and economics of the Essential Facility Doctrine," *St. Louis U. L. J.* 32, 1987, pp. 433–60; D. Reiffen and A. N. Kleit, "Terminal Railroad revisited: foreclosure of an essential facility or simple horizontal monopoly?" *Journal of Law & Economics* 33, 1990, p. 419.
5 The network owner will necessarily lose revenues from denying or restricting rivals' access and so must make up the loss from higher output prices.
6 Congestion and full capacity utilization on physical networks has important implications for service quality and potential for access policy. In many cases, delays and curtailments are the typical response, but new users may also be blocked (as in telecommunications) or the system may fail altogether (e.g., outages on electric systems). Thus, coordination between the network owner and rivals in complementary markets is often crucial, defining a fundamentally different default role for regulation. A busy signal or failure to initiate or complete an internet-based transaction because of congestion in a virtual network can create inconvenience and lost business. But it is worth noting that policies for dealing with congestion and capacity problems on physical networks have not developed for virtual systems.

7 The intensity of lobbying efforts for new or different access regulation or the frequency of private suits are possible barometers of when action might come.

8 In some situations, industry self-regulation can avoid or delay governmental intervention.

9 Policy goals are numerous, e.g., universal access, moderate price volatility, lower prices, etc.

10 The consequences of not getting access "right" may also affect what remedies are chosen. This is particularly true in energy industries, where failure carries significant private and social costs.

11 If the network is divested, ability and incentive are eliminated. If complementary assets are divested, ability and incentive may be reduced or eliminated, depending on how many assets are sold.

12 Vertical separation and incentive issues have been central to many restructuring experiences outside the U.S. (e.g., British Rail).

13 Vertical separation has been pursued more aggressively in Europe. For example, rail sector restructuring plans in the U.K., Sweden, Romania and Czech Republic have employed divestiture.

14 Network expansion is particularly relevant is the case of small airline access to airports with a limited number of slots. See, for example, S. A. Morrison and C. Winston, "The remaining role for government policy in the deregulated airline industry," in *Deregulation of Network Industries,* S. Peltzman and C. Winston (eds), Washington, D.C.: AEI-Brookings Joint Center for Regulatory Studies, 2000.

15 Utilities in the northeast battled these requirements, revising their governance structures several times over.

16 Indeed, critics would argue that compulsory access approaches justify the continued existence of regulatory infrastructure and perpetuate enforcement costs. One notable exception is the Civil Aeronautics Board under the Carter Administration, which was budgeted out of existence as airline deregulation proceeded. But few realized how important hubs would become.

17 The term "unbundling" has been used to mean different things. We use the term "functional" to distinguish unbundling under compulsory access from "corporate" unbundling, or vertical separation. See generally, J. G. Sidak and D. F. Spulber, "The tragedy of the telecomms: government pricing of unbundled network elements under the Telecommunications Act of 1996," *Columbia University Law Review* 97, 1997, pp. 1081–61 and J. Hausman and J. G. Sidak, "A consumer-welfare approach to the mandatory unbundling of telecommunications networks," *Yale Law Journal* 109, 1999, pp. 417–505.

18 Divestiture of complementary market assets (as opposed to network assets) may be preferable when it is relatively easy to determine (1) what assets should be divested to eliminate (or sufficiently reduce) the network owner's incentive to adversely affect prices and (2) if there are likely buyers for those assets.

19 The importance of rigorous merger review in the electricity industry was discussed in the *Economic Report of the President,* Washington, D.C.: Council of Economic Advisors, 1997, p. 206. An extreme form of intervention is a moratorium on mergers (e.g., in railroads). While moratoria have some appeal when industries are rapidly restructuring, they are temporary measures to slow or halt network owners' accretion of market power. Post-moratoria policies need to be devised and implemented once the hiatus ends and since moratoria can prevent efficiency-enhancing consolidation, they should be carefully

fashioned to apply to certain types of mergers, unless their proponents can demonstrate that certain conditions are present.

20 Prescribing a minimum number of rivals to which access must be provided is also risky. It is difficult, if not impossible, to predict "how much" access is likely to promote competitive complementary markets or how entry and exit will affect the competitive landscape.

21 Output expansion is a common innovative response in network industries because higher demand resulting from mandated access places a larger burden on the network. Another innovative response to access is an increase in demand for different types of services.

22 See generally, M. Armstrong, "Access pricing, bypass and universal service," *American Economic Association: Papers and Proceedings* 91, 2001, pp. 297–301, M. Armstrong, "The theory of access pricing and interconnection," in *Handbook of Telecommunications Economics*, M. Cave, S. Majumdar, and I. Vogelsang (eds), Amsterdam: North-Holland, 2001; M. Armstrong, C. Doyle and J. Vickers, "The access pricing problem: a synthesis," *Journal of Industrial Economics* 44, 1996, pp. 131–50; W. Baumol, J. Ordover, and R. Willig, "Parity pricing and its critics: a necessary condition for efficiency in the provision of bottleneck services to competitors," *Yale Journal on Regulation* 14, 1997, pp. 145–64; M. Armstrong and C. Doyle, "Social obligations and access pricing: telecommunications and railways in the UK," in *Opening Networks to Competition: The Regulation and Pricing of Access*, D. Gabel and D. F. Weiman (eds), Boston: Kluwer, 1998; N. Economides and L. J. White, "Access and interconnection pricing: how efficient is the "Efficient Component Pricing Rule?" *Antitrust Bulletin* 40, 1994, pp. 557–79.

23 See generally, T. Brennan, "Policy, federalism, and regulating broadband internet access," Resources for the Future Discussion Paper No. 01–02, March 2001; and T. Brennan, "State and federal roles in facilitating electricity competition: legal and economic perspectives," Resources for the Future Discussion Paper No. 03–24, April 2003.

24 See "'When you don't know what to do, walk fast, and look worried' (Dilbert 2003): Hitting the section 2 'refresh' button for in-house counsel following *Trinko*," antitrustsource.com (July 2004). Online. Available HTTP: <http://www.abanet.org/antitrust/source/Jul04-Teleconf7=23.pdf> (accessed July 27, 2004).

Annotated bibliography

Baumol, W. J., *Superfairness*, Cambridge, Massachusetts: MIT Press, 1986.

Baumol, W. J. and Bradford, D., "Optimal departures from marginal cost pricing," *American Economic Review* 60, 1970, pp. 265–83.

Baumol, W. J., Panzar J. C., and Willig, R. D., *Contestable Markets and the Theory of Market Structure*, New York: Harcourt, Brace, Jovanovich, 1982.

Beard, R. T., Kaserman, D. L., and Mayo, J. W., "Regulation, vertical integration and sabotage," *Journal of Industrial Economics* 49, 2001, pp. 319–33.

Boiteux, M., "Peak-load pricing," *The Journal of Business* 33, 1960, pp. 157–79.

Braeutigam, R. R., "Optimal pricing with intermodal competition," *American Economic Review* 69, 1979, pp. 38–49.

Braeutigam, R. R., "An analysis of fully distributed cost pricing in regulated industries," *Bell Journal of Economics* 11, 1980, pp. 182–96.

Breyer, S., *Regulation and its Reform*, Cambridge, Massachusetts: Harvard University Press, 1982.

Brown, S. J. and Sibley, D. S., *The Theory of Public Utility Pricing*, Cambridge U.K.: Cambridge University Press, 1986.

Coase, R. H., "The nature of the firm," *Economica*, 4, 1937, reprinted in *Readings in Price Theory*, Irwin, Chicago: American Economic Association, 1952, pp. 331–51.

Coase, R. H., "The regulated industry—discussion," *American Economic Review* 54, 1964, pp. 194–7.

Dempsey, B. W., *The Functional Economy: The Bases of Economic Organization*, Englewood Cliffs, New Jersey: Prentice Hall, 1958.

Demsetz, H., "Why regulate utilities?" *Journal of Law and Economics*, 55 1968, pp. 62–3.

Gellhorn, E., *Antitrust Law and Economics*, St. Paul, Minnesota: West Publishing, 1981.

Gerber, D. J. "Note: rethinking the monopolist's duty to deal: a legal and economic critique of the doctrine of 'Essential Facilities,'" *Va. L. Rev.* 74, 1988, p. 1069.

Goldberg, V., "Regulation and administered contracts," *Bell Journal of Economics* 7, 1976, pp. 426–8.

Goldberg, V., "Toward an expanded economic theory of contract," *Journal of Economic Issues*, 86, 1976, pp. 256–77.

Harris, M., "Optimal incentive contracts with imperfect information," *Journal of Economic Theory* 20, 1979, pp. 231–59.

Harris, M. and Raviv, A., "A theory of monopoly pricing schemes with demand uncertainty," *American Economic Review* 71, 1981, pp. 347–65.

Joskow, P., "Regulatory failure, regulatory reform, and structural change in the electric power industry," *Brookings Papers: Microeconomics 1989*, Washington, D.C.: Brookings Institution, 1989.

Laffont, J. J., Rey, P., and Tirole, J., "Network competition: I. overview and nondiscriminatory pricing," *Rand Journal of Economics* 29, 1998, pp. 1–37.

Landes, W. M. and Posner, R. A., "Market power in antitrust cases," *Harvard Law Review* 94, 1982, pp. 937–96.

Luce, R. D. and Raiffa, H., *Games and Decisions*, New York: John Wiley and Sons, 1957.

Mankiw, N. G. and Whinston, M. D., "Free entry and social inefficiency," *The Rand Journal of Economics* 17, 1986, pp. 48–58.

Milgrom, P. and Stokey, N., "Information, trade and common knowledge," *Journal of Economic Theory* 26, 1982, pp. 17–27.

Oi, W., "A Disneyland dilemma: two-part tariffs for a Mickey Mouse monopoly," *Quarterly Journal of Economics* 85, 1971, pp. 77–96.

Roth, A. E. and Sotomayor, M. A. O., *Two-Sided Matching*, Cambridge, U.K.: Cambridge University Press, 1990.

Schmalensee, R., "Another look at market power," *Harvard Law Review* 95, 1982, pp. 1789–816.

Sherman, R. and Visscher, M., "Second best pricing and stochastic demand," *American Economic Review* 68, 1978, pp. 41–53.

Simon, J. L., *The Ultimate Resource*, Princeton, New Jersey: Princeton University Press, 1981.

Stigler, G. J. and Sherwin, R. A., "The extent of the market," *Journal of Law and Economics* 28, 1985, pp. 555–85.

Telser, L. A., *A Theory of Efficient Cooperation and Competition*, Cambridge: Cambridge University Press, 1987.

Von Neumann, J. and Morgenstern, O., *Theory of Games and Economic Behavior*, Princeton, New Jersey: Princeton University Press, 1st edn, 1944, 2nd edn, 1947.

Weisman, D. L. and Kang, J., "Incentives for discrimination when upstream monopolists participate in downstream markets," *Journal of Regulatory Economics* 20, 2001, pp. 125–39.

Wildavsky, A. and Tenenbaum, E., *Politics of Mistrust: Estimating American Oil and Gas Resources*, London: Sage Publishing Co., 1981.

Williamson, O. E., "Franchise bidding for natural monopolies—in general and with respect to CATV," *Bell Journal of Economics* 7, 1976, pp. 73–104.

Williamson, O. E., "Transaction-cost economics: the governance of contractual relations," *Journal of Law and Economics* 22, 1979, pp. 233–61.

Willig, R. D., "Consumer surplus without apology," *American Economic Review*, 66, 1976, pp. 589–97.

Index

For Product Safety Concerns and Information please contact our EU
representative GPSR@taylorandfrancis.com
Taylor & Francis Verlag GmbH, Kaufingerstraße 24, 80331 München, Germany

www.ingramcontent.com/pod-product-compliance
Ingram Content Group UK Ltd.
Pitfield, Milton Keynes, MK11 3LW, UK
UKHW021012180425
457613UK00020B/916